D1521101

# Thy Will Be Done

MERCER
UNIVERSITY PRESS

*Endowed by*
TOM WATSON BROWN
*and*
THE WATSON-BROWN FOUNDATION, INC.

# Thy Will Be Done

# A Biography of George W. Truett

Keith E. Durso

Mercer University Press

Macon

and

The Baptist History & Heritage Society

Atlanta

MUP/H792

Published by Mercer University Press and
The Baptist History and Heritage Society

First Edition.

Books published by Mercer University Press are printed on acid free
paper that meets the requirements of American National Standard for
Information Sciences—Permanence of Paper for Printed Library
Materials.

Mercer University Press is a member of Green Press initiative
(greenpressinitiative.org), a nonprofit organization working to help
publishers and printers increase their use of recycled paper and
decrease their use of fiber derived from endangered forests. This book
is printed on recycled paper.

*Library of Congress Cataloging-in-Publication Data*

Durso, Keith E.
  Thy will be done : a biography of George W. Truett / Keith E. Durso. -- 1st ed.
p. cm.
Includes bibliographical references and index.
ISBN-13: 978-0-88146-157-2 (hardback : alk. paper)
ISBN-10: 0-88146-157-1 (hardback : alk. paper)
1. Truett, George W. (George Washington), 1867-1944.
2. Baptists--Clergy--Texas--Biography. I. Title.
BX6495.T7D87 2009
286'.1092--dc22 [B]

2009025194

*For Baptist Christians who, like George W. Truett, are both Christian and*

*Baptist, and ashamed of being neither*

# Contents

# Preface

On March 16, 1971, Leon McBeth, professor of church history at Southwestern Baptist Theological Seminary (SWBTS), in Fort Worth, Texas, opened his chapel address to the seminary's students with these words: "I count it a great honor to speak today about George W. Truett. He was a man without equal. Even today his name has magic to evoke grateful memory for who he was, and what he did."[i] Likewise, I count it a great honor to have written a biography of Truett. In summer 2006, I read a biography of Truett, which was written by his son-in-law Powhatan W. James and published in 1939. After finishing the book, I wanted to read a more recent biography about the famous Dallas pastor. I had always heard that McBeth was going to write one, so I searched the Internet for it, only to discover that no second biography existed. I then decided that if I could not buy a more recent biography of Truett, I would write one.

One day while I was doing some research for this book, a historian asked me what I was working on. "Nobody cares about Truett anymore," he said after I told him. I replied that people in Texas still care about him, and then continued my work. Actually, people outside of Texas still care about him too, and for good reason. During his forty-seven-year pastorate (1897–1944) at First Baptist Church in Dallas, Texas, Truett preached and embodied his understanding of stewardship—that all of one's talents and wealth should be used for the glory of God and the betterment of humanity, and for nothing else. He preached an average of one sermon a day, led several revivals every year, served three terms as president of the Southern Baptist Convention (1927–1929), presided over the Baptist World Alliance for one five-year term (1934–1939), preached extended tours in Asia, Europe, and South America, and helped found a hospital in Dallas. He was also perhaps the most outspoken and eloquent Baptist defender of religious liberty for all people, and his words concerning religious liberty are still quoted by preachers and scholars alike. A man who has done all that deserves at least two biographies.

People who knew Truett would have agreed with one observer who wrote, "One has to hear him to appreciate what I have tried to say. You cannot put George W. Truett on paper."[ii] Perhaps putting the life of any person on paper is impossible, but one can try. In the following pages I have attempted to describe Truett's life for readers, from his birth in 1867 on a farm in North Carolina, through his becoming one of the most influential Baptist preachers of his day, and finally to his death in 1944 at his home in Dallas. Along the way, I have offered a few criticisms of Truett's positions on certain issues, and more could have been made. I have focused, however, on what he did in his life rather than on what I think he should have done, for the words of H. Richard Niebuhr have been with me throughout the writing of this book: "The evil habit of men in all times to criticize their predecessors for having seen only half of the truth hides from them their own partiality and incompleteness."[iii]

In a sermon to traveling salesmen on October 25, 1914, Truett emphasized the "call to mutual helpfulness.... Such call emphasizes the doctrine that we are all mutually dependent. There are no exceptions. We are dependent upon all classes about us, and without ceasing. Think of our indebtedness to the motorman, the butcher, the laundryman, the clerk in the store, the newsboy, the drayman, the cook, the physician and on and on, without end. We are constantly called back to the doctrine of the solidarity of human society."[iv]

During the writing of Truett's biography, I depended "without ceasing" on many people for their assistance and/or their expertise. To these good people, I offer my sincerest thanks. Nancy Passarello, church librarian of Truett Memorial Baptist Church, Hayesville, North Carolina, spent time after church one Sunday afternoon helping me find information about Truett. Mary Fonda and Debra Kenyon, librarians at Moss Memorial Library, Hayesville, North Carolina, provided important information about Clay County, North Carolina. Bethany Jones and Lindsey Walker of the special collections department at SWBTS scanned photographs. Doris Roberson, co-director of the Truett Camp, Hayesville, North Carolina, gave me a tour of Truett's childhood home and allowed me to photograph pictures of Truett and his family. Martha Manning of Druid Hills Baptist Church, Atlanta, Georgia, and Ellen Brown of the Texas Collection, Baylor University, also provided me photographs of Truett.

The following people also provided me with invaluable help, without which I could not have written this biography. Taffey Hall, archivist at the Southern Baptist Historical Library and Archives in Nashville, Tennessee, went beyond the call of duty by e-mailing photos and information, often within an hour of my request, that I could not have gotten any other way. Ruthe Turner, church librarian of the George W. Truett Memorial Library, First Baptist Church, Dallas, Texas, made available her library's resources, which included material that cannot be found anywhere else. Alan Lefever, director of the Texas Baptist Historical Collection, Dallas, Texas, provided me with the crucial resources that enabled me to write this book at my home in Lawrenceville, Georgia. Kent Reynolds of Christian Mission Concerns and Paul Powell, a member of the board of directors of the Robert M. Rogers Foundation and former dean of George W. Truett Seminary, Waco, Texas, provided financial assistance, which helped defray the costs of two brief but fruitful trips to Texas. Mike Williams, dean of Humanities and Social Sciences and professor of History at Dallas Baptist University, and Charles Deweese, former executive director of the Baptist History and Heritage Society, read the manuscript and offered helpful suggestions. Last, but certainly not least, I want to thank my wife, Pam, executive director of Baptist Women in Ministry, for her helpful comments on the manuscript and for her encouraging words.

---

[i] Leon McBeth, "George W. Truett and Southwestern Seminary" (chapel address, Southwestern Baptist Theological Seminary, Fort Worth, Texas, March 16, 1971) 1, TC between 557 and 558/MF 554–590:1. Many citations contain TC and MF references. For example, in the previous citation TC refers to the George W. Truett

Collection, located at AWRL; the 557 and 558 refer to folder numbers. The MF refers to the microfiche reproduction of the TC, which is located at several places, including AWRL, SBHLA, and TBHC. The 554–590 refers to the group of files on the microfiche card to which a particular folder belongs; and 1 refers to the specific microfiche card in that particular group.

[ii] A. T. Robertson, "Dr. George W. Truett in Louisville," *Watchman-Examiner*, April 3, 1930, 442.

[iii] H. Richard Niebuhr, *The Kingdom of God in America* (New York: Harper & Row, Publishers, 1937; repr., New York: Harper Torchbook, 1959) xv.

[iv] "Travelling Men Hear Rev. George W. Truett," *DMN*, October 26, 1914.

Charles Levi Truett  (Courtesy of the Truett Camp, Hayesville, North Carolina)

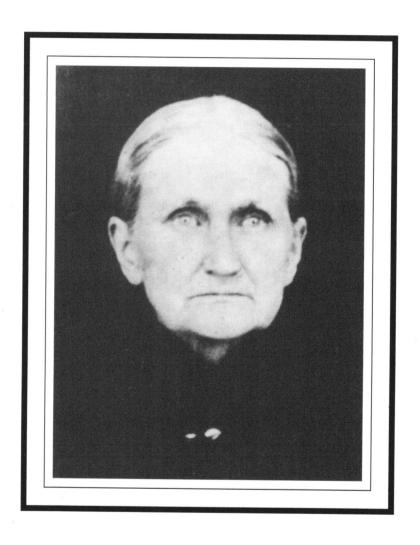

Mary Rebecca Kimsey Truett  (Courtesy of the Truett Camp, Hayesville, North Carolina)

Ferd C. McConnell and Truett
(Courtesy of the Southern Baptist Historical Library and Archives, Nashville, Tennessee)

B. H. Carroll  (Courtesy of Southwestern Baptist Theological Seminary, Fort Worth, Texas)

Truett and Josephine on their wedding day, June 28, 1894
(Courtesy of First Baptist Church, Dallas, Texas)

Truett's graduation photograph, 1897
(Courtesy of the Texas Collection, Baylor University, Waco, Texas)

Truett, early in his ministry at First Baptist, Dallas
(Courtesy of the Southern Baptist Historical Library and Archives, Nashville, Tennessee)

(TOP) Truett (sitting far left) and J. B. Gambrell (standing, front row, far right) watch as C. C. Slaughter turns the first spade of dirt for a new building for the Texas Baptist Memorial Sanitarium, November 4, 1904
(Courtesy of First Baptist Church, Dallas, Texas)

(BOTTOM) Robert H. Coleman
(Courtesy of Southwestern Baptist Theological Seminary, Fort Worth, Texas)

Truett, c. 1910  (Courtesy of First Baptist Church, Dallas, Texas)

Truett in West Texas, c. 1940  (Courtesy of First Baptist Church, Dallas, Texas)

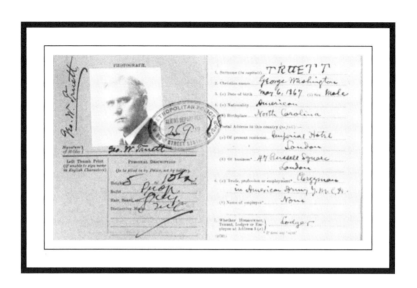

(TOP) Truett's 1918 passport
(Courtesy of Southwestern Baptist Theological Seminary, Fort Worth, Texas)

(BOTTOM) Truett in his chaplain's uniform, 1918/1919
(Courtesy of First Baptist Church, Dallas, Texas)

James A. Francis and Truett, 1919  (Courtesy of First Baptist Church, Dallas, Texas)

George W. Truett
(Courtesy of Southwestern Baptist Theological Seminary, Fort Worth, Texas)

(TOP) Truett (standing just left of center) on the steps of the Capitol, May 16, 1920
(Courtesy of the Southern Baptist Historical Library and Archives, Nashville, Tennessee)

(BOTTOM) Truett on board the *S. S. Berlin*, 1934
(Courtesy of First Baptist Church, Dallas, Texas)

(TOP) J. H. Rushbrooke, Josephine, and Truett in Burma, 1936
(Courtesy of Southwestern Baptist Theological Seminary, Fort Worth, Texas)

(BOTTOM) Truett at the grave of Ann Hasseltine Judson, Burma, 1936
(Courtesy of Southwestern Baptist Theological Seminary, Fort Worth, Texas)

(TOP) Truett after his first plane ride, 1936
(Courtesy of the Truett Camp, Hayesville, North Carolina)

(BOTTOM) Truett and FBC deacons pose outside the home of Cullen F. Thomas, May 28, 1937. J. B. Cranfill is second from Truett's right; Thomas is to Truett's immediate left. Truett's brother-in-law Oscar M. Marchman is in the second row, third from right.  (Courtesy of First Baptist Church, Dallas, Texas)

(TOP) Annie Truett Milliken, Joanne Milliken, Josephine, and Truett shortly arriving in Atlanta for the Baptist World congress, July 17, 1939
(Courtesy Druid Hills Baptist Church, Atlanta, Georgia)

(BOTTOM) J. H. Rushbrooke watches as Truett addresses the Baptist World Alliance congress, Atlanta, July 1939
(Courtesy of the Texas Collection, Baylor University, Waco, Texas)

Truett delivering his presidential address at the 1939 Baptist World Alliance congress  (Courtesy of the Southern Baptist Historical Library and Archives, Nashville, Tennessee)

Annie Truett Milliken, Mary Truett Gilliam, and Jessie Truett James, with their parents, c. 1939 (Courtesy of First Baptist Church, Dallas, Texas)

Robert H. Coleman watches an intense Truett leave his office to preach, 1941
(Courtesy of the Southern Baptist Historical Library and Archives, Nashville, Tennessee)

From the *Dallas Journal,* November 20, 1923
(Courtesy of Southwestern Baptist Theological Seminary, Fort Worth, Texas)

(TOP) Truett (seated far left) and Louie D. Newton (standing far right) watch as Edward R. Carter and Mayor George Lyle shake hands, April 19, 1942
(Courtesy of Druid Hills Baptist Church, Atlanta, Georgia)

(BOTTOM) Truett's funeral, July 10, 1944
(Courtesy of First Baptist Church, Dallas, Texas)

Josephine and Truett in West Texas, c. 1940
(Courtesy of First Baptist Church, Dallas, Texas)

Cover of brochure for the opening of the George W. Truett Memorial Hospital, November 30, 1950  (Courtesy of First Baptist Church, Dallas, Texas)

# Chapter 1

# Thrown into the Stream, 1867–1890

On a hot summer day in July 1943, George W. Truett, the seventy-six-year-old pastor of First Baptist Church, Dallas, Texas, was talking with his good friend Louie D. Newton, pastor of Druid Hills Baptist Church, Atlanta, Georgia, under a tree at Newton's home. Having known each other for thirty-four years, the two ministers discussed their ministries and life experiences, but soon the conversation turned to death. Truett, his health having begun to fail, eventually asked his friend to preach his funeral sermon: "Louie, when you come to have my funeral, if you can say in all consciousness that my thought has been to follow the will of God, Thy will be done, then I'll be happy."[1] A year later, Newton traveled to Dallas to fulfill his friend's request and, with a good conscience, used Jesus' words in the Lord's Prayer, "Thy will be done," as one of his texts. These four one-syllable words epitomized Truett's passion in life, a life that began in a small mountain town in southwestern North Carolina and then took him all over the world, providing him with numerous opportunities to do what he believed he was born to do—preach the gospel of Jesus Christ.

*Two Vital Christians*

Two years after the end of the Civil War, the bloodiest war in the history of the United States, George Washington Truett was born in a log cabin near Hayesville, North Carolina, on May 6, 1867, the seventh of eight children born to Charles Levi Truett and Mary Rebecca Kimsey Truett. The country into which Truett had been born was undergoing dramatic changes. The Civil War had not only demolished slavery, but it had also ruined much of the South's physical and financial resources. Also, while southern African Americans were technically free, the "black codes" passed in southern states relegated freed slaves to second-class citizens by denying them the right to vote, serve on juries, buy or lease land, and attend public schools.[2] Immigration also changed America, for 15 million people, mostly Europeans, emigrated to the United States from 1840 to 1890, bringing with them strange customs and strange political and religious beliefs.[3]

George Truett's paternal great-grandfather, Levi Truett (c. 1775–1830), had emigrated as a young man from England to Swannanoa, Buncombe County, North Carolina, near Asheville. Around 1795, he married Susanna Morgan (c. 1775–c. 1860), whose parents had emigrated from Scotland. The Truetts had eight children, the third of whom was Jeremiah (1800–1888). Jeremiah married Mary Kyle (c. 1801–1876), who was of Irish descent, and together they had eight children. Their fourth child, Charles Levi Truett (1830–1925), was born in Buncombe County, North Carolina, on April 10, 1830. He married Mary Rebecca Kimsey (1830–1911) on May 22, 1851, and they too had eight children: William Thomas (Tom) (1853–?), James Lafayette (1854–1946), Sarah Caroline (1856–1936), Charles Spurgeon (Spurgeon) (1860–1941), Marion Lee (1861–1863), John Harvey (Harvey) (1865–1908), George Washington (1867–1944), and Luther Jeremiah (1869–1941).[4]

George Truett's maternal grandfather, James Kimsey, was a well-known Baptist preacher in Georgia and North Carolina. Kimsey was born in 1803 in Towns County, in north Georgia, and died there in 1870. He converted to Christianity at age twenty-seven and soon thereafter began his preaching ministry, which lasted forty years. He pastored rural churches in Georgia and North Carolina and was a sought-after evangelist. Kimsey never took notes for his sermons, nor did he use outlines when preaching. One man described his preaching as "almost irresistible." Kimsey was also a powerful exhorter—that is, someone who, at the end of worship services, urged people to make a decision.[5]

An article written soon after Kimsey's death described the last two days of the preacher's life:

On Monday morning, the eleventh of April (1870) his condition showed plainly to the bystanders that he could not live long. This being suggested to him by a friend, he summoned all his remaining strength, and in the full possession of all the faculties of his mind, commenced exhorting the crowd of bystanders around his dying bed; and with but momentary intervals, continued his exhortations until Tuesday afternoon, when his breathing stopped and he sank down in death without sigh or groan, remarking that *his work was done*.[6]

A younger brother of Kimsey, Elijah (1812–1896), whom the Truett children called "Uncle Lije," was also a Baptist preacher, and, despite his lisp, he too was a powerful exhorter. As a young boy, George Truett attended several services led by his great-uncle. During these and other services, Truett was probably exposed to the preaching style that characterized many Baptist country preachers in the late 1700s and well into the 1800s. John Broadus, a professor of New Testament and homiletics for thirty-six years (1859–1895) at the Southern Baptist Theological Seminary, described such preaching, particularly outdoor preaching, as that of a "sing-song or 'holy whine'," during which preachers' voices rose and fell in order to relieve their voices from strain and fatigue.[7] That holy-whine preaching would not come from the lips of Elijah Kimsey unless he was certain that the Holy Spirit was with him. Truett recalled watching his uncle bend over the pulpit and tell his congregation, "The Spirit of God is not with me. We must wait and pray."[8] When Kimsey felt the Spirit move him to preach, however, nothing could hold him back.

An incident that occurred long before Truett was born, yet one he heard relatives recount numerous times, typifies his uncle's passion for preaching once the Spirit inspired him. Methodists were holding revival meetings daily at eight and eleven in the mornings, and at four and seven in the afternoons and evenings. One morning before sunrise, Kimsey pled with the Methodist ministers in charge of the revival to allow him to preach, saying, "Brethren, my soul is on fire. I want to preach to these people.… This camp-meeting has been going on for days and nobody is being saved." When the ministers asked when he wanted to preach, Kimsey responded, "The sooner, the better, brethren. The fire is burning in my soul."[9] The ministers told him that he could preach at the 8:00 a.m. service. He began preaching, first to the whole crowd and then to individuals, sometimes from behind the pulpit, other times among the congregation. Other ministers soon joined the preaching while scores of people from the surrounding area began arriving at the meeting. Hundreds of people were converted during that "morning" service, which lasted well past sunset.[10] When Kimsey died on May 7, 1896, his family had the following epitaph inscribed on his headstone: "He went and done what the Lord commanded."[11]

The stories about his grandfather Kimsey and the ministry of his Uncle Lije undoubtedly influenced Truett's understanding of God, preaching, and ministry, but the most influential people in Truett's life were his parents, whom he described as "two of the most vital Christians I ever knew."[12] His father, Charles L. Truett, served in the Confederate army as an infantryman during the Civil War. He was a private in William H. Thomas's North Carolina Legion.[13] John Stewart, a fellow soldier, described Charles as his "ideal Christian and soldier." Stewart noted that he never heard or saw Charles say or do an unkind thing, even in dire circumstances.[14] James Britton (J. B.) Cranfill, who knew Truett's father as an older man, described him as being "as honest as Abraham, and as openhearted as Daniel. It has never been his [nature] to believe that it is right at any time to use deceit.... He has never been on the fence on any question. He stands for the right, as God gives him to see the right, and while he never gives offense to any one who differs from him in opinion, all his neighbors know that he stands for righteousness in every sphere of life, and would, at any time if need be, seal his convictions with his blood."[15]

Prior to the Civil War, Charles married his wife, Mary, in 1851. They resided and farmed in Cherokee County, North Carolina, in the southwest corner of the state. The Truetts and their first four children were still residing in that county in 1860.[16] Later they moved to Clay County, which was formed in 1861 from the eastern part of Cherokee County and a small section of western Macon County.[17]

The land in southwestern North Carolina was so poor for farming that farmers considered themselves fortunate if their crops brought in $25 in a year.[18] Wanting to stay in southwestern North Carolina, but also wanting his children to receive the best education possible in that part of the state, Charles eventually moved his family to a 250-acre farm two miles west of Hayesville, in Clay County, living first in a log cabin and later, as the family grew, in a two-story frame house.[19] Trees covered most of the farm, and the rugged terrain made farming difficult. Yet the Truetts made the best of what they had, raising corn, wheat, oats, rye, and hay, and tending their hogs, sheep, cattle, horses, and mules. Drinking water had to be hauled several hundred yards. Water for washing and bathing came from a nearby brook.[20]

A man with little formal education, Charles believed that if his children were to succeed in life, they would have to receive a good education. Part of that education was the building of good character, which he believed could be nurtured by reading good books and periodicals, all of which he insisted that his children read. Some of the books in the Truett home were the Bible, John Bunyan's *Pilgrim's Progress*, Richard Baxter's *Saints' Everlasting Rest*, J. M. Pendleton's *Christian Doctrines*, and Fox's *Book of Martyrs*. Periodicals in the home included Baptist state papers such as the *Religious Herald* (Virginia), the *Biblical Recorder* (North Carolina), the *Tennessee Baptist*, and the *Watchman-Examiner* (New York). Also available in the Truett home were the printed sermons of several preachers, including those of Jeremiah B. Jeter, a Baptist minister and the first president of the Southern Baptist Foreign Mission Board; James P. Boyce, a Baptist minister and founder of the Southern Baptist Theological Seminary; J. B. Hawthorne, a Baptist minister and evangelist; Moses D. Hogue, a Presbyterian minister; Dwight L. Moody, an evangelist; and Charles H. Spurgeon, perhaps the greatest English Baptist preacher of the nineteenth century.[21]

The greatest spiritual influence on Truett was his mother, Mary, whom he called "the greatest Christian I ever saw."[22] Later in life he recalled that as a little boy he often found his mother crying in the morning while his father and older brothers were working on the farm. He always asked his mother why she was crying, but she told him that he would not understand. After breakfast, she would tell Truett and his younger brother, Luther, to remain in the house while "she would go away with face suffused with tears, and she would come back in a little while...singing, with a smile on her face fairer than the morning." Baffled by the change in their mother's moods, Truett and Luther decided one morning to follow her. They found her in the orchard near their house, face down on the ground, praying. More than forty years later, Truett vividly remembered the scene:

> She was down on her face before God. I can remember until yet the surpassing pathos of her prayers. She said: "Lord, Jesus, I never can rear this houseful of boys like they ought to be reared, without thy help. I will make shipwreck with them, without thy help. I cannot guide them, I cannot counsel them, I cannot be the mother that a woman ought to be to her children, without God's help. I will cleave to thee. Teach me and help me, every hour." I heard her like that, and then she came back, singing every morning.[23]

### Truett's Childhood

The Truett home was a stopping place for many people, including Masons and ministers. As a child Truett often sat on his father's knee, listening to him and other Masons talk.[24] Truett also listened to many country preachers who stayed at the Truett home and discussed the great truths of the Bible.[25] He also heard many of those "old preachers in the country places, with their white locks about their ears, sometimes standing on their staffs as they came to the simple pulpit platform, and with tears running down their cheeks they have asked the question: 'What boy here will have my mantle?'" While Truett listened to those preachers, his "heart...burned like some irrepressible volcano as" he "heard them ask that question."[26] This question "deeply impressed" him, and he often wondered if those ministers played a part in his becoming a minister.[27]

The Truett home was a happy one, though it knew its share of sorrows. On July 13, 1863, the Truetts' nineteen-month-old son, Marion, died. Then in 1872, Spurgeon, one of Truett's older brothers, contracted scarlet fever. Spurgeon survived, but the illness left him deaf. His father taught him to read lips and always corrected his punctuation. People could understand Spurgeon when he talked, and he became adept at reading lips. His family pronounced their words slowly and distinctly so that he could understand them. Having to do this perhaps accounts for Truett's ability to speak clearly and precisely later in life.[28]

Another tragedy, at least in the eyes of young boys, occurred when Truett and Luther's pet squirrel died. When they buried the animal, Truett preached the funeral sermon with such sincerity and passion that his younger brother began to cry. "Don't cry, Luther," Truett comforted his little brother. "Don't cry, the squirrel will rise again." With those comforting words of assurance, Luther filled in the grave, helped set a headstone, and placed wild flowers on the grave.[29]

Charles Truett moved his family from Cherokee County to Clay County so that his children could attend Hayesville Academy, located just outside of Hayesville. Originally, the school was named Hicksville Academy, which was owned and operated for many years by Professor John O. Hicks, known as "the father of education" in that part of the state.[30] Hicks had arrived in southwestern North Carolina in 1850 and eventually started and taught in several schools in which students paid for their education and textbooks. On August 12, 1870, Hicks purchased the land on which he would build the Hicksville Academy.[31]

Some of Hicks's former students recalled that he was "a man with boundless energy" and "a fearless user of the rod." Once, a Baptist preacher protested Hicks's whipping of his son. Rather than providing a verbal explanation for his use of the rod, the professor instead started beating the minister with the rod, which ended the "discussion." Hicks moved to South Carolina in 1876, and sold the Hayesville Academy in 1878 to R. B. Chambers, who sold the school a year later to F. A. Fessenden, the headmaster of the school. Fessenden owned the school until 1883, when he deeded the school to a stock company.[32]

When Truett attended Hayesville Academy, the school included grades 1 through 12. The female students wore blouses and wool skirts, the male students "dark brown homespun trousers, long black frocktail coats, and brogan shoes. The boys also wore black string ties, tied in a bow, and white pleated-bosom shirts that had to be starched and shining."[33] Truett often walked the two miles to school, which, according to his biographer, he attended a few months a year for at least ten years from 1875 to 1885 before beginning to teach at a school in Crooked Creek, Georgia.[34] In his 1886 diary, however, Truett recorded that he was attending a school run by T. Neal Kitchens during spring 1886 and that he was still taking exams.[35] Truett's biographer might have had the dates wrong, which would mean that Truett did not start teaching in Crooked Creek until fall 1886. Or, when Truett wrote that he attended Kitchens's school, he might have used the word "attended" to mean that he was in charge of the school as a teacher, and his references to taking exams might denote that he was taking classes somewhere while he taught at Crooked Creek. Fortunately, an understanding of Truett's life does not depend on knowing exactly when he began his teaching career.

As a student Truett excelled in language, literature, and history, but not math.[36] Though a serious boy, he got into some mischief when the right opportunity availed itself. "There was a boy in our class who always had to be told the answers," recalled Ella Davidson Ritch, a classmate of Truett's at Hayesville Academy. One time "George whispered 'personal pronoun' when the answer should have been a verb."[37]

Being an inquisitive child, Truett spent much of his free time reading newspapers and magazines in the home and devouring the books in his father's library. He read rapidly and perhaps had a photographic memory. Biography was his favorite genre.[38]

Another activity that Truett enjoyed was participating in debates. Children from the surrounding area often gathered at the vacant log house on the Truett farm to hold meetings for their "Log Cabin Debating

Society." Subjects for the debates were decided when the children arrived, forcing them to give extemporaneous speeches.[39] Such experiences would prove to be valuable for Truett, for they taught him to think on his feet and gave him the confidence to do so.

The Truetts were Baptists and attended Hayesville Baptist Church, which had been founded in 1850 and was located a mile south of town at the intersection of Murphy and Hiawasee wagon roads. Charles and Mary were noted for their faith, although Charles did not make a profession of faith until he was middle aged. Both of Truett's parents insisted that their children attend church on Sundays and that they shun card-playing, dancing, and other ungodly activities.[40]

Truett began thinking about spiritual matters when he was six years old. As he was "listening to a sermon by an earnest country preacher," he recalled many years later, "there came to me a distinct deep sense of my need of God's forgiving grace." That need stayed with him throughout the day. In bed that night he yearned for someone "to come…to tell me how I could get right with God, who was so great and good, about whom the preacher had taught me much that day."[41] No one came, however, nor did he seek anyone with whom he could share his thoughts.

Five years later during a revival meeting, Truett was again struck with a consciousness of his sin. In a sermon many years later he referred to that event:

> As vividly as though it were yesterday I can remember my burden, my pain, my loneliness, my fear. I was shrinking. I was timid. I could not venture to speak to anybody. Oh, if somebody could have divined my situation and have taught me! I knew I was wrong. I knew I was a sinner. I knew I was lost in my old nature. I had the sense of alienation from the holy God and of condemnation on my own head and heart, because of personal sin. I knew it all, but I could not see the way. I groped in darkness.[42]

Why he felt too timid to speak with someone, particularly his mother, remains a mystery. But he kept his struggles to himself and continued to "grope in darkness" for another eight years.

*Truett's "News and Notes" for 1886*

Truett's older brother James described Truett as "a clown among the people of the community, a jolly youngster who could give and take a joke, the chief song leader of Clay County, who got more music from the singing bee on Sunday afternoon than anybody."[43] Such a description of Truett would baffle people who only saw photographs of him or who only observed him during worship services when he was older. Most of the photographs of Truett portray him as a stern, intense man with piercing gray-blue eyes, and he rarely sang in public. Yet Truett's 1886 diary supports James's observations. In the diary, which Truett titled "News and Notes by G. W. T. from Jan. 1 to Nov. 28th 1886," he recorded many of his thoughts, dreams, and activities. These entries reveal him to be not only a hardworking farm boy, but also a typical male teenager interested in girls, music, and having fun.

From the time Truett was old enough to do manual labor, he joined his siblings and parents in the arduous work on the farm. He picked cotton, pulled corn, plowed the land, split rails, cut logs and hay, cleared fields, built fences, dug ditches, and tended hogs, sheep, cattle, and horses. Such work often left him "tired! tired!!"[44]

Along with working on the farm, Truett found time to enjoy himself. He loved music and singing, and attended a "singing school" in December 1885 at the nearby Hayesville Methodist Church. On January 2, 1886, the final day of the school, Truett noted that a large crowd had gathered "to witness the exercises of the day. Several short complimentary 'talks' were delivered by the students, among them your 'unworthy,'" referring to himself. "The 'good times' we had," he added, "will long be remembered by many boys and girls."[45]

Despite never having declared his faith publicly, Truett attended the Protestant churches near Hayesville and participated in their ministries. He helped organize a Sunday school at the Hayesville Baptist Church on Sunday, January 17, after which he "attended Preaching" at the Methodist church and "contributed 5¢ [$1.14][46] for the support of the ministry."[47] This diary entry highlights two aspects of church life in small, rural communities in the late nineteenth century. Because many churches could not afford a full-time pastor, they often shared a minister. Members would gather for Sunday school and then attend a "preaching" service at their own church if their pastor was in town or at another church if he was absent. Thus, growing up, Truett attended services at the churches of three Protestant denominations: Baptist, Methodist, and Presbyterian. Such experiences shaped his understanding and appreciation of other Protestant denominations. Later in life Truett noted that he had "learned, early in life, to appreciate God's people of various religious denominations and to learn of the great and good work that they are doing in the world."[48] The morning services at these churches centered around the sermon, which is why people said that they had attended a "preaching" service rather than a "worship" service. Whatever occurred before the sermon was considered to be "preliminary" to the main event: the preaching of the gospel. On Sunday evenings church members often attended "singing," when the "preliminaries" took on a more central role.

Truett often recorded his opinions about the quality of Sunday-school classes and of sermons he heard. The Sunday-school class he attended at the Baptist church during the spring was always good and interesting. In one diary entry he proclaimed his Sunday school to be "[t]he most interesting in the country."[49] He recorded when new members joined that class. For example, he noted that one Sunday nine people joined the Sunday school, including Lenora Tidwell and Nannie Bristol. He "was glad to see them 'coming out from among the world.' 'Go on noble woman in your work! Go on!'"[50] Truett described some of the sermons he heard at the different churches during the spring as "admirable," "very good," "good," and "excellent."[51] Not all the sermons he heard rose to such heights, but even those that did not were still "serviceable" or "pretty good."[52] Most of the time during preaching, Truett was only a congregant; however, one Sunday during preaching at the Presbyterian church, he "tried" to lead the singing.[53] In his opinion, he failed.

Truett took several exams during spring 1886. On Thursday, April 15, he took "[a] very rigid examination in Grammar.... Hope I came out victorious." The next evening he went to Hayesville "and stood for an examination in Physiology," which he passed. The following Monday he took a "strict" history test about which he recorded, "Made several mistakes."[54]

In the midst of studies and examinations, Truett and other boys found time to enjoy themselves. In his diary entry for March 31 he noted, "School progressing finally. We are having a 'rich' time. To-day some of us boys went down to the river or at least started in that direction. We had to go through the bottoms. At times we had to run for life to keep from miring up in the mud. It seemed like...the 'bottomless pit' was our stopping place. We were a 'sight,' when we got back to the school house. 'The way of the transgressor is hard.'"[55]

One of the topics that appears frequently in Truett's diary is his relationship with women. Truett escorted many women to Sunday school, preaching, singing, socials, and debates, and he appears to have been smitten by more than one. "Had some 'jolly' talks with some 'jolly' girls," Truett recorded one day.[56] As April Fool's Day approached, he wondered whether he would receive a card and was ecstatic when he did: "Hurrah! Whoopee! I received an 'April Fool' this morning. It was a 'crackin' one. Shall keep it for future reference. Oh that it was a reality! Phew!!"[57]

Truett described Mary M. Rogers, a niece of J. G. Mashburn, the Baptist preacher in Hayesville, as being "an intelligent looking young lady." After noting in his diary that she had visited the school one day, Truett wrote, "'Aint she a purty gal'! 'Hush she'll hear you'!"[58]

Meeting girls was also on Truett's agenda when he attended church. On Sunday, May 9, for example, he and some friends went to preaching at a church in New Hope, North Carolina. The "excellent" sermon caught his attention, but so did "several pretty girls" in the congregation.[59]

On May 28, Truett took two "rigid" examinations in grammar and algebra, but he "came out victorious. Never missed a single thing." After the exams, the students listened to a speech before eating lunch, about which he noted: "ate an 'awful sight.' I felt so good." After lunch he took a walk with some girls and confessed that he "felt perfectly free for I was through the examination." While in town with his mother the next day, many people complimented Truett for his speech on "The New South," which he probably gave during a function the previous evening.[60]

During the spring, Truett attended and often participated in Friday night debates, which were a source of entertainment for the citizens of Hayesville and the surrounding area. One Friday in February, Truett was the leading disputant on the affirmative side of the question, "Should Education be made compulsory?"[61] Truett did not record whether his side won or lost. On April 9, disputants debated the question, "Does George Washington deserve more praise for defending A[merica]. than Columbus for discovering it?'"[62] Truett and his brother Harvey were on the negative team, which won. The debate for April 20 concerned whether western North Carolina was "as good a country as any portion of the nation." Truett was on the winning, affirmative side. The debate, he noted, had much "lively discussion! Much interest manifested."[63] The debate for May 27 concerned the hot topic whether "parents exercise a greater influence than teachers in forming the characters of the young." Truett, Harvey, and others argued the affirmative. The youngest member of the Truett family, Luther, was part of the negative team. "The house was filled to overflowing," Truett recorded, and despite neither side winning, the "[d]ebate was pronounced by all to be a complete success."[64]

Truett attended other debates, although he did not record whether he participated in them. One debate of interest, however, occurred on May 14 concerning whether "the U. S. [should] suppress Mormonism." He quoted in his diary what was probably the prevalent opinion of that era: "Yes,…it should."[65]

Also during the spring Truett recorded his contributions to churches and the amount he spent on clothes. To Methodist and Baptist churches, he contributed a total of 40¢ ($9.09). He also paid 10¢ ($2.27) for Sunday-school literature and $13.50 ($306.92) for a suit.[66]

In the midst of his many educational and social activities, Truett also turned his attention to others less fortunate and to reflecting on his future. He made two visits during the spring to a young man dying of consumption. After the second visit, Truett recorded that the man's health was declining rapidly: "Poor fellow! he must shortly go."[67] Personally, Truett understood that his life after spring 1886 would be much different. He noted on May 6, his nineteenth birthday: "To-day I am 19 years old. Trust that my future life may be better than the past. Life is beginning to seem like a stern reality. The future of my life can not be summed up in joyful expectations. Evidently, there is serious work ahead."[68]

### A Glorious Time

During the first part of summer 1886, Truett worked on the family farm and helped his father round up cattle that had strayed off the farm, a seemingly harmless endeavor but one that could be dangerous. Truett briefly described one such occasion in his diary entry for June 10: "Pa and I went to the Mts. yesterday. Had good luck. Killed a large rattlesnake on the 'Ball Spring Ridge.' It had 9 rattles and a button."[69]

Truett also had opportunities to speak to Sunday schools at nearby churches and write two articles. Along with a friend, he traveled to Brasstown, North Carolina, on June 17 so that on the following morning he could address the Sunday school of the town's Baptist church. Many members of the "large audience" who heard his brief address complimented him on his speech, but in his opinion, such compliments "were undeserved." That evening he spoke nearly fifteen minutes to a small Sunday-school class at Mount Pisgah, North Carolina, where he raised "$1.25 [$28.42] for S. S. literature."[70]

Truett's refusal to accept positive comments about his speeches was a characteristic he developed early in life. Complimenting oneself or being complimented on a job well done was anathema to Truett and apparently in the Truett home as well. When asked late in life whether he was proud of his children, Truett's father replied, "I can not say I am proud of my children, for I do not like that word 'pride'; it is connected, you know, with the fall of Satan. But I am humbly thankful for them."[71] Throughout his life, George Truett often expressed his own unworthiness to speak to audiences.

In June 1886, Truett wrote two articles he hoped would be published. An article sent to the *Hayesville News* dealt with the end of the previous school term.[72] The second, which he sent to a Baptist publication, concerned the "progress of the Church and S[unday] S[chool] cause in our country."[73]

Work on the Truett farm continued during the early part of the summer, interrupted only by inclement weather. An incessant rain halted work in late June, which frustrated Truett. With the wheat needing to be harvested and the cornfield needing to be weeded, he became "very restless. Wish we could be at work."[74] Four days later, the rain stopped, enabling him to go to town to buy a pair of shoes for $2.50 ($56.84) and to finish cutting the wheat. The change in weather and the resumption of physical activity brightened Truett's spirits. "Feel *better*," he recorded on June 26.[75] The rains resumed, however, causing him to become "pretty restless" again. Yet even in his restlessness and frustration, he noted optimistically, "There is no cloud, but what has a silver lining."[76]

Also during late June, some friends, Herschel and Amanda Cobb, ate dinner with the Truetts after church one Sunday. Herschel, who was going to study law, impressed Truett and encouraged his young friend "to do likewise." Amanda also impressed Truett, who described her as "wealthy, intelligent, and best of all *exceptionally pretty*."[77]

In July, Truett and his brother Harvey traveled to Franklin, North Carolina, to attend a school probably designed to help adults further their education. The boys resided most of the month at the Alleghany House for $10 ($227.35).[78] While at the school, Truett attended lectures on geography, physiology, grammar, and spelling. On July 7, he heard a "*grand* lecture on Physiology," during which he "saw a human skeleton" for the first time. The students also went that day to a telephone office, where a message was sent to a town twenty miles away and a response was received in a minute and a half.[79] During his month-long stay in Franklin, most of the lectures impressed Truett, but the one on "Education and Labor" by Mr. Finger, the school's superintendent, on July 20 did not rise to Truett's "expectations. He is not a forcible speaker." Yet Truett still found something worthy in the lecture: "While it was not distinguished for eloquence, still there were many practical thoughts embodied in it."[80] The following day, however, Finger redeemed himself with a one-hour lecture Truett described as "*excellent.* There was *much practical* information embodied in it."[81]

During his stay in Franklin, Truett did the same things that he would have done had he been in Hayesville: escorting women to social functions; attending debates, Sunday school, and preaching; and contributing financially to various ministries. His first evening in town, however, would prove to be the most important event that summer, for that night he met J. G. Pulliam, an evangelist, who would play an instrumental role in Truett's spiritual life.

Pulliam had been converted under the ministry of Amzi Clarence (A. C.) Dixon, who, from 1880 to 1882, pastored First Baptist Church, Asheville, North Carolina. During a routine pastoral visit to a deacon's home one winter afternoon, Dixon was sitting in the parlor, shivering and waiting for the deacon's wife to get ready for the visit. Pulliam knocked on the door and asked to see the deacon. He then sat down next to Dixon, and while the two men shivered and waited together, Dixon asked Pulliam if he was a Christian, to which Pulliam replied, "You have no use for me; you are looking for the well-to-do, like all the church folks." Dixon assured him that the Lord, churches, and preachers needed men like him. Before long, Pulliam professed his faith in Christ, and the two knelt in prayer. Later, Dixon baptized Pulliam, who then "became a rough and ready evangelist."[82]

Pulliam preached a revival in Franklin while Truett was in town. Pulliam's preaching impressed Truett, who briefly commented on seven of the evangelist's sermons, some of which surpassed others. The evangelist's July 4 sermon was "good," as was his July 8 prayer meeting "talk." Pulliam's sermon "Development the result of exercise" on July 15 was "*excellent*," as was his sermon two days later. On Sunday morning, July 18, he preached a "*grand*" sermon titled "The Christian's Rest," which he followed that afternoon with a "*good*" sermon on "The duty of Christians to the poor." The last of Pulliam's sermons, "Woman's Influence," was, according to Truett, a "*success.*"[83]

Truett did not merely listen to Pulliam's sermons while in Franklin; he also spent time with the evangelist, noting in his diary seven conversations he had with Pulliam.[84] Truett did not record any details about these conversations, although he wrote that Pulliam had given him "some *good* advice," "some good 'hints' concerning my prospects, desires, etc.," and "excellent advice."[85] Since evangelists are called evangelists for a reason, the two undoubtedly talked about Truett's relationship with God. Perhaps in Pulliam, Truett had finally found someone with whom he could share his soul and who could help pull him out of his spiritual darkness.

Truett and Harvey returned home to Hayesville on July 27. On August 9, Truett started teaching students aged seven to twenty-two in a one-room schoolhouse at Crooked Creek, just across the North Carolina state line in Towns County, Georgia.[86] The day before he started teaching, Truett heard his thirty-year-old cousin Fernando (Ferd) C. McConnell preach in Brasstown. According to Truett, McConnell "is certainly a *grand* man. He seems to be a *perfect* orator."[87]

While teaching at Crooked Creek, Truett often boarded with various families during the week and returned home on the weekends. He taught everything, including the alphabet, history, geography, and first-year algebra. The number of students eventually grew from thirty-two to fifty.

Discipline at the school was a problem and, when necessary, Truett maintained it by wielding a hickory stick, often with vigor. Most parents did not mind if he had to whip their children, but one father did mind and threatened Truett. Weighing only 150 pounds at the time, Truett stood his ground and persuaded the man to see things from his point of view. The man did and eventually became a strong supporter of Truett.[88]

On Sunday, September 19, Truett recorded that "'Nigger' preaching [was] in full blast to-day" in Hayesville. That evening he attended a revival at the Methodist church, where he heard a minister preach a good sermon, which was followed by an exhortation by Rev. Mashburn, the Baptist preacher in Hayesville. After a prayer by another minister, "there was a *great* feeling by the Christians. It seemed like 'The walls of Jericho would surely fall down.'" After the service, Truett "lectured to the 'darkies' awhile. Never before did I hear the like."[89]

Also during the Methodist revival, Truett's friend and confidant J. G. Pulliam was leading revival services at the Baptist church in Hayesville. On Sunday afternoon, September 26, he preached an "admirable" sermon.[90] Truett had canceled school at Crooked Creek the previous two weeks so that his students could work on their family farms. He returned to Crooked Creek on Monday, September 27, "and for various reasons postponed school another w[ee]k. Have been attending Preaching at the Bapt[ist]. Ch[urch]. by J. G. Pulliam. An interesting meeting all the while preaching excellent."[91] Although Truett did not elaborate on his reasons for cancelling classes for another week, he perhaps had been experiencing some spiritual struggles and wanted to continue attending the revival services at the Hayesville Baptist Church.

During the service on Sunday morning, October 3, Pulliam preached his "farewell sermon," which Truett described as "*excellent*," before leaving for another preaching engagement.[92] That evening, however, Pulliam shocked everyone when he walked into the sanctuary, marched down the center aisle, and had a brief conversation with Mashburn. The pastor then informed the congregation that Pulliam had returned to Hayesville, having been convinced that God wanted him to continue the revival services for another week. Truett recalled that "[t]he impression made by" the evangelist "was immediately in evidence." Pulliam then preached on the text "The just shall live by faith and if any man draw back, my soul shall have no pleasure in him" (Heb. 10:38). The evangelist talked about faith in Christ, how Christ was humanity's only Savior, and about the danger of rejecting Christ's call to salvation. At the end of the sermon, Pulliam invited people to declare publicly their faith in Christ.[93] Truett described that eventful moment in his diary: "While sitting on my seat, I felt my need of Religion and I began to ask God to save me. Then my mind became absorbed and I lost myself until I found myself on the floor praising God. Mr. Aleck Thompson also professed faith in Christ. It was a glorious time."[94]

Walking home from church that Sunday night, Truett, assured of his salvation, was captivated by the beauty of the stars. They "seemed to be one great galaxy of mighty choirs praising God," he later recalled, "and all about me nature seemed in unison with the divine will. I thought I would never, never, never know what it was to step aside, to stray, to blunder, to err again."[95]

Early on Monday morning, before Truett rode his pony to Crooked Creek, his mother made him some coffee and breakfast while he told her that he was willing to do whatever God wanted him to do.[96] Apparently, however, the assurance that he would "never, never, never know what it was to step aside, to stray, to blunder, to err again" was short-lived, for later that day "every dog out of the pit seemed at my heels. Doubts came, darts pierced, temptations smote, and clouds enshrouded."[97]

That evening, Truett returned to Hayesville to attend the revival. At the beginning of the service, Mashburn asked for those who wanted to join the Hayesville Baptist Church to come forward, which Truett did. He gave testimony of his "Christian experience" and was accepted as a member of the church.[98]

The revival at the Baptist church finally ended on Wednesday evening. After Pulliam's sermon, Mashburn, to Truett's "utter amazement," turned abruptly to him and said, "Brother George, won't you exhort" the people "to turn to Christ?" Truett overcame his fear and began walking down the aisle, pleading with the people to surrender their lives to Christ. "I was carried away with my passionate concern for my neighbors and friends," he said many years later, "everyone of whom I knew," and soon they all "crowded to the door.... Then...it dawned upon me what I had done; and in unspeakable humiliation to myself I sat down." Soon thereafter, he quickly left the building, walked home as fast as he could, and went to bed. When his parents came home, his mother went to his room. "I told her," Truett recalled, that "I felt humiliated and ashamed beyond human speech at what I had done. And she kissed me [and] said, 'My boy, all that is the temptation of the devil to silence you as a witness for Christ. I doubt if ever in all your life you will give a more effective testimony for Christ than you gave tonight.'"[99]

Despite Truett's abrupt departure from church that Wednesday evening, many people from then on asked him if he felt called to preach. Truett assured them, however, that he was not; he was a teacher whose goal was to attend college and become a criminal lawyer.[100]

The Sunday after his conversion, the person responsible for beginning Sunday school at the Hayesville Baptist Church was late, so Truett "opened up" the school "for the first time." For some reason, doing so troubled him, as he confessed in his diary: "Oh! how unworthy do I feel in that position."[101] The following week when the person in charge of starting Sunday school was late again, Truett started the class. He noted in his diary, "The Lord pardon me if I committed an error in doing so."[102]

Two weeks after his conversion, Truett again doubted his conversion experience. He wondered whether he "had not utterly missed the right road and made shipwreck of my soul." A young man, perhaps Charley Curtis, whom Truett mentioned in his diary, sensed that Truett was troubled and asked to talk with him. They took a two-hour walk in the woods, during which Curtis talked about the highs and lows of being a Christian, just what Truett had been experiencing. In his diary entry for Sunday night, October 17, Truett recorded that Curtis's "experience and words strengthen me."[103] The meeting seemed to answer some of Truett's nagging questions, whatever they were, so much so that he later recalled, "When we came back from that walk in the woods I had passed an epoch in my life, the glory of which two hours has stayed with me ever since."[104]

After his conversion, Truett continued teaching at Crooked Creek, singing, commenting on sermons, contributing money to Christian ministries, socializing with girls, and attending and participating in debates. Truett noted his participation in two debates during fall 1886. Once again he was on the affirmative side in the debate over compulsory school attendance, though he did not record a decision.[105] In late October he was also on the affirmative side in the debate on whether "a law prohibiting the manufacture and sale of alcohol beverages would be of national benefit." The debate ended with no decision.[106] Truett debated the prohibition question at Crooked Creek in November and was again on the affirmative side. He did not record the decision, but did note that the debate was "very interesting."[107]

On Saturday, November 13, Truett heard his "Uncle Lije" preach a "good sermon" during a Saturday service at the Hayesville Baptist Church. Kimsey was undoubtedly in town to attend Truett's baptism, which occurred in the Hiawassee River on Sunday afternoon, November 14. Later that day Truett recorded in his diary: "I am endeavoring to serve God according to his Word, and if I am blinded and mistaken and doing wrong in publicly testifying for Jesus, then, the Lord forgive me for it. I want to do the will of Jesus and I humbly pray that he may help me."[108]

Fall classes at Crooked Creek ended on Friday, November 26. The next day, on his way home, Truett stopped at the Baptist church in Hayesville "for preaching." The congregation was "jarred" when it learned that the church clerk had resigned. The congregation then voted Truett to be the clerk. Despite feeling "unqualified" for the position, he promised to "do *the best* I can." During the service he contributed 50¢ ($11.37) for the purchase of a ledger book, which brought his total contribution to Christian causes for the year to $1.65 ($37.51). After the service he and a friend traveled to Bell Creek, where Truett gave a fifteen-minute speech on "Our Country and People." After returning home Sunday morning, he attended preaching and then a baptismal service. With the Crooked Creek school closed for the rest of the year, Truett ended his diary for 1886 almost plaintively with these words: "Don't know what I'll do now."[109] Truett was always looking for something to do.

*A School of His Own*

After the school term at Crooked Creek ended in November, Truett noted in his diary: "It was indeed trying to talk to the parents and children for the last time. Their expressions of kindness, friendship and affection will never be forgotten."[110] He would not return to teach at the school because he had already made other arrangements to teach elsewhere in 1887. Truett had dreamed about starting his own school at Hiawassee, in Towns County, Georgia, much like the one he had attended as a boy. He chose Hiawassee because it was located near the center of the county's population and could be easily reached over fairly decent roads. Moreover, his cousins, the McConnells, lived near the town. The most "prosperous and influential" family in that part of the county, the McConnells did whatever they could to help their kinsman. Particularly helpful was Ferd McConnell, who helped his cousin start the school.[111] Thus, in January 1887, Truett and McConnell opened their school in the Hiawassee courthouse.

The school was open to all children, and parents paid $1.00 ($22.49) per month. If parents could not pay their children's tuition, Truett credited their account. Eventually, a white-framed building was erected. In time enrollment increased to over 300, a number that included 23 preachers and 51 school teachers who wanted further training. Truett preached regularly at chapel and vesper services and led Friday night prayer meetings.[112]

Teaching provided Truett with an opportunity to pass on the knowledge that he had received. Teaching also enabled him to earn the money he would need to attend college later. He dreamed of attending either Carson-Newman College in Tennessee, Wake Forest College in North Carolina, or Mercer University in Georgia. Wanting to be a lawyer, Truett purchased and read Blackstone's *Commentaries on the Laws of England*, and when time permitted, he attended trials in Hayesville and Hiawassee.[113]

Truett perhaps offered his first public prayer during a worship service at the Hayesville Baptist Church or perhaps during a Sunday-school class. Like his first attempt at exhortation, he considered his first public prayer a failure: "I was able to pray only one sentence," he observed many years later, "only one, for my tongue did cleave to the roof of my mouth, and I could not think of another word to say."[114] It would be a gross understatement to say that Truett would eventually overcome his timidity to exhort and to pray publicly.

If Truett was intimidated by praying in public, he apparently had little difficulty praying privately, and sometimes, even unknown to him, with good results. One day in August 1887 or 1888, a moonshiner known as Uncle Jimmie Barrett was transporting a jug of whiskey to a man in Hiawassee. Around noon on his journey to town, the moonshiner heard someone walking in the woods. Not wanting to be caught with his contraband, Barrett hid in some bushes. He saw the man, who was George Truett, "under a tree" and determined that the man "warnt a-spying on" him. Instead, Barrett listened to Truett pray "for the town of Hiawassee and the people in it." He did not pray specifically for Barrett, but, the moonshiner recalled in an interview seventy years later, "I knew I was included." From that day forward, Barrett tried to live a better life. He joined a church, but only on the condition that he be allowed to help build the church building. His eleven children also became Christians.[115] Truett never heard of Barrett's experience, but for someone who debated and preached against the evils of alcohol for fifty-eight years, he would have been pleased.

During his teaching career at Hiawassee, Truett participated in his first "soul winning" experience. One morning during chapel service, a boy named Jim, "a strange, eager, lonely-looking lad" of sixteen, hobbled to the front row and sat down. Truett thought that the boy was a beggar, and after the service, he approached the boy to discover his need. Jim told Truett that he wanted to attend school and to become "somebody in the world." Doctors had told the boy that he would always "be a cripple.... But I want to be somebody."[116] Truett immediately enrolled the boy in school, giving him free tuition and books.

A few days later, Truett called Jim into his office to find out more about him. The boy told Truett that his father had been killed in a mill accident. Because the money his father had saved was soon depleted, Jim's mother, a washerwoman, decided to move to Towns County, hoping to build a better life for her family. Jim wanted to attend Truett's school to help his mother and "be somebody in the world." Classes were about to start when Jim finished his story. As the boy was about to leave, Truett put his hand on Jim's head and said, "I am for you, my boy. You are my sort of boy. I believe in you thoroughly, and I want you to know that I love you." A few weeks later during Friday night prayers, Jim sat in a corner "by himself to keep the boys off his worn and wasted limb, and getting up, sobbing and laughing at the same time, he looked at" Truett and said, "Teacher, I have found the Saviour, and that time you told me that you loved me started me toward Him."[117] Jim went on to become an itinerant preacher in the North Carolina mountains.[118]

While teaching at Hiawassee, Truett returned home to Hayesville on the weekends, which enabled him to fulfill his duties as the clerk of his church. The minutes for the church conferences from November 1886 to October 1888 still exist. These records contain many of the normal affairs that go on in a church, such as the addition of new members, the deletion of members who joined other churches, the progress of committees, and the names of committee members. On November 27, 1887, for example, Truett noted that his father was appointed to a committee assigned to investigate the building of a "Ch[urch]. house in Hayesville." Truett also recorded on that day that the church "agreed to elect a pastor for the ensuing year. Rev. J. G. Mashburn was unanimously reelected by acclamation."[119] During that era many churches issued yearly calls to ministers.

Under the heading "Sabbath" between the entries for November 27, 1887, and December 24, 1887, Truett recorded what was undoubtedly a thrilling experience for his family: "Preaching today by the pastor. The door of the Ch[urch]. was opened. Rec[eive]d Spurgeon Truett by experience. He was baptized by the pastor in the afternoon."[120]

On New Year's Day 1888 members of the Hayesville Baptist Church elected Truett to be their Sunday-school superintendent.[121] The following

May the church chose the twenty-two-year-old Truett and his father to "aid in the settlement of a difficulty in" a Nantahala, North Carolina, church, which had requested help from the Hayesville church.[122]

With his duties as the principal of his school in Hiawassee and as the church clerk and the Sunday-school superintendent of the Hayesville Baptist Church, Truett could not say, "Don't know what I'll do now," for he had plenty of work to keep him busy. As the number of students at his school steadily increased, he realized that he needed help. Consequently, Truett hired his brother Luther to teach math and Young W. Jones, a graduate of Mercer University, to teach some advanced classes. The Georgia Baptist Convention and the Home Mission Board of the Southern Baptist Convention supplemented Truett's salary at Hiawassee and paid Jones's salary. Thus, it was no surprise that Truett accompanied his cousin Ferd to the Georgia Baptist Convention meeting in Marietta, Georgia, in spring 1889.

### A Thrilling Sensation at the Convention

One man who attended the meeting in Marietta was the father of William D. Upshaw. Mr. Upshaw owned a farm in Cobb County, Georgia, and was a deacon in a Baptist church. His son William remained at home in bed, having suffered a spinal injury while hauling wood on the farm. When the elder Upshaw returned from the convention, he stood by William's bed and said, "Well, my son, we had a thrilling sensation at the convention today."[123]

That "thrilling sensation" occurred after Ferd McConnell reported on Christian education, which included the mountain schools, of which Truett's school was one. At the end of McConnell's report, he shouted that mountain children "are there like gold for the touch of the miner's pick and they are fit to stand in the presence of kings, packed full of brains and character waiting for a chance. If you don't believe me I'll show you! George! Where is George Truett?" As he scanned the audience, McConnell could not find his cousin. Shocked, Truett stood where he was, hoping that no one would recognize him. "Brethren, I do believe he's got skeered and run off," McConnell laughed. But someone recognized Truett and shouted, "Here he is!" Having been discovered, the young, mountain schoolteacher reluctantly trudged to the podium, where, according to John E. White, pastor of Second Baptist Church, Atlanta, Georgia, he looked like a defendant being cross-examined, "half-frightened and vastly embarrassed by the focus of eyes." To make matters worse, McConnell boasted that his cousin could "speak like [Charles H.] Spurgeon. George, tell them what the Lord has done for you, and what you are trying to do up in the mountains."[124]

After overcoming the shock and embarrassment of being put on the spot, just as he had been at the Hayesville Baptist Church soon after his conversion, Truett began to speak in that voice one later contemporary described as being "like honey and lava melded into burning words that were penetrating and unforgettable."[125] Truett told the audience:

> I never saw such a great, big, fine body of men as this before in all my life. The truth is, I am so scared my knees are making war on each other, and I hardly know which one of my father's boys I am. But I have been impressed as this discussion on education has proceeded, that some of the people of this convention do not seem to realize what they have in Mercer University. They have not been with me up in the mountains; they have not seen the gleam of Mercer's light gliding over the mountain tops and lighting up the valleys; they have not seen the boys who are catching the radiance in their hearts, and they have not seen the homes that have been blessed, the churches that have been quickened, and the lives that have been inspired and transformed by Mercer's marvelous influence![126]

Truett reported that the mountain students were hungry to learn despite their impoverished circumstances, that the mountain schools were trying to help them, and that these schools could benefit churches. Mountain children, like all children, had hopes and dreams and needed an environment that could aid in fulfilling their hopes and dreams.

When Truett finished his fifteen-minute impromptu speech, McConnell took the podium and said, "As Brother Truett is not a preacher, he is not entitled to free tuition at Mercer University, but while he has not the money to pay his way, yet I want him to go." Calder B. Willingham, a wealthy layman from Macon, Georgia, rose and announced, "I'll give to his school, but I want to do more than that. I want the honor of giving that young man a college education. If he will come to Macon, I will pay his expenses at Mercer University until he graduates." Then, after Archibald Battle, president of Mercer University, declared, "We must have you, sir, at Mercer," the convention responded with "long, loud, rapturous applause."[127]

J. B. Hawthorne, pastor of First Baptist Church, Atlanta, and whose sermons Truett read growing up, noted after the convention that he had heard some of the world's greatest preachers, but "never in my life has my soul been more deeply stirred by any speaker than it was that day at Marietta by that boy out of the mountains. My heart burned within me and I could not keep back the tears."[128] When asked what he thought about Truett, Hawthorne responded, "I quit thinking. I just surrendered. I gave up everything. He just absolutely swept that crowd. He's the greatest potential public speaker I've ever seen."[129]

As a result of his Marietta speech, Truett received an opportunity of a lifetime: a free college education that would launch him into a legal career. Yet that was not to be, for two of his brothers, Tom and Harvey, had moved west to Texas, and soon the rest of his family followed.

*Texas Fever*

Tom was the first Truett to move to Texas, "where life was easier, where money was more plentiful, and above all, where one 'could get on in the world.'"[130] In 1877, the twenty-four-year-old North Carolinian and his wife, Joan, boarded the first train he had ever seen and moved to Whitewright, Texas, seventy miles northeast of Dallas.[131] Harvey, who had served as a superior court clerk in Clay County in 1886, followed his older brother to Texas in 1887. They wrote "glowing reports" to their parents about the land in Texas, and when Tom later returned to North Carolina for a visit, he described the glories of Texas for his father. Charles, however, was not as anxious to leave North Carolina as were his adventurous sons. After returning to Texas, Tom kept a little notebook in which he recorded several reasons that his family should move to Texas and sent them to his father. Charles, who by then had caught "Texas fever," eventually discussed with Truett and Luther the possibility of moving to Texas, and the boys encouraged him to sell the farm and move west. Once Charles decided to move, he quickly sold the farm, and ten days later, in early 1889, he, his wife, Spurgeon, and Sarah moved to Texas.[132] James, who had been teaching school in Tennessee, moved to Texas four years later.[133]

Truett and Luther, who also had decided to move, remained behind to finish the spring 1889 term at the Hiawassee school. Before leaving for Texas, Truett asked his students to sign an eight-by-five-inch autograph book "for memory." Some of the students wrote short messages; others quoted poems. One student wrote a short prayer: "May your life be clad in the beauty of a thousand stars." R. J. Ritchie expressed sentiments that many people felt about Truett: "Ever since I first came under your instruction, I have realized that in you I had a warm friend." Truett's assistant, Young Jones, wrote, "That it has been my happy privilege to labor with you in the Hiawassee High School for the past seven and a half months is one of the sweetest experiences I have ever enjoyed, and one of the sweetest through which I ever expect to pass this side of Heaven. Tonight they end. If I but knew our future days would be so pleasantly and profitably spent, I could then more easily say 'Good-by.' Whether we spend our days in sadness or in joy, we must part. May God's blessing go with us."[134]

After putting the academy in the hands of a friend, Tom O'Kelly, Truett and Luther followed the rest of their family to Texas in summer 1889. By moving west, Truett left behind his opportunity for a free college education at Mercer University, but he still took with him his dream of becoming a lawyer. His brothers Harvey and Luther would become lawyers in Texas, but Truett never would.[135] Another calling awaited him there.

*Appalled but Called*

The Truetts settled in Whitewright, a town in Grayson County that had something Clay County did not have: rich farmland. Founded in 1878, Whitewright had a private school, a public school, Grayson Junior College, a newspaper, and several businesses. A post office was built in 1888, and by 1900, the town had 1,804 residents.[136] As they had done in North Carolina, the Truetts joined a Baptist church and became faithful members.

Moving to Texas from the Blue Ridge Mountains of southwestern North Carolina proved to be difficult for Truett and Luther, at least at first. Leaving their work and home was difficult, but their parents, now nearly sixty years old, had ventured out in faith, so why not them? As the two young men traveled west, the trees became smaller, the land flatter, and the temperature hotter. Arriving in Texas during the summer, they learned what "hot" really meant. One can imagine one of the boys, who had grown up among tall, beautiful trees, trekked in mountains, and breathed mountain air, turning to the other upon arriving in Whitewright, saying, "We left home for *this*?" Indeed, after only a few days of living in the scorching heat of North Texas, Luther confessed to his brother, "George, this is awful. I don't believe I can stand it much longer. If I had known what we were getting into here, I would have stayed in the mountains." George responded, "Amen, brother. You said it."[137] But they had left the North Carolina mountains and would reside in Texas the rest of their lives.

During his first summer in Whitewright, George worked on the family farm. Then in fall 1889, he and Luther entered Grayson Junior College. In order to prepare himself for a legal career, George studied Greek, Latin, history, English literature, theme writing, public speaking, and math. The college also had several literary societies, which provided him opportunities to hone his speaking and debating skills.[138]

Truett joined Whitewright Baptist Church, where he taught a Sunday-school class and eventually became the Sunday-school superintendent. He also often preached in the pastor's absence. Truett did not, however, consider his preaching to be "preaching," nor did he stand behind the pulpit when he "preached." Such a place, he believed, was reserved for ordained ministers, God's chosen instruments, of whom he was not one.[139]

Later in life, Truett recalled his first "sermon" before "his own home folk":

> I will say that when I came to preach my first sermon it was only thirteen minutes long. I preached on that great text from Jesus: "Ye are the light of the world" [Matt. 5:14a]. In thirteen minutes I said all I knew to say on that text. But I shall never forget the faces of the people and their warm hand clasps when it was over and how one after another said, "I prayed for you. I love you. I helped you all I could." That first sermon to the home folk is a great occasion in the life of any preacher.[140]

The sermons Truett preached in his pastor's absences eventually sank his dream of becoming a lawyer, for many people in his church determined that he should be a preacher. Some members talked to him privately about entering the ministry, but he always assured them that God had called him to be a lawyer. His protests, however, did not persuade anyone. Eventually, his fellow church members took matters into their own hands.

One Saturday evening in 1890, Truett attended his church's monthly conference. As he entered the sanctuary, he thought it odd that the sanctuary was full, for usually only a few people attended such Saturday meetings. After the conference and the pastor's sermon, a revered, frail-looking deacon stood up and talked in generalities about the duties of individuals and of groups. While the deacon was speaking, Truett thought, "What a remarkable talk he is making—perhaps he thinks it is his last talk."[141] Then, Truett recalled, the old deacon "got painfully specific and personal."[142] The deacon said, "There is such a thing as a church duty when the whole church must act. There is such a thing as an individual duty, when the individual, detached from every other individual, must face duty for himself; but it is my deep conviction as it is yours—for we have talked much one with another—that this church has a church duty to perform, and that we have waited late and long to get about it. I move, therefore, that this church call a presbytery to ordain Brother George W. Truett to the full work of the gospel ministry."[143]

Someone seconded the motion, but before the vote was taken, Truett rose to express his horror at the church's decision. "You have me appalled," he cried; "you simply have me appalled!" Truett pleaded with them to wait six months. The members, however, responded that they would not wait six hours: "We are called to do this thing now, and we are going ahead with it."[144] They had determined that God had called Truett to preach, and they would not back down. The church then voted unanimously to ordain him.

Truett finally realized that the church would not give in to his pleas. He remarked years later, "There I was, against the whole church, against a church profoundly moved. There was not a dry eye in the house—one of the supremely solemn hours in a church's life. I was thrown into the stream, and just had to swim."[145]

After the church conference, Truett talked to his mother about what had happened. "Son, these are praying people," she responded. "These are Christ's people. These are God's people and you saw how they felt. They felt that they couldn't—even in the face of your plea, your protest, your exhortation to delay—they couldn't [delay your ordination]."[146] She also told him that she had prayed daily since he was an infant for God to call him to the ministry.[147]

The church requested that several ministers hold an ordination council to examine Truett before the Sunday morning worship service the next day. Included in the group was J. G. Mashburn, the man who had baptized Truett and who was visiting Truett's parents. After a sleepless night, Truett went to church and was examined by the ministers before the whole church. He again expressed his desire to become a lawyer, yet confessed that he was now willing to follow God's leadership, wherever it led, "even though it should be the humblest little spot in all the world."[148]

*Another Option*

Truett's ordination forced him to change his plans about becoming a lawyer. He would not do his pleading in a courtroom but in a church sanctuary. To prepare himself for his ministerial vocation, Truett planned to finish college before attending seminary. But soon after making these plans, Benajah Harvey (B. H.) Carroll, the most influential Baptist pastor in Texas, presented Truett with another option.

At the time of Truett's ordination, Baylor University was mired in a $92,000 ($2,162,751) debt. The university's board of trustees needed to find someone to replace J. B. Cranfill, who had worked as Baylor's financial agent but had accepted a position as superintendent of Baptist mission work in Texas. As R. F. Jenkins, pastor of Whitewright Baptist Church, prayed about the Baylor situation, Truett's name repeatedly came to mind. The pastor, however, considered the job at Baylor to be too much for a twenty-three-year-old man who was unknown to Texas Baptists and still a student in junior college. Despite his misgivings, Jenkins wrote to Carroll, pastor of First Baptist Church, Waco, and chairman of Baylor's board of trustees. Jenkins told Carroll, "There is one thing I do know about George Truett—wherever he speaks, the people do what he asks them to do."[149]

Needing an agent who could quickly get Texas Baptists to support Baylor financially, Carroll wrote to Truett, asking to meet the young preacher in order to discuss Truett's becoming Baylor's financial agent. On November 12, 1890, the two men talked at a Mr. Crouch's home in McKinney, Texas, where Carroll was preaching during a missionary conference. After talking with the Waco minister for several days, Truett became impressed with Baylor and told Carroll that he would pray about becoming Baylor's financial agent before making a decision. Truett had already started praying about the situation while at the Crouch home, for, according to Mr. Crouch, "George Truett seemed to stay on his knees just about all the time."[150] Evidently, Truett knew there was serious work ahead.

When Truett returned to Whitewright, his physical appearance shocked his mother, who stated that he looked like he had seen a ghost. Truett told her that he felt sick, which he was—with the measles. He was so ill that his family and friends thought he might die. During this time, Truett contemplated whether he should accept Carroll's offer.[151] Accepting the offer would delay his plans of attending a seminary, or it might even change his life's direction again. But with another option in front of him, he had to make a decision, one that he was convinced was the will of God.

# Chapter 2

# Becoming a Faithful Preacher
# of the Gospel, 1891–1907

Theology in the mid-1800s and early 1900s experienced challenges that many American Christians believed undermined the Christian faith. For some, Charles Darwin's theory of the biological evolution of the human species, first presented in his book *Origin of Species* (1859), challenged the belief in humanity's unique status as God's special creation. According to Darwin, humanity, instead of being created fully developed in one day, which many Christians believed was taught in the book of Genesis, had evolved from lower life forms over the course of numerous centuries. Moreover, many biblical scholars and theologians influenced by European scholars utilized a new interpretive method called "higher criticism" to study the Bible. For example, theologians for centuries had maintained that Moses wrote the Pentateuch, the first five books of the Bible. When scholars used the method of higher criticism, however, they proved to their own satisfaction that the Pentateuch had not been written by Moses but by several authors. Such an approach to the Bible, in the minds of many Christians, including Southern Baptists, challenged their belief that the Bible was the inspired Word of God.[1]

The term "social gospel" also came into use during the early twentieth century to describe a movement, popular mainly among northern American Protestants, that attempted to apply biblical and theological teachings to social reforms, such as poverty. For many social gospelers, the key to Christianizing culture lay in reforming society, not primarily in saving souls. Two prominent Northern Baptists involved in the Social Gospel movement were Shailer Mathews, a New Testament and theology professor at the University of Chicago's divinity school, and Walter Rauschenbusch, a church historian at Rochester Theological Seminary. Rauschenbusch's 1907 book, *Christianity and the Social Crisis*, presented a biting attack on the social evils of the era and the Christian church's failure to deal with them. According to Rauschenbusch, "the essential purpose of Christianity was to transform society into the kingdom of God by regenerating all human relations and reconstituting them in accordance with the will of God."[2] Many Baptists in the South feared that the Social Gospel, which they believed to be more "social" than "gospel," would infect southerners, thereby converting their churches from focusing on evangelism to embracing socialism. Opponents of evolutionism, higher criticism, and social gospelism often called the adherents of such "isms" modernists, a precursor to the term "liberals."

As a newly ordained minister, the twenty-three-year-old George W. Truett did not have to struggle with evolution, higher criticism, or the Social Gospel in the winter of 1890. Instead, he had to grapple with B. H. Carroll's offer to become the financial agent of Baylor University, located in Texas, a state many people in the eastern part of the United States in the late nineteenth century considered to be an uncouth, undeveloped, and uneducated section of the country populated by a bunch of ungodly hicks. Such an opinion of Texas and Texans existed well into the twentieth century. Long after Dallas had become a large city and an influential financial center in the Southwest, easterners still considered the state to be uncivilized. For example, before Mrs. D. W. Jones of Dallas returned home from a trip to Charlotte, North Carolina, in 1933, friends asked her to stay, for they told her that once she crossed "the Mississippi you leave God and civilization behind." And although the North Carolinians considered their native son George W. Truett to be a great preacher, they saw him as "a sort of missionary among the savages."[3] Yet among these Texas savages, Truett, in the words of J. B. Cranfill, would "flower into greatness,"[4] first in the hearts of Texas Baptists and then in the hearts of many Baptists and non-Baptists in the South and beyond.

*Saving Baylor*

Texas Baptists founded Baylor University in 1845 at Independence, Texas, nine miles north of Brenham. The university opened the following year on May 18, 1846, with one teacher and twenty-four men and women students. In 1851, the university was divided into male and female departments. Texas Baptists formed another university, Waco University, at Waco in 1861. Eventually, according to Leon McBeth, Baptists had to decide whether "to divide their support between two mediocre colleges, or pool their resources to create one first-class university."[5] Thus, in 1886 Texas Baptists decided to consolidate Baylor with Waco University in an attempt to create a first-class university, which would be located in Waco. Baylor's female department, called Baylor Female College, relocated to Belton, Texas, that same year.

While recovering from the measles at his parents' home in Whitewright, Texas, in fall 1890, Truett prayed about becoming Baylor's financial agent. He accepted Carroll's offer and boarded a train to Waco in January 1891 to meet Baylor's board of trustees. William D. Upshaw, whose father described for him the "thrilling sensation" that had occurred when Truett spoke at the 1889 Georgia Baptist Convention meeting, was a guest at Truett's home several years after the Baylor debt retirement campaign. During that visit, Truett told Upshaw, "Brother Will, I prayed with almost every revolution of the car wheels: 'Lord, if I am not your man for this great task, please do not let me reach Waco.'"[6] The train reached Waco safely, thereby confirming for Truett that he was to be Baylor's financial agent.

After arriving in Waco, Truett went to Carroll's home, where the trustees soon assembled to meet the man whom Carroll had found to lead Baylor out of debt. Most of the trustees were older men and civic and religious leaders in Waco. They hoped that Carroll had found them a jewel, a man of wisdom, power, and persuasion. To put it in biblical language, the trustees wanted and needed a messiah who would save the university. What they saw before them was a young man, still evidencing the effects of a grueling bout with the measles. Truett could tell by the look in the trustees' eyes that they were underwhelmed. Carroll, famous for his lengthy sermons, gave an unusually brief speech, at the conclusion of which the trustees chatted a few minutes until one man finally saw a way out of the uncomfortable situation, saying, "Well, Dr. Carroll, we'll be going now." Truett, however, would not let them leave before he had made his appeal. He acknowledged that no one in Texas knew him, but that Carroll had convinced him that God wanted him to take the job. Truett also confessed that he did not know how he would retire the debt, but he was convinced that if they all trusted God, God would help them. Yet if God was not in the campaign, Truett would fail, and if God was not in it, he did not want to be in it either.[7] Moved by Truett's earnest response, the trustees accepted him and placed the fate of the university in his hands. Thus began what Carroll and Truett later called "a great battle" to save Baylor.[8]

Shortly after meeting the trustees, Truett moved into the Carroll home, which became his base of operations for the next twenty-three months. Carroll, forty-seven years old at the time, frequently had young preachers stay with him, often for free, and he welcomed anyone who needed counsel or comfort.[9] Although a sensitive man, Carroll had a strong personality, and at 6 feet 3 inches tall and weighing 240 pounds, he was quite an intimidating figure. He read widely and rapidly, averaging 235 pages a day for thirty-five years.

During his stay with the Carrolls, Truett developed a close relationship with the influential Baptist pastor, talking with him and discussing philosophy, theology, and ministry. The time they spent together undoubtedly influenced Truett, who often acknowledged his indebtedness to Carroll, but without being specific. Later in life, Truett called him "the greatest personality I ever touched."[10] Three areas that Carroll might have influenced Truett's thinking, or at least reinforced his thinking, concerned the importance of the pastorate, the necessity of stewardship, and the significance of eschatology, or the doctrine of last things.

For Carroll, being a preacher was the most glorious calling in all the earth. One young man who heard him preach the convention sermon at the 1892 Baptist General Convention of Texas (BGCT) meeting in Belton remembered Carroll saying, "I magnify my office whether poor or rich, whether sick or well, whether strong or weak, anywhere, everywhere, among all people, in any crowd, Lord God, I am glad that I am a preacher, that I am a preacher of the glorious gospel of Jesus Christ."[11] In numerous sermons to his congregations and in addresses to fellow preachers, Truett would express similar sentiments. For example, at the Kansas City Ministers' Conference in 1907, Truett told the pastors, "We are not to be clergyman, we are to be preachers of the gospel of the Christ of God. We are Jesus Christ's preachers, preachers called and consecrated by the Holy Ghost into the glorious service" of God.[12]

Concerning stewardship, Carroll stressed that Christians lived under the Lordship of Christ.[13] Consequently, every man, woman, and child should tithe (give 10 percent of their earnings) and contribute to the ministries of their church, their state convention, and their denomination. Carroll also believed in taking special offerings to support causes beyond his own church, and he led his church to adopt a budget plan to manage the church's finances.[14] Once Truett entered the pastorate, he became famous for his preaching on stewardship and for his taking special offerings at churches and at convention meetings.

Carroll's eschatology also might have influenced Truett. Carroll held a postmillennial rather than a premillennial understanding of Christ's Second Coming. Postmillennialists believe that Christ will return to earth after a thousand years of peace has been produced by the spreading of Christian principles throughout the earth. Premillennialists contend that Christ's return will precede and produce that thousand-year period. According to Carroll, premillennialists were too pessimistic and lacked the faith that the preaching of the gospel and the power of the Holy Spirit would achieve their purposes on earth. Carroll, however, contended that postmillennialists were biblical, optimistic, and fueled by the faith that God was now working through the church to create the millennium on earth.[15] Postmillennialism would have appealed to Truett, for he was an optimist. Also, that his mentor was a postmillennialist would also add weight to Truett being one also. Yet a British Baptist who would hear Truett preach in 1918 asked himself whether Truett was a premillenarian or a postmillenarian. "[I]t was not long before I discovered," the man confessed, "that he was greater than both."[16]

One trait of Carroll that did not influence Truett was the Waco preacher's love of a good verbal brawl.[17] Despite enjoying debating as a teenager and as a student at Grayson Junior College, Truett eventually stopped being involved in public debates, whether face to face or in print. Instead, he relied on other like-minded friends to express his position on many issues, or he worked behind the scenes, often quite forcefully. When attacking an opponent or an opponent's position, however, Truett usually spoke or wrote in general terms, letting his audiences or readers connect what they heard or read with what was happening in church circles or in society. He rarely publicly humiliated individuals by name.

In February 1891, after moving into the Carroll home, Truett began his work as Baylor's financial agent. J. N. Marshall, a pastor in Llano, Texas, and a Baylor alumnus, perhaps extended the first invitation to Truett to speak on behalf of the Baylor campaign. The district association of Baptists in Marshall's area was scheduled to meet at the Llano church on a Saturday, and despite the reservations of the church's deacons, Marshall invited Baylor's new financial agent to address the association during the Sunday morning worship service. Truett preached on 1 Corinthians 3:21, 23, "All things are yours...and ye are Christ's and Christ is God's," to a full auditorium. Forty-five years later, Marshall still remembered how the young preacher

> rose to the highest heights of the noblest pronouncements of impassioned oratory just like George can always do. It would be futile to undertake to report the sermon. No one could do it justice, though to this day the message, its spirit, its passionate, fervent delivery, its matter, and its electrical effect [are] as clear on the tablet of memory as if it had been delivered yesterday. The audience was moved as one rarely sees people under the spell of a spiritual,

rapturous appeal. Everybody seemingly was in tears. I glanced over, and my deacons were simply boo-hoo-ing. Oh, what a heavenly hour![18]

Marshall's account of the sermon contained a brief description of Truett's preaching voice, one that could easily describe the young minister's voice throughout his ministry. Marshall noted that Truett "began speaking quietly in measured sentences, and, as he spoke, his manner and his speech took on an intensity and earnest persuasiveness that has always characterized this great preacher."[19]

Other accounts of Truett's voice support Marshall's description. One journalist, Peter Clark Macfarlane, who heard Truett preach in 1912, noted that he spoke in "short smashing sentences." He spoke slowly and softly at times, but then his voice would roar "like a storm in a mountain. Sometimes, again, it was like the hoarse murmur of many waters, and rose like a wave of the sea higher and higher, to curl and break in spray of white-hot whispers that searched the corners of the auditorium like hissing jets of stream."[20] Later, in 1927, a lawyer commenting on Truett's voice said to a writer for the *Homiletic Review*, "You'll notice he follows the old order: Begin low, speak slow; rise higher, take fire."[21]

Recordings of sermons made in the 1930s and early 1940s support the preceding descriptions of Truett's voice. In these recordings one can hear Truett begin his sermons as if he were talking with a friend and then eventually hear that intensity and roar as his voice explodes into the microphone. His voice rises and falls much like the old revival preachers of the eighteenth and nineteenth centuries. One can also hear what can be described as a holy quiver, the drawing out of words like "oh" and "great." In the next two paragraphs, transcribed material from one of Truett's recorded sermons has been formatted to give readers a sense of what his listeners heard. Italics indicate a rise in the volume of Truett's voice, while capitalization represents an even greater increase in both volume and intensity. Underlined letters indicate a drop in Truett's voice.

In his sermon *Doing God's Will*, probably preached on October 6, 1940, or July 19, 1942,[22] Truett described relationships that should not be neglected, one of which was the husband-wife relationship. He used two illustrations to emphasize the tragedy of neglecting such an important relationship. The first illustration came from the life of Thomas Carlyle, a nineteenth-century English author. "I think one of the most pathetic things in literature," Truett lamented,

> is to read Carlyle's confession after his wife, Jane, had died. He found her diary and read it. And in that diary he saw the indictment of that wife of her *hunger* for old Carlyle's love, of *her longgging*, that he would faithfully care for her, that he *loved* her, *THAT NOBODY MEANT TO HIM WHAT SHE* meant to him. And that *strong-minded-woman* was forgotten and overlooked and neglected by the *strong-minded-MAN!* And you would see Carlyle's confession, "Ohhhh, if I had only *known* that Jane really cared at all." He might have known, he ought to have known.[23]

Truett then used a scene from George Elliot's novel *Amos Barton* to emphasize the same point. Amos worked all the time and neglected his wife, Milly. Upon returning home one evening, he found Milly desperately ill. She died shortly thereafter. Truett described Amos's grief and sense of failure with these words:

> And Amos Barton was over*whellLLMED* and smitten with a *greaaAAT blowwWW*. He staggered as one out of some terrible dream, coming into half awakening consciousness. And they got ready to bury Milly, the wife. George Elliot described it as she alone could describe it with biting words, vivid phrases. And after they got through with the funeral yonder, at the cemetery, and covered over the mound and left the flowers ther*rrre*, and the people went awa*aaay*, George Elliot pictures Amos Barton, the husband, creeping back to the *grave and flinging himself across it and WAILING out his heart-breaking cry,* "MIlly! MIlly! *I DID care for you more than I cared for anybody. I DID love you beyond anybody.* Do you *hear me now?"* No, she doesn't hear now—it's too late.[24]

After listening to the recorded sermons of Truett, readers of his sermons and addresses, and even his articles, cannot read his "ohs," his "greats," or his sentences punctuated with exclamation points without having a sense of how they actually sounded. But the voice Marshall's congregation actually heard was the voice Baptists all over Texas would hear for the next twenty-three months as Truett pleaded with them to save their university from the cancer of debt.

Despite the power of Truett's pulpit presence and his haunting voice, the Baylor campaign apparently did not begin well. Truett's son-in-law and biographer, Powhatan W. James, asserted that Texas Baptists "loved Baylor. It was their pride and joy."[25] Yet Joseph M. (J. M.) Dawson, a close friend of Truett, painted a different picture: "Not every Baptist in the state was concerned for the relief of his denominational school; in fact, there was an appalling indifference to the claims of higher education."[26] Dawson's observation appears to have been correct, for early in the campaign Truett wrote to Carroll, lamenting the apathy of many Texas Baptists toward Baylor. "I cannot but daily weep at the indifference of pastors," he confided to his mentor. "The papers too, it seems to me, are practically against the work."[27] Truett could not fathom why he, a newcomer to Texas with no ties to Baylor, could care so much about the university, whereas many Texas Baptists could care so little.

Despite the campaign's inauspicious beginnings, Truett persevered. Early in the campaign he developed the attitude that "[w]e can get along at Baylor without their money, perhaps, but not without their friendship. People are the important thing. Win the people and they will cheerfully give the money."[28] Thus, Truett did not just want their money; he wanted their hearts. Such an attitude was as apparent as it was effective. A Texas pastor described the results of one of Truett's visits to the Texas Panhandle this way: "[A]s is always the case," he "won the hearts of our brethren in that section to him and to his work."[29]

To win the hearts of Texas Baptists, Truett worked tirelessly for Baylor. For nearly two years, he traveled across the state on trains and horses and in buggies and oxcarts, speaking wherever he could and asking Baptists to liberate their university from debt. Even when not traveling, he spent most of his time trying to eradicate the university's debt. Samuel P. Brooks, a Baylor student during the campaign and later Baylor's president (1902–1931), recalled observing Truett in his office writing hundreds of letters on behalf of the university. Brooks also worked for Baylor as a recruiter during his student days, and the university's president, Rufus Burleson, once sent Brooks on a recruiting trip with Truett to an association meeting in central Texas, where the two young men slept on benches. "George was a good sport," Brooks recalled. "His method of rest was like some social cure-alls, of the temporary sort. When he got tired on one side he merely turned over."[30]

Right before Truett was scheduled to speak to the association one evening, a country preacher told the gathering, "If a man wants to preach, he don't have to know nothing. The Book merely says, 'preach the Word,'" which was hardly a rousing endorsement for higher education. Truett was then asked to preach a sermon, not to speak on behalf of Baylor, which he did. According to Brooks, when Truett finished his sermon, "an old gentleman...jumped from his seat, threw his arms around the preacher and kissed him smack on the cheek. By that time all were up shaking hands and shouting. The meeting was ours." Having earned the right to make an appeal for Baylor, Truett spoke the next day about the university's debt. At the conclusion of the speech, many people walked to the podium and "turned their pocket books upside down. It was not much but some gave their all."[31]

During the campaign Truett used the *Baptist Standard*, at that time an independent newspaper owned by M. V. Smith and J. B. Cranfill in Waco, to inform Texas Baptists about the sacrifices many people had made for Baylor and to remind them that sacrifices still had to be made. In one article Truett noted that "[o]ur successful Mexican pastor, Rev. M. G. Trevino, of San Marcos, has just sent his watch for the University."[32] In another article Truett called on all Texas Baptists to participate in the campaign. People were making a "fatal mistake," he wrote. "Only a handful of our pastors have yet laid the matter before their churches, and taken a collection. Perhaps they have been overwhelmed by local work, and have imagined that this work would be done without their help. They are mistaken.... O, brethren and sisters, is there one of us who can be willing not to bear some part in this great struggle?"[33]

Many Texas Baptists had signed promissory notes to Baylor, which they had not paid, nor did they intend to pay. Truett either returned the notes or received payment; he wanted cash, not promises. Most of the donations to the university were gifts of one to ten dollars. Instead of cash, some people gave jewelry, one man donated a young cow, another man gave a bale of cotton, and a child sold her chickens and contributed the proceeds. Even Truett gave to the campaign. After making one plea, he put a $500 ($11,754)[34] check into the collection plate, all the money he had saved to attend college.[35]

In fall 1892, Carroll took a leave of absence from his Waco pastorate to help with the campaign and often accompanied his protégé on fund-raising tours. At one stop a large crowd was expected, but a rainstorm the night before the meeting resulted in a much smaller attendance. Carroll addressed the gathering first, after which the assembly sang a hymn. During the hymn, Truett scribbled a note on a card, which he handed to his mentor. He informed Carroll that he would not ask for donations because the crowd was small. On the other side of the card, Carroll scribbled these words before handing it back: "Never take counsel of your fears or appearances; do your whole duty, and you may unfearingly leave the results with God. Certainly, you will ask the people present to make their gifts today."[36] Truett followed Carroll's advice. "Women gave the rings from their fingers," he recalled many years later, "and men gave their watches and purses. It was one of the days of God's right hand among his people. It marked an epoch in their lives."[37]

While on the Baylor campaign trail during fall 1892, Truett preached a revival in a Baptist church in Lampasas, Texas, which lasted twenty-four days and nights. In a letter to an unidentified recipient, he described the revival as "a most gracious meeting," during which fifty people made professions of faith. At the end of the revival he made a plea for Baylor that raised $1,000 ($23,508). Truett's preaching so impressed the members of the church that they called him to be their pastor. He declined, however, believing that he should graduate from college before accepting such an important position. The revival made a profound effect on him as well:

"The meeting gave me a fresh zeal for the Lord's work. Above all things on earth, I would be a *faithful preacher*. Cost whatever it may, of money, social position, personal honors, of poverty,—let me to the end of my earthly pilgrimage, be an humble, faithful preacher of the gospel. I count it the sublimest privilege this side of heaven."[38]

By early 1893, twenty-three months into the campaign, Truett and Carroll had raised $91,200 ($2,168,531), only $800 ($19,022) short of retiring Baylor's debt. Carroll told him that he knew three men who would give $100 ($2,377) each, and Truett knew a man who was ill and might give to the university. When he visited the man and told him how much he needed, the man wrote a check for $500 ($11,889). Upon receiving the check from Truett, Carroll lifted his head toward heaven and said, "*It is finished*."[39] Truett wept.

Completing the Baylor campaign early in 1893 proved to be fortunate, because that year a financial panic swept the country as foreign investors and American businessmen liquidated their paper assets for gold, forcing banks to limit credit, slowing the economy, causing a rise in unemployment, and resulting in a five-year depression.[40] In the words of Cranfill, "The banks everywhere were imperiled. Business institutions fell like giant oaks before a devouring storm."[41]

In their article "Account of a Great Battle," published in the March 1893 issue of the *Baptist Standard*, Truett and Carroll informed Texas Baptists that Baylor's debt had been retired. During the campaign, they had "released without a word of reproach, more than $45,000 of old notes, and $25,000 of pledges made" to the university since 1890, noting that "[i]f notes and pledges had been money, we would have been free [of debt] long, long ago." The two men then alluded to some problems they had encountered during the campaign. They had been humbled by the "long and arduous struggle," but "[i]f any man wants to claim any of the glory of this campaign that may justly be ours—he is welcome to all of it. The prize is not worth a dispute. So far as it is earthly it is but a shining bubble— empty and momentary. It will burst in the hand of him that seizes it, leaving in its grasp only emptiness and disappointment. So far as it is heavenly let heaven arbitrate it." Moreover, if they had hurt anyone, even unintentionally, they asked for forgiveness, and if anyone had wronged them "personally or hindered our work by distrust, or whisperings or public opposition—if any one has made our work longer or harder by withholding needed sympathy, prayer and cooperation, so far as it touches us we do now publicly and heartily and freely forgive it forever as God for Christ's sake has forgiven our sins."[42]

Carroll and Truett also emphasized that few wealthy people contributed to the campaign and that "the love of the poor, the masses, has won this fight." They praised the help of the many women who "have never doubted, never discouraged, never asked questions even, never imposed a condition, but lovingly and promptly responded to every call for help. Their promises were synonymous with fulfillment. That the Lord may bless them forevermore is the fervent prayer of two weary but grateful men."[43] The two ministers also praised the numerous pastors and laymen who could not be named, but if "our cold breasts could be opened," Carroll and Truett proclaimed, "the autopsy would reveal their names written on our hearts."[44]

One can safely say that after Truett traveled all over Texas on behalf of Baylor, many Texas Baptists considered the university their pride and joy. With the debt retired, an exhausted Truett returned home to Whitewright to rest. Then in September 1893, he entered Baylor as a freshman. Commenting many years later on his decision to attend Baylor, he remarked, "I had not only talked the people of Texas into giving $92,000 to Baylor, but I had also talked myself into attending there."[45]

*Studying and Pastoring in Waco*

When Truett matriculated at Baylor in fall 1893, he did so, according to McBeth, as "the youth that saved Baylor University; every Baptist leader in Texas knew him, admired him, trusted him."[46] Truett attacked his studies like he had attacked the debt and apparently was a decent student. He studied, according to Brooks, "like some boys play marbles—for keeps."[47] Of the classes Truett was known to take, his lowest grade was a 70 in Botany; his highest, a 95 in three classes: Greek Orators, Horace, and Horace Satires.[48] He also took Bible classes in the Bible Department, which was organized in 1893.[49]

Shortly after beginning his studies at Baylor, Truett "timidly accepted the call" of East Waco Baptist Church.[50] In a 1925 interview, he recalled that the church paid him $400 ($9,511) "a year for experimenting on them.... I continued to be pastor there all through my four years at the university. Before I finished they had raised my salary to one thousand dollars [$25,788]."[51]

Later in fall 1893, Truett filled in for Carroll, who had fallen ill, for three days during an eight-week revival at First Baptist, Waco. In a letter to an unidentified recipient, Truett described the meeting as "the most wonderful...I've ever seen.... Following this meeting I continued [the revival] a week at my church—East Waco—with gratifying results. Would have continued longer but took another spell of something close akin to the 'grippe' and had to stop."[52]

The following year Truett's responsibilities at his Waco church continued to expand. He informed the recipient of a February 24, 1894, letter that he was busy but "very happy," for "[n]o other work I've ever done for God has even half so much delighted my heart as has my *pastoral* work—where you study the life of every *individual* member   that you may be able to 'give to each one his portion in due season.' Thus seeing the varied temperaments and relative needs of the members, sermons come to me like birds in flocks, some-times."[53]

Sermons were not the only things flocking to Truett; people were too. So many were joining East Waco Baptist Church that he noted in his February 24 letter, "We hope to enlarge our house of worship right soon to accommodate the crowds—the house will not hold the people."[54] Despite the economic depression ravaging the country, construction on a larger sanctuary, which cost $10,000 ($254,720), began in summer 1895. The first service in the new, debt-free building was held on December 24, 1895.[55]

While studying at Baylor and pastoring his Waco congregation in 1894, Truett was also courting a young Waco woman. During the Baylor debt retirement campaign, B. H. (Harvey) Carroll, Jr., kept pestering Truett about meeting Judge Warwick H. (W. H.) Jenkins's daughter Josephine, an 1890 Baylor graduate.[56] Jenkins was one of the Baylor trustees at the Carroll home in January 1891 who had grave misgivings about hiring Truett as Baylor's financial agent. Carroll also often talked to Josephine about Truett. Eventually, Truett and Josephine met each other and spent an evening talking. Following this first meeting, Truett left Waco on a fundraising trip, and Josephine did not hear from him for a long time. She learned, however, that he had returned briefly to Waco several times, but had not contacted her. One day she received a note from Truett, informing her that he would like to see her when he returned to Waco. Josephine did not reply to his note, but when Truett arrived home and made his request again, she consented to see him on the last night before he was to leave town again. She was cool towards him that evening, but eventually their friendship grew. On June 28, 1894, Truett, now twenty-seven years old, married the twenty-two-year-old Josephine. B. H. Carroll, Sr., performed the ceremony.

In June 1897, the thirty-year-old Truett graduated from Baylor with an AB degree. Chosen to be the commencement speaker, he titled his address "The Inspiration of Ideals." He began the address with these words: "Every intelligent life must be a journey toward an ideal. This ideal is a *pattern* in the mind, held up before its eye, for imitation, realization and guidance. Aspiration is life's universal law. What we call *progress* is but society following after and translating into life, the visions of the mind."[57] Both individuals and nations are guided by "some vision of what *ought* to be and *may* be; and the individual or nation, unstimulated by such vision, is speedily hastening into decline and the grave."[58] We live in an age, he told the audience, that "sneers at 'visions,'" preferring practical things such as houses and horses, railroads and factories, lands and gold. But all progress emanates from someone's vision, and "[i]n its last analysis, the builder of states is the one who sees visions and dreams dreams."[59]

Likewise, great painters see their paintings before they ever paint them; great generals mentally fight their battles before they take the battlefield; and great statesmen imagine their speeches before they ever utter them. Books exist first in their author's minds before they become printed, and "[w]hat are inventions and factories and institutions but the incarnation of ideals?"[60]

Every great epic in history, Truett noted, began with the incarnation of a great ideal in a courageous leader. Martin Luther's ideal understanding of the responsibility and "freedom of action in religion…set tyrants and thrones to tottering, and led to the banishment of the dark night of the Middle Ages, and the advent of a mighty mental and moral reformation." Oliver Cromwell's ideal of personal rights in church and state "became a weapon powerful enough utterly to destroy that citadel of iniquity: 'The Divine right of Kings.'" The ideal of the structure of the earth set Columbus on a path that "determined the destiny of millions."[61] America's "great ideal of the worth and freedom of the individual, has made the United States an asylum for the earth and put her flag foremost among all that float in the galaxy of nations."[62]

Ignoble ideals exist too, Truett warned his fellow graduates, and shape the character of individuals and nations. One example he used to stress the insidious power of a reprehensible ideal was the lust for wealth, which he called "the Black Plague of America's individual, social and national life." When a pagan emperor of China was asked to license the opium trade, he refused, stating that he would never do anything to contribute to the misery of his people. "And yet," Truett exclaimed, "Christian England gladly derived an immense income from this very traffic; and Christian America 'jumps at the chance' of obtaining revenues from businesses still more infamous and destructive. We talk much of heathen idolatry, but there was never a heathen temple crowded with more eager devotees, than in the temple of mammon in this land of alleged civilization and Christianity."[63]

Because ideals mold people into their image, Truett could do nothing greater than to present his fellow graduates with the highest ideal in human history. Thus, he ended his address with the following words:

### Comrades of the class of '97

Passing by all the ideals of men, many and mighty as they are,—I hold up before you *the one ideal and inspiration for every day and duty of life.* "He is no empty abstraction nor bloodless theory," but He is *Jesus of Nazareth,* "in whom dwelleth the fullness of the God-head bodily." In Him alone is fulfilled those needs of highest manhood and noblest character, that forever enthrone Him the one Master and Model of the world. As you see His faithful portrait, drawn in the simple words: "He went about doing good"—know that all education that aims only at *self-improvement,* stamps its possessor as a twin brother to the miser who gloats over his gathered gold. Study Him, and know that there can be no heroism save in self-sacrificing interest for others. From Him learn the strength of patience, the glory of self-control, the nobility of self-denial. Study Him as against mighty odds[.] He resists temptations and holds up the great truth that bread and power and fame are not so vital as *fidelity* to *principle.* Plant your feet where His have walked, and let His great, magnanimous, unselfish life flash out its rebuke to every lull of conscience and every sordid vision that may assail you. And when you pass through that valley whose waters moan with the soul's last struggle, may His glory rest upon your face and may His welcome make you happy forever![64]

After graduating from Baylor, Truett planned to spend a year studying at the Southern Baptist Theological Seminary in Louisville, Kentucky, and then return to spend the rest of his life in Waco. Several churches wanted Truett to be their pastor, but he was content in Waco.[65]

During the summer of 1897, the Truetts celebrated the birth of their first of three daughters, Jessie. Also during that summer, First Baptist Church in Dallas, Texas, contacted Truett about becoming its pastor.

### Accepting the Call to First Baptist Church, Dallas

On May 9, 1897, Charles L. Seasholes, pastor of First Baptist Church (FBC), Dallas, tendered his resignation. Having pastored the church for a little more than five years, Seasholes gave the following reason for his leaving: "I believe that my work in Dallas is done."[66] Thus, FBC members had to start their search for the church's ninth pastor in its twenty-nine-year history.

Eleven people had started FBC on July 30, 1868, when "Dallas was a straggling Western village."[67] Eleven years later, W. E. Penn, an evangelist, preached a tent revival at the church, which produced many conversions, including those of Edgar Young (E. Y.) Mullins and Colonel and Mrs. Christopher Columbus (C. C.) Slaughter. Mullins later became president of the Southern Baptist Theological Seminary in Louisville, Kentucky. Slaughter, frequently called the "Cattle King of Texas," was a wealthy cattleman and a Dallas banker, who, by 1906, owned over a million acres and 40,000 cattle.[68] He contributed thousands of dollars during his life to FBC and numerous worthy causes.

The men charged in summer 1897 with the task of finding FBC's next pastor moved quickly. William L. Williams, a founding member, a senior deacon, and the chair of the pastor search committee, asked J. B. Cranfill for a recommendation. Cranfill "promptly" suggested Truett. Cranfill also informed several of the church's prominent members of his recommendation, including Waid and Margaret Hill and their daughter, Mary Hill Davis.[69] B. II. Carroll and James Bruton (J. B.) Gambrell, superintendent of missions for the BGCT, also highly endorsed Truett, who was no stranger to FBC, having preached there in September 1891 during the Baylor debt retirement campaign.[70] Consequently, the church's pulpit committee wrote several letters to Truett, who informed the committee that he was happy in Waco and was planning to attend seminary for a year. The church, however, called him anyway. On Wednesday evening, August 4, 1897, Williams announced the pulpit committee's decision "that Rev. Geo. W. Truett of Waco be called as pastor." Of the seventy-seven members present at the meeting, seventy-four voted for the recommendation. The committee was then charged with notifying "Truett of the call and in case he does not accept, to report other names to be voted upon."[71]

FBC members had good reason to doubt that Truett would accept their call. Although the Dallas pastorate was a prestigious one, he had previously rejected a lucrative offer from an even more prestigious church. Prior to his graduating from Baylor, First Baptist Church, Nashville, Tennessee, wanted him to be its pastor. The church asked him to preach a trial sermon and offered him a salary of $3,000 ($77,366), three times the amount he was earning at his Waco pastorate. Truett declined that offer.[72] At a meeting during which his rejection was discussed, one member of the Nashville church exclaimed, "If that young college boy can not be tempted by the pastorate of a great church like this and the large salary we offer, even before he graduates, then I am in favor of calling him without ever seeing him." Although Truett informed the Nashville church that God wanted him in Waco, the church unanimously called him, sight unseen. People from all over Texas advised him to accept the offer.[73] Truett, however, remained firm in his decision.

After FBC, Dallas, called him, however, Truett met with church leaders to discuss moving to Dallas. At the meeting he learned that the 715-member church had a debt of $12,000 ($309,465) and that church policy prohibited the taking of special offerings for missions and other benevolences. Moreover, only 5 percent of total gifts could be given to "outside" causes. Truett informed the leaders that he could not abide by such a policy, for he insisted that he "must be free to take special offerings whenever the need for them appears. If I am to become your pastor, then you must agree that I can be free to present an appeal for missions and benevolences whenever the denominational program calls for it."[74] Without such freedom, he would reject the call. The leaders accepted Truett's condition because he had not been a pastor long and would soon learn the FBC way of doing things; however, FBC would soon learn the Truett way of doing things, and church life for FBC members would be different from then on.

Truett preached the morning and evening sermons at FBC on Sunday, August, 29, 1897, after which he accepted the church's call. Three days later the church set his salary at $1,800 ($46,420).[75] He preached his first sermon as FBC's pastor on September 12, 1897. The church's minutes for that day record that "Rev. Geo. W. Truett having accepted the call to the pastorate of this church, entered regularly into the work on this day."[76] Although he would have many absences from his FBC pulpit, Truett would pastor that church "regularly" for nearly the next forty-seven years.

Truett soon tested his freedom to take up special offerings. On Monday, September 20, 1897, the day after his second Sunday in Dallas, he wrote to Josephine, who was still in Waco. After noting that he was feeling well, except for some pain in his toes, Truett mentioned that she was obviously "anxious about yesterday."[77] He undoubtedly had informed her about his plan to take a special offering during his second Sunday at the church.

Sometime before the morning worship service on September 19, Truett called a meeting of church leaders to discuss taking an offering for state missions. They kept their word about giving him the freedom to do so, but they also cautioned their pastor that the church was unaccustomed to such offerings and that he should not be disappointed when the congregation did not respond as he hoped. When asked how much the people would give, the leaders predicted $25 ($645) at most. Truett responded that they must be joking because "Colonel Slaughter here will give at least one hundred dollars [$2,579]."[78] The deacons laughed at Slaughter's being put on the spot, but also perhaps at their pastor's naiveté.

Despite knowing the church's "scrupulous" policy of not having "public collections," Truett told Josephine that he preached a sermon titled "Free Will Offering." "The result," he noted thankfully, "was amazing," for that morning the church collected $250 ($6,447) for state missions. He told his congregation that the offering would be open through the following Sunday and that he hoped to raise between $300 ($7,737) and $400 ($10,316). "Of course," Truett continued, "they think this a *marvel*, but if they'll stick to me and let me stick to them, they'll think much wider than they do now." He had not emphasized the offering too forcefully, yet even so "it was all a glorious service. God was surely with me." After describing for Josephine some events at the evening service, Truett added, "I forgot to tell you" that in the morning service, "Col. Slaughter was present, listened to the sermon with all the intense interest of a keen business mind" and "gave $100.00."[79]

Soon after that "glorious service" on September 19, Josephine joined her husband in Dallas. By the time the Truetts moved to Dallas, the city had become the center of Baptist life in Texas. Buckner Orphans Home was there, as were the offices of the BGCT. Early in 1898, the *Baptist Standard* was relocated there from Waco. Moreover, Dallas was becoming a modern city. In the early 1890s the city was what many people would have considered to be a dump, and for many it really was because they often dumped refuse, animal carcasses, and other garbage onto the sidewalks. People also often complained of hogs running wild in the streets, which created "stinking mud holes."[80] Despite the elimination of many of the city's swine and sanitation problems by the end of the 1890s, the Cleaner Dallas League was still attempting to make Dallas a cleaner place to live.[81]

At the beginning of the twentieth century, Dallas had a population of 42,638 and was becoming known as a cotton, railroad, and financial center in the Southwest. The city also had many of the amenities of a big city, such as telephones, electricity, and several daily newspapers.[82] Dallas was a predominantly middle-class city with a large African-American population, which ranged between 15 and 23 percent throughout Truett's ministry in Dallas. Religiously, evangelical Protestantism influenced much of the city's religious life and outlook. Along with Baptists, several groups had established churches in Dallas, including the Disciples, Presbyterians, Methodists, Catholics, Episcopalians, Congregationalists, Seventh-Day Adventists, Lutherans, Unitarians, Mormons, and the Salvation Army. The first Jewish families arrived in Dallas in 1872, and by 1890 three Jewish congregations existed in the city.[83]

As the thirty-year-old Truett began his Dallas ministry in September 1897, his future looked bright. He had become a well-known and respected Texas minister and was the pastor of a prestigious church in a prominent Texas city. In that city he and his wife would have two more children, Mary (1904) and Annie (1906).[84] Yet Truett's bright future in 1897 soon turned dark. Just five months after he moved to Dallas, a tragedy struck that almost caused him to leave the city and quit the ministry.

In his response to the welcome address at the BGCT meeting in Waco in November 1898, Truett briefly reflected upon a year that had been extremely difficult for him. In just five sentences he undoubtedly alluded to an event that had devastated him for many weeks earlier in the year. Despite the ambiguity of his words, however, everyone at the meeting knew what he was talking about:

> Every man here has a chapter all his own, written from the experiences peculiar to his own heart and labors. Some of us have been men of sorrows nearly all the year. Some of our nights have been so dark and lonely and long that we wondered if morning would ever come again. Ah, some of us know something at least of what Gethsemane meant to Jesus, for we have entered into the fellowship of His sufferings. But whatever our tears and toils in the sore conflict, His grace has been sufficient for us; and here today we raise our Ebenezer, saying to all the world: "Hitherto our God has helped us."[85]

The event that almost destroyed Truett personally occurred in February 1898.[86] Captain Jim C. Arnold, chief of the Dallas police department and a member of Truett's congregation, went quail hunting two or three times a year on John H. Boyd's farm, eight miles east of Cleburne, Texas. Believing that his pastor needed some time off, Arnold invited Truett to accompany him. The two men traveled by train on Thursday morning, February 3, to Cleburne, where George W. Baines, pastor of First Baptist Church, Cleburne, met them and took them in his carriage to the Boyd farm. Baines, Arnold, and Truett spent the afternoon in a fruitless hunt. Truett wanted to return home that evening, but he consented to stay another day.

The three men hunted all the next morning, again without success. After lunch, Baines wanted to return to Cleburne and Truett to Dallas, but Arnold, wanting his pastor to shoot at least one quail, insisted that they try one more time. Around 3:30 p.m., Baines was hunting by himself and decided to return to the farmhouse; Truett and Arnold were together. Baines heard two shots approximately ten seconds apart, after which he observed Truett running toward the farmhouse with his hat in his hands. Baines ran to Truett, who exclaimed, "Oh, Brother George, I've shot Captain Arnold."[87] The second shot Baines had heard occurred when Truett shifted his shotgun from one arm to the other, discharging the gun and wounding Arnold in the right leg.

When the two men returned to Arnold, Baines sent Truett to get help before he and Arnold retied the tourniquet that Truett had helped the chief tie around his leg. When Truett returned, he and Baines put Arnold into a carriage and took him to the farmhouse. Once a physician arrived, Baines and Arnold tried to convince Truett to return to Dallas so that the chief's wife could be informed about the accident, but he refused to go. He told Baines privately that "he would rather die than leave." Baines later recalled, "I never before saw such terrible suffering. And this added to the chief's pain."[88] Truett finally consented to return to Dallas. D. W. Milam, who sat near him on the train from Cleburne to Dallas, told the *Dallas Morning News* that Truett "was terribly shocked over the unfortunate occurrence and well nigh prostrate."[89] Upon arriving in Dallas, the distraught pastor notified the necessary people about the accident and then went home, where he castigated himself for his "carelessness" and "inexcusable awkwardness."[90]

While Truett was traveling back to Dallas, Arnold informed Baines that he was worried about his heart, for several members of his family had had heart problems. He asked two physicians to examine his heart, which they did. Once the physicians determined that the chief could be moved, Baines and a physician accompanied Arnold on a train to Dallas early Saturday morning. After the chief had been settled at his home, Baines returned to Cleburne that afternoon. The following morning he received a telegraph notifying him that Arnold had died of a heart attack at 8:10 p.m. on Saturday evening.

The news of Arnold's death devastated Truett and the entire city of Dallas. On the night Arnold died, friends and family members heard

Truett in his bedroom repeating to God, "My times are in thy hands." He repeatedly told Josephine, "I will never preach again. I could never again stand in the pulpit."[91] Because Truett was so tormented, Cranfill, who had moved to Dallas with the *Baptist Standard* in January, preached at both services on February 6.[92]

Baines returned to Dallas to preach Arnold's funeral sermon on Wednesday, February 9. Mourners filled FBC's sanctuary and watched as six pallbearers took their places at the front of the sanctuary. After Arnold's casket was brought in, the chief's family walked down the center aisle to their seats. Then, according to a *Dallas Morning News* article:

> Walking as if in a dream, his eyes half closed, his fists convulsively clenched and his face wet with the streams from his eyes, came the innocent cause of all this grief. A universal sigh of pity was heard as Rev. George W. Truett, the pastor of the church, sank into his seat just behind Mrs. Arnold and buried his face in his hands. His wife and several other relatives sat by him and tried to comfort him. It was easy to see that he was undergoing a terrible mental strain. He came near fainting several times during the services.[93]

Still grieving over the death of his friend, Truett probably did not preach on the following Sunday, February 13, for the "Church Notes" section of the *Dallas Morning News* for that day, which listed the preachers at several Dallas churches for that Sunday, did not contain any reference to FBC. The following Sunday, February 20, however, that section of the paper noted that Truett would preach during both Sunday services.[94] One FBC member recalled that "[w]hen Brother Truett came into the pulpit, he looked terrible. His face was drawn and his eyes were so sad. When he stood to preach, he remained silent for a long moment. You could have heard a pin drop. When he began, somehow he sounded different. His voice! I shall never forget his voice…as we heard for the first time the note of sadness and pathos which later we came to know so well. It seemed to carry the burden of all the grief in the world."[95] On Sunday evening, nearby Methodist and Presbyterian churches cancelled their evening services so that their members could support Truett.

The event that pulled Truett out of his paralyzing malaise occurred one night during his ordeal when he had a recurrent dream, the content of which was not publicly recounted until 1939. He woke up Josephine three times that night, telling her that he had just seen Jesus standing by his bedside and that each time the Lord had said to him, "Be not afraid. You are my man from now on."[96] Henceforth, Truett never doubted the reality of Jesus. When, in 1917, he privately told his son-in-law Powhatan W. James about the dreams, James asked him what Jesus had looked like. Truett responded, "He looked just like I had always pictured him in my mind, beautiful and glorious beyond all words."[97]

On Friday, February 25, Truett sent Baines a postcard informing his friend that he would be unable to travel to Cleburne, perhaps for a revival, and that life for him would never be the same:

> My Heart's Beloved Bro.—
>
> Do not expect me next week. What work I may be able to do, I must do here. I have wanted to write you, but I could not. My heart is completely broken, and all life hereafter shall be different from the past. On that tragic Sabbath, when I heard the worst, I laid forever the burden at His [Christ's] feet, and He has my heart. There is no bitterness nor complaining. I now know what Gethsemane meant to Jesus. I have been in that lone garden with Him. My heart is knitted unto you as never before, and the contemplation of Heaven is made sweeter by the thought that you, the loved comrade gone and I shall be together there.[98]

People who knew Truett well noted that he emerged from the Arnold tragedy a changed man. One FBC member remarked, "That week's ordeal was heart-breaking for the pastor; but there is no doubt it is the crucial experience of his life. It is the event which molded him more than any other. No one could come to him with a sorrow greater than his sorrow. His vast capacity for helping people in trouble, as well as his power in the pulpit, was born of the tragedy which remade him."[99] The Arnold tragedy almost caused Truett to leave Dallas a dispirited man, yet a year and a half after that dreadful accident, the first of many invitations came to Truett to leave Dallas a wealthier man.

Truett became a member of Baylor's board of trustees in 1898, a position he held for nearly forty-six years.[100] In appreciation for what he had done for the university, Baylor conferred upon him a D. D. (Doctor of Divinity) degree in 1899, the first of several honorary doctorates bestowed on him.[101] The university appreciated his work so much that the June 12, 1899, issue of the *Dallas Morning News* announced the following: "Rev. George W. Truett, pastor of the First Baptist church, returned from Waco on Saturday night and filled his pulpit yesterday, morning and evening. At the morning service he announced that he had been elected to the presidency of Baylor, over his own expressed wishes."[102] Such news thrilled the Baylor alumni, faculty, and students as much as it horrified FBC members. The newspaper article stated that Truett's willingness even to consider the offer caused "[t]he members of his congregation" to be "very much worked up over the status of things and a number are apprehensive that they will be called upon to part with him."[103] More than a week later, the *Baptist Standard* announced that Truett still had not made a decision. "[I]f the Baptists and citizens of Dallas have any influence to keep him," the *Standard* continued, Truett would decline the offer. "[M]any of his most intimate friends believe that he ought not to leave so large a sphere of usefulness."[104]

Baylor's offer was quite tempting. The pace at FBC was fast, and the slower pace of a college presidency appealed to Truett. Moreover, Josephine secretly hoped that her husband would accept the offer so that she could be closer to her family. But they did not leave Dallas. When Truett announced to his congregation that he had declined the Baylor presidency, the congregation sang "Praise God from Whom all Blessings Flow" while many members wept for joy.[105]

As the blessings of God flowed upon FBC, so did other offers flow to Truett. In October 1901, another temptation came from Waco for him to leave Dallas, this time from the members of Waco's First Baptist Church, who called him to be their pastor. B. H. Carroll had resigned as pastor in 1899 to work for the Texas Baptist Education Commission. At the close of the morning service on October 6, Truett's good friend Cranfill stepped to the pulpit and asked that the church adopt a letter he then read. The letter, probably written by Cranfill, expressed the sentiments of the congregation that Truett "ought not to accept the call" and that God "wills for you to stay with us." Then, in an expression of Dallas pride, or perhaps arrogance, Cranfill maintained that Truett could not be more useful anywhere else, for "Dallas is the key to Texas, Texas is the key to the South and the South is the key to the world. Dallas is to the life of the great Southwest what the heart is to the body. From it the influences that shall shape the destinies of our great State radiate like the sunbeams radiate from the great king of earthly light. As is Dallas, so shall North Texas be; as is North Texas, so shall be the State; as is the State, so shall be the South."[106] When Cranfill finished reading the letter, FBC members unanimously voted to adopt the letter by standing. Then non-church members in the congregation stood in support of what had just been read.

After his morning sermon the following Sunday, Truett informed the congregation that he had made his decision, and he then read the letter he had penned the previous day to the Waco congregation. The *Dallas Morning News* reported that "the interest" while Truett read the letter "was breathless."[107] The call of such a prestigious church honored him, he said, and "[f]rom the moment I received the news…my heart has been exercised, it seems to me, to its deepest depths to find out God's will concerning my duty in the matter…. My decision is reached and is herewith announced: I must decline the acceptance of your call…. This, dear brethren and sisters, is the conviction of my heart as to what my duty is, and it is my reply to your call."[108]

The congregation left church that morning extremely happy, yet the offers for Truett to leave Dallas kept coming. Over the next six years, at least seven other churches called him to be their pastor, all of which he rejected: Calvary Baptist Church, Kansas City, Missouri (1903); Memorial Baptist Church, Philadelphia, Pennsylvania (1903); First Baptist Church, San Antonio, Texas (1904); First Baptist Church, Seattle, Washington (1904); McFerran Memorial Church, Louisville, Kentucky

(1906); Walnut Street Baptist Church, Louisville, Kentucky (1907); and Broadway Baptist Church, Louisville, Kentucky (1907).[109]

Truett had more difficulty convincing some churches of his decision than others. The deacons of Calvary Baptist Church in Kansas City, for example, notified him that their church had "disregarded" his rejection and had unanimously voted to call him anyway. "Our minds were immovably centered upon you," the deacons informed him, and they would pursue him until all attempts had been exhausted. Although the deacons knew that "the matter of salary will have no weight whatever in influencing your decision," and although they were reluctant to mention money, they did inform Truett that his salary would start at $3,000 ($72,922) and be raised to $4,000 ($97,230).[110] The deacons were right; money did not influence him.

### Spreading the Word beyond Dallas

Truett was in constant demand to preach, hold revivals, and deliver speeches, and his church granted him the freedom to accept numerous outside speaking engagements. In 1902, he received an invitation to preach to cowboys for a week during the summer in the Davis Mountains between Dallas and El Paso. Years later he described these men as "brave, brawny men of the plains. Mighty men. Great fathers, honest as sunlight for the most part."[111] These meetings became so popular that, in 1915, Truett and ranchers in the area helped fulfill the dream of Leander R. Millican, a Baptist missionary in Texas, by establishing a permanent encampment, now called Paisano Baptist Encampment, located between the West Texas towns of Alpine and Marfa.[112]

In addition to preaching to the cowboys, every year Truett preached numerous revivals, which lasted from seven to fourteen days, in Texas towns such as Bryan, Cisco, Hico, McKinney, and Pecos. He also preached revivals in his own church and churches out of state. The *Dallas Morning News* kept its readers informed about such meetings, often citing the number of conversions or noting that many people asked for prayer.[113]

Truett was also in demand to preach baccalaureate sermons. For example, to the 1904 graduates of the University of Texas (UT), he preached what one newspaper article described as "an able effort, being fraught with elevating thoughts and good advice."[114] People join gangs, Truett lamented in his sermon, "like dumb driven cattle," and like birds "they sit with wide-open mouths waiting for them to be filled with anything that may be dropped into them."[115] Such an attitude dishonors God. Instead, study the great questions of life, Truett challenged the graduates, and "[d]o your own thinking. Have your own convictions. Believe them so strongly that they will become as real a part of your being as is your hand or your heart."[116] He closed his sermon by exhorting his "young friends" to "fix your heart on" Christ "as your soul's sufficient hope and as the only true inspiration for rightly meeting the intricate questions and momentous duties of human life."[117]

Truett also gave two major addresses outside of Dallas during the first eight years of the twentieth century, one concerning the influence of the printed word, the other concerning the sacredness of human life. In May 1902, he traveled to St. Paul, Minnesota, to address the annual meeting of the American Baptist Publication Society (ABPS) on the topic "The Leaf and the Life," in which he emphasized the wide influence the printed page had on nations and individuals. According to Truett, literature conserves and disseminates truth. "The printing press is man's greatest mechanical triumph," he asserted, for by it "we not only become heirs of the thoughts of the wisest and best men of all the ages, but we have also the transcription of the very thoughts of God."[118] Despite its power, importance, and influence, the printed page, Truett maintained, "can never supersede the divinely sent preacher" whom God uses to evangelize and civilize the world.[119] Yet neither can preachers replace the printed page; they are inseparable. Thus, together, Luther preached and Erasmus wrote their way to the Reformation, and Christ, the incarnate Word, and the Bible, the written word, are "the binomial word of God." Spoken words and written words stand or fall together.[120]

Truett emphasized that the printed word also affects national life. The Bible, for example, was distributed throughout Europe, helping to spread Protestantism throughout that continent. But when people could not assemble lawfully and preachers were imprisoned, "[t]he iron preacher, the press, could go where the flesh and blood preacher could not go," and "the leaves from the press were being silently carried from country to country, from city to city, and from house to house."[121] England, North Germany, and other nations accepted the teachings of the Bible and have flourished ever since. Yet, Truett warned, France replaced the teachings of the Bible with those of Voltaire and other infidels, resulting in the Reign of Terror.[122] Thus, the leaf can both raise and destroy nations.

The printed page can also shape the destiny of individuals, Truett contended. He used the lives of Richard Baxter, William Wilberforce, Thomas Chalmers, John Wyckliffe, John Huss, John Bunyan, and others to illustrate "the amazing expansion of thought by means of the printed page. The reproductiveness of truth, by means of the press, may never, even approximately, be measured. Truth may thus be looked upon as a seed, with limitless powers of self-propagation. The author of a good book may die, but his thoughts, being fastened on the printed page, live on to cheer and inspire the reader to noblest endeavors."[123]

The printed page is a two edge sword, however. Just "as good literature has the power to uplift and ennoble and transform," so also "does bad literature have the power to corrupt and drag down and destroy."[124] Books are people's companions, and people can be judged by the type of books they read. Thus, reading bad books, like associating with people of dubious character, corrupts character because, Truett asserted, that which is seen makes a lasting impression, whereas that which is heard is transient.[125]

Truett challenged parents, teachers, and preachers to heed what children are reading. Agitators and reformers talk constantly about the damage alcohol does to people, "[b]ut the multiform, corrupting literature of the day, schools the reader for every vice in the whole catalogue of crime. Off by themselves, unsuspected boys and girls are reading these subtle and foul productions, thus feeding their minds upon corrupt visions of life, and hopelessly poisoning their lives at the very fountainhead."[126] Thus, Truett emphasized the necessity for homes to have religious and denominational newspapers readily available. Even in poor homes, "the weekly visit of a noble religious paper, supplemented by the occasional visit of the good book," can affect the lives of its inhabitants. "The picture of such a home passes before me now," Truett said, probably referring to his childhood in Hayesville, North Carolina. Though poor, the parents in his home used every extra dollar to buy good literature for their children, and that literature shaped those children to become effective workers for Christ. "Oh, how can parents and teachers and preachers be oblivious to this transcendently important matter of right literature?" Truett wondered. "Carelessness here is worse than being foolish, it is wicked."[127]

Truett ended his address to the ABPS with this plea: "O brothers, I pray Almighty God that your heart and mind from this hour may be found under a spell, from which we shall have neither the wish nor the power to be disenchanted, and which spell shall hold us until we pass into eternity, that we will give and pray and toil and lay our every power under tribute to enthrone Jesus Christ in the realm of all the literature of this whole broad earth."[128]

Truett presented his second major address during his first decade as FBC's pastor at a peace conference held at Baylor University on November 19–21, 1907. Other speakers included the United States attorney general in Dallas, a United States congressman from Texas, and the governor of Texas. The themes for the conference were phases of international peace and arbitration. A crowd of 2,000 filled Carroll Chapel to hear Truett's address, "Why Save Human Life?"[129]

"The civilization of any people may be faithfully read in its estimate of human life," Truett declared.[130] History provides numerous examples of civilizations and butchers, such as Napoleon, who rejected the sanctity of human life. Yet we do not have to look to the past to find such examples, for the current world situation is replete with "ambitious and selfish men."[131] Even now, Truett emphasized, Russia is persecuting Jews, and even "in our own fair land—foremost among all the nations in the progress of liberty and in the sway of religion—even here, we are grievous offenders against the sanctity of human life. That terrible trinity of horrors—suicide, lynching, murder—still mock us with her awful carnival in every section of our great country." The United States must learn from the Son of God "the priceless value of human life," Truett warned, and it must recognize that people of all "races and classes" bear the image of God or else it is doomed.[132]

We breathe the air "heavy with materialism and commercialism," Truett continued, and we must be reminded constantly that the essence of life cannot be judged by the things that a person or nation possesses. "No country can be truly called rich," he said in words reminiscent of the Social Gospel, "where human life is held as a cheap thing; where vast plague spots are willingly allowed to infect her cities; where conditions are such that hordes of defenseless women and children live in squalor and sordidness, dwarfed in body and mind, with life's horizon little larger than that of the beasts that perish."[133]

Not only must we recognize the value of human life, but our estimation of such life must also be "thoroughly Christian." Truett noted optimistically that "Jesus' revolutionary words, 'Blessed are the peacemakers: for they shall be called the children of God' [Matt. 5:9]…are slowly but surely cutting their way through every civilization of earth."[134] Yet, ironically, while the nations of the world are "loudly affirming their love of peace," they are simultaneously "making colossal preparations for war. And our own beloved country seems to be at the head of the column."[135] The United States spends over $200 million ($4.6 billion) annually on its military, but we do not even have anybody to fight. "Does it not all seem incongruous? Is not the spectacle absurd?" Truett asked rhetorically. Rather than spending millions on useless armaments, he contended that nations should spend "[a]s little money as possible" on the military, just enough for national defense, but "as much money as possible for great educational and Christian enterprises,—surely this is the road along which our feet must travel, if the blessings which this generation enjoys are to be transmitted to those that come after us."[136]

At the close of his address, Truett reminded the audience of Pierre Fritel's painting "The Conquerors," which depicted the great military leaders of the past as they marched through scenes "too appalling for speech. Such is the picture of great military leaders, with their conquests."[137] But Truett then concluded his remarks by directing their attention "to another picture, the picture of the march of the Prince of Peace," who

> [t]hrough the centuries...has marched, a beneficent and all-conquering Presence, with hands ever outstretched in blessing.... In Him is found the proper conception of human life and the proper relation towards it. And that nation does most for men and most for God which does the most to carry the world to that golden age foretold in prophecy, when the nations shall beat their swords into ploughshares, and their spears into pruning hooks, and when all shall acknowledge that the Prince of Peace is King of Kings and Lord of Lords.[138]

While on his numerous speaking engagements away from home, Truett wrote thousands of letters. Often on the first pages of letters to friends and colleagues, he wrote "On the Wing" to indicate that he wrote the letters while traveling. Josephine, obviously, needed no hint that he was traveling. A few letters Truett wrote to her on his travels in the early 1900s have survived.

While attending a meeting in Hillsboro, Texas, in early January 1900, he wrote to Josephine, who was in Waco visiting family, informing her that he had just received her "gracious letter," about which he exclaimed, "Oh, how it did help me!" She had chastised him for his previously brief letters. He pled guilty to brevity, "but," he reminded her, "I have written them."[139]

In December 1901, while in Waco for a preaching engagement at Baylor, Truett received a "gracious letter" from Josephine, which did his "soul good," he told her. "The meetings are indescribably glorious. Between twenty and thirty of the young men & women professed [Christ] last night. And scores are asking the way." One of C. C. and Mrs. Slaughter's sons, also named C. C., "is mightily interested and I believe he will soon be converted," Truett noted hopefully. The Slaughter's other son, Allie, however, "does not seem to be interested.... His is a pathetic case—you know why. But C. C. is terribly aroused. I talked about an hour with him yesterday and he sobbed like his heart would break. God save him!" He then asked Josephine to call Mrs. Slaughter to let her know that "my whole heart goes out after her two boys here."[140]

Although he was excited about the people's response during the Baylor meetings, Truett confessed to being a little homesick:

> I do yearn so much to see you and the little girl. God bless and keep you both safe and happy! Don't work too hard my darling. Do take thorough care of yourself—and know that you have the deepest, fondest, truest love from my poor heart, and that you become tender and sweeter to me every hour we live and labor together for our Saviour and I hope He has a long life for us together, and that He means to do good through us continually, to the poor, sinful, needy world.[141]

On June 28, 1902, his tenth wedding anniversary, Truett wrote Josephine from his parents' home in Whitewright, having arrived there from Sherman, Texas, after visiting his brother Harvey, who had consumption. "Poor Harvey is in bad condition," Truett noted sadly. "He leaves tomorrow for Colorado. He just can sit up. I fear that the end is not far away." If possible, Truett indicated that he would go with Harvey and his wife, but circumstances would not allow it. Instead, Truett told Josephine, "you and I are going to send Charlie Penland with them—at our expense—to stay with them 2 or 3 weeks." Truett was going to Denison, Texas, the next day to perform a wedding, but his plans after that were uncertain. He apparently had planned to be away from Dallas for several more days, but several church members were "sick and calling for me.... So, I am in a strait about the conditions about me."Although his ministry necessitated that Truett be away from home often, leaving Josephine behind was difficult, as the following sentence illustrates: "Life seems so blank and barren without you, my darling."[142]

*Incarnating the Healing Ministry of the Gospel*

The fame Truett received resulting from his speaking engagements across Texas and in other states and the influence he had on thousands of people who heard him are immeasurable. A little more than four and a half years after accepting FBC's call, he involved himself tirelessly in an endeavor that would affect the lives of thousands of people for generations—he helped establish a hospital. Although Truett's name is often the only one associated with such an undertaking, others also played crucial roles.

Charles McDaniel Rosser, a Dallas physician, played one of the most important roles in what would become the Texas Baptist Memorial Sanitarium (later Baylor Hospital). In 1900, he and several other Dallas physicians who believed that the city needed its own medical college met on August 14, at the office of J. B. Titterington, a Dallas physician, to discuss the formation of such a college. They then placed an advertisement in a city newspaper inviting all interested parties to meet at the city hall on August 16 to discuss starting the college. Only fifteen of the fifty-five physicians who attended the meeting, however, supported the school. Rosser informed the dissenting physicians that Dallas would have a medical college despite their opposition.[143] Nearly a month later, on September 15, a charter for the University of Dallas Medical Department was filed with the state of Texas. Approximately 100 students began classes on November 19, 1900, in a building in the 1300 block of Commerce Street.[144]

The medical students received their clinical training at Parkland Hospital, a tax-supported institution, but it was not within walking distance of the medical college. Thus, three times a week the students rode to Parkland in a wagon pulled by two ponies. The administrators and staff of St. Paul's Sanitarium, a privately-owned Catholic hospital, had opposed the creation of the medical college and would not permit the students to use their hospital for training.[145]

To provide students with the best education possible, the directors of the new medical college realized that the school needed its own hospital. Rosser asked his friend J. B. Gambrell for advice. Gambrell, who, along with his wife, had joined FBC in December 1897,[146] suggested that Rosser secure the backing of influential Baptists. The physician then set out to find a building to house a hospital, and after getting advice from Gambrell and two other FBC members, J. B. Cranfill and Robert C. (R. C.) Buckner, Rosser bought a two-story, fourteen-room mansion on Junius Street for $22,500 ($573,120), which was then remodeled into a functioning hospital named Good Samaritan Hospital.[147]

Good Samaritan and the medical college operated independently for three years, but that situation changed in 1903. While attending the American Medical Association's 1903 convention in New Orleans, Rosser invited the Austrian physician Adolf Lorenz to hold clinics in Dallas. Known as the "bloodless surgeon of Vienna," Lorenz was famous for using manual manipulation instead of surgery to correct congenital joint and bone deformities. He accepted Rosser's invitation and arrived in Dallas on May 20, 1903. Because of the great demand, Lorenz held two clinics every day, rather than just one, and extended his stay two additional days.[148]

On May 23, Dallas honored Lorenz at a banquet at the Oriental Hotel on Commerce Street. In a letter nearly three decades later, he reminisced with Rosser about his Dallas visit, including the banquet. "I remember the big hotel dinner," Lorenz recalled, "not overwhelmingly good, but richly spiced with lengthy speeches praising the bounty of God and the riches of glorious Texas."[149]

Truett was among the Dallas dignitaries who spoke at the banquet. His speech addressed the topic "Hospitals the Result of Christian Influence." "Whatever makes for the benefit of the race has its origin in Christianity," he noted triumphantly. "The Christianity of the divine physician does not stop at bandages and medicines, but takes the sufferer to a hospital where every attention, care and kindness may be bestowed."[150] At the end of his speech, Truett challenged the audience with these words: "I raise a question at this time, a notable period in the history of our city, if, with the rapid growth of the city, there should not be erected a great humanitarian hospital, which would illustrate the glorious result of Christian influence in the community?"[151] Rosser recalled the impact this speech had on the banqueters: "Classical and colorful as were other addresses," Truett's speech "was applauded as nothing else that night."[152]

According to Rosser, Slaughter, who had attended the banquet, telephoned Truett the next morning and told his pastor that he would donate $25,000 ($607,685) to the founding of the hospital. When Gambrell heard about Slaughter's offer, he told Truett to decline it: "You can't begin a million-dollar hospital with $25,000 from a millionaire. Go, sit up with him. He will give you $50,000 [$1,215,369] just as easily."[153]

The process of building the "great humanitarian hospital" moved quickly. On June 17, 1903, the trustees of Baylor University and a committee of fourteen prominent Dallas citizens, including Truett, Gambrell, and Cranfill, met in Waco and agreed to relocate the university's medical branch in Dallas.[154]

On June 18, Truett announced that Texas Baptists supported the building of the humanitarian hospital about which he had spoken at the Lorenz banquet. Experience had shown, he said, that such institutions needed the support of a

> well-organized body, which shall be directly chargeable with and responsible for their policies and practical operations. Already large and liberal contributions have been received for this great enterprise. As stated in the preliminary announcement touching this matter, the intention of this institution is to represent in spirit and management the broadest humanitarian and benevolent purposes of Christianity. It will not be restricted at all by denominational lines, but its doors will be open alike to men of all religious persuasions and to men of none, and to all reputable members of the medical profession.[155]

The first contribution to the new hospital came from the widow of the late Dallas police chief, Jim C. Arnold, who gave $2,500 ($60,768) in cash. George W. Carroll of Beaumont, Texas, pledged $10,000 ($243,074), and Slaughter, $25,000, not the $50,000 Gambrell had predicted.[156] Nevertheless, Slaughter would eventually give far more than that first pledge.

In October 1903, Texas Baptists paid $22,500 ($546,916) for Good Samaritan Hospital, which was then renamed Texas Baptist Memorial Sanitarium.[157] Later, when some people suggested renaming the institution after Slaughter, he pointed out that "Slaughter Hospital" might not be the best choice for a name.[158] In early November, the board of directors of the new hospital issued a statement announcing that Buckner had been elected president; Truett, secretary; and Slaughter, treasurer.[159] A few days later at the BGCT meeting, Texas Baptists unanimously adopted a resolution presented by Truett that they assume oversight of the hospital.[160]

On March 11, 1904, the Texas Baptist Memorial Sanitarium "threw open its doors for the service of suffering humanity."[161] Those doors, however, would soon be shut. Eight months later, at the BGCT meeting in Waco, Truett, after presenting the report of the sanitarium's board of directors,[162] addressed the gathering on behalf of the sanitarium and explained why the hospital should be closed. Since its opening, he noted, the sanitarium's fourteen-room building had been "overtaxed," resulting in needy people having to be turned away. The directors realized that a new building, estimated to cost $250,000 ($6 million), had to be built if the sanitarium was to meet the needs of the people. A groundbreaking ceremony for the building, which Truett called "an auspicious and eventful occasion," had been held the previous Saturday, November 4, next to the old Good Samaritan Hospital building.[163]

Despite the astronomical price, the benefits of funding such an expensive endeavor far outweighed the costs, Truett assured the audience. Experience had taught him, he lamented, "how Baptists have lost more than we can begin to measure, by so long neglecting this so thoroughly practical, this broadly humanitarian, this exceedingly Christly work."[164]

Apparently, some Texas Baptists had opposed funding the sanitarium. These detractors, according to Truett, were Baptists in name only, for no "true" Baptist could oppose such a ministry. "True Baptists," he proclaimed,

> stand squarely for what Christ stood for; and the great commission of Jesus
> Christ, the great underlying principles of the gospel of Jesus Christ, certainly

include the healing idea, as well as the ideas of missions and Christian
education. And so I say, it will be an epic in Baptist affairs in this great State
and the West, when the Baptists round out this part of their Master's
commission, and bring to full fruition, in a great institution, the incarnation
of the healing idea of our Savior's gospel. Brethren, when this is done, it will be
an epic in Texas Baptist affairs.[165]

Another benefit of supporting the sanitarium would be the influence it
would have on people. "Catholics," Truett told the convention messengers,

> have put their emphasis, to an amazing degree, on the great work of healing the
> bodies of men, and they have thus stretched out their hands of influence and
> taken hold of tens of thousands of people who would otherwise be in Baptist
> and Protestant churches. They have unceasingly stretched out their tentacles of
> influence and power, through their great hospitals and orphanages and kindred
> institutions. These institutions save life. These Catholic people have gone out
> on this idea, quietly driving down their stakes, building up their enterprises, so
> as to conserve human sympathy in the practical ways named, and thus in this
> country especially, have they hastened forward and built up their mighty
> system.[166]

Likewise, Truett wanted "Baptists, for Christ's sake, and for
humanity's sake," to put down their own stakes and stop squandering their
power and influence by continuing to neglect "the healing idea in the
gospel of Christ."[167]

Healing people's bodies is no "little thing," Truett emphasized. He
had talked with many patients in state-supported hospitals about their
spiritual lives and prayed "with them while their feet touched the river
death." Many of these patients had asked him, "'In heaven's name, why
cannot the Baptists have such a place, where they can go to be treated, and
if they die, can die amidst their own people?' And in heaven's sight, I ask
the same question to-day."[168] In Truett's opinion, Baptists should be able
to die among their Baptist brothers and sisters.

A little more than three months after the convention, the sanitarium's
directors voted unanimously on February 25, 1905, to close the hospital
because they feared that the patients' well-being would be jeopardized by

the construction of the new building. Thus, on March 11, 1905, just one year after opening, the sanitarium closed its doors and would not reopen until October 1909.[169]

*Persuading People to Give*

Truett had the amazing gift of persuading people to give financially to various causes. As a teenager in southwestern North Carolina, he had gained fundraising experience by raising money in rural churches for Sunday-school literature. Now Truett used that experience in Texas and elsewhere to ask not for nickels and dimes, but for hundreds and thousands of dollars. Obviously his reputation as the young man who saved Baylor from debt made him the logical choice of churches and other organizations to help them raise money. Concerning Truett's fundraising prowess, Gambrell wrote, "It may be reasonably doubted whether there is a man in all America who has a greater power to get people to give money, and he never makes anything but a direct appeal to the intelligence and to the conscience of the people to give as a matter of duty to God and humanity."[170]

Truett's primary responsibility for raising money was for his own church. From his second Sunday at FBC in September 1897, he never ceased taking special offerings. In an April 1906 form letter to each FBC member, for example, Truett aimed his words "directly to your heart and conscience concerning" the offering for home and foreign missions. He asked the people to pray every day for this cause and that they would make their offerings "prayerfully, joyfully, thoughtfully."[171]

After moving to Dallas, Truett often used the *Baptist Standard* to encourage Texas Baptists to support state and foreign missions, retired pastors, the construction of church buildings, Christian colleges, and Buckner Orphans Home.[172] According to Truett, the responsibility for the success of special offerings "rests most of all upon the preachers."[173] "God help us!" he wrote in one article. "For a pastor to be a trifler with his position as the heaven-appointed leader of the flock, is nothing short of an awful sin against the Lord Jesus Christ and the precious souls for whom

He died."[174] Truett constantly emphasized the crucial role of pastors in fundraising.

Whatever the cause, Truett put his whole heart into it, and no cause consumed as much of his fundraising energies during his first decade as FBC's pastor as that of funding the sanitarium. In his address concerning that institution at the 1904 BGCT meeting, Truett noted that some people had already contributed large amounts of money, others smaller amounts. The people listening to him at the convention meeting had the opportunity to contribute and do something worthy with their money. Texas Baptists "in one year, probably, spend enough on costly and foolish tombstones to build this institution," Truett said in a mild rebuke. "And I ask today, in the name of our Savior, if we cannot have a monument that will not only stand to the perpetual honor of our beloved dead, but will stand at the same time, for the practical service of suffering men and women and little children, until our Lord shall come again?"[175] He estimated that fifty individuals would probably contribute the necessary funds to construct the new central building of the hospital, while churches, mission societies, and other individuals could contribute the furnishings for the hospital rooms. "Where are these fifty people?" Truett challenged the audience. "A half dozen have answered—where are the others?"[176]

Also during the address, Truett promised that he and the other directors would personally visit people in order to ask them to contribute to the sanitarium.[177] To that end he kept a couple of notebooks in which he recorded the names of individuals and churches that could donate money. In his notebook "Notes for Sanitarium Campaign," he listed ninety-one churches that could give $1,000, thirty-four that could contribute $500, and sixty individuals that could give between $500 and $1,000. He also listed ninety-nine names of associational leaders who could be contacted on behalf of the sanitarium.[178]

In a pocket notebook, Truett recorded information about numerous potential donors. Following are some examples from this notebook: B. N. Aycock of Midland, "worth 50,000, cd give 250+"; Mrs. S. L. J. Brown of Cleburne, "No children-Widow -60 yrs-Able- at least 1000"; W. Gary

Burton of Fort Worth, "wife dead-Bapts-He once active-father noble old Bapt. 'Memorial'"; Mrs. Dr. M. J. Crow of Stephensville, "Bapt-60 yrs. old-wealthy-No children-Husband dead";[179] and Mrs. Mary E. Lott of Goliad, "Large ranch-(About 60 yrs. old) Husband died few mos. ago (Hope a Xn [Christian]) Able to do nobly-('Expects to help later')."[180]

The sanitarium directors kept Texas Baptists informed about the institution's finances. In a June 1905 article in the *Baptist Standard*, Truett, Gambrell, and Buckner expressed their "confidence...in God and in the brethren, that the needed funds to keep the work going may be provided week to week." The fundraising trio had sought "to lay the great matter on the hearts of a few who have money, and what is better, who find joy in serving God with their money." Some people had responded positively, yet "[w]e are daily looking for others, and expect to find them, because we have not one doubt that this enterprise is of the Lord."[181] In a November article in the *Standard*, Truett informed Texas Baptists that the first public collection for the sanitarium had just been taken at the BGCT meeting in Dallas, during which $30,000 ($729,222) in cash had been given and nearly $90,000 ($2,187,665) pledged.[182]

At the 1906 BGCT meeting in Waco, Truett presented the report of the sanitarium's directors, in which they stressed again what they had emphasized since Baptists had begun to support the hospital: "The scope of the institution is to be as broad as the spirit of Christ and the needs of humanity. There will be no discrimination as to creeds, people of all creeds and of no creeds sharing alike in its benefactions.... True Baptists could not operate such an institution on a narrower basis, for Baptists have ever unwaveringly contended for absolute liberty of conscience in religious matters."[183] The directors had also contracted for a sixteen-room building on property adjacent to the sanitarium. This building would be used for a science building and for a nursing school. Truett noted that a few people had donated $87,132 ($2,071,803) and that Slaughter had already contributed $25,000 and loaned more than $50,000 ($1,188,888) so that construction on the new sanitarium building could continue.[184]

After presenting the directors' report, Truett, as he had done in 1904, spoke about the need to fund the sanitarium. He declared that every Christian falls into one of three categories: "a tramp,...a thief, or...a trustee."[185] "We have the money" to finance missions, colleges, and numerous benevolences. "We have the money," he thundered again. "Oh, the word now to sound is the doctrine of trusteeship for Christ! 'Ye are not your own. Ye are bought with a price [1 Cor. 6:20].' All that I am as a money-maker, or preacher, or physician, or teacher, or whatever I may be, belongs to Him. We want to sound out the word all over Texas, that a man makes a shipwreck of his life, and puts precedents in his family that will damn his children for generations if he fails to square his life by the doctrine that he is a trustee for Jesus Christ."[186]

To help the members of the audience choose to become trustees, Truett told them about a recent experience he had had while traveling through the outskirts of Dallas. There one evening he

> saw a man, all bedraggled and weatherbeaten, picking little bits of rags out of the old piles of refuse hauled out of the city. Tell me, what is the difference between him and the men who are living to get money with which to get more money? At last they all are only rag-pickers. We must show our men and women who have money, which is God-given, and who have the ability to get money, which gift is also God-given, that every man of them is only a rag-picker if he does not use that money as a trustee for Jesus Christ.[187]

As was his custom, Truett challenged pastors to lead their churches in contributing to the sanitarium. If they failed, they would irreparably harm their church members, particularly children, who "ought to be made unselfish while yet in childhood, before" they become "cramped and narrowed and drawn by the lust for gold, if you don't link them with such a cause as this."[188] If, however, preachers supported the sanitarium drive, it would succeed, for "no cause faithfully espoused by Christ's preachers ever went down into the ditch. I will go with a crowd of Baptist preachers, on a mission for Jesus, down to the very belching mouth of hell, confident of success, if they will have one spirit and keep one step.... God has made them the leaders."[189]

A statewide fundraising campaign for the sanitarium was scheduled for 1907, but other fundraising campaigns delayed the sanitarium's campaign. To ensure that the construction continue, Slaughter loaned the sanitarium's trustees $100,000 ($2,275,982).[190]

*Ministering through State and National Conventions*

Truett got an early start in his involvement in Texas Baptist denominational affairs. While pastoring his Waco congregation and attending Baylor in 1894, he also served as the secretary of the executive board of the BGCT and was a member of that board until his death in 1944.[191] Truett also served on several committees of the BGCT and was often chosen to present a committee's report to the convention, for who better to turn a committee report into an event than a man whose "adjectives and adverbs take on spiritual quality as the dull black wire takes on the electric current"?[192]

Many of the reports he presented were routine, stating facts, suggesting plans, and challenging the faithful to more consecrated service. The report of the BGCT's executive board, which he presented at the convention's 1896 meeting in Houston, was anything but routine. Truett spoke of the "political storm" that had been raging among Texas Baptists, a storm that had been caused by "an agent" who had been "undermining the mission work [of Texas Baptists], drying up the mission spirit, and sowing down our once fertile fields with salt." The agent had "persistently, ruthlessly and openly, in public print attacked this board, its methods and work, charging it directly and indirectly, and by various methods of innuendo and insinuation, with misappropriation, wanton extravagance and reckless waste of public funds." The agent had publicly accused Cranfill, a past corresponding secretary of the convention, of embezzlement and, by implication, the board of directors also.[193]

The board, Truett emphasized, had patiently endured the agent's charges and had sought to counter his deleterious effects on the convention's work. "This year," however, "the situation became appalling."

The board could no longer put up with this man's machinations, and the time had come

> to name the agent who (with what motives and purposes we leave to God's judgment) has so long abused the patience of this convention, trifled with its verdicts, despised its authority, traduced its boards and this year has reached a climax of aspersion of its work, until these inquiries demand an answer. Is there no end of patience? Shall sickly sentimentality about peace forever usurp the throne of justice? Shall we wait until the mission cause, now bleeding, is stamped out of existence? Who, then, is this agent? His name is S. A. Hayden, of Dallas.[194]

A member of the BGCT's executive board and the editor of the *Texas Baptist and Herald*, Samuel A. Hayden had written a letter in 1894 to other board members, complaining about the excessive salaries of the convention's leaders, the meager salaries of missionaries, the rising debt of the BGCT, and the decline in work by Texas Baptists. When a committee appointed by the board found his charges to be groundless, Hayden began publishing his accusations in his newspaper, claiming that the superintendent of missions earned an exorbitant salary while missionaries earned a pittance, that other convention leaders used their authority to control churches, and that churches, not the convention, should direct mission work.[195] The convention again investigated such charges, but again found nothing to support Hayden's allegations.

At the end of the 1896 report, which was signed by Truett and W. H. Jenkins, the board's president and Truett's father-in-law, the board recommended that Hayden be denied a seat at the meeting. The messengers rejected the recommendation, voting instead for a public reprimand. At the BGCT's 1897 meeting in San Antonio, however, messengers refused to seat Hayden by a vote of 582-104.[196] In response, on April 28, 1898, he filed a $100,000 ($2,578,881) damage suit against fifty Texas Baptists, including Truett, for refusing to seat him. In all, four trials were held in Dallas, during which the defendants remained defiant. In a 1902 article for the *Baptist Standard*, Truett noted that Hayden's inexcusably shameful antics would not "even squint at intimidating the Baptists of Texas from conscientiously doing what they conceive to be their duty to Christ and His cause.... No, Texas Baptists will not be at all terrified by such lawsuits," even though they were embarrassing. Nevertheless, Truett proclaimed that God had sustained all the defendants through their "severe trials."[197]

Hayden won a $30,000 judgment after the first trial, but lost on appeal. The next two trials ended in hung juries. The fourth trial ended with Hayden winning a judgment for $15,000, which the Texas Supreme Court reversed. Finally, seven years to the day (April 28, 1905) after Hayden filed his first suit, Cranfill, a defendant in the lawsuit who bore the main brunt of Hayden's attacks, settled out of court with Hayden for $100 ($2,431) plus court costs.[198]

Truett's attendance at the 1907 BGCT meeting in San Antonio was notable not for any address he made or report he presented but for a comment made to one man. That man was John Franklyn (J. Frank) Norris, who had recently resigned his pastorate at McKinney Avenue (now Highland) Baptist Church in Dallas, to become the business manager of the *Baptist Standard*. Norris had begun his pastorate at McKinney Avenue in June 1905, and according to his own calculations, the church's membership had grown from thirteen to 1,000 by the time he accepted the job at the *Standard*.[199] Several of the new members at McKinney had come from Truett's congregation. Among other things, Norris had insinuated that their pastor was an inter-denominationalist, which for many Baptists was as "sinful" as being a modernist.[200] Such an accusation obviously did not please Truett.

At the BGCT meeting in San Antonio, the *Standard*'s new business manager addressed the messengers on the importance of the religious press, particularly the denominational paper. The mission and character of such a paper, Norris contended, was to communicate the gospel, educate its readers, unify the denomination, and defend the gospel. The paper should be run by the best people and should never be used to promote the agendas of its editors, particularly political agendas:

Editors of a high-class religious journal may have their personal political convictions, but they violate a most sacred trust when they venture to use the columns of a religious paper in the advocacy of the claims of any politician, from Constable to Governor, or defend any political issues, from road working to tariff legislation. It is unpardonable for the editor of any great denominational paper to purposely or knowingly allow his name to be connected with any of the present day political schemes.[201]

Many years later Norris briefly described in his autobiography what happened when he finished speaking at the 1907 meeting: "Dr. George W. Truett came up to me and put his arm around me and said, 'My lad, the world will hear from you.' Of course, he has forgotten the prophecy, but I haven't. That may be the reason why I have done some things that I perhaps ought not to have done." Norris then offered this warning: "Great preachers should be very careful how they put their hands on young ministerial sprouts."[202] Norris did not elaborate on those "things" he "perhaps ought not to have done," but some of those "things" he did to Truett, who, in Norris's mind, had only himself to blame.

Along with his work among Texas Baptists, Truett also became actively involved in the national body of Baptist churches in the South, the Southern Baptist Convention (SBC). His response to the welcome address at the 1898 SBC meeting in Norfolk, Virginia, caught the attention of the participants. In part of his address he called on the Holy Spirit to embolden Baptists to live a vigorous Christian life: "Come, Spirit of God, and teach us *here*, as we never knew it before, that Christianity is not only truth embodied in a creed, but that it is infinitely more—it is *truth embodied in a life*—it is *truth* in *action, out on the field* of *battle*."[203] As a result of his address, the assembly chose Truett to preach the convention sermon at the 1899 SBC meeting in Louisville, Kentucky.[204]

For the 1899 convention sermon, the thirty-two-year-old Truett preached on the topic "The Subject and the Object of the Gospel." Ministers must preach boldly with the convictions of the ancient prophets, he challenged his fellow preachers in the audience, for the gospel "is not a conundrum to be guessed at, or a theory to be speculated upon, but it is a divine revelation which is to be implicitly accepted and followed with the deepest heart-throb of our lives. Christ's preacher is not here primarily to teach Christian evidences or apologetics, but his message is like that of the prophet of old—'Thus saith the Lord.'"[205] Being constantly on the defensive is contrary to the gospel. Instead, we must preach "positive truth rather than the refutation of passing error." In a jibe against scholars and preachers who accepted the teachings of higher criticism, Truett advised ministers not be consumed with refuting such teachings, for "[i]t is not the chief business of God's minister to answer the last fool who has escaped from the mortar in which he was brayed." Preach the gospel, Truett advised, for it needs no defense but itself.[206] The subject of the gospel, therefore, must always be that men and women are "saved through the blood of Jesus Christ."[207]

Truett also addressed what he described as "a great itch abroad in the land demanding 'reform,'" a common theme of the proponents of the Social Gospel. Of course, he maintained, reform is needed in both church and state, and Christ's preachers must speak out against sin wherever they encounter it. Yet Christ's gospel goes deeper than mere social reforms. Jesus changed people from the inside out, not from the outside in. "Though corruption reigned on every side and sin was defiant, yet" Christ, Truett maintained, "pointed men, not to outward conditions or questions, but to the eternal verities of God. The emphasis of His message was put upon God and not upon man. It was so with the twelve [apostles]; it was so with Paul; it was so with John the Baptist; it was so with God's prophets of old; it is so with every successful winner of souls."[208] Thus, Christians are primarily missionaries, not social reformers.[209] Converting people to Christ, the object of the gospel, would result in converting society for Christ. Truett emphasized this theme throughout his ministry.

Much of Truett's work for the SBC during his early years as FBC's pastor came as a member of various committees. In 1903, for example, he presented the report of the committee responsible for studying the convention's mission work in the United States. Southern Baptists, the committee concluded, were numerically strong but developmentally weak;

that is, they were strong in baptizing people but "distressingly weak" in discipling them. In recent years, the committee noted, many Southern Baptists had been flocking "by the thousands" to live in cities where, because of their shallow faith and the temptations city life thrusts upon them, many had strayed from their faith.[210] Thus, Southern Baptists had to immerse their people in the knowledge and duties of the Christian faith, not merely in water.

### Pastoring a Growing Church

While doing committee work for the BGCT and for the SBC and while attempting to secure funds for the sanitarium, Truett pastored a growing neighborhood church. When he began his pastorate at FBC in September 1897, the church had 715 members, a Sunday-school enrollment of 250, and a building valued at $40,000 ($1,031,552). The estimated total amount of contributions was $3,300 ($85,103), of which $250 ($6,447), or 7.6 percent, went to missions and benevolences. Truett was the only paid staff member.[211]

After becoming FBC's pastor, Truett, like his mentor B. H. Carroll had done at First Baptist, Waco, led his church to adopt a budget system and to use pledge cards in order to help structure the church's finances. Truett also stressed that members tithe their income, something that had not previously been done.[212] His leadership helped turn the church's financial situation around, but the church was still $12,000 in debt. That debt was soon retired, not by the pastor's persuasive oratorical skills but by death. The church received $12,800 from the will of a Dallas man who had no church affiliation. He had left all his property to FBC because of the church's reputation for good works.[213]

At the end of Truett's first decade at FBC, the church's membership stood at 1,385, and Sunday-school enrollment at 902, having reached a high of 1,178 in 1904. The year 1906 was the best financial year during Truett's first decade in Dallas, when total contributions amounted to $46,491 ($1,105,451), with an astounding 86 percent going to missions and other ministries, such as the Texas Baptist Memorial Sanitarium. For five years (1901, 1904–1907) contributions to outside causes exceeded contributions to FBC's local work.[214]

As the membership of FBC grew, so did Truett's need for assistance. Women had contributed to FBC's growth. Like many large city churches during the latter part of the nineteenth century, FBC hired "Bible women" to visit prospects, report on people needing assistance, and supervise mission Sunday schools.[215] As vital as the ministry of these women was, Truett needed someone to help him personally.

On November 30, 1903, the church called Robert H. Coleman as Truett's pastoral assistant. Coleman owned his own music publishing company in Dallas, and during his publishing career, he edited and published nearly thirty hymnals and songbooks, which sold millions of copies.[216] Coleman was more than just a pastor's assistant, however. He was an ordained deacon and later became superintendent of FBC's Sunday school (1910–1946). He also led the congregational singing and often chauffeured Truett, who never learned to drive. In Truett's absence Coleman led Wednesday evening prayer meetings and sometimes preached and conducted funerals.[217] Moreover, he and Truett became close friends. Many people compared their relationship to that of the biblical characters David and Jonathan.

By the end of 1907, Truett had become entrenched in his life's calling: being a faithful preacher of the gospel. The Arnold tragedy helped turn Truett, already a sensitive man, into an even more compassionate individual. His church members, who monetarily had thought in terms of hundreds of dollars, had begun, like their pastor, to think in terms of thousands dollars. Encouraged by his wife, Josephine, and helped by his assistant, Coleman, Truett had extended his ministry throughout Texas and parts of the United States. That ministry, during the next nine years, would expand to include Baptists in other parts of the world.

# Chapter 3

# Saved to Serve, 1908–1916

During George W. Truett's first nineteen years in Dallas, the city had come a long way since its founding as a small village in 1868. In 1914, for example, the Federal government chose the city as one of the sites of the newly established Federal Reserve Bank. Presidents and presidential hopefuls deemed Dallas to be worthy of their visits. President William McKinley visited the city in 1901, and four years later a crowd of 25,000 welcomed President Theodore Roosevelt. In 1909, President William Taft received a warm, Dallas welcome.[1] Governor Woodrow Wilson of New Jersey, who would win the 1912 presidential election, visited Dallas in October 1911 to speak at the tercentenary celebration of the King James Version of the Bible, which was held at First Baptist Church (FBC) Dallas.[2]

While Wilson was addressing his Dallas audience in October 1911, in Germany, and seemingly unrelated to the lives of Dallas's citizens, a German general, Friedrich von Bernhardi, put the finishing touches on his book *Germany and the Next War*, which the *New York Times* called "the clarion summons to all Germans to prepare for war against England and whatever allies the latter can win over to her side."[3] In the book Bernhardi contended that "[w]ar is a biological necessity of the first importance, a regulative element in the life of mankind which cannot be dispensed with, since without it an unhealthy development will follow, which excludes every advancement of the race, and therefore all real civilization."[4] Yet not only is war a biological law; it is "a moral obligation, and as such, an indispensable factor in civilization."[5]

In response to Bernhardi's book, Reginald Brett (Lord Esher), a British historian and politician, contended that Bernhardi, with his "crude and juvenile" ideas, belonged to the Middle Ages.[6] Indeed, many American Christians would have agreed with Brett, for the twentieth century was to be the "Christian century." By 1900, for example, more than fifty mission boards in the United States had already sent out approximately 5,000 missionaries and staff throughout the world.[7] Membership in American churches continued to grow during the first two decades of the twentieth century, thereby creating the illusion that humanity was marching toward the glorious day when Christ would reign supreme over all the earth. William Warren Sweet described the attitude of American Christians this way:

> Many, if not most, of the Christian people of America were fully convinced that the world was entering upon a new and glorious age in which ballots, not bullets, were to be the weapons in a new kind of warfare, to bring in the reign of justice and right. Most thought a big war impossible. For everybody was saying that no nation was rich enough to bear the cost of maintaining for any length of time the burden of modern warfare. The optimism of these years blinded most Americans to the fact that across the Atlantic was a veritable powder mine ready to explode at any moment.[8]

The European situation, however, had little interest for Dallas citizens, for they were more interested in their thriving city. Nearly 300 lawyers, 250 physicians, and 61 dentists provided Dallasites with legal and medical services. Fighting crime and fire were 100 policemen and 145 firemen. Numerous businesses dotted the city, including 5 cigar manufacturers, 12 post offices, 20 dairies, 20 retail coal outlets, 120 boarding houses, nearly 150 restaurants, 200 saloons, and 400 grocery stores. Twenty-five public schools and six "colored" schools educated the city's youth. A small number of service industries had also blossomed in Dallas: 57 blacksmiths kept the city's equestrian-minded citizens riding their horses, 2 masseuses helped relieve the muscles of tense Dallasites, and 400 prostitutes, all listed in the city directory, serviced other tense customers. Most of these women worked in an authorized area just north of downtown called Frogtown, also known as "the reservation."[9]

The years from 1908 to 1916 were busy ones for the pastor of FBC, Dallas. Truett continued to preach the gospel to Baptists and other Christians in Dallas, in Texas, and throughout the United States, and he had the opportunity to preach to non-American Baptists. Yet wherever he preached and to whomever he preached, Truett's message was the same: Christians are saved to serve.

*Serving His Church*

From 1900 to 1914, Texas Baptists experienced steady numerical progress. The number of Baptist churches increased 32 percent (2,740 to 3,623); baptisms, 135 percent (10,479 to 24,623); and Sunday-school enrollment, 274 percent (57,353 to 214,687). Total gifts increased 482 percent ($347,556 [$8,852,943] to $2,021,676 [$43,258,859]).[10] During this period FBC also experienced numerical growth. Just as people had flocked to East Waco Baptist Church in the early 1890s to hear Truett preach, so also did they flock to FBC to hear him. A *Dallas Morning News* article on April 1, 1907, described the previous day's worship service at FBC: "Rev. George W. Truett preached yesterday at the First Baptist Church to large audiences. The congregation has so outgrown the present church structure that the enlargement of the building is declared to be imperative."[11] Two weeks later the newspaper noted that many worshippers had to sit in a large Sunday-school room to listen to the sermon.[12]

To accommodate the growing crowds, FBC members voted in May 1907 to spend $80,000 ($1,820,786) to enlarge their building. The completed building would be 16,900 square feet and would contain two auditoriums divided by movable partitions. Together, the auditoriums would seat 2,000 people. A gallery would extend along three sides, adding an additional 1,000 seats. Several smaller rooms near the auditoriums could hold 1,000 chairs. Worshippers in these rooms would not be able to see the pulpit, but they would be able to hear the preacher. The basement would contain a 6,600-square-foot auditorium, and a roof garden for socials could accommodate 400.[13]

The remodeling of the building did not begin until spring 1908. At their meeting on March 2, 1908, the deacons recommended holding worship services at the Majestic Theater during the remodeling. Beginning March 22, the church rented the theater for $25 ($581) per Sunday. During the deacons' meeting on March 30, M. H. Wolfe, who chaired the building committee, "very graciously offered to personally provide the expense of the rental for" the theater. The deacons accepted the offer "with much appreciation."[14] The building renovations were completed quickly, allowing FBC members to hold their first service in the renovated church building in December 1908.[15] The additional space in the new church building proved to be a blessing from 1908 to 1916, as FBC's membership grew from 1,400 to 2,507, and as Sunday-school enrollment increased from 1,641 to 3,262.

Although Truett was the driving force at FBC, he did not minister alone. He had the help of numerous volunteers, such as deacons, trustees, and Sunday-school teachers. Josephine Truett, for example, participated in FBC's Sunday-school ministry. On the first Sunday in January 1914, she started the T. E. L. (Timothy, Eunice, and Lois) Sunday-school class. Robert H. Coleman helped start the class by recruiting "volunteers." Mrs. M. B. Slaughter recalled walking into church that morning and looking for a class to attend. Coleman was sitting on the rostrum, and when he saw Slaughter, he said to her, "Mrs. Truett is organizing a class today and you are to be in it." Slaughter described Josephine as her "best friend through all of the years, and a glorious teacher of God's Word."[16] Josephine's class, which started with eight members, eventually grew to 500, had its own budget, and was influential in the church.[17]

Coleman resigned as Truett's assistant in 1909 to become the business manager of the *Baptist Standard* and to spend more time on his personal business interests. He returned to assist Truett once again in 1915, accepting a three-quarters-time position.[18]

On February 2, 1910, T. Adolphus Johnson began his FBC ministry as the church's secretary, a position he would hold for forty-four years. Known affectionately as "Brother Dolph," Johnson, like Coleman, wore many hats: church secretary, church clerk, Truett's personal secretary, secretary of the deacons, chief financial accountant, and business manager. He also chauffeured Truett.[19] As part of his duties, Johnson kept the church's membership roll and helped prepare male converts for baptism. He also attempted to involve these men in the church's ministries.[20] Johnson also mailed thousands of letters encouraging members to tithe and reminding them how much they "owed" on their pledge and how much was "due" on a certain date. His letters often contained the phrase, "with us, giving is a vital part of our worship," a concept that expressed well his pastor's understanding of stewardship.[21]

FBC placed a lot of trust in Johnson. Early in his FBC ministry, the church did not have a safe, so he took the Sunday offerings home, where he and his wife, Annie, counted the money. Dolph deposited the money on his way to church on Monday. It is estimated that he handled more than $8 million during his ministry at FBC.[22]

As part of their contribution to their church's ministry, FBC members canvassed Dallas looking for prospective members. People interested in the church filled out cards that were then given to Truett, who would send them a letter; to the Sunday-school superintendent; and to other officers of the church.[23] The numerous hours FBC members invested in their church's ministry were partly the result of Truett's sermons, in which he often challenged his people to be involved in ministry. For example, in a December 27, 1908, sermon on the Good Samaritan, titled "The True Neighbor" (Luke 10:36–37), Truett contended that a religion consisting only of empty words was a travesty:

> Oh, the farce of it!... [I]f a man's religion is not practical, if it doesn't cause him to stretch out his hand to lift up the fallen and to succor the afflicted; if it doesn't unloose his tongue so that he speaks the word of good cheer to him that is weary; if it doesn't cause him to seek to dry the tears of the widow and to stop the cries of the orphan, it is a blasphemy and a farce.... Oh, for practical religion! Practical religion, Christ's religion, the true religion, seeks ever more to help others. Such religion finds its expression in great deeds. It doesn't chiefly vent itself in vapory speeches.[24]

If FBC members did not understand Truett's call to service in December 1908, their pastor emphasized it again for them nearly four months later in a sermon from the book of Joshua. "God's work is so vast," Truett observed, "and the work to be done so diverse, the tasks so many, the places to be filled so numberless, that not in all his army may one soldier be spared. Indeed, we are saved to serve" in such a great army.[25] No one can be spared,

> [n]ot even the least child baptized…, not the humblest needle woman in our church…, not the noble carpenter, who toils his best at his work and goes into his modest cottage in the evening time with barely enough to keep the wolf from the door…. Not the simple young fellow going on with the great fight for mother and the younger children since father died—he cannot be spared. That is Christ's program. No other theory of church membership is rational, no other theory of church membership is righteous. Every man coming into Christ's army takes the holiest and highest and the most solemn pledge outside those heavens to give the King his best and to render service in the noblest and most heroic fashion.[26]

FBC members also contributed financially to their church's ministries. Contributions during the nine-year period from 1908 to 1916 totaled $571,775, of which 71 percent went to outside causes. Remarkably, in each of those years the church gave more money to such causes than to its own ministries.[27]

While Truett continued to serve and challenge his Dallas congergation, opportunities for him to leave FBC continued to come. As it had done in 1904, First Baptist Church, San Antonio, Texas, called Truett to become its pastor in 1910 and then again in 1915. First Baptist Church, El Paso, Texas, also called him in 1910. In October 1913, members of the pulpit committee of Greene Avenue Baptist Church in Brooklyn, New York, informed Truett that they had prayed about who should replace their pastor and that their hearts had "been deeply touched when" they had "presumed to reach away out to Dallas." The committee wondered whether he had "become so thoroughly wedded to the Southland that it would be quite impossible to persuade" him to leave Dallas.[28] To all these requests,

Truett responded that he would remain in Dallas, the city he loved, and at the church he loved even more, "a church," he professed on his fifteenth anniversary at FBC in 1912, that was "dearer to me than my heart's blood."[29]

FBC members also loved their pastor, and they took care of him. By 1908, the church was paying the Truetts' $600 ($13,947) rent on their home. That year Truett received a salary of $3,000 ($69,734), the same salary he had been receiving from at least 1904. In 1916, he received $5,000 ($97,435), the same salary he had received the previous three years.[30]

Sometime around 1913, FBC provided a home for the Truetts, which they, not the church, owned.[31] While Truett was negotiating with contractors to build a house at 5105 Live Oak Street, the church intervened and paid for it. Knowing their pastor's incredible generosity, however, FBC members insisted that Josephine receive the deed so that her husband would not be able to give their house away.[32] The house was quite spacious, with a large office for Truett downstairs and five or six bedrooms upstairs.[33]

At a Thursday evening reception on September 16, 1915, friends and FBC members presented Truett, who never learned to drive, with a 1916 model 53 Cadillac that seated seven passengers. The price of such a car ranged from $2,080 ($44,278) to $3,600 ($76,636).[34] In his remarks at the reception, Truett noted that his "wife and three girls think this church and this city are next to heaven itself." He praised his wife, whom he described as his greatest human inspiration and to whom he was greatly indebted. He was indebted also to the city of Dallas and to his church for its care of his family and for its harmonious spirit.[35]

While experiencing the joys of preaching to a congregation of thousands of worshippers every Sunday and pastoring people whom he loved and who loved him, Truett also experienced the sorrow of personal losses. His brother Harvey finally succumbed to consumption on January 25, 1908. Truett also experienced the loss of perhaps the two greatest spiritual influences in his life: his mother and his mentor, B. H. Carroll.

On August 2, 1911, Truett's eighty-year-old mother died at Whitewright. She was survived by her husband, six surviving children, thirty grandchildren, and fourteen great-grandchildren.[36] On Wednesday, November 11, 1914, Carroll died at Fort Worth, where he was president of Southwestern Baptist Theological Seminary. The following afternoon at First Baptist Church, Waco, twenty-four years to the day after he first met Carroll at McKinney, Texas, Truett preached Carroll's funeral sermon. In the first few sentences of the sermon, Truett expressed the loss that most Texas Baptists felt:

> In the days of John Chrysostom, the golden-mouthed preacher, the people said, "It were better for the sun to cease his shining than for John Chrysostom to cease his preaching." Something of that same feeling must be in our hearts to-day as we are called to face the exodus of the greatest preacher our State has ever known. How difficult it is to realize that B. H. Carroll has fallen on sleep! When did Death ever deal Texas Baptists before such a staggering blow? Shall we ever see his like again?[37]

Perhaps many of the mourners would have answered the last question with, "Yes, in George W. Truett."

### Serving Texas Baptists

One of the many feats for which Carroll was known was his founding of Southwestern Baptist Theological Seminary. While on a train near Amarillo, Texas, in spring 1905, he became convinced that God wanted him to start a new Baptist seminary in the Southwest. In August, the Baylor Bible Department became the Baylor Theological Seminary. Two years later, on November 9, 1907, the Baptist General Convention of Texas (BGCT) approved the separation of the seminary from Baylor and the founding of a new seminary. Five days later the trustees of the new school, which included Truett, J. B. Gambrell, J. B. Cranfill, and C. C. Slaughter, met in Truett's office in Dallas, elected Carroll as president of the seminary, nominated and elected the faculty, and gave the seminary its name, Southwestern Baptist Theological Seminary.[38] Truett served on the seminary's board of trustees until his death in 1944.

One of the first things the seminary's supporters had to do was find a suitable location for the school. Remaining in Waco was not an option because many people feared that either the seminary or the university would dominate the other.[39] Truett chaired the committee to find a location for the seminary. Many people, including Carroll, believed that Dallas was the natural location for the school, for the city had become the center of Baptist life in Texas. Truett, however, did not want the seminary in Dallas, preferring that the school remain tied to Baylor and perhaps fearing that it would interfere with his efforts to fund the sanitarium and support Buckner Orphans Home.[40] His friendship with the Baylor president, Samuel P. Brooks, and his love for Baylor also played a part in his wanting the seminary to remain in Waco. If, however, the seminary was to be located in Dallas, Truett suggested that it be located in Oak Cliff, a Dallas suburb.

The Oak Cliff suggestion, however, disturbed Carroll, who sent his protégé a seven-page letter, the opening sentence of which set the letter's tone: "I think the time has come for me to speak frankly concerning the Oak Cliff property as a proposed location of our Seminary." Carroll emphasized that he and the other seminary employees were "not working for *A TWO BY FOUR* institution. We believe that it has the approval of God and the favor of men.... We confidently believe that inside of five years it will have FIVE HUNDRED students" and will continue to grow. "Now HAVING THESE CONVICTIONS," Carroll continued emphatically, "it is not our purpose to handicap the future by injudicious location." He listed several reasons that Oak Cliff would be inadequate, among which was that "[o]ur Preacher Boys in Oak Cliff could not benefit from your pulpit ministrations." Moreover, the Oak Cliff suggestion seemed to insult Carroll: "It seems to me that you, yourself, having built up as you have such an institution as the Sanitarium would be unwilling to connect your fame with a little $60,000 [$1,410,490] plant in Oak Cliff as the site of the Seminary of THE SOUTHWEST. It would add nothing to your fame; indeed it would DETRACT from it greatly."[41] Ultimately, in summer 1910 the seminary moved to Fort Worth, Texas. Thus, Truett's reluctance to move the seminary to Dallas helped Fort Worth gain the school it had vigorously sought to have.[42]

Whereas Truett played a negative, almost reluctant role in the seminary's search to relocate, he involved himself intimately in the process by which the BGCT would eventually acquire the *Baptist Standard*. He was a frequent and popular contributor to the *Standard* during the years from 1908 to 1916, having at least 149 of his sermons and articles published in the paper. For three of those years (1907–1909), J. Frank Norris owned the paper. Although professing to shun publicity, Truett and his associates worked hard at creating a positive public image. In his autobiography Norris gleefully emphasized that "everywhere" Truett "went, he would always send me the daily papers giving wonderful accounts of his great crowds and meetings, and I published them.... There would be no comment, just a large envelope of clippings from the daily papers. And the boys in the forks of the creek wondered how I got hold of these papers. Of course, Dr. Truett 'detested the publicity.'"[43] Of course, Truett was also good for business, and because Norris was a good businessman, he published at least fifty-eight of Truett's sermons and articles.

During his ownership of the *Standard*, Norris upgraded the pictorial content, added local interest stories, improved the styling, used a better quality of paper, and increased subscriptions.[44] Yet as Leon McBeth observed, despite improving the quality and content of the paper, "Norris brought controversy and confrontation to the pages of the *Standard* and while this increased subscriptions, it threatened the fragile peace Texas Baptists had achieved since the demise of S. A. Hayden. Apparently Norris adopted some of the Haydenite views and soon had alienated most of the influential Baptist leaders of Texas."[45]

Norris's caustic style of journalism, particularly his personal attacks in late 1908 and early 1909 on supporters of gambling, also irritated those "influential Baptist leaders of Texas," including Truett, who was probably still mad at Norris for coaxing several FBC members to join McKinney Avenue Baptist Church when Norris pastored the church. In 1909, Truett and J. B. Cranfill headed a Dallas group of Baptists who persuaded the paper's board of directors to fire Norris, the paper's majority stockholder and editor. Instead, Norris fired the directors. The pressure on Norris to relinquish control of the *Standard* continued, however, until he finally resigned in October 1909. When Norris left Dallas in November to pastor First Baptist Church, Fort Worth, a group of Dallas Baptists, which included Truett, Gambrell, Robert Coleman, and R. C. Buckner, bought the *Standard.* Norris always believed that Truett was the driving force behind his removal from the paper.[46] The new ownership then named Gambrell as editor and Coleman as business manager. Five years later the group sold the paper to the BGCT.

The Dallas Baptists who bought the *Standard* in 1909 probably thought they had rid themselves of a colossal nuisance in the person of Norris. Yet Norris had an insatiable drive to succeed at whatever he did, and being pressured to sell his paper only served to fuel his desire to succeed even more. He had moved away from Dallas, but Fort Worth was not that far away, and he would make sure that Dallas Baptists, and even Baptists across America, would have to deal with him.

Things went quietly for Norris during his first year and a half in Forth Worth. In summer 1911, however, while preaching a revival in Owensboro, Kentucky, he witnessed the conversions of many people and experienced the "liberation" of trying to be a sophisticated preacher. Concluding that trying to be such a preacher had stifled his Fort Worth ministry, he returned to his pastorate to win souls, not respectability.[47]

On the first Sunday after returning from Kentucky, Norris preached a sermon titled "If Jim Jeffries, the Chicago Cubs, and Theodore Roosevelt Can't Come Back, Who Can?"[48] Other outlandish titles followed.[49] During his sermons Norris often wandered around the platform, shouting, laughing, joking, weeping, removing his coat, rolling up his sleeves, and taking off his tie. He was also known to jump from the platform onto a table, where he called on sinners to repent and be saved.[50]

Norris's preaching style was often vicious, a trait he had learned early in life. When Norris was seven years old, his alcoholic father caught him emptying the elder Norris's liquor bottles, a crime for which the inebriated father beat his son mercilessly with a blacksnake whip.[51] When the younger Norris grew up, he eschewed his father's practice of using a whip to flog transgressors, choosing instead to use words as his weapon. J. Frank zealously attacked sin with a vengeance, and as the title of one of his sermons reveals ("The Ten Biggest Devils in Fort Worth, Names Given"), he assailed individuals with the same zeal, often naming names.

Attacking sin and accusing individuals by name, however, often got Norris into trouble. When many people whom Norris expelled from his church joined College Avenue Baptist Church, Fort Worth, he called the church's pastor, C. V. Edwards, a "long, lean, lank yellow egg-sucking dog" for accepting the wayward members.[52] Consequently, the pastors' association of Fort Worth expelled Norris from its organization.

Other scraps in which Norris was embroiled had potentially deadly consequences. Once, someone shot at him while he was sitting in his office.[53] Later, while Norris was embroiled in a public feud with Mayor W. D. Davis concerning vice and corruption in Fort Worth, an arsonist set fire to Norris's church building on January 11, 1912, which was quickly put out. On the evening of February 4, a fire at Norris's home was soon extinguished, but another fire that evening at the church burned the building to the ground. No one doubted that the fires were the work of an arsonist or arsonists; the question concerned who was responsible. Norris accused Davis, who accused Norris. On March 1, a grand jury indicted Norris for perjuring himself during his grand jury testimony concerning the fires. On March 28, the day before Norris's perjury trial, another grand jury indicted him on two counts of arson. After a three-week trial, the jury acquitted Norris on his perjury charge.[54] In January 1914, he won an acquittal in his arson trial.[55] Such brushes with the law did not damper Norris's enthusiasm for conflict; they only emboldened him and fueled his ego as he continued his attacks on sin and sinners. These tragic events in the Fort Worth pastor's life could only have reassured the Dallas Baptists who had forced him to sell the *Standard* in 1909 that they had made the right decision.

While working to wrest the *Baptist Standard* from Norris during the fall of 1909, Truett was also preparing his address for Baylor University's first homecoming celebration, held November 24–25, 1909. An article in the *Standard* described the event, attended by 5,000 people, as "[t]he greatest educational rally and celebration in the history of Texas." Green and gold, the school colors, adorned badges and ribbons worn by people, and houses, buildings, and vehicles were decorated with green and gold festoons and ribbons. At 7:00 p.m., on Wednesday, November 24, students and visitors gathered at a bonfire. According to the *Standard*, "Not only did the younger element let themselves loose, in [a] weird war dance about the flames to the accompaniment of gongs and rattles and deafening shouts, but staid lawyers, business men and preachers laid aside their dignity to utter college yells and songs that had not echoed on the ambient air for decades and scores of years." An hour later, nearly 3,000 people gathered in Carroll Chapel to hear Truett's address.[56]

Truett developed his address around Baylor's past, present, and future. He called many of the names of the people who had played a part in the founding and growth of the university and who had sacrificed to make Baylor what it had become. If, however, the gathering in Carroll Chapel failed "to recognize the tremendous debt that the Present owes to the Past," he cautioned, "we shall make a mockery of this epochal occasion," which is the celebration of "the growth of sixty-four years of fidelity, and sacrifice, and blood."[57] The Baylor of today, Truett proclaimed, stands where it has always stood—"for thorough scholarship…for the democracy of merit…for a lofty patriotism…[and] for a living Christianity."[58]

As for Baylor's future, Truett emphasized the audience's debt to future generations. We must bless those who follow us just as we have been blessed by those who have preceded us. The "greatest peril of the land to-day is secularism," Truett warned. "Its baleful spirit enters the home, the church, the school, every realm, however high and holy…. The hypnotic word of our present day vocabulary is material success." We can bless our descendants by maintaining a university "great enough and religious enough to lift the people above their material and selfish interests…. On grounds of the highest patriotism, therefore, we are called upon to build and make mighty a Christian school."[59]

Truett also described the "ominous trend" in the United States to divorce religious denominations from their colleges and universities. Driving such a trend, according to Truett, "is organized wealth." Baylor, however, will never succumb to the almighty dollar, for "no amount of money can for one moment tempt her to submit to a divorcement between culture and faith. The religious convictions of the human heart are of the profoundest, and at the same time the broadest. Baylor will not barter these for any mess of pottage, however large." In contrast Baylor will continue to welcome people "of every creed and of none, saying to them that no training can be truly liberal which is not truly Christian." Against the trend to sever Christian schools from the denominations that gave them birth, Truett proclaimed, "Baylor will remain true to the traditions and ideals of the fathers. She will not be ashamed of the noble denomination that has founded and fostered her. But she cannot be what she ought to be in the world without the constant and noblest loyalty of her children."[60] Truett ended his address with a paraphrase of Psalm 137:5–6: "O Baylor, noble, beloved Alma Mater, if ever we forget thee, may our right hands forget their cunning, and our tongues cleave to the roofs of our mouths!"[61]

An important issue Baptists and other Protestants confronted during the early twentieth century concerned Christian union, or the incorporation of all Protestant denominations into one Christian organization. Truett was assigned to a BGCT committee charged with studying this subject. He presented the committee's report at the 1913 BGCT meeting in Dallas. The committee members deplored the divisions existing "among the lovers of Jesus, and the many evils resulting therefrom. We long for Christian union. We pray for it and will labor for it, on a Scriptural basis," but only on that basis.[62] The scriptural basis on which Christian union could be achieved was as follows: "[a]ll people," Protestant or Catholic, who profess Christ as Lord and Savior "are our brothers in the common salvation"[63]; every person is responsible to God for his or her response to God's offer of grace, which eliminates infant baptism; and the church must be comprised of baptized believers and must be separate from the state.[64]

Realizing that many Protestant organizations and the Catholic Church would not agree with the committee's understanding of a biblical basis for union, the committee emphasized that Texas Baptists "stand ready at all times to co-operate with all our fellow-Christians and our fellow-citizens, whether Protestant or Catholic, whether Jew or Gentile, in every worthy effort for the moral and social uplift of humanity, as well as for the equal civil and religious rights of all men in all lands. We would freely co-operate in all good works."[65] The only limitation to such cooperation would be if Texas Baptists were prohibited from preaching what they believed was taught in the Bible. The messengers at the BGCT meeting unanimously approved the report.

Throughout his ministry, Truett followed the guidelines set forth in the committee's report. Wherever he went, he preached what he considered to be the teachings of the Bible and never shied away from his Baptist beliefs. Even so, many non-Baptist organizations and churches in Dallas and around the country invited him to speak. They knew what they were getting when they invited him, and what they got evidently pleased them.[66]

Another avenue through which Truett served Texas Baptists was by attempting to guide ministers in their calling, particularly their call to preach.[67] In 1914, he delivered six addresses to the students of Southwestern Baptist Theological Seminary, four transcripts of which have survived. Truett began his first address, "The Preacher as a Man," as he often did—by expressing his "feelings of painful self-distrust as to" his "fitness" to speak about preaching. Then the great preacher followed this statement about his unworthiness to address young preachers with the following: "I am too busy a man to find time for the preparation of addresses with any literary finish, even if I had the gifts of such literary effort. Every day now with me is a busy, strenuous, crowded day."[68] Truett was a busy man; he knew it, and he often made sure others knew it too. Worse ways to begin a series on preaching might exist, but Truett's opening remarks to the "preacher boys" at Southwestern would rank high on the list. The members of the audience undoubtedly looked past such self-deprecating and unnecessary remarks and focused on what the famous minister had to say rather than on what he feigned to be.

Truett told the young ministers that "the note which breathes throughout" the Bible is that preachers must be absolutely convinced that God had called them to the ministry.[69] Moreover, God's preacher must "be the right kind of man. Oh, it is a crime, my brothers, for God's preacher to be the wrong kind of man. If he be unfair, if he be unwilling, if he be little in magnanimity, let angels weep."[70] Because being "the right kind of man" is so important, Truett emphasized that preachers must focus on their character more than on their words, for "[w]hat a man is himself counts for a great deal more than anything such a man will say. Character is power!"[71] Congregations will hear your words, he seemed to say, but they will feel your power.

Preaching, Truett emphasized, "is not a business…for prigs, or for fops, or for triflers, or for tricksters, or for elegant lecturers, or for dainty gentlemen, or for dawdlers—it is a business for *men*. It is the most masculine business in the world; it is the most robust, it is the most vital, it is the most heroic, and it calls for character to match the cause that we espouse."[72] In order to maintain the character so vital to being God's preacher, Truett warned the young ministers to guard themselves against "the two most insidious and fatal of all the temptations" preachers face: "the love of gain" and "the love of power."[73]

For his second address, Truett chose "The Preacher as a Student" for his topic. He challenged the seminarians to develop early the crucial habit of studying. He told his audience that he studied more in his twenty-first year as a pastor than he did in his first year. "Does that sound wretched to you?" he asked. "Does that chill you? Then I would lay my credentials on that little church table, and get back to the farm or the store or the shop."[74]

Since students need resources in order to learn their subjects, Truett discussed three indispensible textbooks preachers must master. The first was the Bible, "the Word of God, the book divine, *the* book." Nothing can take its place.[75] The second textbook encompassed general literature. Read and devour "the masterpieces," not junk, like sermon outlines.[76] "[T]he book of human nature" comprised the third textbook. Sit among the people, not on a pedestal, Truett told his audience. Live among them, not in a library, for preachers "must *know* the people. We must be men out among the people, and hear their cry and feel the desperate battles they fight."[77]

In his third address, "The Preacher in the Pulpit," Truett emphasized that preachers should be serious when they enter the pulpit, for it is their "throne" and from there they "must rule in royal fashion." Stupid, ineffective preachers, he remarked, are "the most serious handicap of true religion, and the most lamentable scandal."[78]

Truett maintained that every sermon must gather around the two great themes that run through the Bible: the stream of sin, which "runs as a dark current all through the Bible," and "the stream of salvation," which flows as "the stream of light, of healing, of life."[79] Preachers "must emphasize" the "painful fact" that sin separates individuals from God. "Alas," he cried, "many preachers are tempted to soft-pedal the damning fact and effect of sin."[80] But along with damnation, preachers must preach salvation. Remember, Truett advised, that no "sinner in the world however desperate his life, however deep his plunge, however horrible his mire, however sadly lost his estate" is beyond the reach of Christ.[81]

Truett's fourth address centered on the theme "The Preacher as a Soul Winner." Filling people's souls with the saving knowledge of God's grace comprised the primary task of God's preacher, not filling their heads with theology or burdening them with the problems of economics, politics, poor sanitation, inadequate housing, or alcohol abuse. Addressing such problems are important, Truett maintained, but they should never supersede the preaching aimed at regenerating and transforming the individual.[82]

To be soul winners, preachers must possess five "living convictions": that their primary object as ministers "is to win people to God"[83]; that humanity "is doomed" without the gospel[84]; that the gospel is sufficient to meet every need "of a beaten and condemned world"[85]; that churches, large and small, are the agents through which God seeks to win the world[86]; and that every Christian is a soul winner.[87]

The next major speaking event for Truett after he delivered his final address on preaching at Southwestern in fall 1914 came in January 1915 when he traveled to Houston, Texas, to address a group of businessmen on behalf of the city's Baptist Sanitarium and Hospital. Texas Baptists became involved with this hospital primarily through the efforts of D. R. Peveto, a Baptist minister who, in 1907, enlisted the help of other Baptists to purchase a dilapidated, seventeen-bed hospital. The BGCT assumed ownership of the hospital in 1910.[88]

"Your business and mine is not primarily to make a living," Truett informed the Houston entrepreneurs. "Making a living is a mere incident. Making a life is the thing we are here for, and the supreme contribution that you and I can make to this world, through which we are passing rapidly, is to offer it in ourselves the right kind of life."[89] Such a life can only be lived in "the business of service" to our neighbors, whoever they are and wherever they may be.[90]

Several times in his address Truett used an oratorical device, one that he used frequently in his addresses and sermons, in which he repeated a phrase to emphasize a point. In the following example, he repeated "It is not enough" before disclosing to the businessmen the essence of the "right kind of life":

> It is not enough, my fellow-men, for men to be financiers, important as that is. It is not enough for men to be clever, and every man ought to be as clever as he may. It is not enough for a man to be brilliant. It is not enough for a man to be popular. The supreme thing for which you and I are here is that we shall be helpers in the service of humanity. To default at this point means that we have missed the great program that the Master of life designs for us. The highest conception of life, I repeat, and the true conception, is that life is a trusteeship, a stewardship, and all that I have, all that I have, is to be dedicated without reserve on the altar for the welfare of humanity.[91]

One way in which people can live that "right kind of life," according to Truett, is by investing themselves in the right kind of institution, one that "reaches down its hands to the deepest depths of human need and looks after the alleviation of the pain and the wounds and the hurts of human life."[92] Such an institution does not discriminate on the basis of social class, Truett declared. At the Texas Baptist Memorial Sanitarium in Dallas, for example, "charity" patients, those "helpless" men and women who have been "beaten into the dust by the wounds and misfortunes of life," receive "the best of skill and attention" that the wealthier patients receive.[93] The Houston businessmen could link their lives with the physicians and scientists who heal bodies by financially supporting the Baptist Sanitarium and Hospital.

Truett reminded his audience of the greatest lesson of life—that "to give is to live, and that to withhold is to die."[94] To emphasize this point, he quoted a poem from memory, which he often did in his addresses and sermons:

Carve your name high over shifting sand,
Where the steadfast rocks defy decay—
All that you can hold in your cold, dead hand
Is what you have given away.

Build your pyramid skyward, and stand,
Gazed at by millions, cultured, they say—
All that you can hold in your cold, dead hand
Is what you have given away.

Count your wide conquests of sea and land,
Heap up the gold, and hoard as you may—

All that you can hold in your cold, dead hand
Is what you have given away.

Culture and fame and gold—ah, so grand,
Kings of the salon, the mart, a day—

All that you can hold in your cold, dead hand
Is what you have given away.[95]

Another ministry with which Truett helped Texas Baptists was in funding educational institutions. The idea of Christian higher education always had a special place in the hearts of many Texas Baptists. From 1845 to 1912, for example, they started fifty educational institutions.[96] Yet, as John W. Storey observed, names such as Austin Female Academy, Burleson College, and others "stand as ghostly reminders of not only the Baptist commitment to but also the difficulties of sustaining academic institutions."[97] Thus, the idea of having institutions of higher education always far exceeded the financial support of such institutions.

Throughout his ministry, Truett advocated that Texas Baptists were obligated to fund Christian educational institutions at home and abroad. In an address to the Texas Baptist Laymen's Convention in 1913, for example, he stressed the limits of the state educational system and the necessity of Christian education. The state, he contended, cannot provide an adequate education for Christians, which for Truett was not a bad thing. Because "[t]he state cannot, by the very genius of civil government, take care of the Christian religion," churches must provide that which the state cannot. Such a statement did not mean that Christians should reject state education. "We are for state education, patriotically for state education," he maintained, "but we are the more for Christian education."[98] Christian education, for example, can discuss who Jesus Christ is, but the state "cannot enter into the domain of religion. It matters what a man thinks of God, what a man thinks of Jesus Christ, does it not my brothers?" Because what people think of God and Jesus is crucial, churches must teach them. Moreover, what if the state were to teach that Martin Luther "was nothing but a renegade monk"? Such an answer "might satisfy our friends the Roman Catholics," Truett remarked, "but not us." Thus, failing to "provide grandly for the Christian school" was not only insane; it was an act of infidelity.[99]

Truett continued his support for Christian education when, in December 1915, Texas Baptists embarked on a four-year campaign to raise $1 million for Christian education in Texas. The campaign was fully underway in January 1916, with the intention to raise one fourth of the goal, $250,000 ($4,871,758). FBC members launched the campaign when, at the end of the worship service on January 16, 1916, they donated $25,000 ($487,175), or one tenth of the year's goal. To help the campaign, FBC granted Truett a leave of absence for several weeks, during which he raised $265,906 ($5,181,718).[100] The other yearly collections during the four-year campaign were successful, yet promises of financial support always exceeded actual cash, forcing other campaigns to be waged.[101]

### Serving the Baptist Denomination

Truett's ministry beyond Texas mirrored that in his home state. He preached revivals, spoke at camps, raised money for churches, and addressed convention meetings. Prior to preaching revivals, Truett often wrote the host pastor, reminding the pastor of his and Truett's roles in the meetings. To Edwin C. (E. C.) Dargan, pastor of First Baptist Church, Macon, Georgia, Truett wrote in preparation for a 1909 spring revival: "Now, you will keep in mind that I am not an evangelist, but only a busy pastor, going for a few days to help another busy pastor in some quiet meetings in the name of our Master. The services for the several days that I am to be with you are to be under your suggestion and direction."[102] After returning to Dallas, Truett would then write the host pastor, noting that memories of the blessed occasion would remain with him for a lifetime. "[M]y heart turns with most grateful recollections to you and your noble people," Truett wrote Dargan. "The memory of my recent, brief stay with you and with them, will come to me, again and again, like some sweet dream of the morning. It grieved me to the very depths of my heart, that I could not stay with you for 10 days more."[103]

Truett also helped congregations raise money for their new church buildings. In December 1910, he traveled to Conway, Arkansas, to assist the Baptist church there to raise the last $10,000 ($225,127) for its new building. The church's pastor, John Jeter Hurt, informed the readers of the *Baptist Standard* that 1,500 people heard Truett preach in the town of 4,000 people. The collection started when he began his sermon, and within an hour, more than 200 gifts and subscriptions had been collected, totaling $10,125. Hurt also added, "Two Methodists and one Jew subscribed three times each."[104]

Truett did not limit his ministry to Baptists in the South, for he often preached to Baptists in the North and East. His revival in 1910 at Green Avenue Baptist Church, Brooklyn, New York, met "with great success."[105] During fall 1914, he spent a lot of time in the East. In September, he preached twice at Dudley Street Baptist Church in Boston, Massachusetts.[106] The next month, while in Chicago en route to Toronto, Canada, to speak daily at the Baptist Convention of Canada, he wrote to James Marion (J. M.) Frost, founder and secretary of the Sunday School Board of the SBC. Truett informed Frost that on his return trip to Dallas, he was scheduled to stop in Canton, Ohio, to address the Ohio Baptist State Convention. "It is an exceedingly responsible mission for which I am now going," he told Frost. "Please pray for me, that every utterance I may make on this trip, both as to matter and manner, may be according to the will of God."[107] Another swing through the North and East in 1915 took Truett to Chicago and Philadelphia. Along with speaking at four non-Baptist institutions in Chicago, he addressed groups at First Baptist Church, Evanston, Illinois; First Baptist Church, Chicago; and the Baptist Social Union of Chicago. While in Philadelphia, Truett spoke to the Philadelphia Baptist Social Union; First Baptist Church; Chestnut Street Church; and the Baptist Ministers' Conference.[108]

Although Truett spent a lot of time serving Baptists outside the South, he was a Southern Baptist and spent much of his time serving the Southern Baptist Convention (SBC). On the Sunday of the 1910 SBC meeting in Baltimore, Maryland, he preached at the city's First Baptist Church. Richard H. Edmonds, editor of the *Manufacturers Record*, recalled that "[l]ong before the services commenced, every available nook and corner had been filled, even to seating people on the pulpit steps and around the platform leading to the pulpit. Hundreds of people were standing around the doors and out in the vestibule, and hundreds were turned away unable to get in. The sermon was worthy of the occasion." Edmonds noted that during the sermon, he could "scarcely see a single dry eye. I have never seen an audience so deeply affected. I have never seen so many men and women alike in tears."[109]

In the sermon Truett warned that selfish nations, individuals, and churches were travelling paths that would lead to their destruction. He pled for Christians to live sacrificial lives because God would reward them no matter how insiginificant their positions in the world seemed to be. "Shall the mother who slaves her life away so that her boy might preach the gospel to the world be any less rewarded than he?" Truett asked. "No matter how great his success—I say no."[110] A news report from Baltimore declared that he had delivered "one of the most eloquent sermons that has ever been heard in this city."[111]

On Sunday afternoon in the Lyric Theater, Truett presided over "a mammoth meeting," during which he pled for more family devotionals. "The decay of family piety means the deterioration of every holy thing under heaven," he bemoaned. "Parents are leaving the religious training of the young entirely to the Sunday school. What about the prayer in the home, the old-fashioned family altar, the reading of the Bible and the singing of hymns before retiring" for the evening?[112] Truett's performance in Baltimore had Southern Baptists heralding him as the "Spurgeon of Texas."[113]

Except for a brief trip to Canada, Truett's ministry through mid-1911 was confined to American Baptists and other Protestant denominations in America. That situation changed, however, in June when he delivered the closing address of the second Baptist World Alliance (BWA) congress (meeting) in Philadelphia, Pennsylvania.

Baptists had organized the BWA to fulfill their desire for greater unity among Baptists throughout the world. In July 1905, Baptists from twenty-six countries gathered in London, England, to hold their first congress. Along with fostering greater unity among Baptists, the BWA was formed to preach the gospel, facilitate cooperation among Baptists, address social issues, promote religious liberty, and ease human suffering.[114]

Organizers of the second congress assigned Truett the topic "Baptists and the Coming of the Kingdom in America." In April 1911, he wrote to B. H. Carroll, asking him for his "faithful" and "best council" concerning the address. "The occasion is a painfully responsible one," Truett emphasized. "Advise me freely and fully," he asked his mentor, "for which I shall be profoundly grateful. Get the great occasion before you—see the Baptists from all the world there, even from all the lands where it yet means the most [illegible] persecution to be a Baptist—remember the diversities of opinion among the Baptists there gathered—call to mind our progress and perils, our outlook and opportunities, what our future should be." Truett had already thought of several things to say, but Carroll's "suggestions will greatly vitalize my own thinking and I will be greatly reinforced by the thought that *you* will approve what I am going to say."[115]

The responsibility of preaching at such an important gathering obviously weighed heavily on Truett, for despite having preached for eighteen years, he felt the need to ask Carroll for advice. Moreover, he apparently felt the need to have his mentor's blessing and approval for what he would say. Whether Carroll responded to Truett's request is unknown, but one can surmise that he did.

Approximately 7,000 Baptists gathered in Philadelphia June 19–25, 1911, to attend the BWA congress. Grace Baptist Temple hosted most of the sessions, and a nearby church, Memorial Baptist Church, hosted overflow meetings.[116] Other speakers during the week-long meeting included J. B. Gambrell, Walter Rauschenbusch, Shailer Mathews, and two African-American Baptists, E. C. Maurice and Booker T. Washington, both of whom presented a plenary address.

At the meeting's closing session on Sunday evening, June 25, Truett followed the addresses by John Humpstone of New York ("Baptists and the Coming of the Kingdom in Non-Christian Lands") and John W. Ewing of London, England ("Baptists and the Coming of the Kingdom in

Europe"). Truett compared the past week "to a great council of war where God's men have surveyed the battle-field and have taken cognizance their forces. The issue is the conquest of the world for the Saviour, and we have seen and felt as never before that the victory is as certain as the promise of God."[117] Such optimism, however, must not be blind to the "manifold perils" that threatened America's role in the battle.

One peril threatening America was the growth of the cities. Truett noted that in 1800 only 3 percent of the American population lived in cities, but that percentage had increased to almost 40 percent. Two contrasting social conditions met in those cities—people living in opulence, flaunting their wealth, and people living in abject poverty, rotting in their slums.[118]

The peril of the "saloon power" also lived in cities, thriving and cursing everything it touched. Truett described the liquor industry as a "syndicated power," a "leech...sucking the blood from the veins of our Republic," an "anachronism of our modern civilization," and a "rich fiend and chronic criminal of all centuries." He called on Baptists to fight this "evil force" and its allies, the "scurvy politician and the gambler and everything and person that worketh and maketh a lie."[119]

A corrupt press constituted another peril. Baptists want a "free press," Truett affirmed, one that was neither "censured by the Sultan, nor sizzled by some Czar." Yet many newspapers sift "through the sewers and cesspools for matter with which to fill its columns.... It plunges its accursed beak into the putrescent carcasses of crime and virtue, and it parades it all before a waiting world."[120]

Immigration created another peril for America. Many of the current immigrants coming to the United States, according to Truett, were different than the ones who came previously, when "[i]n the long-ago God seemed to sift all Europe to get a composite and universal people for working out here on this continent the civilization, that should point the way for the world.... All Europe seems to have been sifted in that early day by the Almighty that he might get wheat here to plant to bring on a harvest that should point the way for the healing of the nations."[121] Truett thanked God that the nations of the world continued to send "us many of their noblest and bravest sons and daughters."[122] Nevertheless, he decried the insanity of an unregulated immigration policy that allowed immigrants to strain American institutions to the breaking point.[123]

The peril of wealth, one of Truett's favorite topics, also threatened America. Nowhere in the annals of history can such an accumulation of wealth be found as in America, Truett proclaimed. Such wealth staggers and appalls us. We watch and wonder if America can withstand

> this heaving, boiling sea of the vast accumulations, and that virus in American blood which cries out to get rich quick and to get more and still more of material treasure. For money all our ideals have been tainted, and for money all our ideals have been in danger. That passion for money is this hour to a terrible degree dictating terms to society and seaming our highest patriotism and stifling intellectuality. That nation, that civilization, has a dismal future before it if it shall put money before men.[124]

"But what have I said this for?" Truett asked. "To chant a dirge? No, no. To sound out a jeremiad? No. But to beat a charge."[125] Even though such perils challenge us, Baptists have numerous resources from which we can draw in order to wage the great battle against sin. We have millions of Baptists in North and Central America with whom we can work, Truett proclaimed. We live in a propitious time, for "[t]his is democracy's hour" and "the triumph of democracy, thank God, means the triumph for Baptists everywhere."[126] We also have at our disposal a unique mission and message. Any denomination, Truett contended, that does not have its own unique message and mission that it will not relinquish "is guilty of criminal sin against God and man."[127] What, according to Truett, could not Baptists relinquish?

> Absolute loyalty to the person and authority of Jesus Christ; personality *and* religion, and therefore no proxies, nor sponsors, nor deputies in the Kingdom of God; the right and of the duty of private judgment; the Church of Christ a spiritual institution and therefore the inexorable necessity of a regenerate membership! And in such a regenerate membership and in such a spirituality of church organization there is a death-blow to infant baptism and to

hierarchies and to government of churches by State. Certain great age-long contentions we cannot yield, and in the varied distinctiveness of our mission and message we have one of the world's most inspiring opportunities.[128]

America's role, then, in winning the world for Christ was to become Christian. America could not help the nations of the world emerge from spiritual darkness, Truett argued, unless "she be Christian through and through"; however, because "hermit nations" no longer exist, America cannot continue to hide her sins. Foreigners have asked why ghettos blighted American cities, why a half million children slave in its factories, why greedy businesses corrupt its commerce, and why corrupt politicians pollute its political process. Foreigners have asked us if Americans are even Christians. "The only thing that can save America, and through her a large part of the world," Truett declared, "is that America shall be Christian through and through and first of all the people of God."[129]

In order to Christianize America, Truett maintained that churches must recover their passion for lost souls, another of his favorite topics. Any church that has lost "that passion is but a grinning, ghastly skeleton of a church," and any preacher who has lost "that passion is no longer an evangelical preacher, preach whatever he may and however eloquently he will. The only thing that can save our churches is a living orthodoxy. The only thing that can save America and Britain and all the world is a living passion worthily voiced by the lips and lives of God's people, to bring a lost world to him. That is the call to America."[130]

After the BWA congress, J. M. Frost wrote two letters to Truett, congratulating him on his BWA address, although Truett could not fathom why such a pitiful address should be praised.[131] He appreciated Frost's assurance, however, that the address, despite being "poorly reported, and printed without my seeing it at all, has in it some things that ought to be said, and will do good, heartens and helps me more than I can tell you....You always say such gracious, heartening words about my poor efforts that I am ever under inexpressible obligations to you."[132]

*Serving His Beloved City*

Despite his extensive ministry outside of Dallas, Truett always returned home to minister in the city he loved. One way he served Dallas was by working to eradicate the social problems he believed were ruining the health of his city. Although the term "social gospel" was odious to Truett and most of his fellow Southern Baptists, Rufus Spain contended that Baptists in the South "*did* develop a social consciousness."[133] They might not have used the term "social gospel," but many of them preached and lived a gospel with social implications. For Truett, such preaching and living meant serving his community by supporting the Texas Baptist Memorial Sanitarium, seeking to eliminate gambling at the Texas State Fair, promoting Sabbath observance, campaigning for prohibition, helping African-American ministries, trying to eliminate prostitution, and commenting on war. Remaining silent on such issues was, for Truett, unthinkable and unpatriotic. In a sermon in July 1914, he insisted that "every preacher" must "declare moral principles, and…use them as a battle axe with which to bring to the dust the false trees about us. It is our business so to enunciate moral principles that they will cut their way through the world."[134] When speaking on moral issues, however, he contended that preachers must hold civil leaders accountable by proclaiming "great principles," not by demeaning personalities.[135] Thus, preaching the gospel held the key to eradicating social evils Harlan Mathews, a contemporary of Truett, summarized his friend's confidence in the power of the gospel to cure social ills: "He has believed always that the gospel of Christ is the solution of every problem and the panacea for every moral, social, economic, political, and industrial evil known to men."[136]

Securing funds for the construction of a new building for the Texas Baptist Memorial Sanitarium, which had been closed since March 11, 1905, kept Truett busy. While on one of his many trips, he informed E. C. Dargan: "Much absence and many unusually exacting duties have seemed to make it impossible for me to reply earlier to your letters. You will appreciate the unusual pressure of work upon me, just now,—extra work, incident to the rounding up of needed funds for the Sanitarium. I write to you with pencil, because I am 'on the wing,' and no ink is at hand."[137]

While in West Texas at the annual cowboy meeting in summer 1908, Truett and J. B. Gambrell secured cash and subscriptions for $10,000 ($232,446) for the sanitarium.[138] Later in the fall, at the BGCT meeting in Fort Worth, Truett spoke on behalf of the sanitarium, after which $140,000 ($3,254,247) was raised. At the meeting C. C. Slaughter contributed another $50,000 ($1,162,231), bringing his total contribution to the hospital to $75,000 ($1,743,346).[139] Then, early in 1909, he offered to donate $1 for every $2 given by other sources in order to finish and equip the new sanitarium building.[140]

After being closed for five and a half years, the sanitarium reopened to accept new patients on October 14, 1909. The new hospital contained 6 large wards, 114 private rooms, and 250 beds. The central building had five stories and a basement. Two wings of the building had four stories and basements.[141]

For Truett, Gambrell, and others, the hospital was more than a project; it was a means by which to minister. Truett frequently visited patients at the hospital. For example, Edyth Brown, an eleven-year-old patient with a knee injury, entered the hospital in November 1909. Truett visited her often, and on Christmas morning she found a plant and one of his business cards, on which he wrote the following: "To Edyth, the little girl who is over 300 miles away from home and her family at Christmas time. With love, George Truett." At lunchtime an orderly wheeled Edyth to Gambrell's home near the hospital, where she dined with the Gambrell family.[142]

At the 1910 BGCT meeting, Truett presented the report of the sanitarium's directors. During the first year the hospital had admitted 1,673 patients from Texas and fifteen other states and Mexico, treated 474 "outdoor patients," and cared for 726 "charity" patients.[143] Providing free care to indigent patients was important to the directors because "the poor and dependent sick cannot be turned away from a Christian institution. Indeed, the chief glory of such an institution will be to care for such."[144]

At the 1913 BGCT, meeting Truett announced that Slaughter offered to donate $2 for every $3 raised from other sources to help retire the sanitarium's debt and to construct a clinic building, a new nurses' home, and a dining hall and kitchen. The 5,000 messengers at the meeting "forgot their constitutional provision against applause and with mighty hand-clapping, some with tears and others with shouts of joy and glad astonishment, paid tribute to the man who has already showered so many beneficiencies upon Baptists Enterprises in Texas, and especially upon the sanitarium at Dallas. Col. Slaughter and his wife were asked to stand while the convention saluted them." Many Baptists called the demonstration "the most memorable hour almost in the history of the convention."[145]

Another way in which Truett served Dallas was by attempting to rid the city of gambling, particularly horserace gambling, which had been a major attraction at the State Fair of Texas since 1886.[146] The fair, which was held annually for two weeks in Dallas, had an attendance of nearly a million people and provided proponents of horse racing a lucrative opportunity to make money.

While editor of the *Baptist Standard*, J. Frank Norris investigated gambling at the fair in November 1908. On a visit to the fairgrounds, he witnessed forty-eight bookmaking stands and thousands of drunken men and women gamblers. The results of his investigation encouraged the Dallas Pastors' Association, an ecumenical organization to which Norris belonged, to call for a study of racetrack gambling in Texas.[147]

After studying the racetrack gambling issue, the Pastors' Association in January 1909 issued its appeal, authored by Truett, to the citizens of Dallas and Texas. The appeal stated that the association's "profound and inflexible conviction [was] that nothing worthy of our good city and Commonwealth can be helped by immoralities" that harm individuals and society.[148] When a community endorses and accepts vice for financial gain, that "community barters away the very soul of its civilization for a quick and corrupting penny." Such a community is doomed: "Woe to that guilty people who sit down upon broken laws, and wealth, saved by injustice! Woe to a generation fed upon the bread of fraud, whose children's inheritance shall be a perpetual memento of their fathers' unrighteousness; to whom dishonesty shall be made pleasant by association with the revered memories of father, brother and friend."[149] Nothing good, Truett contended in the appeal, could come from a policy that attracts "the outlawed legions of gamblers from other sections, with the brood of evil-doers that follow in their train," corrupting business and homes. Truett concluded that "[g]ambling is essentially dishonest and leads to all manner of dishonest practices. We utterly delude ourselves as a people, if we believe that we can sow to this insidious and undoing evil and not reap the most direful consequences."[150]

The Pastors' Association undoubtedly intended its appeal to influence public opinion against racetrack gambling. At that time Texas legislators were discussing the Robertson Bill, which would end racetrack gambling in the state. On February 22, the House of Representatives passed the bill by a vote of 90-27. The Senate was scheduled to vote during the first week in March. In order to defeat the bill, the Dallas Chamber of Commerce chartered a train and invited the senators to Dallas to investigate Norris's charges.[151] While in Dallas, someone suggested that the legislators who made the trip attend the Sunday morning worship service at FBC.

Having been alerted that several Texas legislators would attend the service, Truett prepared a message specifically for them. He chose Mark 5:9 as the text for his sermon: "And Jesus asked him, 'What is thy name?' And he answered, saying, 'My name is legion: for we are many'" (KJV). This exchange occurred during a preaching tour in Gadera when a demon-possessed man ran to Jesus and asked the Lord why he wanted to torment him. After asking the man his name, Jesus cast out the man's demons, which entered pigs feeding on a nearby hillside. The pigs then ran into the Sea of Galilee and drowned. When the townspeople heard what had happened, instead of rejoicing over the man's healing, they implored Jesus to leave the area. Truett called this scene "one of the darkest pictures that can ever appear in the horizon of any life, and that picture is the misuse of money. When [the demon-possessed man] was healed, when he was clothed with the power of Christ, when the evil ones were expelled, when he was tamed and subdued and renovated and filled with peace and light and happiness and joy, the news of it went out like wild-fire to his neighbors and friends throughout the community. A sensation ever is it, my brothers, when a man is made over!" Yet, Truett lamented, when the man's neighbors arrived at the scene, they uttered "[n]ot one word of joy, not one note of praise, not one hint of pleasure.... O, my brothers, there cannot be found a darker picture than that!"[152]

Why did the townspeople not rejoice? Because, Truett explained, hogs are more important than a man's salvation. Anyone who can witness another person's transformation and "not be smitten to the depths of his soul has a soul that is already dead. It stands out in the New Testament dark with a darkness that no orator and no rhetorician can find words adequately to describe—and gentlemen, the Gadarene spirit is not dead. The Gadarene spirit burns and bounds and lives and shouts today as really as when Jesus walked in this community and delivered the demoniac from the legion of evil spirits." The Gadarene spirit sacrifices people for money; it legitimizes and legalizes every vice for money because that spirit always prefers hogs to Christ. Truett maintained, however, that true wealth can only be found in morality. Wealth purchased by immorality is nothing but "a grinning, chattering skeleton and a colossal fraud. O, the debauchery, as the outlines of this dark picture stand out before us!"[153] "Morality, morality, my brother, is inherently right," Truett exclaimed,

> [even] if men never heard of the Bible.... Morality is man's relation to man, and no man, no corporation, no set of men, have the right, in any relation, to do that which makes it harder for other men to live.... None of us, O my brothers, have the right to make it hard for other people to live. I leave you to look at this tragedy, the tragedy of men who put trade above Christ.... No man has the right to put money above men, and that stands out with a clearness here that makes the blood run faster.[154]

The point of the sermon was obvious. Truett never referred to the horseracing issue, nor did he name anyone who supported gambling, even though many of them were sitting only a few feet from him, making them easy targets for a harangue. Everyone in the congregation, however, knew that he was addressing the peril of gambling. When the Texas senate voted on the Robertson Bill the following week, the bill passed by a vote of 18-12, thus ending racetrack gambling in Texas for the next twenty-five years. How much Truett's sermon helped in defeating the bill is unknown, but Norris, in appreciation for his work against racetrack gambling, received some of the pens used in signing the bill into law from the governor of Texas and several senators who voted for the bill.[155]

In his January 1909 appeal on behalf of the Dallas Pastors' Association, in which he presented the association's arguments against gambling at the Texas State Fair, Truett also presented the organization's case for enforcing Dallas's Sunday laws. Because the pastors supported the separation of church and state, Truett noted, they spoke about Sunday laws in a civil, not a religious context. Human history had shown that people need a break from work, for such a "principle is imbedded in all creation."[156] The appeal emphasized that the association's members had no "desire or purpose to enforce our religious conviction, touching the Sabbath or any other question upon our fellow citizens."[157] Yet nobody could have been oblivious to the fact that the pastors' churches worshipped on Sunday or that such laws supported the pastors' faith. The only way to have tested their disclaimer would have been for the citizens of Dallas or of Texas to vote for another day, say Tuesday, for a day of rest. But as Kenneth K. Bailey observed, in an era when "[d]oubters and village atheists were few,"[158] the likelihood of that happening was practically nil.

Another objection Truett set forth on behalf of the association relating to the neglect and non-enforcement of Sunday laws concerned the welfare of working men and women. Without the enforcement of Sunday laws, "selfish greed would drive helpless labor to ceaseless toil and thus deteriorate the race. It cannot be for the good of humanity that vast excursions be organized for the especial purpose of utilizing the day set apart for rest, in the interest of either private or public greed."[159]

If the 1909 Pastors' Association appeal had any effect on the enforcement of Sunday laws, that effect had worn off by 1915, for during summer and fall that year, the Dallas Council of Churches addressed the issue.[160] Truett remarked that Sunday laws were "humane and righteous" and should be enforced. Failure to do so "would, indeed, be a black Friday for America if the Sabbath should lose its hold upon her people."[161]

Sunday laws were not the only laws Dallas citizens ignored. Like all cities, Dallas had a crime problem. For example, during the one-year period from May 1, 1912, to May 1, 1913, authorities charged 28 people with murder, 5 for reckless driving, 68 for association with prostitutes, 3,202 for vagrancy, and 4,515 for drunk and disorderly conduct.[162] Most Baptists in the early twentieth century, particularly those in urban settings, believed that the consumption of alcohol was an individual sin that had deleterious social consequences and therefore should be eliminated from society, a position not held by everyone.

The Texas battle between prohibitionists ("drys") and non-prohibitionists ("wets") had been fought intermittently since the 1840s. After suffering a defeat by 90,000 votes for a state prohibition referendum in 1887, prohibitionists turned their efforts to local option initiatives by joining organizations to fight the liquor industry. Many Texas Baptists joined secular organizations such as the National Prohibition Party (organized 1869), the Anti-Saloon League (founded 1893), and the Women's Christian Temperance Union (founded 1874). Truett's close friend J. B. Cranfill had been the vice-presidential candidate for the National Prohibition Party in 1892. After the Anti-Saloon League became firmly established in Texas in 1907, many Baptists joined it to work for statewide prohibition. J. B. Gambrell became the superintendent of the league in Texas, and Truett was a member of its board of trustees.

Having eliminated most saloons in North and West Texas through local option votes during the last decade of the nineteenth century, prohibitionists fought a losing battle in 1908 to amend the Texas state constitution. In 1911, the Anti-Saloon League persuaded the Texas legislature to hold a referendum to enact prohibition statewide. In July 1911, after a busy week at the BWA congress in Philadelphia, Truett returned home briefly before involving himself in the referendum campaign. At the morning service on July 2, FBC voted unanimously to give Truett a three-week leave of absence to help rid "Texas of the manifold evils of the legalized liquor traffic." Concerning the church's action, he pledged to "do everything in my power for the promotion of the holy cause of temperance in Texas. I believe that none would ever see a more responsible hour than this, nor ever have a more urgent opportunity to serve God and humanity." Truett added that he would be ashamed of himself if he, as a teacher and preacher of morality, remained silent on such an important issue.[163]

Truett traveled to several cities on behalf of the referendum.[164] Despite his efforts and those of other Baptist and Christian leaders, Texans narrowly defeated the proposed amendment by 6,297 votes.[165] Although disappointed by the outcome, he remained optimistic. In a letter to his friend J. M. Frost, Truett thanked Frost for his "exceedingly gracious words concerning the action of our church here with regard to the great prohibition campaign.... Our noble church stood four square for the triumph of the great temperance cause, and we have abundant reason to believe that our course in such matter has had and will have the favors of Heaven. We did not win the victory..., but we won a colossal victory nevertheless and expect a little later along to win an overwhelming victory."[166] Truett did not elaborate on the phantom "victory," but in a few years he would play a role in a real prohibition victory.

Another social issue with which Dallas citizens, and all Americans, had to grapple in the early 1900s concerned the relationship between black and white Americans. Storey summed up the attitude of most Texas Baptists toward African Americans this way: "Texas Baptists were paternalists who believed the presumed superiority of whites carried with it responsibilities. Allegedly inferior and childlike blacks, instead of being humiliated, were to be under the watchful tutelage of the 'superior' Saxons."[167] Although Texas Baptists proudly pointed to their work among and with their "brothers in black,"[168] these brothers were distant siblings at best. Such an attitude toward African Americans, however, was not limited to southerners; it was nationwide.[169] According to David M. Reimers, even proponents of the Social Gospel, like Rauschenbusch, rarely discussed racial issues.[170] Nevertheless, as Bailey pointed out, "Negroes perceived differences when they crossed the Mason-Dixon line. In the South the color barrier was more precise and the animus aroused by small transgressions more violent and intense."[171]

Truett held an attitude toward African Americans similar to that of many of his fellow white Baptist brothers and sisters, yet he rejected the belief that African Americans were inferior. In a letter to an African-American minister, Truett told the minister what he had "said to many others. The colored people now have great leaders and are growing at a fine rate. They are by no means a weak people, and much of the talk about them is mere foolishness."[172]

Truett undoubtedly had more personal contact with African Americans than most whites, and many blacks in Dallas loved him. He could use pejorative terms to describe them, even as he had done as a teenager, yet rejoice at their receiving the best medical treatment possible. For example, in his 1915 address to Houston businessmen on behalf of that city's Baptist hospital, Truett mentioned an "old darky" who had undergone surgery at the separate facility for African Americans next to Dallas's Baptist hospital and whose "old black mammy…rocked in her grief, and voiced the best she could to the Father of life her cry that he would help them in their helplessness that hour." Yet at the same time Truett proclaimed that he could "never get away from the emotions that surged through my heart" as he observed "five…great scientists, mighty surgeons, conferring about" the man's "exceedingly difficult case."[173]

Whatever the exact nature of his relationship with and attitude toward African Americans was, Truett did not find associating with them, at least during religious functions, to be demeaning. In October 1899, for example, Truett, rather than the Dallas mayor, welcomed "Texas colored Baptists" to Dallas for their annual meeting. In his welcome address he expressed his "great joy in the prosperity" that African Americans were "making throughout the south. There is not a single record of any people in all history that has made a showing more brilliant than the record of your people, in the last twenty-five years. You are advancing religiously, intellectually and materially."[174] Four years later Truett addressed the "colored state evangelical convention."[175] Then, at a 1905 "mass meeting...for the general uplifting of the negro orphans in Texas" held at New Hope Baptist Church in Dallas, whose pastor, Alexander S. Jackson, was called the "Negro Truett" by whites and blacks,[176] Truett delivered an address on behalf of the "colored orphanage" in Gilmer, Texas.[177] In January 1912, he participated in the Man and Religion campaign among the "negro men of Dallas," during which he spoke at three services. He also chaired the committee for the campaign among the African-American men.[178]

Occasionally, Truett specifically referred to African Americans in his sermons. In his sermon on Christ's miraculous feeding of the multitude (Matt. 14:15–16), he addressed the difficult "race question." In the sermon he focused on the disciples' demand that Jesus send the people away hungry. "Send them away," Truett cried, is the method of unbelieving Christians and unbelievers. We do not want the poor, the maimed, or the toiling men and women to bother us. We want to send them away. Sending them away, Truett noted, is also

> the method proposed by some of our clever men, regarding the vexing race question, that ever and anon sends out its warning to the races of the South. Now and then, some man who imagines that his vision is far reaching, and his mind astute, rises and says, "Send the black race where we will never again see them! Send them away!" It is the same cry, in essence and spirit, as that when the disciples of Jesus, despairing over their relation to the needy thousands, proposed to hide their heads like ostriches, and leave the thousands to famish and die. It is not God's plan.[179]

God's plan for the race question, according to Truett, demanded that the stronger race must help the weaker race, which the African-American "race" was economically, socially, politically, and educationally. To ignore that plan, Truett declared, "is to invite the most calamitous consequences.... The principle and spirit of the gospel of Jesus inexorably requires that the strong shall help the weak. The race question, with all its complications and embarrassments, will be settled only by the application of the teachings and spirit of Jesus Christ, in His compassion for a broken, needy, sinful world."[180]

However his relationship with African Americans can be described, Truett was far ahead of many whites. He never exhibited the negrophobia set forth in Charles Carroll's *The Negro a Beast.*[181] Nor would Truett have condoned the actions of the mob that, in March 1910, murdered Allen Brooks, an African American who had been accused of raping a three-year-old white girl, by wrapping a rope around Brooks's neck and yanking him out of a second-floor window of the Dallas courthouse.[182] As Peter W. Agnew observed, Truett's

> kindly paternalism had greater potential for the fostering of mutual cooperation between blacks and whites than the more coldly aloof attitude toward blacks of some of Dallas' other white religious leaders, and in the context of the city in which virulent racial hatred was commonplace in the white population, kindly paternalism practically constituted liberalism. Truett's major concern for society at large was the arrival at a moral consensus of decent people of all races and creeds, and of the achievement of such agreement Truett was confident.[183]

Such an attitude toward the plight of African Americans remained with Truett for the rest of his life. He helped them and ministered to them, yet he expressed little of the outrage with which he attacked other social ills, such as gambling, the violation of Sunday laws, and alcohol.

One social issue that attracted Truett's attention briefly in 1913, and one that brought out his indignation, concerned "the reservation," the authorized area just north of downtown Dallas where hundreds of prostitutes lived and worked. On September 15, 1913, the Dallas Pastors' Association unanimously supported a resolution of the Dallas Council of Churches calling for the abolishment of the "reservation" and voted to support the campaign to rid Dallas "of that district." During the meeting, G. W. Benn, secretary of the council, discussed the plan to turn public sentiment against the reservation. Truett noted that "we are after fallen men as well as fallen women," noting that men create and maintain the conditions that make the reservation possible. E. O. Sharpe emphasized that Christians did not want to persecute the prostitutes but to help them live a more honorable life.[184]

An overflow crowd filled the sanctuary of First Methodist Church, Dallas, on the afternoon of September 21 to begin the campaign to purge Dallas of the reservation. After M. H. Wolfe, president of the Dallas Council of Churches, spoke about the purpose of the campaign, Truett delivered an address titled "The Social Evil and Fallen Men," described by the *Dallas Dispatch* as "one of the most severe excoriations on the violation of laws in this city ever heard in a Dallas pulpit."[185] Truett pitied the prostitutes who lived in that segregated section of Dallas, but not the pimps. He advised treating the prostitutes "kindly" and "as human beings." He also supported United States District Attorney Wilson's suggestion that the state provide homes for such women. Truett described as slanderous the notion that women would starve in such institutions: "Let such women come to the City Commissioners, to the members of the Council of Churches, and say they want a chance. Those men will divide their last crust to keep such a child from want."[186]

In contrast to his pitying the prostitutes, Truett not only pilloried the pimps and the johns who made such a life possible for women; he also denounced the Dallas officials who were sworn to enforce laws, yet did not care to enforce them. Concerning those officials, he asked, "Are we to shrug our shoulders and admit that we are a city of lawbreakers? The overwhelming majority of the people of this city want the laws enforced."[187]

Truett then noted that segregating the prostitutes had failed because "[t]here are more fallen men in this country, incomparably [more], than fallen women. Shall we quarantine the women while the men run loose? It is a colossal, world-wide, ghastly failure. The chief offender in this whole business is the man—and the man goes scot free. I do not propose to brand the poor, deceived thing and let the man go unwhipped." Yet segregation upholds this double standard. If we segregate the women, we should segregate the men too, for they rob these women of their innocence. "I shall not be a party," Truett declared, "to putting a fence around that child while the libertine struts the streets untouched. If God has vials of wrath more for one than for another, it is for the man who does this unspeakable thing."[188] "If we are to have segregation, let's have it," Truett proclaimed. "Let's segregate those men. Let's mark them. Whip, as a vulture from the face of the earth, any man who parades this city with a smirk and ruins our girls."[189]

Truett also addressed the "rumor" that many church members were involved in prostitution. Any man, he thundered, who even rents property for the purpose of prostitution "is worse than the inmates." "You fling it in my face that churchmen do it. Give us the facts," Truett challenged the rumor mongers. "We will discipline him as the vilest rogue. I have but loathing for a traitor striking religion in the back." Such a scoundrel was nothing but "a pusillanimous moral coward."[190]

The "rumor" Truett attacked, however, was true. Darwin Payne noted that if William W. Samuell, a prominent Dallas physician and member of Truett's church, had been "in attendance that Sunday, he must have been squirming" in his seat because he was part-owner of two homes on the reservation.[191] Truett probably never learned about his well-respected church member's real estate activities, for he preached Samuell's funeral sermon on December 14, 1937, during which he described the noted physician as a man "who gave himself unstintedly to the poor and unfortunate as well as to others."[192]

At the final meeting of the campaign on October 5, the ministers of the Pastor's Association passed a resolution urging the abolishment of the reservation. Commissioner Louis Blaylock and John W. Ryan, chief of Dallas police, did not like the idea of disbanding the reservation, but the Dallas County attorney, Currie McCutcheon, did and he gave the prostitutes until 6 p.m. on November 3 to move or to be arrested. Only a handful of prostitutes accepted the help to leave their former profession; most of the others, unwilling to give up such a profitable livelihood, either left Dallas or moved to another part of the city.[193]

Less than a year after the campaign against prostitution, the citizens of Dallas turned their attention to world affairs. The headlines for the June 29, 1914, edition of the *Dallas Morning News* announced the event that would embroil the world in war for the next four years: "Heir to Austro-Hungarian Throne Is Assassinated."[194] The day before in Sarajevo, Austria-Hungary, a Serbian nationalist, Gavrio Princip, assassinated Archduke Franz Ferdinand, heir to the Austria-Hungary throne, and his wife. One month later Austria-Hungary declared war on Serbia, thus starting World War I.

Although thousands of miles from Dallas, the war captured people's attention. In a sermon on October 4, 1914, Truett noted that everyone was thinking about

> the Pan-European struggle, the ghastliest, perhaps, in human history. We are thinking of the appalling loss of life and property; we are thinking of the rivers running red with carnage; we are thinking of strong nations fastening debts on their children and children's children which will take generations to pay; we are thinking of the slowing up of industries and sciences, and institutions; we are thinking of helpless women and children, with burdens too heavy to bear, who weep and wait and wonder what the outcome will be. Today we have come apart to cry unto the Lord God of Sabaoth to stay the carnage and ruin.[195]

In the sermon Truett described several lessons everyone could learn from war, two of which stand out. One was that God might allow the war to rage until the world's nations realize the impotency of their programs and "anchor themselves to God." The other was that without Christianity, "civilization...is a ghastly failure, and will relapse into barbarism.... This terrible war is waged in spite of Christianity. It is the very antithesis of what Jesus is and teaches. I speak of a genuine Christianity, not the so-called Christianity of galvanized formalism; I speak of Christianity in which the Spirit of God is regnant in human life."[196]

Despite the war, the world was not bereft of hope. In comments that perhaps revealed his postmillennialism and portrayed America almost in messianic terms, Truett noted that "[t]he day is coming when our nation will have a chance to pilot other nations in the upward climb, when war will cease throughout the earth, and a civilization in which Christianity is regnant will prevail in these nations."[197]

Yet, as horrible as the European war was, Americans still considered it to be a European problem, one that had little to do with them. Even after 128 Americans lost their lives on May 7, 1915, when a German submarine sank the British passenger ship *Lusitania*, America still maintained its neutrality. The following week an editorial in the *Baptist Standard* addressed the tragedy. The editorial emphasized that the *Standard* had attempted to follow President Woodrow Wilson's desire that the American press maintain a neutral attitude toward the combatants. Moreover, because Americans had only received British accounts of the hostilities, they could not render an impartial verdict about the war. The editorial noted that many Americans wanted to avenge the death of innocent Americans by declaring war on Germany. "We are confident," the editorial noted confidently, "that this will not be done," for sending troops across the ocean to fight in a European war was unfeasible and un-Christian. Additionally, "We would not right the wrong by sacrificing the lives of a hundred thousand men or more because one or two hundred American subjects were put to death."[198] This attitude, however, would gradually change over the next two years.

On a brighter note, in 1915, Fleming H. Revell Company published *We Would See Jesus*, a compilation of twelve of Truett's sermons, all of which had been stenographically reported J. B. Cranfill edited the sermons and contributed a short biographical sketch of his close friend and pastor, and John E. White, pastor of Second Baptist Church, Atlanta, Georgia, contributed a short essay on Truett's character. The book served as a means by which Truett could expand his preaching ministry. People who had never heard him could now read some of his sermons, at least edited versions of them.

On December 1, 1916, less than a month after Truett began his twentieth year as FBC's pastor, the city he loved so much honored him for his ministry in Dallas. The banquet, held at the Scottish Rite Cathedral of the Scottish Rite Masonry, was also intended to begin the campaign to raise $200,000 ($3,897,406) for the construction of a building for the Nurses'

Training School, which was part of the Texas Baptist Memorial Sanitarium.[199]

Truett was the only speaker at the gathering, which was attended by 500 people, including his father. Rhodes S. Baker, a Dallas attorney, introduced Truett, saying, "The name of Dr. Truett suggests great movements and institutions. When we think of great constructive reformations, we think of the big men connected with them.... Men's names are linked with spiritual things as well as material things. In Dr. Truett we have expressed the spiritual life of Dallas. His name is connected with those of three great institutions—the First Baptist Church of Dallas, Baylor University and the Texas Baptist Memorial Sanitarium."[200]

When Truett rose to speak, the audience gave him a long ovation, which he said was not for him but for the great institutions he represented. He praised Dallas for the "harmonious team work" that been the key to the city's growth, and reminiscent of his 1897 Baylor commencement address, "The Inspiration of Ideals," he noted that everyone was required "to help our public institutions, which have the highest ideals and make for the best in everything. Right ideals must find expression in the institutions in our midst."[201]

"The best contribution a man can make to the world," Truett informed the audience, "is a consecrated life," a life of service.[202] "The ideal life," he contended, "is described in this sentence: 'He [Jesus] went about doing good' [Acts 10:38]. You can not improve that definition.... Service is what is needed—service and sacrifice. It is not enough for a man to be a scholar, an orator or a financier—he must be a helper for humanity." Because every person is a trustee, "Every poor and sick and needy child is a legatee of your trust or mine, and woe betide us if we default our trust. As soon as a trust is forgotten, deterioration sets in—be the defaulter individual, city or nation."[203]

Truett also emphasized that the Texas Baptist Memorial Sanitarium not only had helped many sick and injured people; it had benefited the Dallas economy as well, having brought in $3,000,000 ($58,461,090) to the city. Baptists, he reminded the audience, had funded the sanitarium's work from the beginning. Noting that Catholics "deserve a great praise for their wonderful work" in the Dallas sanitarium, he then challenged the Protestants of Dallas to join their Baptist brothers and sisters and "rally to their standard and build their hospital."[204]

At the end of his speech, Truett, as he had done since his second week in Dallas in September 1897, asked people to open their hearts to a worthy cause by opening their wallets: "Will you not make it in your heart this resolution: 'The movement to improve that institution, which is a humanitarian and constructive force in the life of the city, that institution which is nobly helpful in the social welfare and progress of Dallas, shall have my support'?"[205] After the banquet two men asked to visit with Truett the next day so that they could make a contribution. Hal E. White, a member of the sanitarium's board of directors, met him in the hallway and made a contribution of $5,000 ($97,435).

The nine-year period from 1908 to 1916 proved to be productive ones for Truett. In his sermons to American and non-American Baptists, he stressed that the primary goal of preaching the gospel was to save souls, but those saved souls were obligated to serve their neighbors. Truett himself served his church, community, and denomination by raising money and by speaking out on social issues that he believed threatened the welfare of society and individuals. Such service endeared him to many Baptists and non-Baptists. Yet Truett also made a lifelong enemy in J. Frank Norris. In the years to come, Norris would be a thorn in the flesh of Truett and of many Texas and Southern Baptists.

Truett ended 1916 on a high note at the banquet given for him in December. He spoke about the sanitarium, which he loved, and asked people to invest their lives in a worthy cause, which he loved to do. That December America remained a spectator of the bloody Pan-European war, but circumstances would soon change and the United States would enter the Great War.

# Chapter 4

# The Great Journey, 1917–1919

At the beginning of 1917, the United States still remained out of the Pan-European war. With the slogan "He kept us out of war," the Presbyterian president, Woodrow Wilson, had won reelection in November 1916 by defeating his Republican opponent, Charles E. Hughes, a Baptist, by twenty-three electoral votes. While Wilson and Hughes campaigned across America battling for votes, soldiers in France and other countries battled for their lives, using new weapons and causing such misery and terror as had never been seen in human history. The machine gun, for example, made mass infantry charges suicidal, but unfortunately not obsolete, as commanders continued to order thousands of their troops "over the top" of their trenches to their deaths. In July 1916, for example, on the first day of the Battle of Somme, England suffered 60,000 casualties, most in the first half hour of fighting.[1]

The month before the Battle of the Somme, an anonymous French lieutenant described his observations and terror when, in June 1916, he arrived at Fort de Vaux, in Verdun, France:

> We had scarcely arrived…when there came an unprecedented bombardment of twelve hours. Alone, in a sort of dugout without walls, I pass twelve hours of agony, believing that it is the end. The soil is torn up, covered with fresh earth by enormous explosions. In front of us are not less than 1,200 guns of 240, 305, 380, and 420 calibre, which spit ceaselessly and all together, in these days of preparation for attack. These explosions stupefy the brain; you feel as if your entrails were being torn out, your heart twisted and wrenched; the shock seems to dismember your whole body. And then the wounded, the corpses! Never had I seen such horror, such hell.[2]

War might be hell, but it was also a hell of a good business deal for American entrepreneurs. American trade with the Allied Powers (England, France, and Russia) during the first three years of the war rose from $825 million ($17.7 billion)[3] in 1914 to $3.2 billion ($62 billion) in 1916.[4] In April 1917, however, the United States was finally drawn into active participation in the war.

At the November Baptist General Convention of Texas (BGCT) meeting in 1917, M. T. Andrews presented a resolution, which Texas Baptists adopted, urging the Foreign Mission Board of the Southern Baptist Convention (SBC) to take "some steps toward following our soldiers across the seas, and in every way consistent with military order, preaching the gospel to them, and leading them to accept the Savior before they go, as many of them will go to their death."[5] George W. Truett attended the meeting, yet he had no idea that in eight months he would be following the "soldiers across the seas" on what he would call his "great journey."

### The End of Neutrality

A little more than two months after his victory over Hughes, President Wilson, in a speech before the United States Senate on January 22, 1917, proclaimed that any peace between the warring nations must be followed by a concerted effort that "will make it virtually impossible that any such catastrophe should ever overwhelm us again. Every lover of mankind, every sane and thoughtful man must take that for granted."[6] The war must end, the president continued, but how it ends and upon what terms it ends were also important. There "must be a peace without victory" because victory means that the victors will impose their demands on the vanquished, which will only cause resentment and bitter memories. Thus, there must be a "peace among equals."[7]

On February 1, just ten days after Wilson's speech, Germany resumed its unrestricted submarine warfare, in which it vowed to sink any vessel, even passenger ships, deemed a threat. Two days later a German submarine sank the American cargo ship *Housatonic* near the Scilly Islands, off the southwest coast of England. The crew survived, but the incident caused the United States to break diplomatic relations with Germany.[8]

Germany's decision to resume unrestricted underwater warfare pushed the United States closer to entering the war. Prior to this decision, the German foreign minister, Arthur Zimmermann, sent a telegram in January 1917 to the Mexican government, stating that if Germany's submarine attacks brought America into the war, Germany would financially help Mexico attack the United States and regain the "lost territories" of Texas, New Mexico, and Arizona. The British intercepted the telegram, deciphered it, and then eventually sent it to the Americans. The telegram was published in American newspapers on March 1, causing an outcry of bitterness toward Germany.[9]

Germany's resumption of its unrestricted submarine warfare and the country's plans to help Mexico invade the United States finally forced the United States into the war. On April 2, Wilson asked Congress to declare war on Germany. "The world must be made safe for democracy," the president proclaimed. "Its peace must be planted upon the tested foundations of political liberty."[10] Asking for such a declaration was "a distressing and oppressive duty," Wilson confessed near the end of his speech, yet it was the right thing to do, and "the right is more precious than peace, and we shall fight for the things which we have always carried nearest our heart—for democracy, for the right of those who submit to authority to have a voice in their own governments, for the rights and liberties of small nations, [and] for a universal dominion of right by such a concert of free peoples as shall bring peace and safety to all nations and make the world at last free."[11] On April 4, the United States Senate voted 82-6 for the nation to enter the war; two days later the United States House of Representatives also voted (378-50) to join the conflict. With Congressional approval, the United States entered what J. B. Cranfill called "one of the stupidest wars in history."[12]

The majority of American religious leaders supported Wilson's decision to enter the war. Henry Van Dyke, a liberal Presbyterian minister and author of the hymn "Joyful, Joyful, We Adore Thee," advocated hanging anyone who spoke against America's entry in the war. Cardinal James Gibbons, primate of the American Catholic Church, proclaimed that loyal Americans must obey their country's call to arms.[13] Lyman Abbott, a Congregationalist minister, called the war a "twentieth century crusade."[14] Harry Emerson Fosdick, a liberal Baptist pastor, supported the United States' war effort in his book *The Challenge of the Present Crisis.*[15] For most American Christians, the war was "an expression of righteous purpose."[16]

Like Fosdick, most Baptists supported the unfortunate necessity of the United States' entry into the war. Delegates to the Northern Baptist Convention meeting in 1917 pledged their support to the nation in its war effort and urged churches to help the War Department (now called the State Department) fight the liquor industry and all other evils that plagued military camp environments.[17] Messengers at the 1917 SBC meeting approved the report of the Committee on the Present Crisis, which, in part, stated that "the issues involved in the great war concern fundamental human rights and liberties. The cause of democracy is at stake." While Southern Baptists could not claim that they cherished democracy more than other people, neither could they "forget that democracy is peculiarly a part of our religion, that it is interwoven with all our common and cherished beliefs. Deeply as all of us deplore war, ardently as we longed and labored to avert or avoid it, we may be cheered and heartened in remembering that we are moved in entering it, neither by lust nor hate, but by the love of humanity."[18]

While the United States military was planning its war strategy in April 1917, nineteen Dallas Baptist churches were planning a thirty-day spring revival to be held in Dallas's Jefferson Theater during the noon hour. Truett's assistant, Robert H. Coleman, said that the services were "primarily for business men, women and boys and girls, though others will be welcome."[19] Truett preached the April revival, which became an annual event. During the next twenty-six years, he led the spring revival twenty-four times.[20]

In June, Truett preached a fourteen-day revival hosted by Fort Worth's Broadway Baptist Church and College Avenue Baptist Church. The evening services were held under a revival tent and the noonday services in the Chamber of Commerce Auditorium.[21] Truett's twenty-four revival sermons were published in his second book, *A Quest for Souls*.[22] Cranfill, who edited the sermons, contended that these messages revealed "the key" to Truett's life.[23] Also in June, the National War Work Council (NWWC) of the Young Men's Christian Association (YMCA) appointed Truett to preach to soldiers in the National Guard mobilization camps.[24]

Truett's ministry at the military camps during fall 1917 did not detract from his ministry at his church or in his beloved city of Dallas. On September 9, 1917, the day before a vote to ban the sale of alcohol in Dallas County, he celebrated his twentieth anniversary as pastor of First Baptist Church (FBC). In his sermon on Romans 1:14, "I Am a Debtor," he emphasized two truths that he applied to the upcoming vote. Because "all power is a trust," people must use their resources for the betterment of hu-manity. Therefore, Truett contended that the answer to Cain's selfish ques-tion, "Am I my brother's keeper?" (Gen. 4:9), was yes because "our lives are indissolubly linked with everyone who ministers unto us, whether he be [a] laundry man, dairyman, grocer, merchant, legislator or executive."[25]

A second truth concerned how Christians were to fulfill their debtorship to others. "We must recognize our responsibility for everyone," Truett declared.

> By our words, our deeds, our conduct, our votes, we must discharge such debtorship. If men who toil do not have sufficient wages, we must see to it that they receive sufficient wages. If around us are institutions that do evil, that corrupt public morals, we must do away with such institutions.... We can discharge our debtorship to our brothers, to suffering women and children, by putting in the white ballot that will banish the liquor traffic from our fair city. The moral issue now before us is one that goes to the very foundations, and we cannot keep silent. As debtors we are under obligation to help, and bless and serve others all about us.... One boy in our city is worth more than all the

money in all the banks. Let us discharge our debtorship to the boys by voting out the institution [of organized liquor] that would corrupt and debauch them. Let us not sell our birthright for a mess of pottage.[26]

On Sunday evening, a crowd of more than 6,000 people packed the auditorium of the Coliseum at Fair Park to conclude the month-long campaign to free Dallas County of alcohol. Another 1,000 people had to be turned away. M. H. Wolfe, chair of the campaign, presided over the meeting. In his opening remarks he said, "We come to the close of this campaign with the same spirit with which we went into it—with ill will toward none, with good will to all." Truett spoke next and was followed by Edmond D. Mouzon, a Methodist bishop. Mayor Joe E. Lawther closed the meeting with prayer.[27]

Truett began his address by expressing his love for Dallas: "Just twenty years ago today I lifted up my voice for the first time as a citizen of the goodly city of Dallas. As these years have passed…the people of Dallas and all the higher interests of her people have been strengthened and deepened in my love with every passing day. I love Dallas as I love no other spot in all God's great big world. Her people are my people; her institutions are mine."[28] Therefore, he could not remain silent on such an important moral issue as banning the sale of alcohol in Dallas County.

To the crowd of sympathizers, Truett described the horrendous consequences of legalized liquor and why such an industry was "a moral absurdity and an ethical blunder."[29] The liquor industry, he said, destroys individuals by causing them to commit crimes, by damaging their bodies, by ruining their minds, and by destroying their souls.[30] The liquor industry destroys homes, "the citadel in our fair land, both for church and for state."[31] The liquor industry destroys civil government, as "[i]t puts its slimy hands on every election on the face of the earth that it can possibly influence" and as "[i]t puts a fear in the hearts of men who ought to have conscience and courage to repel its insolence with all just righteousness."[32] The liquor industry corrupts economics, for the grain used to make alcohol could "make eleven million loaves of bread a day—enough to maintain all our armies fighting throughout the world to bring to death the reign of autocracy in Germany."[33]

To the anti-prohibitionists' contention that prohibition infringed the civil liberties of the people, Truett declared that "every evil on the face of the earth" made such an argument. Yet "evil has no rights on the earth—not one. Evil is an impertinence; evil is a presumption; evil is an intruder; evil is an interloper;—and our business, please, God, is to drive evil wherever we find it from the face of the earth."[34]

Such harsh words against the liquor industry, however, did not mean that Truett hated the "saloon men" involved in the industry, for he aimed his words at rescuing them from a such "degrading" business. "I believe the saloon men of Dallas know that I am their friend," Truett claimed. "I am the friend of every man on the face of the earth. I would get up at the hour of midnight and go through any kind of weather to befriend any human being."[35] To support such a claim, he mentioned that just in the past few days he had comforted mourners who had lost loved ones. "Time and again," he emphasized,

> I have met with the stricken family of a saloon man yonder in Oakland Cemetery and the other cemeteries of our city. Time and again I have been with them as the sands of life galloped away from the child or wife or other loved one. Once more, I repeat—I believe the saloon men of Dallas know that I am their friend; and because I am their friend, so help me God, I must go to the limit to extricate them from the business that will damn them and their families for time and eternity if they are not extricated soon.[36]

The following day, numerous women stationed themselves outside of polling stations offering sandwiches and cold "soft" drinks to voters and asking them to support prohibition. Dallas citizens voted against prohibition by 687 votes (6,945 to 6,258); however, of the 18,837 Dallas County citizens who cast their votes, 55 percent (10,344) voted to prohibit the sale of alcohol in their county. Consequently, saloon owners had until October 20 to close their businesses.[37] The prohibition victory obviously pleased Truett, who had claimed a moral victory after the earlier defeat to amend the Texas constitution in July 1911.

A month after the prohibition victory in Dallas County, Truett and Josephine had another reason to celebrate. On October 9, 1917, Truett performed the wedding ceremony for his oldest daughter, Jessie, and her fiancé, Powhatan W. James, pastor of Gaston Avenue Baptist Church in Dallas.[38]

Also in fall 1917, Truett was named to a committee of the BGCT's executive committee to raise $25,000 ($404,000) for work among 20,000 soldiers stationed at temporary camps in Texas. In a September letter to Texas Baptists, the committee emphasized that the soldiers were the "bone of our bone, and flesh of our flesh...the flower of our manhood." They need to hear the gospel, for "[a]s these noble young men gather in the camps, their hearts will be tender, while yet the mother's kiss is fresh on their lips. But evils, the most deadly, await them and surround them in the camps, like ravenous wolves, to devour them soul and body."[39]

In early November, Truett also raised money for the YMCA's NWWC, which was trying to raise $35 million ($566 million) nationwide for its ministry to soldiers. He participated in a campaign to raise $2,500 ($40,000) among students at Southern Methodist University (SMU) in Dallas. The SMU campaign was part of a larger YMCA campaign to raise $65,000 ($1 million) from Texas college students. After Truett's address, the SMU students pledged $2,300 ($37,000).[40]

Part of the YMCA's work during the war consisted of supplying chaplains for military camps in the United States and overseas. When the war started in 1914, the U. S. Army had seventy-four chaplains. Although that number had increased to 194 by May 1917 and then to 666 by April 1918, the chaplaincy corps was still inadequate to meet the spiritual needs of soldiers.[41] Thus, by sponsoring chaplains, the YMCA provided a crucial service for the army and its soldiers.

The YMCA also built "Y-huts," in which soldiers could participate in religious, athletic, educational, recreational, and social programs. Military officials feared that soldiers, particularly those stationed overseas, would spend their free time in brothels located near military camps. The officials hoped that the YMCA programs would decrease the incidents of alcohol abuse and venereal diseases.[42]

At the BGCT annual meeting in November 1917, Truett presented a paper supporting the Allies against their battle "against autocracy, as expressed in all ecclesiastical and political systems." On behalf of Texas Baptists, Truett pledged "to our fellow patriots everywhere, and to the civil government of which we are a part, our loyal devotion to the principles inspiring the present titanic struggle of the democracies of the world against the most highly specialized and most powerfully organized autocracy in the world, supported by the most consummate military machine ever organized to support imperialism, against the common rights of humanity."[43]

Also in his presentation, Truett affirmed that the world will be better when "all autocracies are overthrown, and when the right of the people to rule themselves is everywhere recognized." He then applied the principle of self-rule to women. Because Baptist polity had always been democratic, and because every believer was equal in privilege, "we look with grateful favor upon the rapid conversion of the American people to their principle of the indefeasible right of women to express their convictions at the ballot box, along with their brothers."[44] The messengers to the convention adopted Truett's paper, and a year later Texas Baptists voted to begin placing women on the boards of Texas Baptist educational institutions.[45]

The beginning of 1918 found Truett engaging in activities in support of the American war effort. To a men's group at Gaston Avenue Baptist Church, Dallas, on Sunday evening, January 8, Truett spoke on the topic "The World War and the Duty of Men in This the Most Crucial Hour of Civilization." "The principles we are fighting for," he contended, "are not only worth living for, but are also worth dying for. This is no time for cowardice, littleness and selfishness." His optimistic nature led him to predict that "[t]he world is in the remaking, and when the job is finished crowned heads and military despots will be things of the past."[46]

A week after Truett's address at Gaston Avenue, members of the Dallas Pastors' Association, upon Truett's recommendation, promised that, during their next Sunday's sermon, they would stress the need for food conservation.[47] The food-conservation program, known as "Hooverizing," was named for Herbert Hoover, the food administrator in the Wilson administration. "Hooverizing" called for the conservation of fat and sugar and for wheatless Mondays and Wednesdays, meatless Tuesdays, and porkless Thursdays and Saturdays.[48]

FBC participated in the war effort too. By January 1918, more than 100 FBC members had joined the military.[49] The church also welcomed visiting servicemen at church services, and members invited soldiers to their homes after church. On Sunday afternoons the soldiers used a special lounge set up for them in the church to write letters, visit friends, and listen to music. The church also permitted its building to be used as a Dallas registration center for military service.[50]

### The Great Journey

In spring 1918, Truett was among twenty ministers whom President Wilson invited to preach to Allied forces overseas. The twenty included Henry Churchill, president of Oberlin College; Albert Hitch, former president of Andover Newton Theological School; Nolan Best, editor of the *Continent*, Chicago, Illinois; James A. Francis, pastor of First Baptist Church, Los Angeles, California; Philip Howard of the *Sunday School Times*, Philadelphia, Pennsylvania; Henry Sloan Coffin, pastor of Madison Avenue Presbyterian Church, New York City; and Edwin H. Hughes of Boston, Massachusetts.[51] Truett told the *Dallas Morning News* that he had "the matter under very serious consideration."[52] The ministers who accepted Wilson's invitation would go under the auspices of the YMCA, not the United States military.

While Truett pondered the invitation to go to Europe, Southern Baptists in May 1918 continued to ponder an issue that Truett's assistant, Coleman, had brought before the 1913 SBC meeting. At that meeting he announced that, at the 1914 meeting, he would propose an amendment to the convention's constitution to recognize women as messengers at convention meetings.[53] Such a change in the constitution would require a two-thirds majority. The issue proved to be so volatile, however, that he had to postpone offering the amendment for a vote until the 1917 meeting. At that meeting, messengers passed Coleman's proposal, but a question arose concerning whether a two-thirds majority meant two-thirds of the messengers enrolled at the meeting or two-thirds of those voting during a particular session. J. B. Gambrell, president of the SBC, ruled that two-thirds meant total enrolled messengers, which nullified the vote. Finally, at the SBC meeting in May 1918, messengers first amended the constitution by clarifying that changes in the constitution must have a two-thirds majority of messengers when a vote is taken, and then they passed Coleman's proposal.[54]

That Coleman made such a controversial proposal seems odd, for Truett was the logical person to have made the motion, not his assistant. Yet Coleman's leading role in the issue undoubtedly had his pastor's blessing and illustrates Truett's usual modus operandi in controversies: he let others work in public while he worked behind the scenes.

Also at the 1918 SBC meeting, the Committee on the World Crisis issued its report. Although not a member of the committee, Truett presented the report. After stressing once again the purity of American motives for entering the war, the committee contended that the issues of the war were "essentially religious," not primarily personal or political, for they concerned "fundamental human rights and liberties" and "touch the very foundations of moral law."[55] The committee hoped that "as far as may be consistent with military necessity and efficiency, the largest freedom ought to be afforded for religious activity among the enlisted men, to the end that they may have the best possible opportunities for religious guidance and instruction, and that in providing such facilities, all Christian bodies ought to be treated with perfect equity."[56]

By Sunday, June 2, Truett had made his decision concerning Wilson's invitation to preach to troops overseas. At FBC's morning service that day, he preached a sermon on Psalm 66:12: "We went through fire and water; but Thou broughtest us out into a wealthy place" (KJV). The whole Psalm, Truett contended, praises God's goodness for delivering the

Hebrew people "from [the] tyranny that enslaved them" in Egypt and for leading them to the promised land. The nations of the world, Truett noted, have been drawn into a "world cataclysm," their own "fire and water." "We find our hearts sinking within us," he lamented,

> with a faintness words cannot describe, that the world is enshrouded now because of embattled armies as it never was before since the stars sang together in creation's morning. Vast armies now are in the wilderness of Sinai, responding to the call of drum and leader. Egypt is one vast military camp. Mesopotamia is one ghastly battlefield. The hill of Golgotha and the Mount of Olives bristle today with bayonet and cannon. Judea is seamed with military trenches. Jerusalem, the Holy City, resounds with the tramp of marching soldiers. Airships fly over the land where Hebrew prophets taught, and where lived and walked the blessed Savior, Son of man who was also Son of God. Every considerable race on the earth today is involved in this world war. More than forty millions of men are actually under arms, and myriads already lie dead in unmarked graves throughout Europe.[57]

The only place people could look for comfort during such troubled times was to "heaven, in which sits God on His throne, reigning and caring for the children of men." God is sovereign, Truett proclaimed, and will lead "His people 'through fire and water into a wealthy place.'"[58]

Many people, particularly those who had sent loved ones and friends to the battlefields, continued to ask, "Why is America in this war?" Truett responded to such a question thusly: "*Because there was no other course for her to pursue except at the damnation of her soul.* In the other days, my own heart was pierced with the poignancy of anguish concerning the war. War is hideous! War is horrible! War is unspeakable in its atrocity and suffering! But there are some things far worse than war, and America is in this world war to make war against war, to make a war for real peace, a peace based on righteousness, and a peace to last."[59]

America is "a great, peace-loving nation," Truett proclaimed, and had entered the war neither for land nor treasure, for Germany and its allies have nothing that America wants or needs. Germany, in its lust for world domination, has sought to imprison the world in its "tyrannical subjugation"; it has "trampled under foot" all treaties; and it has sought to teach the world "the doctrine of barbarians…[and] savages," which is that "might makes right."[60] Such are the facts, and if given the chance, Germany wants to do to America "what she has already done to poor, weeping, bleeding Belgium," a reference to Germany's brutal invasion of the neutral country in August 1914.[61] "Red-blooded…and right-thinking men," Truett continued, "take their stand in the sight of God's throne and say, please God, the ravages that swept Belgium and Northern France shall not sweep our fair, free land of America! America is in the war on the highest moral aims to which men can give their hearts and lives."[62]

To prove his point, Truett asked the members of his congregation to consider what would happen if a "ruffian" were on the loose in Dallas, assaulting "our aged women, our fair maidens and our little girls." Of course, the congregation would immediately "call that ruffian to account." Likewise, "a vast ruffian, on the scale of the most compact and closely organized militaristic nation in the history of mankind goes up and down thoroughfares of the world," laughing at godliness and seeking to establish paganism everywhere. Any nation that would sit idly by and watch that ruffian debauch the whole world "is already doomed, and deserves to be doomed." Thus, in Truett's mind, circumstances beyond its control compelled "peace-loving, righteous-loving America…to bring all her resources of time and of material treasure, and, if necessary, of precious, patriot blood, and lay them all on the altar, to the end that aggressive autocracy, clearly seeking and demanding universal slavery, shall be checked and brought to righteous account."[63]

Yet even as the "atrocious and terrible" hostilities raged, Truett asked his congregation to consider "certain collateral advantages" of the war. Many people, even "the clever magazine editors and the astute writers in the secular press[,] are sounding a pean of appeal to God for His light and leading, such as you and I never heard before." The war has ended any notion of isolationism and has caused people to think of themselves as world citizens. We have also seen, Truett noted, an increased spirit of cooperation among all social classes and between "capital and labor."[64]

People are learning that laziness is a disgrace and that spending their money on superfluous things is a crime.[65] The most important "collateral advantage," however, is that people have learned the necessity of prayer.[66]

After the sermon, Truett announced that he had accepted President Wilson's invitation to go to Europe. In his letter to the members of FBC explaining his decision, Truett noted that everyone assembled that morning agreed "that humanity has reached the most tragical and responsible hour in all the history of civilization. It is an hour of supreme testing for nations, for ideals and institutions, for churches, for families and for individuals." No person or nation should fail to do its duty. At such a momentous time in world history, "it is unthinkable that preachers and churches should hesitate to give their most loyal support…to our noble Christian President" and others in authority.[67]

Truett confessed that he had felt "inexpressible awe" as he pondered ministering to "the soldiers in the camps and in the blood-sodden trenches beyond the Atlantic, where whole nations are being convulsed with the wrath of men, where the life of the world's finest young manhood is being poured out in rivers of blood, and where God in His might and mercy will surely restrain the wrath of men for human good and for the divine glory." My "heart is filled with yearning to speak to them some word, if possible, that will help them faithfully and victoriously to perform their whole duty."[68]

Truett informed his congregation that he would go to Europe in order to point the "soldiers for all humanity…to the infinite resources of wisdom and forgiveness and hope and life in the glorious gospel of the Lord Jesus Christ…. God help me—I can do nothing else but go, and go with my whole heart to cheer and help the struggling endangered men, as God by His grace and strength may enable me."[69]

After their pastor finished reading his letter, Coleman, Gambrell, Wolfe, and Cullen Thomas presented a resolution to the congregation granting Truett a leave of absence. The resolution stated, in part: "We believe that the call to him to go is equally a call to this church to send him." FBC members resolved to spend more time praying and working to continue God's work during their pastor's absence. They also counted it "a sacred privilege to care for" their pastor's "dear family and his children" during his absence and while "the world is in Gethsemane."[70]

Shortly after announcing his decision, Truett visited the eighty-one-year-old C. C. Slaughter, who was in poor health. Truett knew that Slaughter had been planning "to do something worthy for" the Texas Baptist Memorial Sanitarium. "You may not be alive when I get back," Truett told his wealthiest church member, so "[w]hy not do it before I leave?"[71] At that time, a total of $200,000 ($2.75 million) worth of bonds had been issued, $150,000 ($2 million) of which Slaughter held. When Truett returned to Slaughter's home the next day, the aged philanthropist handed him a tin box with $150,000 of cancelled bonds.[72]

Having made his decision to preach to soldiers in Europe, Truett set about securing funds to finance his journey. He borrowed $800 ($11,014) from a bank, which would not have covered the cost. When FBC's deacons learned that Truett was going to pay for the journey himself, they appropriated $1,000 ($13,768) from a special fund to help their pastor pay his expenses.[73]

During his time as a YMCA chaplain, Truett recorded his thoughts, activities, and prayers each night in a diary. He also wrote daily letters, which were read by a censor, to Josephine. Most of these letters have survived. The *Dallas Morning News* kept its readers informed about many of his activities by publishing excerpts from some of those letters.[74] Josephine also wrote numerous letters to her husband, and while Truett did not receive all of them, enough arrived to keep his "heart singing."[75] Apparently, however, he did not save the letters he received.

At 4:30 p.m. on July 9, 1918, Truett, now fifty-one years old, left Dallas by train "to go on the great mission to the soldiers overseas." The day had been one "of inexpressible emotions," he recorded in his diary. Josephine and the children had impressed him with "[h]ow brave and reassuring they all were, especially the brave, little wife, when I left them.... God keep them in His holy keeping forever!" Truett concluded his diary entry for the day with this statement: "I have committed all to Him, now and forever, as I go on this great journey. He is consciously with us. Our times are in His hands. All is well. Phil. 4:19."[76]

Truett arrived in New York City around 3 p.m. on July 11. He spent his first few days in the city visiting YMCA officials, getting measured for his uniform, sightseeing, and buying things he would need overseas. Necessities for the bibliophile Truett required a trip to a bookstore: "Did what I always do in a Book Store—came away with a pile of books, to read on the journey."[77]

In his support for American involvement in the war, Truett held a "Crusade ethic," which holds that a nation fights for some utopian ideal, such as waging a "war to end wars," and that a clear distinction can be made between the forces of righteousness and the forces of evil.[78] In one of his diary entries, he recorded that "the War *must* be won, no matter the cost, in money, time and life—and that this War must be so fought and concluded as to end wars forever. Autocracy must go in all realms. Aggressive autocracy must be dethroned, for the sake of today and of the long tomorrow."[79] In another entry, he left no doubt as to which side the Allies belonged: "The Am[erican] people have their minds made up about this war and they unhesitatingly believe that our Allied Armies are God's instruments to right the greatest wrong in all human history. It is now with the American people, the 'Sword bathed in heaven.'"[80]

On July 30, Truett finally boarded the ship that would take him to England. He spent much of the day watching "the pathetic sight of the long line of tired boys, with their heavy packs, marching, climbing into the Steamer—and now, asleep! Its wrings my heart. God keep them I pray. How horrible is the crime of those who brought on this war!"[81] Unfortunately, Truett would eventually see worse scenes than tired soldiers sailing off to war.

After twenty-three hours in the New York harbor, a convoy of ships loaded with men and material finally set sail for England on July 31. Truett found it "[i]mpossible to restrain" his tears. No lights were permitted during the evening hours, and many people became seasick, but "not so with me," he added, "yet!"[82]

On Friday, August 2, at dusk, Truett preached a sermon to the soldiers who had gathered on the ship's deck. "Great ships were all about us," he noted in his diary. The troops had "listened so reverently. God was with us. I talked about 'Doing His Will.' It was as soft music to my heart that the boys were so appreciative of my message, and the officers also."[83]

Truett spent much of his time on the ship visiting with Walter R. Lambuth, a bishop of the Methodist Episcopal Church, South, talking with soldiers and sailors, practicing lifeboat drills, studying French, and learning first aid. On the eleventh day at sea, August 10, Truett sighted the coasts of Ireland and Scotland and wrote a brief cable to be sent home immediately upon landing in England. With Germany waging a fairly successful submarine warfare, Truett knew that the convoy was traveling through treacherous waters, for he noted that "one cannot but be serious today in view of the waters through which we are now traveling. A season of prayer in [Bishop Lambuth's] room at 4 a.m."[84] Their ship docked safely at an English port on the morning of August 11.

Disembarking on English soil excited Truett: "Thrilling emotions surge through the heart as one's foot touches old England!"[85] Shortly after arriving, he burned one of his feet in a bath. A Scottish doctor delivered the horrible news that he had to remain in bed a few days.[86] The cable Truett had written aboard ship finally arrived in Dallas on the evening of August 13. While her husband was traveling to England, Josephine had feared for her husband's safety. The one-word cable, "Safe," relieved her anguish somewhat.[87] Earlier on the thirteenth in London, Truett met James A. Francis, one of the twenty pastors President Wilson had invited to preach to the troops and the man with whom Truett would spend a great deal of time in England, Ireland, France, and Germany.[88]

On his first Sunday in London, August 18, Truett, still hampered by his burned foot, noted in his diary how "sweet" it was "to hear the church bells and chimes. It is a sore deprivation that I cannot go out to preach or to hear [a sermon], as the others about me [are]. Lord, graciously help Thy servants, everywhere, to witness for Thee, as they ought, this day!"[89] The war cast its grim shadow all over London, he wrote to Josephine: "Over here, the eye cannot look anywhere without acutely realizing the fact of War—of devastating, horrible War—sorrow, silent but deep, is everywhere. But Hope and Courage and Faith as to the sure triumph of righteousness are also everywhere."[90]

Truett informed Josephine that he would have to "spend some time" in the British Isles before going to France. His roommate for the first few days in London had been Charles C. (C. C.) Selecman, pastor of Trinity Methodist Church, Los Angeles. Selecman, Lambuth, and Truett often prayed together and looked at family pictures in order to keep from becoming too homesick.[91]

August 23 proved to be a frustrating day for Truett. Selecman had already left to minister elsewhere in England, and on this day the "sane, saintly, noble" Lambuth left for work elsewhere. Truett described the bishop's departure as "like parting with a brother." Moreover, Truett had yet to receive a letter from Josephine. Because she had sent her letters to Paris, he had to wait for them to be forwarded to him in London. "Surely I would give the half of my Kingdom for one from you today," he wrote to her, "and the other half for two."[92] The next day, however, several of her letters arrived. "Glorious to get them," he recorded in his diary. "My emotions too deep for words."[93]

His foot having healed enough to travel, Truett preached on Sunday, August 25, at London's Metropolitan Tabernacle, the church that the famed nineteenth-century British Baptist Charles H. Spurgeon had pastored for thirty-eight years (1853–1891).[94] The following evening, Truett spoke at a Canadian hospital, where he watched as wounded soldiers were unloaded from a train. "Language human cannot describe my emotions," he recorded in his diary. "The sites are seared into my very brain."[95] He and another man preached to more than a thousand wounded soldiers, "some with one hand, some with a foot, some with one eye, etc." After the service, Truett talked with some wounded Americans. He described for Josephine how he took one nineteen-year-old boy into his "arms and petted and loved him, and he so clung to me. They were so brave and uncomplaining. Surely, surely, I shall know better than ever to be a murmurer any more about *little* things, when men by the myriads are dying without a murmur, for me, and my family, and my country, and for liberty and civilization. They were so appreciative of my address that it compelled me to put on all the brakes to keep from sobbing like a child."[96]

For the rest of August and into early September, Truett continued to preach to and visit with American and Canadian soldiers in London and in cities on the southeast, western, and southern coasts of England. He also did some sightseeing in London and elsewhere. After visiting Westminster Abbey and an old royal chapel, he noted in his diary entry for September 6: "The influence of the Established [Anglican] Church is seen and felt on every hand. The irresistible feeling one has [is] that too much is made of the mechanical and formal, and not enough of *God*."[97] The experience of worshiping at an Anglican church did not change his mind. While in Oxford sixteen days later, he attended Christ College Cathedral, after which he recorded that "the clear, deep, painful impression" he had felt during the service was "that such religious exercises will never win the masses to Christ."[98]

September 15 proved to be "one of life's highest days" for Truett because he preached six times to 15,000 soldiers, probably in Winchester, approximately seventy miles southwest of London.[99] "I would have gladly crossed the ocean and braved all the perils and hardships for what I have seen and felt today," he wrote to Josephine. "Multitudes—vast multitudes came to the side of our great Savior and King. Impossible to tell you how great it was. Never, never, can I get away from the greatness and blessedness of this day. To God be all the praise, forever!"[100]

While in Winchester, Truett met several soldiers from Dallas, "who followed" him "everywhere." He informed Josephine that he would write a brief letter to each of their mothers.[101] The *Dallas Morning News* published one such letter to Mrs. J. P. Edwards of Dallas: "Dear Mrs. Edwards: This is to tell you that I have just seen your dear son, Kirby, and have had a delightful little visit with him. He is in excellent health and all goes well with him. Be assured that I shall have untold joy in cheering and helping your dear son, and all our Dallas boys, to the limit of my power. Very sincerely, George W. Truett, of Dallas, Texas."[102] Parents cherished these letters and never forgot the spirit and dedication that went into writing them.[103]

Although Truett's ministry in England dealt mainly with white soldiers, he did request to preach to African-American soldiers, who comprised their own units that were often commanded by white officers. "It will be fine to speak to these darkeys," he wrote to Josephine the day before his preaching engagement on September 27. "I always enjoyed speaking to them, as you well know. I asked for the privilege of thus helping them." He asked her to tell Will and Agnes, an African-American couple who helped around the Truett home, that he was "everywhere trying to help their people as well as ours."[104] Truett's time with the African Americans proved to be a success. He assured Josephine that "we had a fine time.... They were radiant in true darkey fashion over my message. I was glad that I could visit them and speak to them. Nobody can get to them as well as one from the South, who knows their characteristics and spirit. They could not thank me enough for my message last night," and he expected "to speak to many more of them on this great journey."[105]

In October, Truett and his traveling companion, James A. Francis, spent nearly two weeks ministering in Ireland. After arriving back in England on October 13, Truett wrote to Josephine from Wales, the opening paragraph of which he penned ambiguously: "Have this afternoon crossed the Irish Sea, and am now in Wales. Am inexpressibly thankful to be safe across these waters. Will have a great story to tell you about it when I see you. No words have I that are adequate to express my gratitude to God for His guidance and mercy."[106]

Often in his letters to his wife, Truett vaguely mentioned incidents about which he would elaborate when he returned home, so the ambiguity about his "great story" would not have caused Josephine much concern; the content of the story would have, however. Truett and Francis had booked passage for Thursday, October 10, back to England on the Irish ship *Leinster*. Truett, however, insisted that they take the next boat, even though their luggage had already been stored on the *Leinster*, and spend a few more hours ministering in Ireland. He eventually talked Francis into staying.[107] The *Leinster* never reached England, however, because a German submarine sank it, drowning 520 persons, including women, children, and many Americans.[108] On Sunday morning, three days after the tragedy, Truett visited a hospital and viewed the bodies of the "American boys drowned on the Irish Sea…. Oh, the gruesome sight! It was burned into my very brain. I wonder if I can ever forget that long row, or rather the long rows of bodies! God comfort the loved ones far away! I felt as I felt standing…the other day, by the graves of the 207 *Lusitania* victims—they died for humanity!" That afternoon on their passage back to England, Truett and Francis passed by the spot where the *Leinster* had been torpedoed. "We were to have crossed last Thursday on that very vessel!" Truett recorded in his diary. "But our plans were changed! 'God moves in a mysterious way.' How great is His goodness!"[109]

After arriving in London at 7 a.m. on October 14, Truett and Francis received word that they would leave for France in the afternoon. They traveled by train to Folkstone, on England's southeast coast, and then crossed the English Channel to France.[110] The next day, one "to be remembered forever," Truett toured "the incomparable battlefields," tested his gas mask, and witnessed the grizzly scenes of "the unparalleled War. The fields, trees, and even the very skies above them seem heart broken." In Neuve Chapelle, he saw "[g]hastly sights" of dead soldiers: "The young boy with hand on heart—The other with Prayer book—ah, what pictures! God pity our poor world! The awfulness of War!"[111]

On the sixteenth he traveled approximately 150 miles, seeing more razed towns, more devastated land, and more dead soldiers. He expressed to Josephine the attitude toward Germany that millions of others held: "One thing is certain—the nation that brought on this titanic, ghastly War should now be made to feel the enormity of its guilt and no premature peace should be made with such nation. The world has been filled with woes too deep and terrible to be described by pen or tongue. The nation that has wrought such world-wide havoc should be given to understand that neither it nor any other nation must ever do this ghastly thing again."[112]

Truett noted in his diary that during one excursion on the sixteenth, he saw a "Crater 130 ft deep, 266 [ft] wide. Shook London."[113] This crater might have been part of the devastation caused at 3:10 a.m. on June 7, 1917, when the British detonated nineteen mines filled with 600 tons of explosives during the Battle of Messines, near the town of Ypres. The explosion, which the British prime minister, Lloyd George, heard and felt at his residence in London, caused 20,000 German casualties. On the evening prior to the detonation, the British general in charge of the attack, Herbert Plumer, remarked to his staff, "Gentlemen, we may not make history tomorrow, but we shall certainly change the geography."[114]

Truett and Francis returned to London on October 17. On the passage back across the English Channel, Truett spoke with several soldiers who insisted that the Allies must win "an overwhelming victory" and must reject "any premature and inconclusive peace." He agreed with such sentiments: "After seeing the long, long rows of trenches, blood-sodden, and the Dugouts, and the mud and blood of them all, and the mutilated cities, some utterly obliterated, and the horribly furrowed fields, and the dying and the dead, and then thinking of the millions who have been banned to the dust by this War, it is idle and irrational and criminal to think of any unworthy peace. God lead our Allies on to do His will!"[115]

Back in England, Truett spent his time preaching, socializing, and sightseeing. Naturally, he missed his family, whose pictures he carried with him "everywhere. They give me untellable comfort," he told his family. "Over great waters, my thoughts travel to you, unceasingly and go heavenward for God's best blessings."[116] Having Francis as a roommate and traveling companion, however, helped assuage Truett's homesickness: "We console each other as best we can, about our far absence from loved ones. He is goodness itself to me—a brother could not be more considerate of me."[117]

His health was fine, Truett informed Josephine, even though the flu had caused many deaths. "The 'Flu' over here—we call it 'Grippe'—is fearful. I have not had the semblance of it and hope to avoid it," he assured his wife. "You must do the same."[118] The 1918 flu pandemic perhaps presented the greatest danger to Truett's life while he was overseas, for disease caused 55 percent (62,000) of the estimated 113,000 deaths of American soldiers. In just four months during late 1918 and early 1919, the flu killed 548,452 people in the United States and twenty-one million people worldwide.[119]

Truett and Francis returned to France on October 26, arriving in Paris at 10:30 p.m. The next week they visited the Louvre and the Eiffel Tower, got measured for warmer clothes, and visited wounded soldiers. The beauty of Paris, even in wartime, and the friendliness of the French people, however, could not conceal the devastation of war. Truett recorded in his diary one day that he had "never seen as many people in black. It is terrible to see so many young women in black. The awful meaning is evident. Oh how France has suffered."[120]

On Sunday, November 3, Truett and Francis traveled nearly 100 miles and spoke at four different camps.[121] The "wounded and often incurably mutilated" soldiers Truett met at two military hospitals on the following Tuesday impressed him because they were "the cheeriest men one ever sees. Not a low note is ever sounded by any of them. It seems a miracle to them every one how they got through without being killed. So, when they look at the stumps of their legs—or arms—they smile reassuringly and say: 'I am here for a good while yet and I expect to play the man to the finish.' This was a common attitude."[122]

On November 7, the two ministers traveled by train from Paris to Brest, on the west coast. The news of the impending armistice caused "a wild riot of joy—on train, in villages, along roads, in the fields, etc."[123] The cessation of hostilities was scheduled for four days later, at the eleventh hour of the eleventh day of the eleventh month of the year.

"Today is probably the most notable day in all history, next to the day when Jesus died on Calvary," Truett recorded in his diary on November 11. "All France is in riot of joy." At the much-anticipated hour, 11 a.m., the people began to celebrate. Never, never, did the world see the like before. Two flags everywhere are waiving—the French and American flags…in [buildings], in windows, in the marches, in the hands of the aged, the women, the children, even in the hands of babies. God be praised forever, for the end that has come and is coming to the incomparable War! Now, may the victorious nations be humble and obedient to the call of the highest. It is a time for prayer. God help us![124]

While Truett was praying, however, the victors were planning how best to humiliate and punish the vanquished. "Humility" was not in their vocabulary.

After two and a half weeks in western France, Truett and Francis returned to Paris on November 25, leaving two days later to visit camps in other cities. On December 2, probably in Chaumont, 168 miles southwest of Paris, Truett experienced "another of life's great days—one of its greatest." He spoke to a group of Frenchmen who were learning English at "The Interpreter's School" so that they could be interpreters for the American and British armies. For nearly an hour, he tried to explain American religious life for them. "The occasion was one of the most challenging and thrilling that I have ever faced or expect to face," he informed Josephine. "These fine men were marvelously alert as I sought to interpret America's doctrine of 'a free church in a free state.'"[125]

Truett and Francis returned to Paris on December 9. A bad cold forced Truett to remain in his room for a few days. When Francis left to preach in another city, Truett noted in his diary that he was "indeed lonely." Despite his cold, he visited the YMCA headquarters and then wrote several letters "to cheer anxious parents in the homeland."[126]

In his December 18 letter to Josephine, Truett described the yearning of everyone to return home and his quandary about what to do next. "The desire to go home is in the air," he wrote; "it is everywhere—and the boys who have to stay over here for some time yet, greatly need the best possible help—they need it now more than ever." He had been asked to spend three months with the American Army of Occupation in Germany. He could not agree to stay that long and would probably only go for a month because he could not wait to get back home. Truett also told his wife that his experiences during the past five and a half months had changed him: "I have seen and heard and felt so much, on this great journey. My whole life must be vitally affected by this journey, henceforth. And we will ever [have] the consciousness that we both did the best we knew to do and could do, in the crisis-hour that came to the world. Our future work will, I trust, be better in every way, because of these great experiences."[127]

On December 21, Truett left for Germany. Francis, who was on a preaching tour, did not return in time to go with him, but he would join his roommate in a few days. Truett traveled with J. Ross Stevenson, head of Princeton Theological Seminary, and two others ministers, all of whom were Presbyterian and "high grade men."[128] The men arrived in Koblenz, Germany, at 11 a.m. on Christmas Eve. Truett and Stevenson took a walk along the Rhine River, just before lunch. "[T]he Scenery in all directions is most attractive," he noted ironically in his diary. "It seems like some awful dream, and not an actual reality, that this country and the others, were until recently engaged in the most desolating War of all history."[129] The men and women bustling about the city and carrying presents and Christmas trees, and the children laughing and playing made the surreal experience even more ironic.

That evening when Truett returned to his room in a modest German home, he found that the owner had placed a small Christmas tree decorated with tinsel on the table next to his bed. A few minutes later he heard some American Red Cross nurses singing "Silent Night" below his window. The kindness of the German landlord and the beautiful singing proved to be too much for the weary, homesick preacher as he fell to his knees and wept.[130]

On Christmas morning, Truett preached during a worship service for YMCA workers, which helped everyone "to put aside some of our poignant homesickness." The return of Francis also lifted his spirits, and they "had a glorious afternoon together."[131]

On December 26, the two ministers left Koblenz and separated to preach in several different cities. On January 6, 1919, they met back in

Koblenz, where they discussed the past ten "most stressful and meaningful days that we have ever lived." Francis had preached nineteen times; Truett, twenty-one.[132]

Also on January 6, Truett informed Josephine that the men of the Thirty-second Division requested that he visit them. Because he and Francis were having problems getting passage home, Truett was able to fulfill that request, which made the men of the division "radiantly happy."[133]

The next day, Truett stayed in bed until noon. He was "almost feverish at the thought of going" home. He wrote to Josephine, "The one thing that has made it bearable for me to be so long and far separated from you, has been the fact of duty—of duty to men who needed the best possible reinforcement from everybody, and who have kept me busy, night and day."[134]

After preaching several days to the men of the Thirty-second Division, Truett received word on January 12 that he could return to the United States. He left Germany on January 13 and arrived back in Paris at noon on January 14, after he and Francis had sat up all night in a crowded, cold train.[135] As the two men prepared to leave, the thought of returning home thrilled their "hearts to the depths. We are as eager about it as two little boys for a promised picnic in the delightful fields and woods."[136]

Back home in Dallas on the evening of January 17, a group of Texas prohibitionists gathered at the Southland Hotel in Dallas to celebrate the ratification of the Eighteenth Amendment, which, in December 1917, Congress had sent to the states to be ratified. The amendment prohibited "the manufacture, sale, or transportation of intoxicating liquors within, the importation thereof into, or the exportation thereof from the United States and all territory subject to the jurisdiction thereof."[137] Several speakers at the gathering declared that the prohibition victory was even greater than the recent military victory over Germany and that it was the greatest cause for celebration since the signing of the Declaration of Independence.[138] If Truett knew about the ratification, such news would have thrilled him. Yet even such glorious news undoubtedly would have taken second place to what he was experiencing that day, for he and Francis had had a "glorious ride to Bordeaux," near the southwest coast of France. "What stirrings of heart as one thinks of going home!" Truett noted in his diary. "Today has been such a happy, glorious day—because I am going home! Home!! Home!!!"[139]

At 5:30 p.m. on January 18, the same day that the Peace Conference began in Paris, Truett and Francis boarded the French steamer *Lorraine*, which set sail that evening for New York City. In his diary the following day, Truett wrote the following pledge to God: "As best I can, I give myself anew to Him who died for me. Living or Dying, in time and throughout eternity, I would be His forever. Oh, for more of His wisdom and sympathy and power, that I may live for Him as I ought!" He ended this entry with the prayer and sentiment with which he closed several entries and letters: "God's will be done on earth as it is in heaven!"[140]

January 28 became yet another never-to-be-forgotten day for Truett because he and his fellow passengers sighted land, "which sight thrilled our hearts. The Band gave glorious music throughout the day. By and by came the sight of New York and the Statue of Liberty. Emotions unutterable filled our beings—to see the homeland again and to set foot upon it." After disembarking, he and Francis took a cab to the Hotel Belmont, where Truett had "[a] glorious supper, a glorious bath, a glorious bed. How happy we are! A glorious letter from Josephine."[141] It was a glorious day indeed.

Truett began his journey back to Dallas on January 30 when he boarded a train for St. Louis, where he would meet Josephine. Also that day he received a letter from her informing him that C. C. Slaughter had died on January 25. "How I shall miss him!" Truett noted in his diary. "My gratitude for him, and my love for him, are inexpressible."[142] The next day at 5:30 p.m he sighted St. Louis. A half hour later, as his train was pulling into the station, he was writing in his diary while looking out a window: "Will my wife be there? Yes, there she is! Thank God, we are together again!"[143]

After spending most of three days in St. Louis, the Truetts left at 6:30 p.m. on Monday, February 3, on the Texas Special. On Tuesday, at a stop in Greenville, Texas, fifty-three miles northeast of Dallas, Truett was surprised to be greeted by his three daughters, Powhatan James, and Robert Coleman.[144] When the Truetts' train arrived in Dallas at 3:00 p.m., a vast throng greeted them at the station. The *Dallas Morning News* described the crowd as being "so dense that numerous passengers who had purchased tickets for the incoming train were unable to get down to the tracks. As [Truett] entered the station he was lifted on the shoulders of friends in order that all of the crowd might be able to see him. Ten minutes elapsed before he could make his way from the entrance to the gates, and after that he had to pass through a crowd of lines about the steps."[145]

A few hours after Truett arrived in Dallas, a standing-room-only crowd packed FBC's sanctuary, which had been decorated with green and the flags of the Allies, to hear him speak about his experience in Europe.[146] On Thursday evening, February 6, more than 1,000 people attended a banquet held in Truett's honor at the Scottish Rite Cathedral in Dallas. Mayor Joe E. Lawther, the master of ceremonies, called Truett "Dallas' choicest citizen, in whom we recognize not only a man of state and national, but international fame."[147] According to Peter W. Agnew, the diversity of people, denominations, and faiths represented at the banquet

> all say something about the bond that existed between Dallas and the one who was, to all appearances, the city's very own holy man. From the point of view of many citizens, Truett's tour of Europe was a lens through which they could direct and focus their desire to participate directly in the Allied cause. From Truett's perspective the trip was an opportunity to exercise a ministerial office for the entire community. At this moment George W. Truett was *de facto* pastor to Dallas—or, more precisely, to Dallas's white middle class which dominated the city in most respects, including laying claim to the prerogative of defining and describing the life of the community as a whole. Dallas citizens' behavior toward Truett indicated that he embodied and exemplified their highest and best attainments and aspirations.[148]

With his duties overseas concluded, Truett settled back into his routine as FBC's pastor on Sunday, February 9.[149] Nearly five months later, on Sunday, June 29, the day after the signing of the Treaty of Versailles in Paris on June 28, 1919, exactly five years after the assassination of Archduke Franz Ferdinand, Truett preached a sermon titled "Blessed Are the Peacemakers." In grandiose fashion, he called the signing of the treaty "the greatest event to transpire since Christ rose from the tomb after He had been crucified on Calvary." With the war ended, the world had to focus its energy on waging peace. Jesus spoke his blessing upon peacemakers during a time when world leaders "won their trophies through the sacrifice of human blood on battlefields" and trumpeted their motto, "Blessed be the war makers."[150]

Truett characterized Jesus' teachings as being radical for his day, yet they "have been ding-donged into the ears of men till they forget how radical and fundamental they are. We are to remember that under these gentle sayings of Jesus are the volcanic fires that will turn the world upside down. His teachings have revolutionized the thinking of the whole world."[151] Jesus taught, for example, that God was the Father of all humanity, not merely some "tribal god, a national deity, not a German god. Woe betide Germany when she thought she had a corner on deity." Jesus also taught "the brotherhood of man." Everyone who needs you is your neighbor, Truett proclaimed. One's neighbor might be next door, or "[h]e might be some cannibal on the islands of the sea, making his breakfast on the flesh of a missionary. Wherever he is, or whoever he is, he is your neighbor and you are to get yourself to him."[152] If our neighbors are in trouble, we must flee to help them. Such a teaching is radical, Truett contended, because it means that a "little nation, going down from Jerusalem to Jericho," will no longer "be fallen upon by a Germany or an Austria, and beaten unto death. The other nations will spring to its relief. That is what this peace treaty, so recently signed, means."[153]

Also in the sermon Truett repeated his conviction that America had entered the war with noble motives and had done so only after Germany continued to sink ships carrying civilians and wounded and sick soldiers.

"We fought for a peace based on righteousness," he declared, yet if we really want peace, we must "agitate" for it. Speaking from personal experience, Truett described for his congregation the consequences of not pursuing such agitation:

> War is gruesome. War is terrible. It is awful! Oh, the irony about the glory of war! It is all lost when one gets close to the battle lines. Beautiful boys with legs torn off, with faces mangled, bleeding and dying! I was on the battlefield and saw them lying dead. I saw one German boy, a youth whose face had never been touched by a razor. A deep, terrible gash had laid bare his heart, and over it was placed his hand. Oh, there is a sorrowing mother somewhere! War is hideous and horrible! War cannot be justified except as a nation springs to the defense of righteousness. We must fortify the forces that make for peace. In all our gatherings we are to agitate for peace; we are to strive for the things that bring men together.[154]

Truett concluded the sermon by proclaiming that Christ was the only hope for the world, for without him, the world was doomed.

Earlier, Truett had turned down an invitation to Paris to confer with President Wilson, Prime Minister George, and the French prime minister, Georges Clemenceau, while the Treaty of Versailles was being drafted. Had he gone, Truett might not have presented such a glowing picture of the signing of the treaty, for he could have observed the deep-seated hatred the warring countries had for one another. Herbert Hoover was in Paris at the war's end and was present during the peace negotiations. Several years after the war, he recorded his observations concerning his time in Paris: "Destructive forces sat at the Peace Table. The life and future of 26 jealous European races were on that table. The genes of a thousand years of inbred hate and fear were in the blood of every delegation. Revenge for past wrongs rose every hour of the day.... These emotions of hate, revenge, desire for reparations, and a righteous sense of wrong were in fever heat."[155] After Wilson had arrived in Paris in December 1919, he asked Hoover his opinion of the situation. Hoover informed the president that the European nations were desperate, and he described individuals as being consumed with "greed, robbery, power, sadistic hate and revenge. But as applied to nations, to crowds, groups or governmental officials I could think of no equivalent expressions. Fevered nationalism, imperialism, militarism, reaction, determination to decimate or dominate hardly expressed it."[156]

Although harsh on all the defeated countries, the Treaty of Versailles proved to be brutally tough on Germany. Forced to admit that it bore sole responsibility for the war, Germany also lost nearly 13.5 percent of its territory and all of its overseas lands. Its army was limited to 100,000 soldiers, and it was forbidden to have tanks, heavy artillery, and airplanes. Moreover, Germany had to pay reparations to Allied countries for all civilian damage suffered during the war.[157] Thus, Wilson's vision of a "peace without victory" proved to be just that—a vision, not reality.

Most Texans probably did not worry too much about the excessively punitive aspects of the Versailles Treaty because they were ecstatic that the war was over. Moreover, many Texans on June 28, 1919, the day on which the treaty was signed, had their sights on Austin, Texas, not on Paris, France, for on that day the Texas Senate, following the lead of the Texas House four days earlier, voted for the adoption of the Nineteenth Amendment, making Texas the ninth state to ratify the amendment. This amendment, which, on June 4, Congress had sent to the states for ratification, prohibited denying "citizens of the United States" of their right to vote because of their gender.[158] The sisters, as Truett had hoped at the BGCT meeting in November 1917, had finally been given the right to express their convictions, along with their brothers, in the voting booths.

*The Seventy-Five Million Campaign*

On February 9, 1919, his first Sunday back in Dallas, Truett made his final entry in the diary he kept on his great journey: "Now, with my whole heart I must give myself to the care of this dear Church and its many related interests."[159] Of the many interests in which Truett was involved after returning from Europe, perhaps nothing captivated his attention and energy as did the Seventy-Five Million Campaign.

In May 1919 at the SBC meeting in Atlanta, messengers adopted the report of the "Committee on Financial Aspects of Our Denominational

Program" recommending "that in the organized work of this Convention we undertake to raise not less than $75,000,000 [$898.9 million] in five years."[160] The next month, at the planning session held at First Baptist Church, Atlanta, the campaign commissioners named Truett as chairman of the Campaign Commission, which determined how to distribute the money that would be raised during the campaign. The commissioners voted to designate a little more than 57 percent of the funds to missions and the rest to educational institutions and benevolences. Also during the meeting, the commissioners chose Lee R. (L. R.) Scarborough, president of Southwestern Baptist Theological Seminary, as the campaign director.[161]

The commissioners assigned a monetary goal, based on membership, for each SBC church, and every church member was asked to pledge an amount to be paid over five years. Southern Baptists were to make their pledges during Victory Week, the eight-day period from Sunday, November 30, through Sunday, December 7.

Truett spent part of fall 1919 promoting the campaign. In late September and early October, he spent two weeks in Georgia and North Carolina. To an audience of 5,000 in North Carolina, he predicted that Southern Baptists would pledge $100 million ($1.2 billion). He proclaimed that

> Baptists have come to the greatest day they have ever seen since Christ was baptized by John the Baptist. I would rather be living for the next twenty-five years and be able to think, to speak and act than to have lived in any 250 years of the world's history. The day of all days for us has come. The need of the world is calling. Look at the world now, with strikes and dissentions, with discord and riots. Can any physician cope with its condition now? There is one—Jesus Christ—and the world is dying for the need of him.[162]

After returning briefly to Dallas from Georgia and North Carolina, Truett left again on October 13 to speak in the Tennessee cities of Memphis, Nashville, and Johnson City. Then, from October 28 through November 15, he spoke in twenty-four Texas cities and towns.[163]

In November, Truett sent a letter to Texas pastors, emphasizing their crucial role in the success of the campaign. He informed the pastors that they "now face the most responsible hour and task in all our lives, and this campaign will be largely WON or LOST by the Preachers!... Oh, our Texas preachers dare not, must not fail, in the epochal hour!" Truett was confident that they would not fail to support their "dear and noble Baptist denomination, whose message and mission are so worthful for the world; for the sake of humanity today, and for all the generations to follow this; above all, for the sake of Him, Whose we are and Whom we live to serve."[164]

The initial phase of the campaign proved to be an overwhelming success. By the end of November 30, the first day of Victory Week, Southern Baptists had pledged over $54 million ($647 million). The forty Baptist churches in Dallas County had a quota of $750,000 ($9 million), but had pledged $1,033,148 ($12 million). Truett reported that FBC had pledged $578,870 ($6.9 million), far exceeding its $300,000 quota.[165]

By the end of Victory Week, December 7, Southern Baptists had pledged more than $76 million ($911 million). Inclement weather during Victory Week caused Scarborough to continue the pledge period for another two weeks. When all the pledges had been tallied in December 1919, Southern Baptists had pledged more than $92 million ($1.1 billion). Texas Baptists, who had set $15 million for their quota and an extra $1 million for other Texas causes, pledged $16.5 million ($198 million).[166] In Fort Worth, even J. Frank Norris had willingly accepted his church's $100,000 ($1.2 million) quota.[167]

The Seventy-Five Million Campaign energized Southern Baptists. The spirit of cooperation found among them thrilled Scarborough, who noted the unity among individuals, editors, pastors, churches, and associations as they all worked together for a common good.[168] Such cooperation undoubtedly thrilled Truett also. While in London during the war, he had observed the necessity of cooperation. "Everybody is expected to cooperate with everybody else, to further our task in the Great War," he wrote to Josephine. "This cooperation is both wise and imperative. One can acutely realize it here so near the actual conflict itself."[169] Such an observation confirmed what he had been advocating for several years, for he believed that the cause of Christ was best served when churches worked together. "The very spirit of Christ," Truett had written in a 1902 committee report for the BGCT, "is cooperation." All of the apostolic churches, for example, had "cooperated in the prosecution of work common to them all." Likewise, modern churches must "cooperate with other like bodies for the furtherance of the interests common to all. Church independence and church isolation are two widely different things, and we need to know it right well."[170]

The success of the Seventy-Five Million Campaign lay in churches working together and fulfilling their pledges made during Victory Week. Along with cooperation, "loyalty to the denomination" became important.[171] At the end of 1919, with thousands of Southern Baptists and their churches cooperating in the campaign, disloyalty was not an issue yet.

The years from 1917 to 1919 proved to be prosperous ones for FBC, despite Truett's seven-month absence during the war. In 1917, total gifts for the year exceeded $100,000 for the first time, and Sunday-school enrollment surpassed 4,000. Membership also rose from 2,732 in 1917 to 3,036 in 1919. As in the previous thirteen years, the church contributed more to outside causes than to its own ministries.[172]

In the minds of many Americans, 1919 became the year in which two wars officially ended: the ratification of the Eighteenth Amendment ended the war to eliminate the scourge of the sale and manufacture of alcohol in the United States, and the Treaty of Versailles ended the war to make the world safe for democracy, to end all wars, and to rid the world of military despots. History, unfortunately, would prove that the cessation of hostilities in both wars was merely a time for the vanquished to prepare for the next wars. Commenting on the end of World War I, S. L. A. Marshall observed, "Almost ten million men and women had been killed in the fighting. More than six million had been crippled or invalided for life. There had been a victory of sorts, but what the victors celebrated chiefly was that mass death, after four years, had taken a holiday. The illusion was that all of humanity would profit by the great lesson."[173] Prohibition would also prove to be illusory.

Truett's ministry to the troops overseas obviously blessed the soldiers who heard him preach, the soldiers who sought his counsel, and the hundreds of parents of soldiers to whom he wrote letters. Although he never got close to actual fighting, he did have to face unseen dangers such as the flu and submarine attacks. Dodging the former and barely escaping the latter, he returned unscathed from Europe to continue his ministry in Dallas.

While in Europe, Truett learned many things about himself, others, and war. He also came home determined to reflect on the issue of patriotism. In the Memoranda section of his diary, he noted the following reminder: "Probe the *motives* of our patriotism. Have not the bastard type which says 'My country r[igh]t or wrong.' Be forever assured of the righteousness of our cause."[174] These are noble sentiments, although he hopefully knew that people often deluded themselves as to the righteousness of their causes as they embarked on causes that were essentially unrighteous.

Although the wars with the liquor industry and with European despots had ended victoriously, Southern Baptists continued in the neverending battle to save souls. With such a glorious start to the Seventy-Five Million Campaign, they believed that the 1920s would undoubtedly be one of cooperation as they all worked together to fight Satan and sin. At least that is what they thought.

# Chapter 5

# Striving Together with Sinking Hearts, 1920–1929

T he 1920s have been called the "Roaring Twenties." Having been "disillusioned by a war that failed to save humanity from itself," Americans, according to Joseph R. Conlin,

> set out to have a little fun, and ended up having a lot. Images of the Roaring Twenties readily flood the mind: college boys and flapper girls defying traditional morality; jazz music; Babe Ruth's Yankees and John McGraw's Giants; Jack Dempsey and Gene Tunney; Bobby Jones making golf a popular sport, and Big Bill Tilden doing the same for tennis. Radio made its debut. Movies became a fixture of life in cities and towns. The automobile, the modern world's amulet of personal freedom, was everywhere.[1]

Fun in the 1920s for many Texas and Southern Baptists meant evangelizing the world and raising the money that would help them fulfill that task. The decade for Southern Baptists began on a euphoric note. During the Seventy-Five Million Campaign's Victory Week, November 30–December 7, 1919, Southern Baptists had pledged to contribute $92 million ($1.1 billion)[2] during the first half of 1920s, which included the $16.5 million ($198 million) pledged by Texas Baptists. Moreover, nationwide prohibition became effective on January 16, 1920, and many Southern Baptists on August 18 welcomed the ratification of the Nineteenth Amendment, giving women the right to vote. Thus, as the new decade dawned, Southern Baptists believed that they were entering a phase of unparalleled growth and success.

Unfortunately, poor economic conditions and dissension quickly quenched the euphoria. As Leon McBeth observed, World War I had ended without making the world any safer for democracy or anything else, and the overseas hunger for American agricultural exports dried up. The end of hostilities reopened the stream of cheap European labor into this country, and wages plummeted. Cotton declined from forty cents a pound, and a combination of drouths and boll weevils further reduced Southern agriculture. Long before the stock market crash of 1929, which marked the onset of the industrial depression, the agrarian South had its own depression.[3]

Blaming one person for the dissension Southern and Texas Baptists experienced would be unfair. Nevertheless, one man did his best to sink the Seventy-Five Million Campaign and to destroy the reputations and careers of people who did not believe the Bible the way he believed it. At the 1926 Southern Baptist Convention (SBC) meeting, George W. Truett presented a paper on Christian education, part of which dealt with that man and his supporters, yet without ever mentioning the man's name:

> That word "co-operation" is a most challenging word for our Baptist people. And, happily, Southern Baptists are increasingly glorifying Paul's expression about "striving together." Their poise and self-restraint and patient continuance in well-doing, in the face, sometimes, of self-appointed, noisy, self-advertised, and sometimes reckless agitators is a chapter clothed with the most significant meaning. Southern Baptists have all along known how to take the measure of men who are manifestly obsessed with their own personal interests rather than with the honor and the furtherance of the great, common, co-operative cause committed to Christ's people. At no time have half-baked and reckless disturbers succeeded in misleading many of our people and diverting them from the common and glorious work fostered by our churches. Nor will they succeed.[4]

Revered Baptist leaders of the past and respected leaders of the present, Truett continued, all of whom were and are "mighty protagonists of co-operation,...have again and again been derided by men from whom we might well expect better behavior.... Such great leaders have had to hear the epithets of 'Pope' and 'Hierarchy' and 'The Machine' again and again. Who can think of it, except with a sinking of heart?"[5]

The main polemicist deriding those "mighty protagonists of co-operation" was J. Frank Norris. During the 1920s, he spent much of his energy, skill, and gifts, of which he had an abundance, attempting to divert the focus and contributions of Southern Baptists to his own causes and to ensure that Baptist university professors were doctrinally pure. Rather than having his heart sink, Norris relished his participation in the religious controversies that characterized the 1920s in Texas Baptist life and in the SBC. As he proclaimed in an undated letter to Truett, L. R. Scarborough, and J. M. Dawson, pastor of First Baptist, Waco, and publicity director for the Seventy-Five Million Campaign in Texas, "the last thing in the world you want now is agitation and that is the first thing I want."[6]

Norris had become a leader in the fundamentalist movement, joining the World's Christian Fundamentalist Association (1919) and the Baptist Bible Union of America (1923). Curtis Lee Laws, editor of the Baptist newspaper *Watchman-Examiner*, perhaps coined the term "fundamentalist" when, in 1920, he wrote that that word best described "those who still cling to the great fundamentals and who mean to do battle royal for the fundamentals."[7]

Long before Laws coined the term "fundamentalist," however, many Baptists had been defending what they believed to be the fundamental truths of Christianity. In 1910, A. C. Dixon, a Baptist pastor in Chicago, joined with two California oil millionaires, Milton and Lyman Stewart, to produce a series of booklets called *The Fundamentals*. Dixon edited the first six booklets, while the Stewarts financed the project. Between 1910 and 1915, twelve booklets were published, and by 1915, three million copies had been distributed, without charge, to pastors, missionaries, seminary professors, seminary students, college professors, Sunday-school superintendents, and religious editors. The authors of many essays contained in *The Fundamentals* defended such doctrines as biblical inerrancy, the virgin birth of Jesus, his substitutionary atonement, his bodily resurrection, his miracles, and his imminent and personal return to establish the Kingdom of God on earth.[8] Most Southern Baptists in the

1920s accepted and defended such doctrines; they did not, however, accept or defend Norris or fundamentalism.

Defining fundamentalism is difficult. George M. Marsden defined the movement broadly, describing it as "a loose, diverse, and changing federation of co-belligerents united by their fierce opposition to modernist attempts to bring Christianity into line with modern thought."[9] More specifically, James J. Thompson, Jr., defined Southern Baptist fundamentalism as being characterized by five characteristics: "First, J. Frank Norris" was "the guiding genius intellect of Southern Baptist fundamentalism. Second, premillennialism furnished the most important theological doctrine of the movement.... An interdenominational impulse, derived from the premillennial conception of the church, formed a third aspect.... Fourth, 'ruralism' played a role in shaping the movement. Finally, fundamentalists advocated local autonomy, spontaneity, and democracy," as opposed to denominationalism.[10]

As Norris and his fundamentalist friends sought to sink the Seventy-Five Million Campaign, they also waged a battle to cleanse denominational schools associated with the SBC and with the Baptist General Convention (BGCT) of Darwinian evolutionists. In July 1925, the nation's attention was drawn to Dayton, Tennessee, where John Scopes, a high school biology teacher, was tried for violating a Tennessee law prohibiting the teaching of evolution in public schools. The noted agnostic Clarence Darrow defended Scopes, while the famed fundamentalist William Jennings Bryan testified as a Bible expert in defense of the law. After an eight-day trial, Scopes was found guilty and ordered to pay a fine.[11] Even before the Scopes Trial, however, Texas and Southern Baptists had been debating the theory of evolution, most making sure that Baptist universities and seminary professors were not Darwinian evolutionists and some, mostly fundamentalists, even hunting for theistic evolutionists.

Money and monkeys dominated the life of Texas and Southern Baptists in the 1920s. For many of them, however, they had too little of the former and too much of the latter.

*Money and Embarrassment*

The enthusiastic participation of Southern Baptists in the initial phase of the Seventy-Five Million Campaign during Victory Week 1919 obviously pleased Southern Baptist leaders. As McBeth humorously observed, "Rejoicing among Baptists knew no bounds; if they had not been Baptists, no doubt there would have been dancing in the streets."[12] In January 1920, Truett announced that his church, First Baptist (FBC), Dallas, had increased its pledge to $606,743 ($6.3 million), more than doubling its quota set by campaign leaders.[13] In May 1920, when Southern Baptists gathered in Washington, D.C., for their annual meeting, L. R. Scarborough, the campaign director, announced that the final tally for all churches stood at $92,630,923 ($958 million), well above the $75 million goal, and that $12,237,827 ($126.6 million) in cash had already been given.[14] Scarborough stressed, however, that "denominational pledges are good: but the payment of these pledges in the coin of the realm is the best show of victory. We will bring on ourselves a South-wide denominational embarrassment if we do not collect our pledges."[15]

The "South-wide denominational embarrassment" so feared by Scarborough began to take shape when the United States experienced a depression in 1920–1921, which was caused by several factors. European countries, which were recovering from the war, began producing more goods. Consequently, the demand for American products declined.[16] Also, agricultural prices dropped drastically in 1920. Total farm income, so vital in the South, had reached ten billion dollars ($119.9 billion) in 1919, but plummeted to less than four billion ($46.3 billion) in 1921.[17] Moreover, the national income, which soared to $75 billion ($776 billion) in 1920, fell to $59 billion ($683 billion) the following year.[18] Although by July 1921 the economy had begun to recover, campaign leaders realized that Southern Baptists were waging an uphill battle to meet their $75 million goal by 1924.

According to Gwin Morris, "It should have been obvious to the leaders that some churches and individuals had made pledges far beyond their ability to pay. Further, it seems that the campaign organizers did not adequately take into account external conditions which might hamper collection of pledges."[19] SBC leaders also should have known that the denomination's assigning quotas for churches, rather than letting the churches themselves determine how much they wanted to pledge, violated the Baptist principle of the autonomy of the local church and that such a violation would cause resentment among some pastors and churches. That numerous SBC churches and their pastors willingly accepted their quotas without a protest, however, was their own fault.

The economic depression was not the only factor that threatened the success of the Seventy-Five Million Campaign. Norris devoted much of his energy to ensure that the campaign failed. Skillfully utilizing his pulpit, radio station, and church newspaper, the *Searchlight*, he portrayed the campaign as a violation of Baptist principles and attacked the integrity of Texas Baptist leaders, whom he characterized as "denominational despots," "ecclesiastical dictators," "the machine," and "the Sanhedrin" (the supreme ruling council of the Jews during Jesus' life).

Although initially supporting the campaign, Norris soon regretted accepting his church's $100,000 ($1.2 million) quota. The poor economic conditions in the South, coupled with an expensive building program at his church, First Baptist of Fort Worth, meant that the church would never be able to fulfill its pledge, for every dollar sent to the campaign meant less for Norris to spend on his own church. To justify his change of heart, he soon began to denounce the assignment of quotas as violating the autonomy of the local church. In a sermon on January 13, 1935, during the time when he was pastoring a church in Detroit, Michigan, while also pastoring his Fort Worth congregation, he recounted for his Detroit congregation how, alone in his office, he had stood firm when confronted by a group of Baptist leaders insisting that he succumb to their will. Norris described the epic day when, at the beginning of the Seventy-Five Million campaign,

> a group of denominational despots called on me in my office, and demanded I
> take their apportionments of $100,000. I quietly informed them I did not

believe in that method, and my conviction was then, and is now, that every church has the right and the sole right of naming how, what, when, and the method of its liberality, and that no set of men on the face of the earth has a right to even suggest what the local church will do, much less dictate to it. But this group of political, ecclesiastical dictators, headed by Dr. L. R. Scarborough,…said to me: "Now, Norris, if you don't cooperate and put on this drive, we will brand you to the ends of the earth as a non-cooperating Baptist, and you will lose out; you will not have any crowds to hear you, your church will disintegrate."[20]

Norris then told his Detroit congregation that "some days before the *ex cathedra* demand of this coterie of ecclesiastical dictators," he had received their letter stating how much each church should pledge. When they threatened him, he reached over, picked the letter up off his desk, "tore it to pieces without saying a word, and then crumpled the pieces in my right hand and cast the pieces at the feet of these dictators, and said, 'That's my answer to your papal demands.'" After a "prolonged applause" by his congregation, Norris added: "And ladies and gentlemen, I would not have any self respect if I had done otherwise."[21]

Apparently, Norris forgot to inform his Detroit congregation that he had accepted the quota, that he had written a congratulatory letter to Scarborough for leading Southern Baptists to "the most notable victory in their history,"[22] and that from 1919 to 1922, his Fort Worth congregation paid a little over $11,000 to the campaign.[23] Revealing such information, however, would have ruined a wonderfully inspiring story, and in Norris's world, a good story, particularly one in which he rose to heroic heights, always trumped the truth. Nevertheless, despite all of his accusations and his trumpeting of the autonomy of the local church, Norris "simply needed the funds to finance his" church's programs.[24] Fighting for the sacredness of the local church autonomy against "the machine" and its "ecclesiastical dictators," however, not only sounded much better than being selfish; it also produced better results.

While Norris worked to convince Southern Baptists to reject the Seventy-Five Million Campaign, Truett strove to encourage (or, in the minds of some, to bully) his fellow Baptists to fulfill their pledges. At a conference in Waco in spring 1921, he recalled that, at the beginning of the campaign, he had heard people scoff at the idea of raising such a large sum of money. Now, however, he predicted that Southern Baptists would become so disciplined in their giving and so visionary in their outlook that they would ultimately give $200 million ($2.3 billion), double what he had predicted in North Carolina in 1919. Baptists needed the campaign, Truett told the audience, because they must be challenged in order to be great, and people cannot become great "with little, pygmy programs.... Great believers are great doers. Our program is identical with the program of Jesus." Furthermore, the world needed the campaign. "All Europe is waiting for our message," he proclaimed. "This is the day of the people in Europe, and Baptists have always been the protagonists of the people. The Macedonian call comes to us, 'Come over and help us.'"[25]

When Southern Baptists met in May 1921 for their annual meeting, they learned that total gifts to the Seventy-Five Million Campaign stood at $25,086,324 ($290.6 million), almost $5 million ($57.9 million) short of the projected giving.[26] The news at the meeting in 1922 was even worse. Scarborough, in his report on the campaign, announced that $35,164,310 ($434.8 million) had been contributed to the campaign, putting Southern Baptists nearly $10 million ($123.6 million) behind schedule.[27] He put the best spin on the disappointing news, emphasizing that the last three years had

> been marked by a period of declining prices in all commodities and labor, excessive and critical world-psychology, interchanging drouths, floods, storms and destructive pests. These years have been the hardest on the pockets of the people in the recent history of this country. Added to these great hindrances, during the last year, especially, the critical mind has prevailed throughout the entire Baptist world. We have turned our eyes and our pens upon ourselves. All of our churches, organizations, institutions and leaders have been under critical review. This has, more or less, caused denominational unrest, disturbed confidence, and put the whole cause on its nerve.[28]

Scarborough's reference to the "denominational unrest" was obviously a veiled reference to Norris's attacks on people who supported and led the Seventy-Five Million Campaign, including Frank S. Groner, secretary of the BGCT, and Scarborough himself. In "The Fruits of Norrisism," a scathing attack on Norris and his beliefs written a few years after the campaign, Scarborough quoted "a deacon of a Baptist church, who is under the dominance of Norrisism…: 'The big trouble is that Drs. Brooks, Truett, Gambrell, Scarborough, Groner and others had misappropriated a considerable amount of funds of the 75 Million Campaign.'"[29] The unnamed deacon undoubtedly got his misinformation from Norris. In April 1922, for example, Norris claimed that the BGCT secretary had misappropriated over a million dollars that had been given to the campaign. When the polemical pastor asked to see the books concerning the campaign, Groner consented. At the agreed upon time, however, Norris did not show up. His explanation, according to Groner, was this: "A fight was on and I know the psychology of the human mind, and I knew when I raised the question about the books…that the fellows from the forks of the creek would line up with me."[30] Then in September 1922, Norris asserted that Scarborough had refused to let anyone see the campaign's financial books and that he had falsified an auditor's report.[31] The effect of such allegations on the campaign is impossible to determine, yet undoubtedly Norris's actions and accusations did not help.

Like other Southern Baptists, Texas Baptists struggled to meet their quotas. In an attempt to collect their pledges, the BGCT instituted a Catch-Up Campaign for three months in fall 1922. The campaign included an All-State Motor Tour that reached almost 2,000 churches, and over the next two years netted $4 million.[32]

To assist the Catch-Up Campaign, Truett wrote an article in October 1922 titled "Some Frank Words with Texas Baptists," aptly titled since it was aimed at rebutting Norris's attacks on Texas Baptist leaders and the Seventy-Five Million Campaign. Although he never mentioned Norris's name, no one could have missed the intent of his article. "[S]hocking as is the very thought," Truett wrote, "it must be apparent to every observant and well informed Baptist in Texas that sinister and strenuous efforts are now being made to divert the attention of our Baptist people from the main things of the [Seventy-Five Million ] Campaign, and, if possible, to obstruct and defeat the success of the Campaign."[33]

"[T]he spectacle of a palpable, aggressive effort to misrepresent and obstruct the work of Christ's cause is a spectacle shocking and ghastly," Truett continued, but history was repeating itself. Recalling Samuel A. Hayden's attacks on the work of the BGCT and the integrity of the convention's leaders twenty-five years earlier, Truett predicted that the current smear campaign would end the way Hayden's machinations ended—"in the frightful shame and hurt of reactionary obstructionists on the one hand, and on the other hand, in the co-operation of the Baptist forces of Texas."[34] Anyone can "criticize,…confuse,…waste,…tear down,…[and] destroy," he maintained. "Anybody can in a few moments bedaub a great painting or wreck a fast-flying train or burn down a bridge or a house, but one would hardly applaud such abuses of personal liberty." The very thought of people abusing their liberty in the cause of Christ "stings right-thinking people to the heart and the shame of it cries to heaven." Yet would such abuse deter Texas Baptists from fulfilling their pledges to the Seventy-Five Million Campaign? "No, no," Truett wrote confidently, "the Baptists of Texas will not allow their zeal for the Savior's cause to be chilled and their efforts for such cause to be sidetracked, no matter how grievously the principles of liberty and co-operation may be misrepresented and abused."[35]

The efforts of Truett and others to promote the Seventy-Five Million Campaign continued to have minimal effect. At the SBC meeting in May 1923, Scarborough announced that a little more than $44 million ($534.4 million) had been raised for the campaign.[36] Soon after the meeting, Truett, along with his wife, Josephine, and Robert H. Coleman and his wife, traveled to Stockholm, Sweden, to attend the third congress of the Baptist World Alliance (BWA). Coleman led the music during the meeting, and Truett preached a sermon titled "An Adequate Gospel for a

Lost World."[37] During the three-month trip, Truett visited nearly every European country, "the Holy Land," and Egypt.[38]

Upon returning to Texas, Truett found that the Seventy-Five Million Campaign continued to flounder. He wrote a letter to Texas Baptist pastors, encouraging them to fulfill their churches' pledges. Some pastors, however, interpreted the letter as an attempt to shame or bully them into paying their pledges. J. Matthew Harder, a pastor in Ralls, Texas, responded to his friend's letter by noting that his congregation had contributed $1,000 ($12,147) a year to the campaign, "[b]ut that is not any thing *now*."[39] Harder chided Truett and other Texas Baptist leaders for having "[t]oo much 'ego' & *envy*.... There are some *home rats* eating up the *sacks*. You don't see them Geo[rge]. If ever Baptist[s] needed a safe leader we need him now. Some of you leaders hurt the cause by being angry with those who don't agree to every thing. We are loosing [*sic*] some of our great laymen['s] support."[40]

If Truett's letter had any positive effect, it was minimal, for when Scarborough presented his report on the Seventy-Five Million Campaign at the May 1924 SBC meeting, he reported the dismal but much-expected news: "The balance necessary to complete the 75 Million objective is $21,167,147.21 [$256.7 million]. We have from now until December 1924 to finish this task. This is the task of titans."[41] Southern Baptists had their titans, but what they really needed were miracle workers, of whom they had none.

Despite the daunting, titanic task before Southern Baptists, Truett remained unbelievably optimistic about their reaching the $75 million goal. In an October article in the *Baptist Standard*, he wrote that he had attended regional conferences and was heartened by the desire of Texas Baptists to work for their denomination, "whatever may be the lurid and reckless agitations thrust upon such work from time to time. Such agitations periodically appear," Truett reminded his readers,

> and Texas Baptists are not deceived by them, nor are they going to be deceived by them. It is glorious to see how a great army of God's people, quiet and conservative, and yet nobly purposeful and aggressive, can go right on with one

mind, one heart, one spirit, in carrying forward our Great Master's cause. Less and less will sensation-mongers and self-appointed regulators get any sympathetic hearing at the hands of Texas Baptists.... Neither in Texas nor beyond will any large group of our Baptist people have any fellowship for heckling and reckless agitations, or for the injection of improper personalities into their work.[42]

Completion Week for the campaign was scheduled for November 2–9. Truett encouraged Texas Baptists to make that week "the most glorious week of our lives" by fulfilling their pledges made five years earlier.[43]

As the Seventy-Five Million Campaign was drawing to a close, the BGCT took action against Norris and his church at its meeting in November 1924, by refusing to seat messengers from First Baptist, Fort Worth. The Tarrant County Baptist Association had taken such an action two years earlier in September 1922.[44] At the Friday session of the BGCT meeting, the first order of business concerned whether to seat those messengers. The convention's special Committee on the Challenge and Credentials presented its report recommending that the convention not seat the messengers. The committee noted that the church had "for years...encouraged, financed, and otherwise supported propaganda, state and Southwide, which has cruelly and unjustly criticized, unmercifully misrepresented and persistently opposed the program, method of work, institutions, causes and elected and trusted leaders, fostered and promoted by this and the Southern Baptist Convention."[45] The committee also noted that First Baptist, Fort Worth, "represents, favors, and supports a movement and a leadership which in spirit and method misrepresents, discounts and brings into shame the great testimony of our truth-loving, Christ-honoring, soul-winning Baptist people throughout the world." Moreover, the church "represents, favors and supports a movement and a leadership which continuously in their own city, county, state and through the Southern [Baptist] Convention sows the seed of discord and division." Consequently, the committee could not "for the sake of denominational fellowship, unity, and the very life of Baptist causes, favor such a divisive and destructive movement, therefore, we must respectfully challenge the right of said messengers to seats in this convention."[46]

Upon the committee's recommendation, the messengers from Norris's church were denied seats at the meeting. Truett did not sign the resolution ousting the church from the BGCT, but according to McBeth, he undoubtedly played a major role in the crafting of the resolution, preferring to hover "serenely above the fray."[47]

In 1925, when Southern Baptists met for their annual meeting, Scarborough announced the expected, embarrassing news: the "27,000 supposedly co-operating churches"[48] had contributed only $58,591,713.69 ($693 million) to the Seventy-Five Million Campaign. Despite not reaching "its total financial goal," however, the campaign "came more nearly doing so than almost any other forward movement conducted by any of the large denominations during the period immediately following the war."[49] Scarborough also emphasized that more than a thousand retired preachers and their dependents had been helped; twelve new hospitals and two new orphanages had been built; all orphanages had become better equipped; enrollment in Baptists schools had increased; the number of baptisms and church organizations had risen; and the SBC had expanded its presence in foreign countries from nine to seventeen.[50] Moreover, as McBeth observed, "The campaign also brought a new spirit of unity, convincing Baptists they could accomplish big things. Baptists became more stewardship conscious, and many churches adopted the budget system to regulate church finances."[51]

Texas Baptists also failed to reach their $16 million goal, ultimately contributing only $8.7 million ($103 million) to the Seventy-Five Million Campaign.[52] Truett's church never came close to raising the $6 million it had pledged, but it was the only SBC church to meet its original goal.[53] If the churches comprising the BGCT were embarrassed by their failure to reach their campaign goal, they could at least take some comfort from the fact that their convention had officially severed its relationship with Norris and his followers. Any campaign that could do that can never be deemed a failure.

*Baptists and Religious Liberty*

When Southern Baptists had assembled in Washington, D.C., in May 1920, more than 14,000 people traveled to the city to participate in religious meetings. A little more than 8,000 Baptists registered as messengers for their meeting, and approximately 6,000 Catholics gathered in the capital city to celebrate the canonization of Joan of Arc, whom the Catholic Church in Spain burned at the stake in 1431.[54] Because no convention activities had been scheduled for Sunday, the Baptists of Washington, D.C., had asked Truett to present an address on religious liberty.[55] Having heard the disappointing news concerning the Seventy-Five Million Campaign, Southern Baptists were ready to hear something that would lift their spirits. Truett did not disappoint them.

At 3:00 p.m. on Sunday, May 16, perhaps as many as 15,000 people gathered at the steps of the United States Capitol. The crowd, which stretched the length of the Capitol building, included Supreme Court justices, military officials, cabinet members, congressmen, senators, and foreign ambassadors.[56] Robert Coleman led the singing of "My Country 'Tis of Thee,'" "Battle Hymn of the Republic," "Rescue the Perishing," and "My Faith Looks Up to Thee." Archibald C. Cree, executive secretary of the Georgia Baptist Convention, prayed, and then J. B. Gambrell, president of the SBC, introduced Truett.[57] With Gambrell sitting to his immediate right, and Coleman to his immediate left, Truett rose to deliver his most famous and often-quoted address, "Baptists and Religious Liberty."

Without notes or a public address system, Truett, as he often did in his major addresses, looked to the past and to the future. Remembering the past was important, he maintained, for "[w]e should be stronger and braver if we thought oftener of the epic days and deeds of our beloved and immortal dead."[58] The Hebrew people, for example, "never wearied of chanting the praises" of their great leaders, nor should Baptists ever weary of harkening back to their "Baptist fathers, who paid such a great price, through the long generations, that liberty, both religious and civil, might have free course and be glorified everywhere."[59] Baptists can proudly and justifiably remember that religious liberty "was pre eminently a Baptist contribution" to the history of the world.[60]

Baptists, according to Truett, have always "been the unwavering champions of liberty, both religious and civil." All people must be free to worship God or not to worship God according to the dictates of their conscience, for such is their "natural and fundamental and indefeasible right."[61] Truett then distinguished between religious liberty and religious toleration:

> Toleration implies that somebody falsely claims the right to tolerate. Toleration is a concession, while liberty is a right. Toleration is a matter of expediency, while liberty is a matter of principle. Toleration is a gift from man, while liberty is a gift from God. It is the consistent and insistent contention of our Baptist people, always and everywhere, that religion must be forever voluntary and uncoerced, and that it is not the prerogative of any power, whether civil or ecclesiastical, to compel men to conform to any religious creed or form of worship, or to pay taxes for the support of a religious organization to which they do not believe. God wants free worshipers and no other kind.[62]

Truett emphasized that he made such praiseworthy claims for Baptists and their support for religious liberty not because Baptists were "inherently better" than others, for they were contentedly happy "to live side by side with their neighbors of other Christian communions, and to have glorious Christian fellowship with such neighbors, and to honor such servants of God for their inspiring lives and their noble deeds."[63] Rather, Truett made such claims because the principle of religious liberty was inherent in who Baptists are. Early Baptists "did not stumble upon this principle" by accident; it molded them from the beginning of their existence and has molded Baptists everywhere into "unyeilding protagonists of religious liberty, not only for themselves, but for everybody else as well."[64]

The foundation of religious liberty, Truett argued, is "the absolute Lordship of Jesus Christ. That doctrine is for Baptists the dominant fact in all their Christian experience, the nerve center of all their Christian life, the bedrock of all their church polity, the sheet anchor of all their rejoicings. They say with Paul: 'For to this end Christ both died, and rose, and revived, that he might be Lord both of the dead and living.'"[65] Everything in Truett's address concerning religious liberty from that point on must be read with the Lordship of Christ in mind, for from that doctrine flows everything else.

If Christ is Lord of conscience, then the Bible, particularly the New Testament, must be the source to which people must look for guidance. After stressing the primacy of the Bible, Truett then contrasted Baptist beliefs with those of the Catholic Church:

> The Baptist message and the Roman Catholic message are the very antipodes of each other. The Roman Catholic message is sacerdotal, sacramentarian, and ecclesiastical. In its scheme of salvation it magnifies the church, the priest, and the sacraments. The Baptist message is non-sacerdotal, non-sacramentarian, and non-ecclesiastical. Its teaching is that the one High Priest for sinful humanity has entered into the holy place for all, that the veil is forever rent in twain, that the mercy seat is uncovered and opened to all, and that the humblest soul in all the world, if only he be penitent, may enter with all boldness and cast himself upon God. The Catholic doctrine[s] of baptismal regeneration and transubstantiation are to the Baptist mind fundamentally subversive of the spiritual realities of the gospel of Christ. Likewise, the Catholic conception of the church, thrusting all its complex and cumbrous machinery between the soul and God, prescribing beliefs, claiming to exercise the power of the keys, and to control the channels of grace—all such lording it over the consciences of men is to the Baptist mind a ghastly tyranny in the realm of the soul and tends to frustrate the grace of God, to destroy freedom of conscience, and to hinder terribly the coming of the Kingdom of God.[66]

Despite the differences between Catholics and Baptists, Truett argued that Catholics had every right to worship according to dictates of their faith. Moreover, he proclaimed that "[a] Baptist would rise at midnight to plead for absolute religious liberty for his Catholic neighbor, and for his Jewish neighbor, and for everybody else."[67]

According to Truett, the New Testament emphasizes the individual; that is, each person must give an account of his or her life to God. Every individual "must repent for himself, and believe for himself, and be baptized for himself, and answer to God for himself, both in time and in eternity."[68] Salvation is a gift of God through Jesus Christ, who is the only Mediator between individuals and God. Therefore, "Let the state and the church, let the institution, however dear, and the person, however near, stand aside, and let the individual soul make its own direct and immediate response to God. One is our pontiff, and his name is Jesus. The undelegated sovereignty of Christ makes it forever impossible for his saving grace to be manipulated by any system of human mediation whatsoever."[69]

Moreover, if individuals are responsible for what they believe, they must be free to discover the content of their belief. "The right to private judgment," Truett declared, "is the crown jewel of humanity, and for any person or institution to dare to come between the soul and God is a blasphemous impertinence and a defamation of the crown rights of the Son of God."[70] Baptists consider any attempt to force people to violate their consciences to be an abomination. Persecution only makes hypocrites, Truett contended, not Christians.[71]

Speaking frankly to his "honored...friends in the audience" who practiced infant baptism and "in the most fraternal, Christian spirit," Truett emphasized that if Christ is Lord of conscience and if individuals must give an account for themselves to God, then infant baptism was "unthinkable." Besides being unscriptural, such baptism "tends to ritualize Christianity and reduce it to lifeless forms[,]...tends...to the secularizing of the church and to the blurring and blotting out of the line of demarcation between the church and the unsaved world," and "has flooded the world, and floods it now, with untold evils."[72]

If individuals must be free to determine what they believe, the church and the state must also be free to fulfill their own functions in society. According to Truett:

That utterance of Jesus, "Render therefore unto Caesar the things which are Caesar's, and unto God the things that are God's," is one of the most revolutionary and history-making utterances that ever fell from those lips divine. That utterance, once and for all, marked the divorcement of church and state. It marked a new era for the creeds and deeds of men. It was the sunrise gun of a new day, the echoes of which are to go on and on and on until in every land, whether great or small, the doctrine shall have absolute supremacy everywhere of a free church in a free state.[73]

When we look back to the early church, Truett contended, we see the "early disciples of Jesus, without prestige and worldly power, yet aflame with the love of God and the passion of Christ, went out and shook the pagan Roman Empire from center to circumference, even in one brief generation. Christ's religion needs no prop of any kind from any worldly source, and to the degree that it is thus supported is a millstone hanged about its neck."[74] Yet in the fourth century, Emperor Constantine wedded the church to the state, thereby beginning "the most baneful misalliance that ever fettered and cursed a suffering world."[75]

In the sixteenth century, men such as Martin Luther and John Calvin left the Catholic Church and began the Reformation. Yet the stories of "these mighty men" comprise "one of the most outstanding anomalies of all history," Truett contended. Although they preached and wrote about the errors of Rome, "they retained the doctrine of infant baptism and a state church. They shrank from the logical conclusions of their own theses."[76] Moreover, like Rome, they became persecutors, with Luther unleashing "the dogs of persecution against the…Anabaptists" and Calvin burning the heretic Michael Servetus at the stake.[77]

The same distressing story of persecution was repeated in England and then in the American colonies, where Baptists fought for religious liberty for all people, not just themselves. These Baptists, Truett proclaimed, "dared to be odd, to stand alone, to refuse to conform, though it cost them suffering and even life itself. They dared to defy traditions and customs, and deliberately chose the day of non-conformity, even though in many a case it meant a cross." Eventually, however, they won the battle, and their principle of a free church in a free state was written into the Constitution of the United States, which, according to Truett "was preeminently a Baptist achievement."[78]

Truett then called the crowd's attention to Alfred Tennyson's poem "The Flower," which describes "the history of the seed of freedom."[79] After a gardener planted a seed that grew into a flower, detractors stomped through the garden, cursing him and his flower. When the flower grew tall, thieves stole the seed, sowing

> ...it far and wide.
> By every town and tower,
> Till all the people cried,
> "Splendid is the flower."
>
> Read my little fable:
> He who runs may read,
> Most can grow the flowers now,
> For all have got the seed.[80]

Baptists hope, Truett noted, that people "of every denomination and creed" will embrace "this splendid flower of religious liberty, but you will allow us to remind you that you got the seed in our Baptist garden. We are very happy for you to have it; now let us all make the best of it and the most of it."[81]

With the past described, Truett then asked his audience to consider the obligations that liberty imposes on a free people. The press must not abuse its freedom by dragging "itself through all the sewers of the social order, bringing to light the moral cancers and leprosies of our poor world and glaringly exhibiting them to the gaze even of responsive youth and childhood." Legislators must pass laws that benefit society. Individuals must take responsibility for their actions, obeying laws that help society function properly and in an orderly manner. Nations must not isolate themselves, for the world has become one "big bundle of life." Nations must no longer shirk their responsibilities to other nations by hiding behind "the murderous question of Cain, 'Am I my brother's keeper?'" Instead, the parable of the Good Samaritan is their heaven-sent law to obey.[82]

Truett maintained that one way for the United States to resist isolationist tendencies was to support the League of Nations, an organization designed to prevent war and settle disputes between countries. He believed that the "moral forces" in America, regardless of their political affiliation, would support the league, which would "put an end to the diabolism and measureless horror of war."[83] Support for the league not only would honor the sacrifices of the millions of people who had sacrificed their lives during World War I; it would also stress the obligations nations had to future generations. To emphasize these points, Truett quoted a section from "The Victorious Dead," a poem by Alfred Noyes:

Make firm, O God, the peace our dead have won,
For folly shakes the tinsel on its head,
And points us back to darkness and to hell,
Cackling, "Beware of visions," while our dead
Still cry, "It was for visions that we fell."

They never knew the secret game of power,
All that this earth can give they thrust aside,
They crowded all their youth into an hour,
And for fleeting dream of right, they died.

Oh, if we fail them in that awful trust,
How should we bear those voices from the dust?[84]

Also in his address, Truett trumpeted the necessity of an educated public, both in the church and in the state. In doing so, he stressed the necessity of Christian universities that are "fundamentally and aggressively Christian." As he had done in 1913 at the Texas Baptist Laymen's

Convention, he noted that secular education was incomplete, whereas Christian schools can incorporate spiritual training in their curriculum. Christianity was the only "inspiring influence" in the world, and without such influence the world "is doomed. Let there be no pagan ideals in our Christian schools, and no hesitation or apology for the insistence that the one hope for the individual, the one hope for society, from civilization, is in the Christian religion. If ever the drum beat of duty sounded clearly, it is calling to us now to strengthen and magnify our Christian schools."[85]

As important as Christian schools are in the church's mission in the world, Truett maintained that evangelism, "the work of winning souls from sin unto salvation, from Satan unto God," is the church's "primary task," and such a task must direct not only the church's mission but that of all Christian "schools,…religious papers,…hospitals, [and] every organization and agency of the churches."[86]

Baptists, however, must understand that the gospel is not an American possession, for it belongs to the whole world. Therefore, according to Truett, Baptists—indeed all Christendom—must "seek to bring all humanity, both near and far, to the faith and service of Him who came to be the propitiation for our sins, and not for ours only, but also for the sins of the whole world."[87] Fulfilling such a calling will be costly, compelling Truett to ask, "Are we willing to pay the price that must be paid to secure for humanity the blessings it needs to have?"[88] Christians claim that they have encountered God in Christ, that they have been born again, that they are friends of Christ's, and that they would prove such claims by doing the will of God. Proving such claims meant, according to Truett, that Christians must live a life of holiness (1 Pet. 2:9) and that they must remember that many of the first Christians paid with their lives to receive spiritual power (Rev. 12:11).[89] To carry forward the work of the early church and the work of the early Baptists, he maintained, "selfish ease must be utterly renounced for Christ and his cause and our every gift and grace and power utterly dominated by the dynamic of his Cross. Standing here today in the shadow of our country's Capitol, compassed about as we are with so great a cloud of witnesses, let us today renew our pledge to God, and to one another, that we will give our best to church and to state, to God and to humanity, by his grace and power, until we fall on the last sleep."[90] If we do that, Truett contended, we can journey forward, singing the words of John Greenleaf Whittier:

> Our fathers to their graves have gone,
> Their strife is passed, their triumphs won;
> But greater tasks await the race
> Which comes to take their honored place,
> A moral warfare with the crime
> And folly of an evil time.
>
> So let it be, in God's own sight,
> We gird us for the coming flight;
> And strong in Him whose cause is ours,
> In conflict with unholy powers,
> We grasp the weapons He has given,
> The light and truth and love of Heaven.[91]

For the most part, Truett received praise for his Washington address. "Since Paul spoke before Nero," Gambrell wrote, "no Baptist speaker ever pleaded the cause of truth in surroundings so dignified, impressive and inspiring."[92] E. C. Routh, editor of the *Baptist Standard*, declared that the address was perhaps "the greatest hour in the history of the Southern Baptist Convention."[93] The *Tennessean* reported that "the zeal with which" Truett "maintained his position on the League of Nations and the general approval accorded by his vast audience, made up mostly of church people, constitute a fair index of the thought and sentiment of church people of the country as to the necessity for a league of nations."[94]

Not all Baptists, however, appreciated Truett's comments on the League of Nations. E. J. Forrester, a Georgia pastor, contended that Truett should not have mentioned the league, for the league "belongs to the realm of governmental policy, and cannot be said in any easily perceivable way, to involve a moral question." Had Truett not been "an appointee of a Convention," he could have said whatever he wanted, but as an appointee, he was bound to refrain from addressing a political subject on which some members of the audience disagreed with him.[95]

According to Forrester, many good people longed for the end of war, but they did not "believe that the League is the best means to that holy end." Moreover, it was illogical and unjust for Truett to claim that those who opposed the league were selfish and on the road to destruction, but logic has never been a virtue of great orators. "As it was," the Georgia pastor continued, "the shrewd Romanists who infect the Capitol must have chuckled when they heard our greatest Baptist preacher, while discussing Baptist Principles and Religious Liberty, as had those who differed from him on the League of nations, such intolerant speech as that which consigned them to a welter of destructive selfishness. It may be observed that there is intolerance of Sword, intolerance of stake, intolerance of prison, and intolerance of—Eloquence!"[96]

The anti-Catholic statements Truett made during his address must be read not only in the context of his understanding of the Lordship of Christ, but also in the context of the religious milieu of his day. At that time, Catholics adhered to the "Syllabus of Errors." This document contained eighty propositions issued by Pope Pius IX in 1864 that all Catholics had to reject, including such concepts as religious liberty (props. 15, 78, 79); the belief that salvation could be found outside of the Catholic Church (props. 17, 18); the rejection of the use of coercion in religious matters (props. 24); free public education (props. 47, 48); the separation of church and state (props. 55, 77); and free speech (prop. 79).[97] In Truett's mind, and in the minds of most Baptists, any organization that condemned such concepts deserved to be condemned.[98] Thus, the Catholic Church's system did not impress him, although as he noted in a 1905 statement to the *Dallas Morning News*, "the age-long conflict between the Baptist and Romanist lines of religious thought…is not personal. It is wholly a conflict of ideas and of doctrines. I am personally glad to be on terms of cordial friendship with many

Catholics,…among" whom was James M. Hayes, rector of Cathedral Sacred Heart of Jesus, Dallas, Texas.[99]

Truett's assertion that "Christ's religion needs no prop of any kind" must also be read in light of his 1909 plea on behalf of the Dallas Pastors' Association, in which he presented the organization's case for the city government to enforce Dallas's Sunday laws. Sunday laws are props, and props by any other name are still props. Moreover, his piece of homiletical hyperbole that Baptists "would rise at midnight to plead for absolute religious liberty" for their neighbors, although a noble sentiment, was an overstatement. While many Baptists would have done what Truett said, and he would have led the charge, others would have risen at midnight to beg for Caesar's coin and support.

Also in the address, Truett overstated his claim that Baptists had always been champions of civil liberties. The SBC, for example, had been formed in 1845 partly in support of slavery, and while many Baptists opposed slavery, others, particularly in the South, vigorously defended it.[100]

### Monkeys and Fundamentalists

During his "Baptists and Religious Liberty" address, Truett warned against allowing "pagan ideals" to infest Christian schools. One "pagan ideal" that drew the wrath of many Christians in the 1920s concerned Darwinian evolution, the belief that humans evolved from earlier life forms. Even Christians who believed in theistic evolution, the belief that God used evolution to create life on earth, often could not escape the charge of being Darwinian evolutionists.[101] Archibald T. (A. T.) Robertson, for example, would have fallen into this category. A world-renowned Greek scholar and professor of New Testament at the Southern Baptist Theological Seminary, Robertson stated one day during a lecture that he did not have a problem with theistic evolution. "I can stand it," the professor confessed, "if the monkeys can."[102] Thus, while Southern Baptists struggled to raise money for the Seventy-Five Million Campaign early in the decade, they also had to deal with monkeys, some in textbooks, others in Baptist pulpits.

Norris proved himself to be a fierce opponent of any monkey business in Baptist schools. In his sermons to rally his congregation against the Darwinian scourge, he shouted, wept, and paraded apes and monkeys in front of his pulpit so that his congregation could see Charles Darwin's relatives.[103] One Sunday, Norris took a monkey dressed in a red suit into the pulpit with him. Whenever Norris made a point, he turned to the monkey and asked, "Isn't that right?"[104] When W. T. Conner, a theology professor at Southwestern Baptist Theological Seminary, heard about this fiasco, he remarked that one monkey in a Baptist pulpit was sufficient.[105]

In October 1921, Norris charged Grove S. Dow, a sociology professor at Baylor University, with advocating Darwinian evolution in his textbook, *Introduction to the Principles of Sociology*. Norris also attacked Samuel P. Brooks, president of Baylor, other Baylor faculty members, Truett, and a host of others, charging that they too held questionable beliefs regarding creation and evolution. Even before Norris's attacks on Dow, however, E. C. Routh had read the professor's book and found some questionable paragraphs. Dow promised to revise those paragraphs and assured everyone that he believed in the biblical account of creation. After talking with Dow and some of his students, Routh determined that the embattled professor was a good Christian man. In a letter to Brooks, Routh noted that several of the passages in Dow's book for which the professor had been criticized had been taken out of context, but also that the book would have to be revised if it was to be accepted by Texas Baptists.[106]

At the 1921 BGCT meeting, members of the Pastor's and Laymen's Conference, including Truett, issued a memorandum stating their opposition to the teaching of Darwinian evolution, to any theory questioning the validity of the Genesis account of creation, and to any destructive criticism based on rumors.[107] Thus, the memorandum both condemned Darwinian's theory and Norris's rumor mongering.

Messengers at the 1921 BGCT meeting also voted to have a committee investigate the curricula at Texas Baptists schools. The committee did not have to worry about Dow, who submitted his resignation in fall 1921.[108] By July 1922, the committee had finished its report. T. V. Neal, chair of the committee, informed the executive board of the BGCT: "Much ado about nothing has engaged the attention of your committee for several months."[109] In its report to the convention in November, the committee stated that "no teacher should be allowed to hold a position in any of our Baptists schools who teaches" Darwinian evolution, discredits the Genesis account of creation, or denies the inspiration of the Bible.[110] The committee found no evidence that Texas Baptists schools, particularly their science departments, "tended to make infidels out of students.... On the contrary, we have found strong evidence that the teachers were diligent in strengthening and stabilizing the faith of pupils."[111] Unimpressed by the committee's findings, Norris "dismissed its members as toadies of the convention, and charged that evidence had been suppressed."[112]

In 1924, Norris helped pressure C. S. Fothergill, an instructor of his-tory at Baylor, to resign. A proponent of theistic evolution, Fothergill hoped that his resignation would result in the condemnation of the persons who had maliciously twisted his beliefs to fit their own political agendas.[113]

In addition to causing a controversy in the life of Texas Baptists, the debate over evolution played an instrumental role in Southern Baptists adopting in 1925 the first confession of faith in their eighty-year history. Called the "Baptist Faith and Message," the confession briefly dealt with such doctrines as the nature and purpose of the Bible, God, "the fall of man," salvation, the church, and eschatology, as well as other topics such as religious liberty, some social issues, evangelism, and cooperation with other denominations. Ironically, or perhaps purposely, the document never mentioned evolution.

After E. Y. Mullins, president of Southern Baptist Theological Seminary (SBTS) and chair of the Committee on Statement of Baptist Faith and Message, presented the committee's report at the 1925 SBC meeting,

Clarence P. Stealey, editor of the Oklahoma Baptist newspaper, the *Baptist Messenger*, asked that the third section of the report concerning "The Fall of Man" be amended to read that God created humanity directly "and not by evolution."[114] In discussing the proposed amendment, Mullins argued that because the committee members had not stated how God created humanity, they did not have to state how God did not do it.[115] Messengers rejected Stealey's amendment by a vote of 2,013 to 905.

Truett was no evolutionist, theistic or otherwise. He briefly referred to evolution as far back as June 1904, when, in his baccalaureate sermon at the University of Texas, he mentioned that many people had been talking a lot about humans descending from monkeys. "Why, they have it all backwards!" he proclaimed. "The tendency is far greater in men to become monkeys than in monkeys to become men!"[116]

During the evolution controversy, Truett, as was his custom, remained in the background. Such aloofness, however, unsettled many Baptists. In April 1926, John Boland, a San Antonio layman, wrote Truett a rambling but impassioned letter expressing his dismay at Truett's silence. Boland, who had known B. H. Carroll, noted that his heart was "pained" because Carroll would have rather died than let "northern modernism" poison the South and southern religious schools. Men such as Brooks, Mullins, and John R. (J. R.) Sampey, professor of Old Testament at SBTS, were modernists, Boland claimed, for "they rejected the clause 'And not by Evolution'" during the discussion of the BFM at the 1925 SBC meeting. "I now hear you are also imbibing the teaching," the layman informed Truett. Boland contended that if he had been misled about everything he believed about God and the Bible, he was "ready to burn my Bible and curse the day God let all you men preach it. If science and evolution is [*sic*] right I want to know it, and thousands of baptist [*sic*] just in my fix to day [*sic*], come out in the open let us all know where you stand.... I'll never give one more dollar to support a preacher or a teacher until I know what he is to preach or teach."[117]

In his reply to Boland, Truett informed the San Antonio layman that he had "evidently been pitifully misled and misinformed about" the men "whose names you have mentioned in your letter. Your letter is such an amazing one that my first impulse on reading it was to ignore it utterly as one is compelled to do sometimes with letters that come to him." Truett believed, however, that Boland was "probably an earnest Christian man seeking to know and do the right, and certainly I would not wish to ignore or mistreat a fellow Christian." To set the record straight, Truett sent him some examples of his "beliefs and convictions," ones that he had "been teaching from my first day as a witness for Christ until now."[118]

What Truett sent Boland is unknown, but the contents probably contained something similar to Truett's response to Stealey, who, in March 1926, had asked the Dallas pastor for a paragraph stating his beliefs about the creation of humanity. Truett answered the editor, expressing his belief that God created humans in the same form as they are today and not by a process of evolution:

> This has been my steadfast testimony, till now. Indeed my convictions on the question you ask are so definite and well known to all who come within the radius of my humble life and labors, that, to answer the question, seems almost a work of supererogation. With my first reading, as a child on the farm, of the Bible record of man's creation, until now, I have believed such record, without hesitation or equivocation, just as I believe, with ever deepening conviction, all the truths recorded in God's Holy Word.[119]

In August 1927, Truett received another letter rebuking him for his spinelessness during the evolution controversy. Alva N. Turner, a former Dallas pastor, had wanted to write his colleague concerning the "storm cloud of evolution" that had "been marring the sky of Texas Baptists," but had procrastinated because the "burden" of his message concerned Truett's "lack of a backbone." Be a Christian and a Baptist like B. H. Carroll was, Turner chastised his famous friend, and you will change things at Baylor. If not, he warned Truett, when the history of Texas Baptists is written, that story will note that, while you were a faithful preacher, you were also "a cowering slave of Policy which, in the presence of Modern Contention, put the splendid personality of his leadership under a bushel and declared that his backbone was nil."[120]

Truett's opponents obviously equated his willingness to work with a diverse group of people with cowardice. Indeed, his circle of inclusion had a widely diverse circumference. For example, when Shailer Mathews, a proponent of the Social Gospel, addressed several Texas colleges' organizations in 1921, Truett invited him to preach at FBC. The presence of Mathews in FBC's pulpit on Sunday morning, March 27, 1921, distressed many Baptists, including A. N. Hall, a pastor in Muskogee, Oklahoma, who expressed his concerns in a letter to Truett. In response Truett informed Hall that Mathews "gave a clear, sound message on the Deity of Christ, faithfully insisting that it is to be Christ or chaos for humanity." Moreover, that Sunday afternoon at the Dallas Open Forum, which was attended by "people of all shades and beliefs and unbeliefs," Mathews, "in the searching questions that the audience put to him" after his speech, "held fast to the contention that there is no way of salvation to anybody except through Christ."[121]

Truett also maintained friendships with theistic evolutionists, such as J. M. Dawson, pastor of First Baptist Church, Waco. The two men were close friends for many years. When Dawson married Willie Turner, Truett performed the ceremony.[122] Many years before the evolution controversy, Truett baptized Turner, whom the Truetts "regarded…almost as a daughter."[123] She was also one of the FBC members whom Norris had persuaded to join McKinney Avenue Baptist Church in the early twentieth century.[124] In a 1929 letter, Truett expressed his feelings toward the Dawsons, writing that "for a long, long time, one of the largest rooms in my heart has been reserved for *you two*—and it is to be *yours* to the end of the earthly days, and then, please God, beyond, *forever!*"[125]

The bottom line for Truett was that he would work with practically anyone who cooperated with him in spreading the gospel and saving souls. Commenting on Truett's emphasis on cooperation, David Brian Whitlock noted that the Dallas pastor "did not fully address the issue of how much diversity the convention could tolerate and still fulfill its mission of world evangelism. Perhaps he recognized the dangers of such an approach; it held the possibility for conflict which would detract from the salvation of souls."[126] Despite the wideness of Truett's circle of inclusion, it was never wide enough to encompass Norris or anyone who used innuendos and lies to defame and undercut the programs, policies, or people for which and with whom Truett worked for a common goal.

*Presidents and Prohibition*

Although the Seventy-Five Million Campaign fell far short of its goal during the first five years of the 1920s, the campaign did highlight what could be accomplished if Southern Baptists worked together for a common goal. As they haggled over evolution and the wisdom of adopting a confession of faith in 1925, they also adopted a new program of financing their convention's agencies. Under this program, called the Cooperative Program, state conventions affiliated with the SBC agreed to send a percentage of their funds to the SBC for its programs.[127] Southern Baptists needed the Cooperative Program as they struggled to stay financially solvent. The excessive pledges made during the initial phase of the Seventy-Five Million Campaign produced visions of grandeur as Southern Baptists secured loans to fund building projects, mission programs, and educational institutions with money that they did not have. By 1926, the SBC had incurred a debt of $6.5 million ($76 million).[128] Debt would plague the convention for many years.

At their meeting in 1927, Southern Baptists honored Truett, who ran unopposed, by electing him president of the SBC. "I appreciate this honor, but from my deepest heart I had hoped it would never come to me," he said after being elected, but a sense of duty compelled him to accept it. With no knowledge of parliamentary procedures, Truett relied heavily on John D. Mell, a Georgia pastor, to handle the procedural aspects of the meeting.[129]

Commenting on Truett's election, J. E. Dillard, book editor of the *Alabama Baptist*, wrote, "No better choice could possibly be made. We need at this time a great heart, a great brain, and a strong hand. We have them. Dr. Truett showed himself a master of assemblies, and he loves every cause fostered by our great denomination."[130] Claude W. Duke, pastor of First Baptist Church, Tampa, Florida, wrote to Truett, complimenting him on his leadership at the meeting: "You presided well, and shunted to Dr. Mell judiciously. I never admired you more than at the convention…. I very sincerely feel that we are at the fork of the road, but not at a danger point of serious moment. We are about done sliding backwards now, we are about at the end of the creed making convention policy for awhile, we are going to unify our forces better…, and we are going gradually to crawl out of the hole."[131] Duke's reference to "the creed making convention policy" probably concerned the BFM, which was adopted at the 1925 meeting. The "hole" referred to the convention's debt.

Unfortunately, two acts of fraud deepened the "hole" from which Southern Baptists had "to crawl." At the 1927 SBC meeting, the Foreign Mission Board quietly announced that its treasurer, G. N. Saunders, had embezzled $103,000 ($1.2 million).[132] The SBC recovered half of the money from Saunders's assets and a fidelity bond required for the treasurer position, but for an organization mired in debt, recovering only half of anything could not be described as a success.

Another blow to the SBC coffers occurred in summer 1928. That summer began well for Truett, as SBC messengers again elected him as president of their convention in May. Then in June, he attended the BWA congress in Toronto, Canada, and read E. Y. Mullins's presidential address, "Baptist Life in the World's Life."[133] Mullins was the president of the BWA (1923–1928) and could not attend the meeting because he was ill. After returning from Europe in August, Truett was vacationing in Virginia when he received a call from Baron D. Gray, secretary of the SBC's Home Mission Board (HMB), which was located in Atlanta, Georgia. "Something has happened," Gray told Truett. "I want to see you. Our treasurer is missing, and I'm afraid he's been knocked in the head."[134] The next morning, Truett took a train to Atlanta. When the two men met, the secretary repeated his concern, saying, "I'm afraid the treasurer has been knocked in the head somewhere." Truett, however, suspected that the treasurer had done the knocking: "I'm afraid the Home Mission Board has been knocked in the head."[135]

The missing treasurer was Clinton S. Carnes. Except for having served time in an Atlanta penitentiary for embezzlement, Carnes had impeccable credentials when he began work at the HMB in 1918. Prior to his employment at the HMB, the Fidelity Trust Company of Philadelphia ran a background check on Carnes and, incredibly, did not discover his past transgression. Thus, the company put a bond on him for $50,000 ($688,386).[136]

About ten days after Truett arrived in Atlanta, auditors tallied the amount of Carnes's embezzlement at $909,461 ($11 million). Truett asked reporters and others who had gathered at the HMB offices to "[t]ell the people that Baptists are honest. Tell them that we will pay all."[137]

To recoup the losses incurred by Carnes's defalcation and to regain their honor, Southern Baptists set aside November 11, 1928, as Honor Day. While canvassing the South during the week before Honor Day, Truett and Archibald Cree, who, after Gray's resignation, became the HMB's interim secretary, sent a "special telegraphic message" to Texas Baptists. The two men assured them that their visits with Baptist leaders and pastors had gone well, and even "[a]mid the dark shadows of the humiliating tragedy of our Home Mission Board come cheering assurance of fellowship and confidence from other Christian groups." One Southern banker, not a Baptist, told the two men: "I believe in the integrity of Southern Baptists just as I believe in the stability of the United States Government. When Southern Baptists fail, the government will fail. They are a mighty people and they can raise this money in one brief hour." The banker's response caused Truett and Cree to exclaim, "What a credit! What a standing! What a confidence! Surely we will vindicate such confidence and maintain such credit on Baptist Honor Day!" Thus encouraged, the two men called on Texas Baptists to give sacrificially "and thus to blot out this humiliating and perilous disaster."[138]

On Honor Day, Southern Baptists raised $389,164 ($4.7 million), of which $8,821 ($107,000) had been contributed by Truett's church.

When coupled with other special gifts, Carnes's bond, and some of Carnes's assets, Southern Baptists eventually recouped $629,683 ($7.6 million) of the stolen funds, or 69 percent.[139]

Honor Day had been held the first Sunday after the 1928 presidential election, which pitted the "dry" Protestant, Republican candidate, Herbert Hoover, against the "wet" Catholic, Democratic candidate, Al Smith. If E. O. Smith of Dallas had had his way, Democrats would never have nominated Al Smith. Instead, E. O. Smith wanted the party to nominate a man of impeccable character who could instill confidence in people. In a letter to the *Dallas Morning News* in February 1928, Smith asked the people of Dallas and America "to draft a man…that will not only carry the confidence of the people" of the United States, "but will hold and keep it as a public servant." Smith was not asking Democrats to draft "a sprout mouthed political preacher or a little politician"; rather, he was suggesting "a man who is one of the world's greatest living souls, a man who would measure up to the standard and meet every requirement as mentioned above. He is a leader, an educator, a statesman, a businessman, a man with executive ability, practical wisdom, both progressive and aggressive, a worker, a man of experience, a man's friend, a servant of the people and a doctor of divinity. That man is in the person of George W. Truett."[140] E. O. Smith's suggestion obviously went unheeded, as Democrats nominated Al Smith when they convened in Houston, Texas, in June 1928.

In the minds of many people, particularly southerners, Al Smith had two obstacles he could never overcome: his Catholic faith and his opposition to the Eighteenth Amendment. In summer 1928, L. R. Scarborough headed a list of over 200 Texas Baptists who signed an article titled "To Our Brother Baptists," opposing the election of Smith. Cullen Thomas, a deacon at FBC and a lawyer, wrote a polite but pointed letter to Scarborough, stating that the signees of the article did not speak for all Texas Baptists. The FBC deacon urged religious leaders not to become partisan pawns of the political process; rather, he suggested that they follow the example of Truett, who had stated in a recent address to a men's Bible class at FBC:

We are in an election year. Not as a partisan, but as a religious teacher, as far as I would be willing to go, would be to urge my fellow-countrymen to give the best thought to have righteous laws regnant over us all and to elect officers of law to serve us that shall function in the highest and most vital way. The pulpit should not be turned into a political platform. The church is not a forum for participation in the present political warfare. Great principles should be enunciated from the pulpit and their application left to be thoroughly carried out as the conscience and judgment of the people may be constrained.[141]

A couple of months after his address to the men's Bible class, Truett felt compelled to respond to reports "in the secular press" concerning current political issues, particularly prohibition. He repeated what he had said to the men's Bible class about preachers not involving themselves in partisan politics from the pulpit. He also added that he could not in good conscience vote for any presidential candidate who did not support the Eighteenth Amendment. Conscience also compelled him "to say that I believe it would be a tragedy, both for America and the whole world, for any man to be elected to the presidency of this great land, who is not in the fullest sympathy with the eighteenth amendment, and with the faithful enforcement of the laws enacted thereunder."[142]

While Truett held firm to his long-held beliefs that preachers should not endorse candidates, no one could have missed whom he would vote for. His non-endorsement endorsement of Hoover, however, did not satisfy many Baptists, particularly Norris, who loved to bait Truett. An October 5, 1928, article in Norris's newspaper, which he had renamed the *Fundamentalist* in 1927, expressed outrage that Smith supporters had been spreading the "diabolical" propaganda stating that Truett supported the Democratic candidate. No one, the article continued, could ever believe that "the great preacher" had endorsed Smith.[143] The *Fundamentalist*'s praise of and support for Truett, however, was accompanied by mild rebuke of Truett for not specifically naming the candidate for whom he would vote. After noting correctly "that Dr. Truett, by both nature and practice avoids controversial matters and rarely ever takes an out spoken position when red-hot issues are discussed," the article listed several examples of Truett's silence on important issues. He "was silent" during the 1909 racetrack fight, until the Sunday prior to the vote in March; during the 1911 statewide prohibition campaign, until the near the end of the campaign; during the "Sunday Moving Picture Show" battle in Dallas; during the "red-hot" evolution battle; and during the battle against modernism in the Baptist World Alliance.[144]

Whereas Truett refused to open his mouth about Al Smith, Norris apparently could not keep his shut. From his pulpit and from the pulpits in other churches, the Fort Worth fundamentalist railed against Smith and his religion. By mid-October 1928, Norris estimated that he had delivered 107 anti-Smith speeches.[145]

When all the votes were finally tallied in November 1928, Hoover received 58.2 percent of the popular vote and 444 electoral college votes to Smith's 40.9 percent and 87 electoral college votes.[146] According to Conlin, "had Smith been a Kansas Presbyterian who never drank cough syrup, he would have lost in 1928. Business and the Republican party reigned supreme because of the general prosperity of the New Era and because a great many Americans were convinced that businessmen were the new messiahs Woodrow Wilson had tried so hard to be."[147] That Smith was a Catholic who imbibed more than expectorants, however, obviously did not help him.

Hoover's election elated the majority of Southern Baptists. When they gathered in Memphis, Tennessee, in May 1929, for their annual meeting, the convention's Commission on Social Service presented its report on Saturday morning, May 11. In part of its report, the commission expressed the sentiments of many Southern Baptists concerning the 1928 presidential election: "It is doubtful whether there has ever been achieved a greater victory for public morals and good government than was achieved in the battle of ballots on November 6, 1928, when American citizens in a manner that could not be misunderstood declared to the world that their government, whether national or state, would not go back into alliance with the blighting, death-dealing liquor curse."[148]

Prior to the commission's report on Saturday morning, a few of the messengers expressed their distress about the convention's alleged liberal leanings. J. W. Porter, a pastor in Louisville, Kentucky, made a motion on behalf of Kentucky Baptists to rescind the invitation that had been given to Mrs. W. J. Cox, president of the Woman's Missionary Union, to address the messengers at the 1929 meeting.[149] Nearly two weeks prior to the meeting, he had written to Truett, expressing his dismay that Cox had been invited to speak. Porter informed Truett that Kentucky Baptists had recently passed a resolution protesting the invitation and that he had written Cox, "asking her, for the sake of peace, and not giving offense not to make the address…. I may be wrong, but in my judgement [sic], it will result in evil and evil only."[150] When Porter addressed the SBC meeting, he contended that the Bible forbade women to speak in church and maintained that Cox had received the invitation only to "please the sisters and get more money." "It's trading God for gold," Porter declared. "Eve tempted Adam. Women would do all right if the petticoated preachers would let them alone." When Truett, who had been elected as the convention's president for the third and final time, put the question of whether the SBC should rescind the invitation, only a few people in attendance voiced their affirmation.[151] When Cox and several other women walked onto the platform, Porter and M. E. Dodd, a pastor from Shreveport, Louisiana, walked out of the meeting.

Although Truett had no problem with Cox addressing the SBC meeting, he did not believe that women should be preachers. Responding to an inquiry by E. H. Owen, a pastor in Karnes City, Texas, Truett maintained that women's work "in Christ's cause is a very large and gracious work, but I do not believe that the Scriptures sanction their becoming preachers."[152]

*Joys and Trials*

For Truett, the 1920s proved to be a mixture of joys and trials and of praise and rebuke. The Truetts' daughter Mary became the wife of Thomas W. Gilliam, III, in November 1924, and their daughter Annie married

Robert Lee Milliken in April 1927.[153] In between those marriages, Truett was named one of the top twenty-five American pastors in 1925.[154]

Much of the joy Truett experienced during the decade came from his church. Total contributions exceeded $200,000 for eight of the ten years, and in three years (1920, 1921, 1923) gifts to outside causes exceeded those to the church's programs.[155] FBC's membership also increased from 3,442 to 6,229 during the decade, and its Sunday-school enrollment grew from 3,789 to 6,164.[156]

By 1929, FBC had hired eight staff members to assist Truett in ministering to such a large congregation. Along with Robert Coleman and Dolph Johnson, the staff included Bertha Mills (director of children's work) Georgine Coley (director of young people's work), Ivy Marie Johnson (secretary of the Sunday school), Mrs. J. H. Cassidy (organist and director of the volunteer choir), Emma Hines (supervisor of the dining room), and Mrs. W. L. Pitts (church visitor). Along with teaching a Sunday-school class, helping train Sunday-school teachers, teaching Bible studies in homes, and attending a weekly dinner with "Business Girls," Pitts averaged 250 calls a month and wrote between twenty-five to fifty letters each month.[157]

For his leadership and hard work, the church paid Truett a handsome salary, which increased slightly from $7,500 ($77,598) in 1920 to $8,000 ($96,832) in 1929. By 1921, however, the church had begun to supplement his salary with an "incidental fund" for books, upkeep on his home and car, and other expenses. In 1929, for example, he received $2,000 ($24,208) for this fund.[158] Despite his salary, Truett was often in debt and had to borrow money, which concerned the church's deacons and is one reason for his receiving the "incidental fund." Some years he pledged his entire annual salary to the church budget, and he returned all the money he received from outside speaking engagements to the churches that had paid him an honorarium.[159] Once, early in his Dallas ministry, Truett paid the rent of an unemployed man. Another time a friend protested Truett's borrowing money to pay the funeral expenses for a poor family.

Truett replied, "That is what money is for, to help others, and that is all it is for."[160]

During the 1920s, FBC's facilities underwent drastic changes. In fall 1921, the church went high-tech when it began broadcasting its services over the radio. By 1926, three Dallas radio stations were broadcasting the Sunday morning and evening services.[161] The sanctuary was remodeled and expanded in 1924, and an education building, later called the Truett building, was built the following year. In 1929, FBC's facilities covered a city block, 268 by 134 feet, on property valued at $1.25 million ($15 million).[162]

With such a successful ministry, Truett had people heaping praise on him left and right, although his father was not one of them. In 1923, an interviewer asked him if he was proud of his son George. Charles Truett responded, "No, I am not proud of George. I am only grateful the Lord is using him. 'Proud' is the wrong word. If it depended on me for George to get bragged on, I'm afraid he wouldn't get much."[163]

As in previous years, however, many people from different walks of life "bragged on" the famous Dallas pastor. For example, after attending a Baptist Young People's Union convention in Georgia, Adelia Brown wrote that when Truett looked into the faces of the audience, "we felt" as if "God was looking into our hearts."[164]

Truett received other flattering words of praise during a September 14, 1922, banquet celebrating his twenty-five-year ministry in Dallas. Baptists at the celebration obviously extolled Truett's virtues, but non-Baptists did so too. Robert S. Hier, president emeritus of Southern Methodist University, remarked, "The great thing about Dr. Truett is power. It is power! He is more than eloquent. He is more than wise. He is a man greater than any other man I have ever heard—a man of power. I am not impressed by his eloquence and his erudition, but I am always overwhelmed by his power."[165] John W. Phelp, a Catholic and the postmaster of Dallas, called Truett a "great man." No other person in Dallas, he continued, reaches the heart of his hearer like George Truett. If you ask me why I believe he is a great leader—yea, why I know he is a great leader—if you ask me why he is successful, if you ask me why he loves you and me, and why we love him, my answer is that he always reaches the heart. I have heard him preach funerals, I have heard him perform marriage ceremonies, I have heard him address business men, and I have never failed to know on any occasion that he had not only reached my heart, but the heart of every hearer.[166]

Praise for Truett also came from unlikely sources. In a January 1929 letter to Truett, David Lefkowitz, rabbi of Temple Emanu-El in Dallas, wrote, "I feel that you have been the finest spiritual influence in Dallas for over a generation."[167] Also that winter, a *Kansas City Star* reporter traveled to Dallas to write an article about Truett. Stopping one afternoon to get his shoes shined, the reporter remarked to the African American polishing his shoes that Dallas had "a great preacher." The man knew that the reporter meant Truett and said, "Yes, we colored folks is mighty proud of Dr. Truett." Surprised, the reporter responded, "You colored folks? Why, he is not your preacher." The shoe shiner, somewhat offended, stood up and said, "Isn't he?... He's been in my house, and prayed with my little girl when she was sick. I sent for him and he come. Yes sir. And he's preached in our church."[168]

Two books appeared in the 1920s bearing Truett's name. In 1923, the SBC's Sunday School Board (SSB) published ten of his addresses and funeral sermons under the title *God's Call to America*, which included his 1911 address at the BWA congress and his 1920 "Baptists and Religious Liberty" address in Washington, D.C. In 1929, the SSB published *These Gracious Years*, which contains nineteen of Truett's Christmas-New Year's messages written between 1910 and 1928. Truett sent these cards to thousands of people each Christmas season. In 1941, for example, he mailed approximately 10,000 cards, each by first class and each addressed by hand and marked "Personal."[169]

Along with experiencing much joy and praise during the 1920s, Truett also experienced sadness and trials. His good friend J. B. Gambrell died in June 1921. Four years later, Truett's ninety-five-year-old father

died in Whitewright, Texas.[170] After Charles died, his son Spurgeon, who
was deaf and had been living with his father, moved to Dallas to live with
his brother George. Spurgeon did not consider preaching to be a job and
liked to say, "*George* never did a day's work in his life."[171] In 1929,
Truett's cousin Ferd McConnell, who had helped Truett start his school in
Hiawassee, Georgia, in 1877, died.

Along with the letters from Turner and from Boland accusing him of
being a coward during the evolution controversy, Truett received other
letters that helped to keep him humble. One such letter came from a
church member. W. C. Biting wrote to Truett requesting that his name be
removed from FBC's membership roll because he was "completely out of
sympathy with the manner in which the finances of your Church are being
administered, and with the result as shown by the fact that this year you
must raise, in cash, a total of $207,500 [$2.5 million], in addition to the
ordinary running expenses and gifts for benevolences at home and abroad."
Despite his request, Biting assured Truett that his "affection for" his soon-
to-be-former pastor "will always be as deep as it is possible for me to 'feel'
toward any other man."[172]

Along with receiving letters during the 1920s criticizing him for
things that he did or failed to do, Truett had to contend with Norris's
involvement not only in the affairs of Texas and Southern Baptists, but also
in the affairs of FBC, Dallas. One way in which the Fort Worth pastor
attempted to undermine Truett's character and ministry was by sending
the *Fundamentalist*, free of charge, to FBC members. Although some
articles in the paper praised Truett's ministry, other articles barely
concealed the utter contempt Norris had of Truett. In his private letters to
friends, however, Norris felt free to express his hostility toward Truett. For
example, in an April 1929 letter to his friend Victor I. Mastors, editor of
the *Western Recorder*, Norris relished in the fact that, at least in Norris's
mind, everything that Truett had tried to do in the past three years had
ended in "complete failure" and "is now common talk."[173] Truett used to
make others cry during his messages, Norris confided happily to his
friend, but now he just blubbers by himself, and "[h]is bitterness and hate

against me knows no lengths, depths or breadths, and it has become common talk."[174] "Truett is indeed very pitiable," Norris continued.

> While I have admired him and appreciated his worth and work, yet I have come to have a contempt mingled with pity for him. For a long time I grieved to see him heading, like Lot toward Sodom, in the direction toward the camp of the modernists.... I am sending my paper to nearly every member of his church and believe me they are doing the talking. Of course it is pro and con. One of his lady members brought me a long list a few days ago. Once she was very bitter toward me and now she is just as strong for me. She tells me that Truett has a very small house Sunday nights and the balconies are empty Sunday mornings, and frequently the attendance of his Sunday School is not what it was two or three years ago.[175]

The truth of Norris's report about FBC's attendance problem is difficult to determine, for he had a penchant for skewing facts. Norris, however, had his own problems to contend with during the 1920s, the most tragic of which occurred on Saturday, July 17, 1926. The fundamentalist pastor had been attacking what he considered to be corrupt city officials. His main target was H. C. Meacham, a Catholic department store owner and the mayor of Fort Worth, whom Norris accused of using city funds to benefit Catholic institutions. According to Norris, on July 17, Meacham's friend D. E. Chipps threatened to kill Norris and then confronted the pastor at his church. After arguing briefly, Chipps started to leave; however, he turned back and followed Norris into his office. The pastor ran to his desk, removed the night watchman's pistol, and shot Chipps three times, killing the unarmed man.[176] After a ten-day murder trial in January 1927, a jury acquitted Norris, accepting his plea of self-defense.[177]

Apparently, Chipps did not die in vain, at least in Norris's eyes, for the notoriety generated by the murder trial proved to be beneficial for Norris and his church. According to Scarborough, the controversial Fort Worth pastor emphasized that by July 1927, one year after the Chipps killing, 2,000 new members had been added to the membership of First Baptist, Fort Worth. Scarborough, however, doubted that figure and contended that evangelism by homicide was not the method advocated in the New Testament.[178]

By the end of the 1920s, Truett had much for which to be thankful. His church membership had increased; he had striven together with thousands of Southern Baptists during the Seventy-Five Million Campaign to raise money for the spreading of the gospel; he had been elected three times to head his beloved denomination; and he had been praised by Baptists and non-Baptists for his ministry. Yet many events occurred during the decade that sank Truett's heart. The Seventy-Five Million Campaign did not reach its goal; loved ones and friends died; and because they rejected fundamentalism, Truett and many of his friends became the targets of a smear campaign headed by Norris.

Truett's rejection of fundamentalism apparently pained Norris, who lamented to his friend Masters, "Oh, what [Truett] could have done if he had thrown himself in the breach for the cause of fundamentalism, but he is gone."[179] Truett was a conservative theologically, not a fundamentalist, and any suggestion that he was an evolutionist or a modernist was ludicrous. As his good friend J. B. Cranfill observed, "One of the most remarkable things about...Truett is that, even in these hectic days of so-called 'fundamentalism,' and 'modernism,' he is lovingly orthodox. He is not identified with the so-called 'fundamentalist' movement because he can say, 'Before fundamentalism was, I am.' He follows none of the new pronouncements of the modernists, saying over and again from his pulpit, 'I believe the Bible just like my mother believed it.'"[180]

The end of the 1920s did not, however, end the financial woes of Southern Baptists, for on October 24, 1929, the headline in the *Dallas Morning News* described the ominous financial news from the previous day: "Deluge of Selling Crashes Stock in Last Hour of Trading." In one hour, the value of stocks on the New York Stock Exchange had plummeted $3 billion ($36 billion), an average of about $50,000 ($605,000) a minute.[181] Few Americans realized that they were about to experience the most serious economic depression in the nation's history. Nor did the end of the decade stop Norris's baiting of Truett. "[E]very chance I get I am going to wade into him," Norris confided to Masters. "Every time there is a joint in his harness I am going to let go the arrow."[182] And Norris had a quiver full.

# Chapter 6

# Owing Himself to the World, 1930–1939

During the 1920s and the 1930s, a new breed of dictators emerged, dictators who sank the meaning of the word to a more diabolical level than it had ever been before. Benito Mussolini became prime minister of Italy in 1922, and Joseph Stalin became head of the Soviet Union in 1929. In Germany, Adolph Hitler was sworn in as chancellor on January 30, 1933, and soon thereafter his political party, the National Socialist German Workers Party (Nazi), took control of the country. A year and a half later, on August 19, 1934, Hitler declared himself to be Führer of Germany. According to David Thompson, leaders like Mussolini, Stalin, and Hitler "rode to power on stimulated waves of fear and anger, hatred and envy."[1] They used the police, the military, and the secret police to eliminate anyone who defied the edicts of their governments. They indoctrinated their citizens and seized

> not only absolute power but totalitarian power, for no limits were admitted to the scope of state competence. Churches were reduced to political impotence, free trade unions destroyed and strikes forbidden, free associations demolished or absorbed. Every agency for molding public opinion—schools, the press, radio, cinema, public meetings—was taken under party control. No element of social life was accepted as lying beyond the direction of the government. Never before in the history of the world had ruthless men enjoyed such complete and far-reaching power over the lives of millions.[2]

During the 1930s, particularly during the first half of the decade, Americans focused their attention on economics, not on dictators, for the Great Depression wreaked havoc on the lives of individuals, families, businesses, and even churches. Texas Baptists, like other Americans, suffered financially. Many Texas Baptist churches had difficulty keeping full-time pastors, and many rural churches had to close their doors. Some churches stopped sending money to the Baptist General Convention of Texas (BGCT), resulting in the reduction of the salaries of convention employees and of mission projects.[3] The convention's debt in 1930 was $1.1 million ($14 million).[4] By 1933, gifts to missions had dropped by 50 percent, and total gifts had dropped by 42 percent.[5] The Southern Baptist Convention (SBC) did not fare any better. To help offset the SBC's financial woes, the convention's executive board in 1933 initiated the Hundred Thousand Club, whose members pledged to give the convention $1 per month above their regular gifts to their churches. From 1933 to 1939, the club raised slightly more than $1.1 million.[6]

First Baptist Church (FBC), Dallas, also experienced a financial crisis during the depression, although the church's predicament was not as bad as that of many other churches. FBC members contributed $232,301 ($2.9 million) to their church in 1930, an 11 percent increase over the previous year. The next year, however, total contributions fell by 19 percent to $189,023 ($2.4 million). The year 1933 was the worst year financially for FBC during the 1930s, when gifts totaled only $124,123 ($1.98 million), a 47 percent decrease from 1930. Even so, 34 percent of total gifts to FBC during the decade went to outside causes.[7] To save money, FBC cut salaries. At least by 1933, George W. Truett's salary had been reduced by 25 percent to $6,000 ($95,992), which was still much more than most Americans made.[8] Manufacturing workers in 1933, for example, earned less than $17 ($272) a week, or $884 ($14,143) a year.[9]

Like all cities, Dallas suffered the effects of the Great Depression, but the discovery of oil in East Texas in 1930 helped prevent a difficult situation from becoming worse. In 1932, 787 companies in Dallas were solely connected with the oil business. Despite the prosperity of some Dallasites, by 1933, 15,000 of the city's citizens had been placed on public relief roles.[10]

Truett did what he could to help those who had lost their jobs or who were struggling just to survive. In December 1931, for example, he exhorted the citizens of Dallas to contribute $100,000 to fund the city's emergency relief fund. Ever the optimist, Truett stated that no one

> would be willing for one moment to ask the age-old and fatally selfish question: "Am I my brother's keeper?" That is the question of the slacker and the defaulter, and to trifle with such question is to invite the most serious consequences. We are bound together in the bundle of life. We can neither live nor die to ourselves. We are to go with true neighborliness to every person who needs us and forgetfulness of this high privilege and duty carries with it a penalty too serious to be thought of except with a shudder.[11]

By 1936, the New Deal programs instituted in 1933 by President Franklin D. Roosevelt's administration had begun to offset the effects of the depression. More Texas Baptist churches began calling full-time ministers, and the BGCT began to spend more money on missions and to raise the salaries of employees.[12]

Truett's plea in December 1931 on behalf of Dallas's poor reflected his life-long attitude toward ministry: Christians were saved in order to help others, at home and abroad, spiritually, mentally, physically, and economically. His ministry during the 1930s can be summarized in a statement he made during a sermon on September 9, 1917, his twenty-first anniversary as FBC's pastor. "The highest debtorship is in the realm of morality," Truett proclaimed. "Debtorship in the realm of morality is greater and more inexorable than in the financial realm. The Apostle Paul, the highest credential Christianity has given to the world, laid down the true principle of life: 'I owe myself to the world.'"[13] During the 1930s, Truett embodied that principle. He did not neglect his congregation or the people of Dallas, but he extended his fame, influence, and ministry throughout the world as he traveled the globe visiting Baptists and preaching the gospel.

*President of the Baptist World Alliance*

In March 1930, Truett traveled to Louisville, Kentucky, to speak at the Southern Baptist Theological Seminary (SBTS). According to A. T. Robertson, Truett's messages on "The Preacher–His Life and Work" "gripped the entire city."[14] The audiences were so large that many people had to sit in a classroom and listen over a loudspeaker. Many more people did not bother to attend the lectures because they knew that there would be no room for them. Robertson described Truett as having "a clear brain that sees things as they are," a "simple Anglo-Saxon speech in which to tell the story of Christ," and "one of the rarest of human voices resonant, searching, haunting, piercing, lingering, unforgettable." "He is a master in telling stories of his own experience," Robertson continued, "and he has had rich and varied dealings with men. Sometime the pathos of these stories melts the hardest hearts."[15]

From Louisville, Truett went to Gainesville, Florida, where he preached a revival at the city's First Baptist Church. Other services during the week were held at the University of Florida's auditorium. Loudspeakers placed in many locations around Gainesville, such as hotel lobbies, churches, and garages, enabled others to hear Truett's messages, which were also broadcast on the radio.[16]

Soon after arriving back in Dallas from Gainesville, Truett received a letter from J. R. Sampey, president of SBTS, informing him about a letter Sampey had received from Benjamin F. Procter, a judge in Bowling Green, Kentucky. The judge had urged Sampey to convince Truett to allow his name to be submitted for the candidacy of the president of the United States in 1932. "If you really want the job, my dear friend," Sampey wrote to Truett, "I am for you. I think you are doing a work more far-reaching than our best statesmen.... I am not sending you the Judge's long letter to me, inasmuch as it would entail serious effort to decipher it. He lives up to his privileges as a lawyer in his chirography. We are still feasting on the wonderful messages you brought us during the Conference on preaching."[17] Obviously, Truett ignored the judge's proposal. As Leon

McBeth wryly observed, "For a man who had turned down the presidency of Baylor University, the job in Washington would hold little appeal."[18]

At the 1930 SBC meeting in May, Truett gladly relinquished his position as the convention's president to William J. (W. J.) McGlothlin, president of Furman University in South Carolina. Afterward, Jessie Truett James asked her father if he felt like a caged bird that had been freed, to which Truett responded: "Daughter, I feel as though I had turned a hippopotamus loose. In fact, I feel just like a boy after school lets out."[19]

To help relieve the stress experienced during the previous three years as the SBC's president, the sixty-three-year-old Truett accepted the invitation of Southern Baptist missionaries in Argentina, Brazil, Chile, and Uruguay, to spend two and a half months in South America preaching revival meetings. He and Josephine left from New York City for Brazil on May 30, accompanied by Mrs. George W. Bottoms of Texarkana, Texas; a Mrs. Jenkins of Louisiana; T. B. Ray, executive secretary of the SBC's Foreign Mission Board, and his wife; O. E. Sellers of the Baptist Bible Institute (now New Orleans Baptist Theological Seminary); Kathleen Mallory, corresponding secretary of the Woman's Missionary Union; Una Roberts Lawrence, a writer for the SBC's Home Mission Board; and John H. (J. H.) Rushbrooke, a British Baptist and secretary of the Baptist World Alliance (BWA). When the group's ship docked in Rio de Janeiro, more than a hundred missionaries, Brazilians, and Americans greeted the Truetts and their companions.[20]

Truett spent nearly four weeks in Brazil, preaching on numerous occasions through an interpreter and traveling well over 3,000 miles in the country.[21] After touring Brazil, he and his companions visited Uruguay and then Argentina. Their ship docked at Buenos Aires, Argentina, on the morning of July 29, 1930.

At the end of one service in Buenos Aires, people responded for half an hour after Truett gave the invitation for people to surrender their lives to Christ, the scene of which, according to William A. Brown, pastor of the First Methodist Episcopal Church, Buenos Aires, "was unprecedented in the history of Missionary work in Argentina."[22] On another occasion, after

Truett preached "The Business Man of Today" at the city's American Club, the audience "gave him a great ovation, and scores expressed their joy at his being in Buenos Aires and wished him to come again."[23]

From Argentina, Truett and his friends crossed the Andes Mountains to Chile, where the Dallas pastor preached in the cities of Santiago, Concepcion, and Temuco. After a brief visit in the country, the group returned to the United States.

In late November 1930, Truett left Dallas again, this time for Nashville, Tennessee, to preach a revival at Immanuel Baptist Church, where his son-in-law Powhatan W. James had been pastoring since 1926. A court reporter transcribed Truett's fourteen revival sermons and his one address to Nashville preachers. These messages were later published in his book *Follow Thou Me.*[24]

Despite his numerous trips outside of Dallas, Truett always found time to involve himself in causes about which he felt passionate. One such cause was prohibition. Although national prohibition had been the policy of the United States government since the ratification of the Eighteenth Amendment in January 1919, anti-prohibition forces had continued to fight prohibition and Americans continued to drink. Having witnessed the destruction that the abuse of alcohol inflicted on society, families, and individuals, Truett had nothing good to say about alcohol. In an undated sermon, he declared, "Laws need to be passed before the nation is submerged in" the evils of drinking. "Parents and teachers need to wake up. Smile about it? Go smile at a casket! Go smile at a dead boy! Too much is at stake here for people to be laughing and joking about the evils of drinking…! Too much is at stake here, too much!"[25] Thus, when anti-prohibition forces had garnered enough support in the early 1930s to repeal the Eighteenth Amendment, Truett and other ministers worked to keep the amendment alive.

With Hiram A. Boaz, a Methodist bishop, Truett traveled throughout Texas, campaigning against the repeal of the Eighteenth Amendment. Truett, however, did most of the talking, for Boaz made only a few introductory remarks before giving his Baptist colleague the remaining time to speak about the great cause of prohibition.[26]

Not all Dallas ministers supported prohibition. In February 1933, Truett and Harry T. Moore, an Episcopalian bishop in Dallas, presented their differing opinions of the Eighteenth Amendment before the Texas legislature's House Committee on Constitutional Amendments. Truett contended that the amendment had made a positive impact on American society, but lamented the fact that after passage of the amendment, "the forces of temperance...went to sleep and fancied the battle had been won for all time." Anti-prohibitionists, however, had kept working to undermine the amendment, for "[e]vil never abdicates nor leaves the switch unguarded." "A true prophet of God," Truett continued, "can not be silent when the moral and immoral forces meet on the great field of battle. This is a great moral question, one that goes to the very foundation of the social order. Moral forces can not sit down and see a license, high or low, in the liquor laws." Since the passing of the Eighteenth Amendment, he contended, the consumption of alcohol had decreased, and only "red-shirted anarchists" contend that prohibition laws cannot be enforced. To the argument that tax revenues from the sale of alcohol would benefit society, Truett countered: "I don't believe men's bodies should be sold to run the Government; I do not believe that women's bodies should be sold in houses of prostitution to support our schools. You build a town with blood money when you build it on immorality." Let the American people decide this issue, Truett argued. If so, they would vote to retain the Eighteenth Amendment.[27]

In his testimony before the committee, Moore emphasized that people used terms like "temperance" and "prohibition" to mean the same thing, which they did not. "Temperance," the bishop maintained,

> is a real Christian virtue, a part of the very life of every Christian, man and woman, but under that does not come the drastic law of prohibition. Temperance comes from inside out, [producing the] courage to be master of one's self, to govern by restraint and to make of one's life that which as nearly as possible follows the pattern of perfection. It differs widely from thou shalt and

thou shalt not. Let's draw clearly a line between the divine message handed down to us and a law that has been imposed upon our citizenship.[28]

Like his Baptist colleague, Moore wanted the people to voice their opinion on such a vital issue that affected their lives. Contrary to Truett, however, the bishop contended that drunkenness had increased since the passing of the Eighteenth Amendment. He wondered "where the people who make" contrary claims "have been. I have had fathers and mothers come to me, since the Eighteenth Amendment became effective, pleading for their sons and daughters."[29]

The cultural and political forces sided with Moore's position on prohibition, which eventually led to the repeal of the Eighteenth Amendment. Many Americans, particularly in urban settings, never accepted prohibition, as speakeasies thrived and bootleggers benefitted financially by supplying liquor to eager customers. According to Richard F. Hamm, several factors led to the amendment's repeal: states had abdicated their responsibility of enforcing prohibition to the federal government; attitudes toward alcohol had changed; prohibition organizations had lost their influence; and the Great Depression had destroyed the argument of prohibitionists that prohibition would produce prosperity. The poor economic conditions also helped "wet" Democrats to be elected to national office, which ensured that the amendment would be repealed.[30] Thus, on February 20, 1933, Congress passed the Twenty-first Amendment, which repealed the Eighteenth Amendment. By December 5, 1933, enough states had voted to ratify the Twenty-first Amendment, thus ending prohibition in the United States.

Whereas the repeal of the Eighteenth Amendment in 1933 obviously disappointed Truett, the year 1934 proved to be a personally rewarding one for him. In April, he traveled to England to speak at the C. H. Spurgeon Centenary Commemoration. Being chosen to present the address honoring the deceased British Baptist minister, whom one historian described as "the most popular and the greatest preacher of his age,"[31] was quite an honor. In justifying the choice of an American minister to speak at the commemoration, Rushbrooke, a British Baptist leader, noted:

It is right that this man should be the world's spokesman on the occasion of the Spurgeon centenary. He is Spurgeon's soul-mate, in a true sense his successor. His resemblances to his predecessor are many and striking. Like Spurgeon's, his doctrinal attitude is conservative, but who, listening to Spurgeon as I once heard him in the Metropolitan Tabernacle, was inclined to ask theoretical questions or to enter upon critical analysis? Spurgeon presented the Christ of whom he himself was a bondslave and with that Christ we were brought face to face. Dr. Truett does the same: through him his Christ speaks.[32]

Truett spent twelve days in England, preaching every day, the highlight of which came at the Spurgeon Centenary, on Wednesday evening, April 25, in the Royal Albert Hall, in London. After expressing his "unfitness to speak in a manner befitting this epochal, world occasion,"[33] Truett spoke for fifty minutes, without notes, about the great Baptist preacher. Truett noted his indebtedness to Spurgeon, whose "printed sermons found their way across the great ocean, and on and on they traveled, until they came to a little mountain home in the remote country. Week by week, I read those sermons, often reading them over and over again, until, like great drops of iron, this man's message entered into my deepest life."[34]

Truett described Spurgeon as "a man of incarnate integrity," whose "mind travelled in a straight line like the light," a man of "moral courage," and "a man of universal sympathies," one who treated rich and poor alike.[35] But preeminently, Spurgeon was a man who preached the gospel, "the one message that will transform human society; that will cure all social ills; that will readily settle the age-old dispute between labor and capital; that will heal racial hatreds, and end war, and abolish national suspicions and antagonisms, and make all men brothers."[36]

Truett challenged his fellow preachers and Christians in the audience to follow Spurgeon's example "to be true shepherds of souls—of all souls, of all conditions, of all places, and always. This is ever to be our dominant passion. We must not, dare not be indifferent to the spiritual welfare of any soul, anywhere."[37]

After the Spurgeon Centenary, Truett returned to Dallas in May. He did not stay long, however, as he returned again to Europe in August in order to attend the BWA congress in Berlin, Germany.

Fifteen years had passed since Truett preached in Germany immediately following World War I. The country had come a long way since its bitter defeat in the war. Germany had already begun to violate the terms set forth in the Treaty of Versailles, prohibiting the country from expanding its military. With the Nazis in control, the German government mandated in July 1933 that all Germans suffering from blindness, physical deformities, and mental illness be sterilized. By the end of the year, at least 100,000 Germans had been sent to concentration camps.[38] Consequently, some Baptist leaders thought that the BWA congress should be held elsewhere. Rushbrooke traveled to Germany to confer with German Baptists, some of whom believed that the meeting should be moved. Fearing that Baptists would choose to hold the congress elsewhere, the German ambassador to the United States, Hans Luther, and the German propaganda minister, Joseph Goebbels, offered their support to the BWA and insisted that the meeting be held in Germany.[39] Ultimately, Baptist leaders agreed to hold the congress in Berlin, August 4–10. More than 3,000 delegates attended the meeting, which was held in the Kaiserdamm exhibition hall. Hanging prominently behind the choir was the Nazi (swastika) flag.[40]

On Tuesday, August 7, participants at the congress elected Truett as the BWA's president, a position that entailed a five-year commitment. Later in the week, in his brief closing remarks to the congress, he challenged members of the audience to stand firm in their commitments to putting the kingdom of God first in their lives, to defending religious liberty for all people, to emphasizing cooperation, and to spreading the gospel. Because "[a]ll saving power is sacrificial," Truett proclaimed, the winning of the world to Christ would be a daunting one, and "[n]o cheap service will win" that battle.[41] Nevertheless, Truett reminded the delegates that before Jesus experienced victory, he had encountered hostility and endured the cross. The BWA's new president then ended his remarks by quoting a stanza from Isaac Watts's hymn "When I Survey the Wondrous Cross": "Were the whole realm of nature mine, / That were a present far too small, / Love so amazing, so Divine, / Demands my soul, my life, my all."[42]

While Truett was sailing back home, Robert H. Coleman, who had attended the congress and returned home before his pastor, presented a report on the meeting to FBC. Coleman noted that Nazi officials, through Reich Bishop Ludwig Müller, head of the German state church, had assured BWA leaders that the 70,000 German Baptists and other members' "free churches," such as Methodists and Presbyterians, would not be forced to join the state church. Coleman also expressed his opinion that "the more cultured people, the best people of the country were not in sympathy with" Hitler or his "ideals. However, the plain man in the street almost worships him. Hitler is improving conditions and the masses of the people are undoubtedly for him. His supporters tell lots of things in his favor."[43] As Erich Geldbach remarked, however, "German Baptists...learned" soon after congress ended "that their newfound freedom was an illusion; they, like all other religious groups, would have to submit to the dictates of the Nazi state. They and the BWA had been victims of massive self-deception."[44] Nevertheless, despite grave reservations on the part of many Baptists, the BWA had met in Berlin. While there, messengers voted to hold their 1939 congress in Atlanta, a choice that caused concern among many Baptists, particularly in the African-American Baptist community.

### "That Man"

Truett's election to head the BWA elated many Southern Baptists, particularly in Texas. For example, the members of the committee responsible for publishing the *Centennial Story of Texas Baptists* in 1936 dedicated the book to Truett, calling him "Texas Baptists' Gift to the World."[45] Not all Texas Baptists, however, rejoiced at his election. J. Frank Norris's long-held disdain for the BWA's new president was equaled by his contempt for the organization itself, which he called "the biggest cuckoo frame-up ever known among Baptists."[46] Rushbrooke, Norris declared to his Detroit congregation on January 13, 1935, was "a rank modernist," but "when he comes South he preaches orthodox sermons." Another BWA supporter, Albert W. Beaven, president of Colgate-Rochester Divinity School, was, according to Norris, "one of the smoothest modernists, and he too when he goes South speaks oily words of orthodoxy." Truett, whom Beaven used "as a wall-flower," was a dupe of the BWA "modernist machine," which had fooled him to go "up and down the land speaking in behalf of" the organization. Although Truett "extends the hand of orthodoxy, yet the hidden voice is that of modernism."[47]

Despite pastoring two large congregations, one in Fort Worth, the other in Detroit, Norris apparently had a lot of spare time on his hands, some of which he dedicated to making Truett's life miserable, or, as Norris wrote in 1929 to his friend Victor I. Masters, shooting his arrows in every "joint" in Truett's "harness."[48]

The Fort Worth/Detroit fundamentalist pastor took every opportunity he had to pin Truett down on theological issues so as to use the Dallas pastor's words against him, and Norris had help in doing so. While vacationing in St. Petersburg, Florida, in February 1931, John Graham attended a revival led by Truett at First Baptist Church, St. Petersburg. Having heard that the revered Dallas pastor did not believe in the verbal inspiration of the Bible, the theory that God inspired the very words of scripture, Graham placed a note in the offering plate requesting Truett to "[p]lease state from the platform if you believe in the verbal inspiration of the Bible, I hear it reported you do not?"[49] The next day Truett responded from the pulpit to Graham's note, declaring his unwavering orthodoxy in terms that should have been clear to anyone:

> You ask me if I believe in the divine inspiration of the Holy Scriptures? I answer, I most certainly do…. You ask me if I believe in the virgin birth and absolute deity of Christ? I answer, I most certainly do…. You ask me if I believe in the vicarious suffering and substitutionary death of Christ for our redemption? I answer, I most certainly do. You ask me if I believe that this gospel plan is the only way out and up for sinful souls? I answer, I most certainly

do.... You ask me if I believe in the Bible doctrine of hell? I answer, I most certainly do.... You ask me if I believe in the literal second coming of our Lord? I answer, I most certainly do.[50]

Norris wrote to Graham, thanking him for the report on Truett and asking him to "kindly write" the Dallas pastor and ask for a written statement concerning "the verbal inspiration of the Scriptures and send his reply to me and I shall be very glad to publish the same." According to Norris, Truett was on record in Texas as rejecting the doctrine of verbal inspiration, so Norris wanted to "publish and broadcast" Truett's statement.[51]

Norris's obsession with Truett was not merely theological; it was personal. In a 1936 article for the *Baptist Standard*, J. N. Marshall, the pastor in Llano, Texas, who, in 1891, offered one of the first invitations to Truett to speak on behalf of the Baylor debt retirement campaign, referred to Norris's personal attacks on Truett. After a prayer meeting at FBC in 1936, Marshall felt compelled to express his "sorrow and pain" to his friend "because of frequent unworthy and ugly thrusts at him" by Norris, who had called Truett "the 'Baptist Pope,' the 'Holy Father,' and other things. I'm sure," Marshall wrote, "that all of his friends have felt incensed and outraged at such treatment. I knew that many telegrams and letters had been sent to him trying to excite some reply. Such had been going on for a long time, and may be, still for all I know."[52] After Marshall expressed his sentiments to Truett, the famed pastor merely remarked, "I have turned all of that over to the Lord. What I am concerned about, J. N., is that our people may be one, that they may do right, go forward, and do the work that will please Christ and glorify him; that's all; that's all." According to Marshall, his friend "seemed to be entirely indifferent to the criticism."[53]

The telegrams and letters to which Marshall referred were usually written by Norris on Saturdays. The date on which he began sending these messages to Truett is unknown, but Norris was still sending them in March 1940. The messages arrived either at Truett's home or office, sometimes at both places, usually before he was to preach on Sunday mornings. Norris's goal was obviously to upset his Dallas foe and perhaps to get Truett to attack him publicly as others did, something on which Norris thrived.

In a diary entry for February 12, 1938, Truett, obviously referring to one of Norris's mischievous missives, wrote: "The wretched letter sent me this afternoon—one copy to the church office and the other copy to my home by the hand of a messenger boy—which letter was carefully sealed and drawn out into several pages, was taken to the Lord and committed to Him and for His management."[54] Several of Truett's friends recalled that these messages contained such things as, "How can you stand before your people today and preach Christ, when your heart is so black and full of sin?"[55]

Eventually, Robert Coleman and Josephine Truett began intercepting the letters and telegrams before they reached Truett. What they did with them is unknown, but they probably destroyed them. Fortunately, however, Coleman saved at least one of the letters, one that Norris penned on Saturday, March 9, 1940, and one that drips with sarcasm and hubris. Norris typed the following instructions on the envelope: "Special Delivery" and "DELIVERY TO BE MADE AFTER 8 AM."[56]

After addressing his letter to "My dear Dr. Truett," Norris claimed that Truett would agree with him that "the basest sin known to man under heaven is the sin of ingratitude. When people have rendered a man great favors he indeed is small who forgets the kindly hand that favored him." "When you jumped on me," Norris continued, "I was very frail in body, timid and unknown. I was preaching only to average crowds and having average results in my meetings, about like results that you and other pastors were having." My "most serious trials and ordeals," however, came not from my "court house experiences, or the conspiracies of the under world" but from you, Truett, when you threw your "weight of...great influence, and that at the time when you were in the zenith of your power and influence—throwing the weight of a great denominational machine against one man according to all the rules of the game was calculated to destroy that man." I have always known that you were the moving force behind such schemes, but I had not known all the details until recently.

Soon, Truett, a book will be published revealing the "midnight caucuses, [and] proceedings of boards and committees, where you thought that you were safely hidden behind the scenes."[57]

Norris was not bitter for what Truett had tried to do to him; rather, he was grateful because Truett had rendered him "a great service when on Monday morning before the Convention met in Dallas twenty years ago you told a group concerning me, 'We will end it right now. It is just like thumping an ox.'" When someone told me what you said, I trembled, "for I knew you could thump me off just like gangsters bump off their victims, except a man can expect more mercy from the gangsters of the underworld than he can from the hands of ecclesiastical dictators."[58]

All of your shenanigans to destroy me, Norris continued, and all of your predictions that I would end up "on the junk heap" have proven to be futile and false. Everything you have said about me and done to me has emanated "from your enraged and angered soul" and has "scared me most terribly." Yet your attacks have "challenged me" and "rendered me a great service." By God's grace, I have risen from being "a frail preacher broken in health, broken in purse, broken in nerves, broken in every way" to "enjoying the best of health, and [pastoring] the two largest churches on the American continent, and [having] the two largest attended Sunday Schools in the world." Moreover, unlike you, Truett, who needs publicity agents to trumpet your ministry, I need no one because the "Associated Press, United Press, and International News, carry regular items on my work."[59]

Both of us are "nearing our eternal and glorious home," Norris reminded Truett. "Perhaps you will precede me, and perhaps not. Then we will have lots of joy in talking it all over when we meet on the other shore." In the meantime, "I wanted you to know now that the multiplied thousands that I have reached in my ministry, and the increasing thousands that I am now reaching—a large part of the credit belongs to you."[60]

Evidently, Truett never responded publicly to Norris's harassments. Once when a fellow pastor began criticizing Norris for his attacks, Truett responded, "Now, now, brother, we don't talk about those things."[61] Privately, however, he did talk about "those things," confiding to friends that the attacks eventually began to bother him. During those conversations, however, he refused to speak unkindly about Norris, nor did he even mention the name of his nemesis, preferring to refer to the polemicist as "that man" or "that man in Fort Worth."[62] As Gwin Morris remarked, of all the Texas Baptist leaders whom Norris attacked, "Only Truett had the good sense to ignore" him.[63]

### A Shepherding Tour of the World

The letters and telegrams from Norris that Truett actually received obviously pained him. Yet such spiteful missives did not reach Truett when he was out of the country, and as president of the BWA, he set out in fall 1935 on what an acquaintance called a "shepherding tour of the world."[64] That November, with the full support of his church, which paid for his travel expenses, Truett embarked on a six-month tour of the Far East to preach in "mystical India[,]…age-old China[,]…Burma (now Myanmar), and…alert Japan."[65] Along with Josephine, he sailed first to England, where they met Rushbrooke, who accompanied them on their journey. Josephine had begun traveling with her husband, making sure that he ate the right foods on his trips.[66]

That FBC would tolerate, much less encourage, Truett's extended absences from his pulpit might seem unusual. However, according to Mildred Lively, who, as a young girl, participated in the church's youth ministry and later became the church's librarian in 1957, "We were taught, as young people, that it was our duty to share our Pastor with the world that needed him so badly."[67] Thus, sharing Truett's ministry with others constituted part of the FBC's world-wide mission ministry; it was an act of stewardship.

After visiting Egypt and Palestine, the Truetts and Rushbrooke traveled to India, where they spent five and a half weeks. They visited many cities, including Bombay (now Mumbai) on the west coast; Ongole, on the east coast; Telugu, in the south; Calcutta (now Kolkata) on the east coast; and New Delhi, in north-central India.

While in India, Truett preached to large crowds and spoke informally with smaller groups of people when time permitted. In Calcutta, he spent three hours one evening, from nine until midnight, speaking to a hostile group at a university. The Indian accompanying Truett warned him that the students would attempt to anger him by asking embarrassing questions, such as why Christian America murdered people for things that they had done and why it had the most crime-ridden cities in the world. The group did ask such questions, and it also criticized America and England for sending Christian missionaries to evangelize Hindus and Muslims.[68]

Truett denied the group's assertion that America was a Christian nation. "If you have the impression that my country is a Christian land, you are mistaken," he informed the students. "It is not a Christian land. There are a great number of Christians there, thank God, and various Christian groups; but ours is not a Christian land. We have wicked, congested cities; and sometimes our men, unrestrained by any thought of mercy or compassion, leap upon a fellow-man and take his life like some simple beast; but we are trying to make a Christian country out of our country. If all of our people would follow Christ and His teachings, we would have a Christian country."[69]

As for the group's criticism of sending Christian missionaries to India, Truett responded, "My dear men, if I had a serious illness and found a sure remedy and heard that you were affected with the same illness, shouldn't I bring you that remedy?" After the meeting, one man told him, "We have no fault to find with your Christ. We believe that he is the light of the world."[70]

In an article published in the April 9, 1936, edition of the *Baptist Standard*, Josephine described for Texas Baptists the strange customs she had observed in India. Men and women go barefooted everywhere, even to church, she wrote, and the traffic in Calcutta "makes one's head go around." The "most surprising thing" she had witnessed was "the great Brahma bulls, that are sacred animals, dedicated to the gods, and this huge animal is allowed to roam at will," eating wherever and whatever it wants while no one objects.[71]

From India the Truetts and Rushbrooke traveled to Burma, where they spent several weeks. They attended a district meeting of Burmese Baptists that was attended by 5,000 people.[72] The Truetts and Rushbrooke also traveled to Amhurst (now Kyaikkami), on the southeast coast of the country to visit the grave of Ann Hasseltine Judson, a Baptist missionary in Burma from 1812 until her death in 1826. "Wonderful woman!" Truett said of Judson. "Inexpressible emotions filled our hearts as we stood by her grave."[73]

In Rangoon, Josephine contracted a tropical fever, which forced her to spend nearly two weeks in bed. After recovering from her illness, she and her husband joined Rushbrooke, who had gone ahead to China. The Truetts had dreamed for many years of visiting China, where Josephine's sister Annie and her husband, W. Eugene Sallee, were missionaries in Kaifong, Honan Province. Annie traveled with the Truetts during part of their visit to China. In a letter written en route to Hong Kong on March 4, 1936, Truett informed his good friend J. B. Cranfill that the previous weeks had been "strenuous" because of "needless travel and much speaking. It has been glorious beyond words to see with my own eyes and hear with my own ears the mighty triumphs of Christ's gospel in these far-off pagan lands. In addition to my daily public messages to the people, I have had many most interesting general conversations and conferences with individuals. Interesting authors and other challenging fellows are found on a ship like this. What a study of human nature such a journey gives."[74]

During his stay in China, Truett preached in several Chinese cities and towns, drawing large crowds of Christians and non-believers. For one sermon, three elderly Chinese, one man and two women, walked forty-five miles to hear him preach.[75] His five days in Canton, Truett informed Coleman in a March 12, 1936, letter, "were days of God's right hand. His gracious hand crowned every service," as the meetings produced 200 conversions. "Never, forever, can I get away from the inspiration and blessedness of these five days in Canton!" he told his assistant. After the

Sunday morning service, 1,200 worshippers remained to observe the Lord's Supper, the sight of which moved "the heart to the deepest depths."[76]

In Hong Kong, the Truetts and Rushbrooke participated in the Henrietta Shuck Centennial, which celebrated the life and ministry of Henrietta Hall Shuck, the first American woman missionary to China. Shuck and her husband, John, began their ministry as Baptist missionaries in 1837 on the Chinese island of Macao before settling in Hong Kong in 1842. She died there two years later at the age of twenty-seven.[77] At Shuck's gravesite, Truett gave "a brief address" and Rushbrooke "offered a most fervent prayer." Although she "did not live long in years," Truett wrote to Coleman, "she lived much, and continues to live on and on, in her notably gracious and challenging life and service."[78]

After several weeks in China, the Truetts and Rushbrooke traveled to Japan, which Truett described as an "incomparably beautiful country."[79] After spending fifteen days there, the trio sailed first to Honolulu and then to San Francisco. From there they traveled to St. Louis to attend the annual SBC meeting, after which Truett spoke at a joint meeting of the SBC and the Northern Baptist Convention, which met following the SBC meeting. During his speech, Truett said that his recent tour of the Far East "was the most laborious, yet the most heartening trip" of his life. From St. Louis, the Truetts returned to Dallas, where he resumed his preaching duties at FBC on May 24, 1936.[80]

After spending nearly two and a half months in Dallas, Truett traveled in early August to the "Far West" for his annual preaching engagement with the cowboys of West Texas. That engagement lasted until August 10. Then, along with Josephine, he traveled to the Baptist encampment in Ridgecrest, North Carolina, where he presented two addresses during the SBC's Foreign Mission Board conference on August 13 and 14. On the way to Ridgecrest, Truett wrote to J. M. Dawson, pastor of First Baptist Church, Waco, thanking him for the recent funeral message that he had preached for Truett's sister, Sarah. "All of us must ever cherish the remembrance of your blessed words, with inexpressible gratitude," Truett told his good friend. "How the years are hurrying away for us all! It matters not how fast they go, if only we are faithful to Him, Whose we are and Whom we live to serve!"[81] After Ridgecrest, the Truetts visited their daughter Mary and her family in Lynchburg, Virginia, and then returned to the North Carolina encampment for Preaching Week from August 23 to 30, before returning home to Dallas.[82]

In fall 1936, Truett participated in the Federal Council of Churches' (FCC) National Preaching Mission, the goal of which, according to the *Dallas Morning News*, was to send speakers to twenty-five key cities, including Dallas, "to rekindle the religious life of those in the churches and to bring the Christian message, and call to Christian discipleship to many who are outside the churches."[83] The week-long meetings, which were held from mid-September through early December, essentially followed the same schedule: morning meetings for ministers and women; luncheons for lay leaders and church workers; noontime evangelistic meetings; afternoon seminars for ministers and lay leaders, and conferences for young people; worship services during the evenings; and large services on Sundays.[84]

Along with Truett, the mission included speakers such as E. Stanley Jones, a missionary in India; Murial Lester, a Christian social worker in London; Francis B. Sayer, Assistant Secretary of State; Douglas Southall Freeman, a journalist; George A. Buttrick, pastor of Madison Avenue Presbyterian Church, New York; and Paul E. Scherer, pastor of Lutheran Church of the Holy Trinity, New York. Organizers of the mission asked Truett to attend all twenty-five meetings, but he could only attend a few of them.[85]

When Mary E. Ponce de Leon, a member of Norris's Detroit congregation, learned that Truett had accepted the invitation to join the Preaching Mission, she wrote to him in August while he was at Ridgecrest for Preaching Week. Ponce de Leon rebuked Truett for associating himself with such an ungodly organization: "Surely, Dr. Truett, you know,—a man of your understanding and ability, spiritually and other wise,—that this [Federal] Council of Churches is nothing but a tool of Communism."[86] Death can come at any moment, she warned Truett, evoking the memory of W. J. McGlothlin, who, according to Ponce de Leon, had tried to unite the Southern Baptist Convention with the "liberal" Northern Baptist Convention. "The scriptures say," she reminded Truett ominously: "'There will come sudden destruction'[1 Thess. 5:3]."[87]

Truett ignored such "advice" as Ponce de Leon's. He saw the Preaching Mission as an opportunity to preach the gospel, as he understood it, to thousands of people he might otherwise never reach. Thus, when the invitation to join the mission had come, he readily accepted it.

Accepting the FCC's invitation to join the Preaching Mission was easy; however, traveling to some of the cities, particularly the mode of transportation, proved to be an obstacle for Truett, at least prior to the start of the mission. "I have not yet taken to *flying*, and am hesitant about such method of travel," Truett had confided in a 1933 letter to a friend.[88] Truett also expressed his concern about flying to his family, which evoked a loving jab from his daughter Jessie. "If you have ridden with Mother for forty years," she kidded her father, "wouldn't you be brave enough to fly in any sort of an airplane?"[89] Truett's love of preaching eventually conquered his fear of flying. After addressing the Oklahoma Baptist Convention, during which he raised $58,000 ($867,664) to help the convention discharge its debt, Truett boarded a plane the next day in Oklahoma City and flew to Chicago. After deplaning in Chicago, a photographer snapped a picture of Truett, who looked like the proverbial deer caught in the headlights; however, he recovered well enough to preach to 10,000 people.[90]

Truett encountered another problem that almost made him quit the mission. He toured with E. Stanley Jones, even though they had different personalities and theological outlooks. They alternated preaching, and each agreed to preach his own convictions. One night in Kansas City, Jones often said, "We believe," referring to Truett and himself. Jones, however, said things with which Truett did not agree, such as denominational loyalty being one of the major stumbling blocks of Christianity. Truett told mission leaders that, while he respected Jones's missionary service, he would not continue touring unless Jones stopped saying, "We believe." "I am a denominationalist," Truett informed the organizers. "I believe in denominations. I do not believe that God meant for all people to be in the same denomination. There are many denominations, and in this way the gospel reaches more people. I wouldn't make a Southern Baptist out of everybody in the world if I could. I want the world to know that though I am in this national preaching mission, I am a denominationalist. Therefore, I request that Dr. Jones say, 'I believe,' instead of 'We believe.'"[91] Truett was granted his request, for he continued with the mission, preaching during two Dallas mission meetings in mid-November and early December.[92]

*Another Great Journey*

Having participated in the Preaching Mission in fall 1936, a weary Truett noted in his diary entry for January 15, 1937: "Have had a graciously restful evening at home—a privilege profoundly prized by me."[93] Though prized, such a privilege was brief because on January 19, he arrived in Orlando, Florida, for a ten-day preaching engagement. After preaching three times on January 24, he wrote in his diary: "I am weary tonight—not *of* the work, but *in* it!"[94]

On May 6, 1937, Truett turned seventy years old. "It is almost impossible for me to realize that I am three score and ten years old today!" he recorded in his diary. "Emotions very deep stir in my heart today. My gratitude to God is inexpressible, for His marvelous and never-ceasing goodness and mercy to me."[95] For a birthday present, the church's Woman's Missionary Society presented him with a check for $15,351 ($221,651), which he announced would go towards reducing the church's building debt.[96] Truett described the gift as "a beautiful, glorious expression, and I must ever keep it in most grateful remembrance."[97]

A little more than three weeks later, on May 28, Mr. and Mrs. Cullen F. Thomas hosted a dinner for their pastor and his wife. Nearly fifty FBC deacons attended the dinner, which was held shortly before the Truetts left on another BWA trip, this time to Europe.[98] On this tour, which would take the Truetts to Baptist regional conferences in England, Wales, Scotland, France, Holland, Sweden, Germany, Latvia, Poland, Romania, Hungary, and Switzerland, Truett would preach two to three times a day and hold the same number of daily conferences.

Shortly before leaving Dallas, Truett wrote to J. M. Dawson, informing his good friend that he and "Mrs. Truett" were leaving soon "on our great journey" to Europe. Truett asked that Dawson and his wife "uphold us in your prayers, to the end that our journey and mission may all be according to the will of God!"[99]

The Truetts left Dallas on Sunday evening, June 13, and arrived in New York City on June 17, after spending a few days in Atlanta, Georgia, and Lynchburg, Virginia. They left New York at midnight on June 18 and arrived at the southern port city of Southampton, England, around noon on June 24. At 3:00 p.m., they left for London, where they met Rushbrooke, who would accompany them while they were in Europe.

After five and a half days in London, the Truetts and Rushbrooke traveled to Cardiff, Wales. During a service there on June 20, Truett so thrilled the congregation that the people asked that the evening events be cancelled so that he could preach again.[100] He enjoyed preaching to Welsh Baptists, for it reminded him of preaching to African Americans. During his sermons in Wales, as many as fifty people at a time would respond, "You said it, say it again." Such interruptions, however, did not bother him.[101] The service the next day in Llanelly, Wales, proved to be as exciting as the ones in Cardiff. "The enthusiasm in the meeting tonight was profoundly fervent," Truett noted in his diary. "The singing was the [most] fervent and victorious that I have heard in all the world. It excels the singing of the Negroes of the South, and that is saying much."[102]

After returning briefly to London, the Truetts and Rushbrooke spent a week in Scotland, where Truett found Baptists to be as pious as Welsh Baptists, yet much more sedate. He described the Scottish Baptists as "dignified and precise. The word 'Amen' never escapes their lips. I wished somebody would say or do something that would let me know whether I was getting anywhere."[103]

The Truetts and Rushbrooke arrived back in London on July 12 and sailed to France the following day. After a day in France, they stopped briefly in Holland before spending three days in Sweden and then three days in the German cities of Berlin and Köningsberg. Truett described the situation in Germany as "very serious, very tense. On every hand there is constraint, there is religious persecution," which, however, had yet to affect smaller groups like Baptists, Methodists, and Presbyterians.[104] All the time he "felt…something in the air terribly suggestive of fear, that there was some premonition that all was not well."[105]

Truett's impressions of Germany were well founded. On the evening of June 30, three weeks prior to Truett's arrival in Berlin, Hitler instigated a three-day purge, known as the Night of the Long Knives, during which a former German chancellor was executed, as were several leaders of Hitler's personal militia, the Brownshirts. Two weeks later, the Führer informed Germans that political dissent would not be tolerated: "Everyone must know that in all future time, if he raises his hand to strike at the State, then certain death will be his lot."[106]

The Truetts and Rushbrooke left Germany on July 24 and arrived that evening in Riga, Latvia. The two men met with the Latvian president, Karlis Ulmanis, whom the Dallas pastor described as "a forceful man."[107] In his report to FBC members after returning from Europe, Truett said that Ulmanis had asked them, "Tell me just what you Baptists aim at; what are your objectives?" They answered that Baptists "stood for indefeasible, unrestricted religious liberty for every person, granting them the privilege to worship God according to the dictates of their own consciences; *that this was asked not simply for our Baptist people, but as much and equally for everybody else for Jews, Catholics, all.*" At this point, according to Truett, the president stood and, sounding surprisingly like Truett, declared, "*THAT IS PRECIOUS, PRICELESS AND OUGHT TO BE THE WAY OF EVERY PEOPLE IN ALL THE WORLD.*"[108]

After three full days in Latvia, the Truetts and Rushbrooke traveled to Poland, spending two and a half days there before leaving for Romania on July 30. They arrived in the Romanian capital, Bucharest, at 5:00 p.m. the following day. On August 2, Rushbrooke and Truett met with the country's Secretary of the Ministry of Cults, the government organization charged with overseeing, and perhaps persecuting, Romanian churches. "The Conference greatly disturbed and distressed us," Truett noted in his diary. "We are profoundly concerned for our churches in Romania. The Lord be their guide and refuge and strength, in these troublesome days."[109] The Romanian situation "saddened" them "in a terrible way," grieved their hearts, and robbed them "of sleep for the three nights and days" they stayed in Bucharest. Despite the ominous situation in the country, Romanian Baptists packed a large hall in the capital city, where Truett and Rushbrooke spoke three times daily, while government officials wrote down their every word.[110]

On August 3, the Truetts and Rushbrooke left Romania for Hungary, where they spent two and a half days. After Hungary, the trio spent two and a half days in Switzerland, after which they returned to France.

Sailing from France on August 13, the Truetts arrived in New York City five days later. From New York, they traveled to Lynchburg, Virginia, to visit their daughter Mary and her family, arriving there around 7:00 a.m. on August 19. Around midnight on August 20, Truett left for Ridgecrest, North Carolina, to participate in Preaching Week. After returning to Lynchburg, he conducted prayer meeting on September 1 at the church where Mary and her family worshipped. After the service, he baptized his granddaughter, whom he called "little Truett." "It was my sacred privilege to baptize the precious Child, at the close of the Church Prayer Meeting," he recorded in his diary. "She was altogether quiet, self-controlled and serious—not at all excited or afraid."[111]

Departing Lynchburg at 9:40 p.m. on September 8, the Truetts arrived in Dallas after a twelve-hour train ride. A "goodly group of loved ones and friends" met them at the station, Truett recorded in his diary. "It was glorious to see them and to realize that we are again at home! God be thanked forever for His guiding and keeping mercy with unto us all!"[112]

In describing his recent visit with European Baptists, Truett told his congregation that he had returned "home more deeply concerned for and more profoundly interested in our age-old doctrine of religious liberty than ever before. I came home to say to you that wisdom has fallen away from us if we sleep at the switch and allow sinister influences to invade this country circumventing religious liberty, if we sleep at the switch and allow such hurtful influences any place in the social order in this country."[113] He urged his congregation to keep their "eyes, ears and minds wide open that religious liberty may not be trampled into the dust and that the church shall not play mentor to the civil government, and that the civil government may not play mentor to the church."[114]

In September 12, 1937, Truett celebrated his fortieth anniversary as FBC's pastor. In his honor, the *Baptist Standard* dedicated almost its entire September 9, 1937, issue to Truett. The issue contained praises from friends, colleagues, and institutions such as Baylor Hospital, formerly known as the Texas Baptist Memorial Sanitarium, whose entry covered a full page. The hospital noted that without Truett, "it would not have existed; his idealism permeates its service as school and hospital. Over quarter of million patients cared for in its beds. Thousands of new-born babes cared for in its nursery. Hundreds and hundreds of doctors, dentists, and nurses trained, graduated, and sent out to lives of high professional service. These nurses and doctors are found on mission fields clear around the world, serving with patience and skill. Hundreds of crippled children sent out to walk in gladness."[115] The September 9 issue also contained brief articles on Coleman and Josephine by Franz M. (F. M.) McConnell, the *Standard*'s editor. McConnell described Josephine as a woman who "kept the home, mothered the children, led the women, kept fully up with the work of the church and the denomination, looked after the pastor's health constantly, guarded him against hurtful foods on this travels in the Orient and in Europe, counseled him in times of stress and perplexity and consoled him in hours of deep sorrow and distress."[116]

The following year, 1938, Josephine had ample time to console her husband when a severe bout of the flu kept him from preaching for nearly two months, from late April to late June. He spent the second month of his illness in Baylor Hospital.[117] Josephine stayed continually with her husband during his hospital stay. After Truett was released from the hospital, she briefly described for her son-in-law Powhatan W. James how severe her husband's illness had been: "My job hasn't been an easy one these past months. It is very sweet to me and a source of comfort to him to know that all through his unconsciousness and delirium from fever or medicine his subconscious mind was just as clear and Christian as his daily life has always been. As you probably know I did not leave his bed side for the four weeks of his hospitalization nor the weeks since." Despite lying in a hospital bed, Truett had continued to preach to and pray for sinners, even though his congregation existed only in his subconscious. "In his talking (in delirium)," Josephine informed James, "he was quoting scripture—preaching—calling men to Christ or praying for them. I feel that his illness was a great revelation of the real man."[118]

A week after his release from the hospital in late June, despite his weakened condition, Truett made one more trip on behalf of the BWA. In July, the seventy-one-year-old preacher took a twelve-day trip to western Canada, where he spoke on eleven different occasions.[119]

Despite his two-month absence from preaching, Truett kept a torrid pace in 1938, even for a man half his age. He preached at least 199 sermons, officiated at 19 weddings, presented 46 addresses, and officiated at 24 funerals. He was absent from Dallas for 140 days, preaching in Canada, West Texas, 8 different Texas cities, and the states of Oklahoma, Florida, West Virginia, Missouri (twice), North Carolina, Virginia, Tennessee, and Colorado.[120]

In an interview published in February 1937, Truett had been asked to give advice to students. Quoting Benjamin Franklin, he responded, "'Value time, for time is the stuff of which life is made.' And over the gateway to the tomb of many a man who has failed might be written the cause of his failure in these two words, 'He dawdled.'"[121] Many things could be said about Truett, but never could it be said that "he dawdled." Having made two lengthy trips on behalf of the BWA to two continents, and one brief trip to Canada, Truett had one more major task to fulfill as president of that organization—presiding at the 1939 BWA congress in Atlanta.

### A Baptist Avalanche in Atlanta, 1939

The choice of Atlanta to host the 1939 BWA congress was controversial. According to Frank H. Leavell, secretary of the SBC's Sunday School Board (SSB), the city apparently was ill-prepared to host such a meeting. He wrote to Truett in November 1937, informing the BWA's president that the city's auditorium was a death trap, part of the roof having already fallen in, and the hotel accommodations were inadequate to house the thousands of people expected to attend the congress. Leavell wondered whether the BWA should hold its congress in Philadelphia or Washington, D.C.[122]

Leavell also alerted Truett to another obstacle that threatened the BWA's holding its congress in Atlanta: several SBC leaders had "received communications from some of the colored brethren indicating an issue will be made in the matter of seating the delegates in the auditorium. Deplorable as that would be, should it eventuate, that is not the only issue to be considered. Some of the Atlanta pastors say that they see no way in which that matter can be handled without provoking a disturbance which might go to doubtful ends."[123]

Organizers of the 1936 Preaching Mission had encountered a similar problem concerning racial issues when the mission held one of its meetings in Atlanta. According to *Time* magazine, an editorial in the *Atlanta Constitution* stated politely but pointedly that, although "[t]here should be earnest and full co-operation by the Christian people of Atlanta in the constructive and inspirational meetings to be held during the next four days," many of Atlanta's white ministers did not want a "public controversy" and insisted that the mission rescind its stipulation that at least one African American be included among the speakers during each mission stop. According to *Time*, despite pleas from mission participants and local African-American ministers, "the Preaching Mission followed its schedule, 100% white."[124]

The thought of having a "100% white" BWA congress horrified many people, both whites and blacks. Responding to a letter in March 1937 from Wifrid L. McKay, a Canadian, Truett attempted to counteract the "amazing statements" about the religious conditions of Southern blacks that McKay had read in his hometown newspaper. Truett noted that he had often worked with African-American Baptists, preaching for them, speaking with them, and holding "conferences with their various and sundry committees about the Christian work, both local and general. It has been my delight all the years to help them in every way that I could, and my case is not exceptional—it is the spirit of our white Baptist people everywhere in this section, so far as I have ever known or heard." Truett admitted "that the negroes have their own churches and denominational organizations, which policy is just as they prefer. Time and time again, however, negroes may be seen in our white congregations, both in the local churches and in general meetings, and they are made welcome there." In concluding his letter, Truett stated, "The leaders of these two races, living side by side, are continually praying, planning and striving to make the relations between the races just what our Savior and Lord would have them to be."[125]

In a September 1938 letter to Truett, M. McElroy Flynn, pastor of an African-American Baptist church in Shreveport, Louisiana, wrote that he had heard rumors that "Negro Baptist[s] will be 'jim-crowed'" at the BWA congress in Atlanta. If that was true, "Baptist colored people face a grave and growing crisis" and "are reluctant to lead our people into such embarrassments." "Feeling that 'jim-crow' religious meetings are in absolute contradiction to the teachings of Jesus," Flynn continued, "we are asking that you will please do all in your power to make it comfortable for the colored brethern [sic] at the 1939 meeting. As we march on toward Atlanta we shall expect the banner of 'Brotherly Love' to be our guide and the order of the day."[126]

Despite the several obstacles to Atlanta's hosting the BWA congress, the city held the organization's sixth congress on July 22–28. Thousands of Baptists from around the world descended on the city, in what one

African American from Atlanta described as a "Baptist avalanche."[127] The official registration for the congress was 12,445 messengers, but perhaps as many as 67,000 people attended one of the sessions. The baseball stadium of the Atlanta Crackers was set up to host nine sessions, while churches and the city's auditorium held smaller sessions. Many visitors stayed in Atlanta hotels, while others lodged in boardinghouses, at campgrounds, or in the homes of Atlanta families.[128] During the congress, Truett noted in his diary: "What crowds are here! Nothing to equal it, I suppose, in all the history of Baptists."[129]

As for the fear that African Americans would be humiliated at the congress, the thirteen African-American members of the organizing committee and the twenty white members, including Louie D. Newton, an acquaintance of Truett since 1909 and pastor of Atlanta's Druid Hills Baptist Church, made sure that such humiliation never happened. According to Ernest A. Payne, a British Baptist historian, "One of the most noticeable features of the Atlanta Congress was the large part played by the negro Baptists. Never before at a great international religious assembly have negroes shared so fully in both the preliminary arrangements and the actual proceedings. That this took place in the Southern States of America gave it added significance." Payne also noted that even "the geographical labels which had been placed for convenience on certain of the stands were removed to avert even the suspicion that they might imply a colour distinction."[130] Apparently, laws prohibiting the "mingling of the races" had been suspended during the congress, although whether segregated seating was enforced cannot be determined from the proceedings of the congress.[131]

Truett had visited Atlanta several times in his life before arriving there in July 1939. His first visit to the city occurred while he was teaching school in Hiawasee, Georgia, in 1887. He and his cousin Sam E. McConnell traveled to Atlanta to see President Grover Cleveland, who was visiting the city. The two young men stood in mud for two hours waiting for the train that would take them to Atlanta. At that point in his life, Truett had never been to a big city, nor had he ever seen a train. After hearing the president speak, the cousins ate dinner at a restaurant offering diners all the pancakes and syrup they could eat for only 25¢ ($5.62). On the Sunday of their trip, they visited First Baptist Church, Atlanta, to hear J. B. Hawthorne preach. After the service McConnell remarked to his cousin, "George, some day you will be pastor of a great church like that, and people will travel for miles to see and hear you." Truett gave his usual response to such predictions, stating that his life-long dream was to be a lawyer, to which McConnell responded: "Yes, I know, but I will live, I hope, to see you preaching somewhere, and I stick by my prophecy— people will travel further than we have traveled to hear Dr. Hawthorne to hear you."[132]

Fifty years later in Atlanta, McConnell's "prophecy" concerning his cousin came true. On Monday night, July 17, 1939, Truett, along with Josephine, their daughter Annie Truett Milliken, and their eight-year-old granddaughter, Joanne Milliken, arrived in Atlanta. *Time* magazine described the scene at the city's train station:

> A 300-voiced choir and the Georgia State Girls' Military Band burst into "Praise God From Whom All Blessings Flow." A huge throng of Atlantans, ringing Terminal Station Plaza, cheered and handclapped as a white-haired man, large of frame, square of face, firm of jaw, stepped from the station. Atlanta's Mayor William Berry Hartsfield, a representative of Georgia's Governor Eurith Dickinson Rivers, Baptist ministers white and black greeted him—Rev. Dr. George Washington Truett, best-known Baptist in the world.[133]

The greeting at the station thrilled Josephine, but the motorcycle escort of Atlanta policemen from the station to the Biltmore Hotel unsettled her. She noted that had the Atlanta police officers run red lights in Dallas, they "would have gotten a ticket for us."[134]

To open the congress, Baptists held a parade in Atlanta on Saturday, July 22, another one of Truett's "never-to-be-forgotten" days.[135] A crowd of 125,000 lined the streets as nearly 50,000 Baptists marched or rode slowly in cars through downtown. Along the parade route, flags from every country, including the swastika, hung from buildings. The parade, which began at noon, halted briefly at the junction of Peachtree and Ponce de Leon streets as Mayor Hartsfield presented Truett with the key to the city. The parade ended at the Atlanta Crackers' stadium, where Truett opened the first session congress at 2:00 p.m., with an attendance estimated between 40,000 and 67,000.[136]

On Sunday afternoon, July 23, Truett delivered his presidential address, titled "The Baptist Message and Mission for the World Today." Fifty years earlier when he spoke to a modest crowd at the 1889 Georgia Baptist Convention in Marietta, Georgia, Truett was an unknown school teacher in North Georgia. Now, just as his cousin Sam had predicted, Truett was a world-famous pastor about to preach to the thousands of people who had filed through the turnstiles of the baseball stadium and to a host of others who would listen on the radio. Many years later, Newton recalled standing alongside the Atlanta fire chief and watching the turnstiles click. "Now when that thing clicks 67,000," the chief told Newman, "you stop. We can't admit any more than that because I think all reasonable people know that we have got to be able to get those people out of that place in the event of any unexpected development." When the number hit 67,000, no one else was let in. Later, while sitting in the stadium's press box with the mayor, the fire chief, the police chief, and other Atlanta dignitaries, Newton asked the fire chief "to look down there in the street— Ponce de Leon—and tell me how many people you would estimate are standing out there who can't get in." The chief responded, "I believe that 20,000 to 25,000 people are out there."[137]

Truett had written out his address and given copies to journalists, yet, as was his custom, he spoke without notes. For nearly an hour, on a "blisteringly hot Atlanta afternoon,"[138] he proclaimed the Baptist message of religious liberty and the Baptist mission of evangelism. Fortunately, congress organizers had the address recorded. On the recording, one can hear Truett, as he had been doing for the past forty-eight years, drawing out many of his words and utilizing the preaching delivery of old revivalist preachers: "Begin low, speak slow; rise higher, take fire."

In his introductory remarks, Truett spoke of the precarious world situation, stating that the messengers had "assembled in one of the most ominous and fateful hours our world has ever known. Stupendous influences and changes now mark the world.... [M]aterialism stretches its dark shadow throughout all realms, and among aaall peoples in the world. And the ghastly fact of persecution, religious and racial, confronts us in the face and many places wher'er we turn." Economic, political, educational, social, moral, and religious changes "sweep the world as ocean currents sweep the seas." Class struggles, misunderstandings in national and international affairs, "the awful philosophies of terror and hate," and "wars and rumors of wars—all these conditions are such as to cause us to know that we are now facing one of the most fateful days in all the history of civilization."[139]

Indeed, at the time of the 1939 BWA congress, the world was teetering on the brink of world war. Italy had invaded Libya in 1931 and then Ethiopia in 1935. In Spain, a civil war, begun in 1936, had raged until April 1939. In 1937, Japan had invaded China, capturing most of the coastal provinces. Germany had annexed Austria in 1938 and then seized Czechoslovakia in 1939.[140]

With the world in disarray, no matter where "we turn," Truett said, "the acutely searching question is pressed upon us: have Christians an adequate solution for the world's ills?" Of course we do, Truett answered. "We would say with the poet, 'We know of a world that is sunk in shame, / Of hearts that faint and tire; / And we know of a Name, a *Name*, a Name / That can set such world on fire.'"[141]

That name is Jesus. Although "He was born in the first century,... He is equally applicable in His mercy and grace for all the centuries." And despite being "born in little Bethlehem," Truett continued, "He belongs alike to all countries. He was born a Jew, but He belongs alike to all races. And His call is to Saxon, and Teuton, and Mongolian, and Latin, and Slav, to come penitently to Him, and if they will thus come, they shall have His forgiving grace and His empowering help." Jesus alone is the answer to the world's ills, and the only authority for Baptists is the Bible, the Word of

God, and "Christ, as revealed in that Word, is our Prophet, Priest, and King, our one authoritative and final teacher, our atoning and competent Savior, our divine Savior and Lord."[142]

As he had done in his 1920 address on the steps of the Capitol, Truett emphasized the individual's responsibility to God. Referring glowingly to E. Y. Mullins's teaching on soul competency, Truett noted that the late seminary president "stated one sentence that may well crown his name with immortality and may well mark the historic significance of our Baptist people. His sentence is that the individual is competent under God, in matters of religion…. He does not mean by that statement a'tall to imply that the individual is self sufficient in himself a'tall. But that his sufficiency in the world religious and spiritual is competent under the guidance and blessing of almighty God. Now from that bedrock *all* our Baptist principles emerge."[143]

Because individuals are responsible to God alone for their religious beliefs, Truett maintained that individuals must be free from civil and ecclesiastical tyranny. When the first Baptists in America "refused to stultify their consciences" by conforming to the requirements of state churches, the civil and religious authorities persecuted them. But these Baptists continued to fight for religious freedom "until they saw to it that" such freedom "was written in the Constitution of these United States of America that state and church are separate functions and must be forever separate and free."[144]

Again, reminiscent of his 1920 address, Truett emphasized the theological differences between Baptists and Catholics. He added, however, that no one man, alluding to the pope, should be the head of an ecclesiastical system. Even the apostle Peter, Truett claimed, "evidently did not find out that he was a pope a'tall. He was a married man…[and] fallible," for even the apostle Paul publicly rebuked him.[145]

Despite their differences with Catholics and others, Baptists, according to Truett, welcome and accept "without any hesitation…anybody who accepts Christ as his personal Savior." Anyone who does that, "whether it be in this Protestant communion, or the Catholic communion, or in some other communion, or in no communion a'tall, is our brother in Christ."[146]

We live in a world that needs to hear the gospel, Truett said, and all Christians are called to know what they believe. "It is conviction that convinces," Truett maintained. "The *pulpit is no place for a religious stammerer....* It is *conviction* that convinces everywhere."[147] Every Christian "of every name needs to get *back* and see to the reincarnation of the John Bunyan spirit. Incarcerated he was for twelve years in jail. He was by and by offered his freedom if he would put his conscience in shackles. And the great old hero of the faith made the sublime reply, 'I'll remain in this prison til the moss grows over my eyebrows, before I'll make a slaughterhouse of my conscience or a butchery of my principles.'[148] That sort of reincarnation is needed in the world today."[149]

Truett then returned to the subject of religious liberty, calling on Baptists in the United States "to keep their ears and eyes *alertly* open to the end that perversions of religious liberty, *abuses* of it, may not be allowed...in this land of ours. Our fathers purchased this great principle of freedom for us with a *greaaat cost.* And it's our great business *now not to forget it, nor allow anybody else to forget it,* in this whole country."[150]

Religious liberty is the "great business" of Baptists, Truett maintained, because such liberty owed its genesis, in great part, to Baptists:

> The great journalist Whitelaw Reid declares that the most outstanding and remarkable fact of modern times is the rise of the American nation. He states a greaaat truth. But we can amend it. I think you'll agree to it, the most revealing and outstanding and hopeful fact of our modern civilization was not the *discovery of the United States of America, but the discovery of religious FREEDOM* and its compatriot, civil freedom. And again I must say that such discovery was preeminently a Baptist discovery. I hurry on to say, it was not because our Baptist people are inherently better than our fellow Christians of other names. I would make no such arrogant claim. It *waaas and IS because* our Baptist people have certain convictions...which cannot be bartered awaaay for *ANY* price, whatsoever, and therefore this great day to which we come, that our American people keep wide open eyes to the insidious and easy

encroachments that can come against religious freedom and the doctrine of the separation of church and state here in America.[151]

Truett then briefly discussed three examples of such "insidious encroachments." The first concerned the Congressional debate as to whether church employees should be included in the "federal pension trough of the United States." He protested against such inclusion and highlighted "the ominous fact" that Christians had pressured Congress into debating that issue.[152]

The second encroachment concerned the use of public funds for sectarian purposes. "Again, and again, and again, in this place and that and the other," Truett lamented, "the proposal is openly made that taxes be taken out of the public treasury and applied for the support [and] the maintenance of sectarian schools." Then, in words that drew applause and laughter, he spoke directly to Baptists: "Now, if right here I'm speaking to any Baptists who have been enthralled a little bit by such beguilement, let me beg them to repent speedily of their inconsistency and go and sin no more."[153]

The proposal to establish diplomatic relations between the United States and the Vatican constituted Truett's third example of the encroachment upon the separation of church and state. Such a proposal, Truett contended in words that drew two rounds of applause, was unreasonable, for the United States had no more business recognizing the pope as the temporal sovereign over a little plot of land than it did granting such recognition to the leaders of the Presbyterian, Episcopalian, or Methodist churches in the United States, "or the moderator of the least Baptist association in the far off mountains of North Carolina."[154]

In order to present the Baptist message of religious liberty to the world, Truett continued, Baptists must look to their "immortal dead," and, in doing so, they will see

a galaxy of immortal names…written on our Baptist banner. There is John Bunyan, the immortal allegorist. There is John Howard,[155]…the great philanthropist. There is John Clifford,[156] the mighty champion of men's rights everywhere. There is Alexander MacLaren,[157] the peerless Bible expositor of his generation. And *there is Charles Haddon Spurgeon, perhaps the most glorious gospel preacher the world has ever seen since the days of Paul.* And there are our great missionaries [William] Carey[158] and [Adoniram] Judson[159] and [Luther] Rice[160] and Henrietta Hall Shuck, and...John E. Clough,[161] and an unnumbered host of mighty names. These great names, how much they mean in our Baptist vocabulary and history and heritage.

There is Roger Williams, the outstanding protagonist of religious liberty for *America* and the whole world. There were our great Baptist leaders [B. H.] Carroll, the Pauline preacher; and [J. B.] Gambrell, the sane philosopher; and [R. C.] Buckner, the immortal friend of orphan children. There were great editors who pleaded for our Baptist fellowship...and that we reach out and take the world in our program, such editors as...[R. H.] Pitt[162] of Virginia and others and others too numerous to name. There were our great teachers like Augustus Strong,[163] and John A. Broadus, and E. Y. Mullins, and A. T. Robertson. There was John Hope,[164] modest, noble John Hope, whose noble deeds have not only enhanced the glory of Atlanta but enhanced the glory of the Southland and the whole country. And *there was Booker T. Washington,* a world citizen, who like Moses has led and continues to *lead his* people out of the land of bondage into the Promised Land.[165]

After spending nearly forty-five minutes expounding the Baptist message of religious liberty, Truett used the remainder of his address exhorting Baptists to embrace their mission: evangelism. We must be "world-wide missionary enthusiasts," he exhorted his audience, "*WORLD*-wide. The religion of Christ re*fuSES* to va*CATE its suprema*CY, *everywhere.* And Jesus Christ re*fuSES* to be enrolled in any Pan*theON, anywhere. Chrr*RIST* must be Lord of all,* or he'll not be Lord a`tall."[166]

As he closed his address, Truett declared that the current world situation demanded that the gospel be preached everywhere in the world. Many parts of the world are shrouded in the night of violence and tyranny, he noted, yet we must remember that in other parts

it's glorious morning, and the morning gets fairer and wider and larger with every rising and setting sun. And one day it shall be morning everywhere. "Weeping may endure for a night, but joyyy cometh in the morning."[167] [Jesus

Christ] must reign till He hath put aaall enemies under His feet. One day war will be under His feet, God hasten it. One day intemperance in all of its hydra-headed manifestations shall be under Christ's feet. One day death shall under his feet. Ohhhh, without any defeatist spirit, but with full courage and confidence, let us give ourselves afresh from this congress to the conquest of the world. Who wouldn't want to sing, "Bring forth the royal diadem and crown Him Lord of all"?

Let ev'ry kindred, ev'ry tribe,
On this terrestrial ball,
To Him aaall majesty ascribe,
And crown Him Lord of all.

[Who wouldn't want to sing it? Who wouldn't want to sing it?]

Ohhhh, that with yonder sacred throng,
*Weee* at his feet may fall,
*WEEE LL join* the everlasting song,
And crown him Lord of all.[168]

With his presidential address behind him, Truett spent the rest of the congress presiding over other sessions and making shorter speeches to various groups. During his two weeks in Atlanta, he spoke on numerous occasions to several different audiences, met with reporters, and took the time to answer questions from people who gathered around him after his speaking engagements. His willingness to answer questions patiently impressed thirteen-year-old Edwin Gaustad, who eventually became a world-renowned church historian at the University of California, Riverside: "The closest that I got to him was when many admirers clustered around after a session to press questions upon him. (I was too timid to ask any.) He dealt with the questions as they were raised: never hurried, never impatient. We didn't know the word 'cool' in its contemporary sense then, but he struck me as 'cool.'"[169]

The final meeting of the congress was held on Friday, July 28, thus ending Truett's five-year service as president of the BWA. "My relief was unspeakable," a relieved Truett wrote in his diary, "when I handed the President's gavel to the new President, Dr. Rushbrooke."[170]

After the congress, C. C. Whitmire of Westminster, South Carolina, wrote a letter to Truett in which he described Truett's presidential address as "the most profound message I ever heard fall from the lips of man."[171] A Catholic, however, who either had read about or heard the address provided Truett with a different evaluation of the address. In an undated and unsigned note to Truett, the man wrote:

> Your statement[s] concerning the Pope, or rather His Holiness the Pope
>     (The Baptists not-withstanding) are amazing in one who claims to be a
>     follower of Christ.
> Christ said to his Apostles (and by no means to Johnnie Smyth 1600 years
>     later): "Whosoever despises you despises Me and whosoever despises Me,
>     despiseth Him Who sent Me...." [Luke 10:16].
> Consequently—by despising His Holiness the pope, the visible head of the
>     only true Church, founded by Jesus Christ Himself, you despiseth Jesus
>     and Him Who sent Him....
> This to you and to your 60,000 who had the misfortune of listening to your
>     absurds.
> *STULTORUM INFINITUS EST NUMERSUS* ["Infinite is the number of
>     fools"]. (Just fits you and your followers.)[172]

Truett might have been a fool, but he always signed his letters and provided a return address.

Prior to the BWA congress, in spring 1939, Zondervan Publishing House published Powhatan W. James's biography of his famous father-in-law. Although initially hesitant about having a book written about him, Truett eventually relented, though not without some embarrassment: "It is painfully embarrassing to me to have to think of a book about myself. May it be for good and not for evil."[173] He expressed similar sentiments to his friend J. M. Dawson: "If only the story may be used by our gracious Lord and Master, for the furtherance of His blessed cause, even in the humblest way, then, indeed, shall I be inexpressibly grateful."[174]

Josephine hoped that her son-in-law's book would provide a more accurate picture of her husband. "I really know better than most any body about my husband," she wrote to James in 1938. "I have heard more of his sermons than any other dozen people. I have felt every time I read what people say about him that most of it is pure theory." She hoped that James would show that her husband's lengthy 1938 illness had left no lasting, ill effects, but also "that he isn't an iron man and that he must not presume on nature."[175]

During the 1930s, Truett often presumed on nature, preaching hundreds of sermons and presenting numerous addresses on four continents. If he was not an "iron man," he came close to being one. Believing that he owed himself to the world, he had fulfilled that debt by the time he handed the BWA president's gavel to Rushbrooke at the end of the 1939 congress. Although he was beyond retirement age, Truett would continue to "presume on nature" during the remainder of his life. In 1939, he was seventy-two years old and was approaching the day when he would be "hushed to sleep" and pass into "the Yonderland, forever to be with the Prince of Love and with others 'loved long since and lost awhile.'"[176] But until that day arrived, he would hold firm the attitude he expressed often: "Happy if with my latest breath, / I may but speak His name; / Preach Him to all, and gasp in death, / 'Behold, behold the lamb.'"[177]

# Chapter 7

# That Last Sleep, 1940–1944

In 1915, shortly after J. M. Dawson accepted the call of First Baptist Church in Waco, Texas, to become its pastor, George W. Truett gave his friend some advice about not setting a time limit on how long Dawson should stay at his new church: "No, Brother Joe, don't fix any boundaries for your term of service. I think the average length of changing pastors since Dr. Carroll has been a year and a half. You may stay here six months, six years or sixty. Leave your tenure in the hands of God. Take my favorite scripture, 'Thy will be done!'"[1]

At the beginning of 1940, God's hands had held Truett as the pastor of First Baptist Church (FBC) in Dallas for a little more than forty-two years. The city's population had grown from 42,638 in 1900 to 294,734 in 1940,[2] and like the city's population, Truett's ministry and reputation had also grown. Since accepting FBC's call in 1897, Truett had expanded his ministry from one city church to encompass Baptists around the world, and he had gone from being a Texas Baptist hero to being compared with the greatest Baptist preacher in the nineteenth century, C. H. Spurgeon. At the dawn of the 1940s, however, Truett's ministry was nearing its end.

Occasionally during his ministry, Truett looked to the day when death would silence his voice. When he did so, he expressed one of the two wishes he hoped would be granted when that day came. One wish concerned preaching; the other concerned the place where he would die. In a sermon preached on September 8, 1912, his fifteenth anniversary at FBC, Truett related how his grandfather James Kimsey, who, although quite ill, had died preaching on his front porch. "I should like to go like that," Truett told his congregation, "to the last, to the last, witnessing for Jesus."[3] He also wanted to die in Dallas. On Sunday evening, September

9, 1917, the evening before the vote to determine whether the sale of alcohol could be banned in Dallas County, he addressed a packed auditorium at the Coliseum at Fair Park in Dallas. In his opening remarks to his fellow prohibitionists, Truett first proclaimed his love for the city and the people of Dallas and then expressed his wish for the final moments of his life: "[W]hen I come down to the last day of my earthly work, if my wish is carried out, I shall take that last sleep side by side with the people of Dallas."[4]

Truett's two wishes revealed his two passions in life: his love for preaching and his love for people, especially the people of Dallas. In July 1944, he would be granted both wishes.

*A Shepherd of Souls*

In a 1912 article about Truett for *Collier's* magazine, Peter Clark Macfarlane wrote, "The W.—I do not know what it is for. It does not matter. It is an unsignifying detail. It may stand for Washington. It may stand for a whirlwind. George W. Truett, by any other initial or cognomen, would burn up his soul as fast." Macfarlane then described the Dallas pastor as "a mile-a-minute sort of person. He seems to have entered the world on the run and never to have slackened his pace."[5] Indeed, a year later J. B. Gambrell wrote that many people had predicted that his good friend Truett "would soon wear himself out with his abundant labors."[6] The predictions made early in the twentieth century concerning Truett's burning himself out at an early age proved to be unfounded. In 1941, Eugene P. Alldredge, editor of the *Quarterly Review*, compiled statistics about Truett's forty-four-year ministry at FBC. By that year, the Dallas pastor had preached 270 revivals, or 6 per year; delivered 1,200 addresses, or 2 per month; presided at an average of 6 church dedications per year; and presented 16,060 "special talks" during revivals, conferences, and denominational meetings.[7] In 1942, the year in which Truett celebrated his seventy-fifth birthday, he preached 251 sermons, officiated at 28 funerals and 47 weddings, and delivered 50 addresses. He was away from Dallas for 153 days.[8]

During his long ministry at FBC, Truett was absent from Dallas approximately 40 percent of the time.[9] Apparently, such absences eventually began to take a toll, at least on attendance. His diary entries for Sundays in the early 1940s often contain notations about his preaching to "vast throngs" at FBC's services. Other observers, however, noted that attendance at the services dwindled during Truett's last years and that the sanctuary's two balconies were seldom used.[10] Despite Truett's frequent absences, FBC's membership increased by a little more than 600, from 7,200 in 1940 to 7,804 in 1944. Although Sunday-school enrollment decreased during those years, from 4,885 to 3,940, total gifts increased from $174,341 ($2,576,494)[11] to $256,302 ($3,019,441).[12]

As he grew older, Truett took a little more time off from his work and occasionally would go a week or two without preaching, but he usually worked seven days a week. If reading is a hobby, then he had one hobby. He was a member of the Dallas Athletic Club, where he ate many meals and got many massages but no exercise. Commenting on Truett's lack of an exercise regimen, Powhatan W. James contended that his father-in-law "may have mowed the lawn in the long ago, but that is doubtful."[13] Suffice it to say that Truett got his exercise during his work as a shepherd of souls.

Truett's primary function as a pastor was preaching, a task for which he spent hours preparing. At one Wednesday evening prayer service in September 1941, he challenged Sunday-school teachers to "dig and dig and dig!"[14] In doing so, he was only exhorting them to do what he had been doing for forty-eight years as a pastor. Truett's weekday diary entries for 1941, 1942, and 1943 often ended with these words: "In my library tonight." A typical Saturday entry ended like the one for January 18, 1941: "In my library tonight, seeking further preparation for tomorrow. May God mercifully help me, to do His will wholly, in the services tomorrow!"[15]

No presentation was too insignificant for Truett to "dig." In 1941, one of his close friends told Joe W. Burton, secretary of education for the Southern Baptist Convention's (SBC) Home Mission Board: "I have known him to withdraw and pray and study and outline what he would say when he was going to speak to a newspaper boy about his soul."[16]

To prepare for his preaching ministry, Truett studied at his home office, which, after being extended twice, covered almost half of the downstairs of his home. Depending on who counted, between 3,600 and 5,000 books lined the walls of his study. If he did not have an evening engagement, he retired to his office around 7 or 8 p.m. and studied until midnight, when Josephine would tap on the floor above the study, signaling for him to come to bed.[17]

Truett delivered his sermons extemporaneously. He told Burton that he often wrote ten to fifteen pages of a sermon, which he would then condense into a brief outline often written on an envelope. He would then study the outline repeatedly before placing it in his pulpit Bible, but he would not use the outline during the sermon. "No one," Truett said, "not even Mrs. Truett, would understand my abbreviations; sometimes a letter stands for a word." He did not use his outlines because he wanted to look "straight into the eyes of the hearers [rather] than at notes."[18]

FBC's worship services during Truett's ministry were marked by their solemnity. In a 1929 article in the *Kansas City Star*, A. B. Macdonald quoted the "pastor of an old downtown church, apologizing for his sensationalism," who said, "In a downtown church you have to pull that sort of stuff to draw the crowds. If you don't the picture shows will get them." Macdonald mentioned this pastor's approach to worship to an FBC deacon, who responded, "This isn't a show, it's a church; and it's a downtown church, too, right in the business district of Dallas; but there isn't money enough in the world to put a freak of any kind, a 1-man band, a whistler, a comedian, or any other 'stunt' in Dr. Truett's pulpit."[19]

When he was not leading a worship service, Truett, according to his niece Josephine Nash, was the "life of the party" at family gatherings, was always "very talkative, with lots of hilarious anecdotes," and "had a contagious laugh. His blue, blue eyes often spoke as much as his words!" But her uncle's demeanor changed drastically, she recalled, when he preached, for "he was *very serious*—preaching God's word was serious business! He would never, never 'warm up' the congregation with something breezy or humorous.... I do recall my mother mentioning, on the rare occasion, when something he said had caused a slight little titter across the congregation, how extremely *embarrassed* he was and he would *groan* over his 'ineptness' afterwards!!"[20]

When he preached, Truett was usually dressed in a dark suit, white shirt, and dark tie. He planted his six-foot, 210-pound frame directly behind or just to the side of the pulpit. He used few gestures and often stood erect with his hands in front of him. According to Nash, at one point in his ministry, her uncle "had a habit as he made important points" of slipping "his left hand in his pants pocket," a tendency Josephine Truett considered to be a distraction. To break her husband of that habit, "one Sunday she *sewed up* the offending pocket—Bad idea! When his preaching got intense, the habit kicked in—the hand searched for the pocket—which wasn't there—and his mind shut off like somebody had pulled the switch. Aunt Sittie [Josephine], sitting in her pew and looking dead-center, froze like a block of ice. She said she thought her heart stopped beating!... [S]he never did *that* again," Nash added, "and I think it broke his habit."[21]

Truett was more than just a preacher; he was also a pastor who made sure that he was available for personal conferences when he was in Dallas. He gave people who sought his advice all the time they needed, but no more. When Truett sensed that they had finished their business, he pressed a small buzzer under his desk, alerting the church secretary, Dolph Johnson, to enter the office and announce the next appointment.[22]

Numerous couples asked him to officiate at their weddings. Most of the ceremonies were simple affairs and were held either in Truett's church office or at his home. On many days he often officiated at more than one wedding. On March 29, 1941, for example, he recorded in his diary: "Today has been the busiest day of my life for weddings—I have officiated at the marriages of six couples today. This is the record, thus far."[23]

Many of the people who found their way to Truett's church office did so because they were experiencing personal problems. For example, after moving to Dallas in the early 1940s, Grace E. Wilson confided to Truett that she was afraid to sing in public. He told her: "Well, Gracie, you know I've never gotten over being afraid of speaking in front of people. By the time I walk to the platform and to the pulpit, I'm afraid. But I get my eye on a person and then my mind on the subject, then I do my best."[24] Indeed, Truett became quite anxious before he preached, even after preaching for four decades. Before preaching, he paced while occasionally referring to his sermon outline. His daughter Jessie recalled watching him pace for three hours before preaching to ministers at the Baptist encampment in Ridgecrest, North Carolina, even though he had preached many of those sermons elsewhere.[25]

Many people whom Truett counseled unburdened their souls to him. Although he often noted such conferences in his diaries, he never recorded the details. "Serious conferences with troubled souls were had in the Church Office today," he wrote in his 1937 diary. "One often wonders how God can bear the sorrows of humanity."[26]

Truett also ministered to people through the thousands of letters he wrote. He often spent two or three hours in the afternoons dictating letters.[27] "I have written many letters to all kinds of individuals, men, women and young people," he told Burton in 1941.

> This is a constant ministry.... Every contact is different. Sometimes one hears that a man is sick, or has lost a loved one, and that affords an opportunity for a letter of condolence. The letter can go on in the most tactful way to point out that there is no sickness beyond Christ's healing power. Frequently such letters are followed by an invitation from the person, saying that he would talk further about Christianity. Thus we follow up to make every contact count for Christ. One of the largest ministries a minister can have is through letters.[28]

Truett also mailed thousands of books during the course of his ministry. Many people received a copy of his *These Gracious Years*, published in 1929, and to bereaved families he sent, with a short, personal inscription, a copy of F. B. Meyer's *Peace, Perfect Peace*. He also gave couples he married a copy of Meyer's *Lovers Alway.*[29]

When in town, Truett preached the funeral sermons for deceased church members and for many non-members. He preached a particularly difficult one on December 29, 1942, following the death of J. B. Cranfill, who had died the previous day. Truett noted in his diary that Cranfill had been "a great friend" and "one of my most faithful and inspiring friends."[30] Truett, however, did not officiate at the funerals for family members. His older brother Spurgeon, who had been living with the Truetts since 1925, died on February 13, 1941, after a two-week illness.[31] Truett's younger brother, Luther, died at his home in McKinney, Texas, on October 2, 1941, after an extended illness. During Luther's illness, Truett made several trips to McKinney, which saddened him greatly. "It wrings my heart to see how he is wasting away," he recorded in his diary after one visit.[32] On the day his younger brother died, Truett wrote, "It comforts the heart beyond all words, to reflect that the dear, patient poignantly suffering loved one is well now, and to be well forever, in the House of Life above."[33]

### A Mirror of His Ministry

In many ways the last years of Truett's life mirrored his entire ministry. He attended celebrations in his honor, ministered during a world war, preached revivals and at camps, accepted invitations to speak at special events, and continued to be involved in the affairs of the Texas Baptist Memorial Sanitarium, whose name was changed to Baylor Hospital in 1921.

On February 16, 1940, Truett and Josephine traveled to Mary-Hardin College (formerly Baylor Female College, now the University of Mary Hardin-Baylor), in Belton, Texas, to attend a banquet honoring Truett for his long ministry to Texas Baptists. During the ceremony, he received a scroll, which read in part: "In appreciation of him as a wise leader—as a first citizen of Dallas and a citizen of the world,—whose influence blesses all nations—as a disciple of Christ—as a tender and forceful interpreter of the Word of God—as a pastor for more than 40 years of a great and consecrated Baptist church."[34]

Truett's long-time friend Louie D. Newton, pastor of Druid Hills Baptist Church in Atlanta, Georgia, delivered the main address of the evening. "The secret of the power and influence of Dr. George W. Truett's life," Newton said, "is his selflessness. His uncompromising surrender to the will of God challenges the admiration of his fellowmen everywhere, Christian and non-Christian. It can truthfully be said of George W. Truett that he is God's man."[35]

Both Josephine and Truett made brief remarks at the ceremony. After receiving a thundering ovation, Josephine remarked that everything the speakers had said about her husband was "all true." She challenged the young women in the audience to study hard and to set high Christian standards for themselves because "a home never rises above the ideals of the woman in it."[36] When Truett spoke, he expressed his gratitude for the remarks made about him and his hope that the college would build more buildings on its campus, place more equipment in its classrooms, and raise more money for its endowment.[37] Celebrations honoring Truett, such as the one at Mary-Hardin College, were held often during his ministry.

Tragically, the United States entered another world war during the last years of Truett's life. On December 7, 1941, despite inclement weather, a good crowd gathered at FBC's morning service, and eleven people joined the church, two of whom requested baptism. Many people stayed after the service to observe the Lord's Supper. The atmosphere at the evening service, however, was subdued, for the news of Japan's attacks in the Philippines and on Pearl Harbor had become public knowledge. After the service, the Truetts listened to the radio reports "filled with the terrible War news. God help us all," Truett wrote in his diary, "and may His will be done, in all the lessons and outcome of the awful conflict!"[38]

As it had done during World War I, FBC ministered to soldiers in the Dallas area. It provided a "Soldier Center," a large lounge/reading area, where soldiers could relax and feel at home. When the ministry expanded, the church hired Mrs. E. E. Partain to direct the center. The church also placed cots in the basement rooms of FBC's Sunday-school building for soldiers on leave who could not find lodging in Dallas.[39]

Truett supported the Allied cause during the war, but unlike his support during the first world war, he did not think that victory would be a panacea for the world's ills. He was perhaps speaking autobiographically during one sermon when he declared, "During and immediately following [World War I] many said: 'Now we may look for a long era of peace and good will, of law and order, or righteousness and justice.' But alas! We find ourselves in the same battle, the same scramble, the same selfishness, the same lawlessness and disobedience." Never one to remain long on a discordant note, however, Truett cautioned his congregation not to become overly discouraged: "Now, we must alertly guard ourselves lest we be filled with despair about the moral welfare of the world and allow the days of biting fear and discouragement to benumb us."[40] Whatever doubts, fears, or discouragements the members of his congregation might have been experiencing, only one word, Truett promised, could describe the eventual outcome: "It is Victory! It is victory for any of you in this great throng who will come to God with all your battles, doubts and sins and struggles and defeats and losses and failures! It is Victory! It is victory if you will stay yourself on God!"[41]

Unlike World War I, during which Truett spent six months in Europe, the Second World War did not interrupt his ministry at home. He continued to preach revivals in and out of Texas, including the annual spring revival in Dallas, which had begun in 1917, and the revival for the cowboys in West Texas, an engagement he had fulfilled, when his schedule permitted, since 1902.

Of the many invitations to preach at special occasions during the last years of Truett's life, three stand out. While preaching in Georgia in April 1941, Truett also addressed the Georgia Baptist Convention, which was meeting in Marietta. That event brought back fond memories, which he noted in his diary entry for April 19: "This afternoon['s] service was used as a vivid reminder of my Mission Speech in 1889—just 52 years ago, this month, to the Annual Meeting of the Ga. Bapt. Convention here in Marietta. I was unexpectedly called out by F. C. McConnell, to speak, while the subject of Christian Education was being discussed. This was before I was a preacher. It was an unforgettable occasion, 52 years ago!"[42]

While preaching a revival for Druid Hills Baptist Church, Atlanta, in April 1942, Truett also spoke at the celebration of Edward R. Carter's sixtieth anniversary as pastor of Friendship Baptist Church, the oldest African-American church in Atlanta. Carter, whom Truett described as "a glorious man of God,"[43] had requested that his white, Baptist colleague preach the sermon at his anniversary celebration.[44]

Another invitation to preach also brought back fond memories for Truett. On Sunday afternoon, May 2, 1943, he and Josephine traveled to Waco, where on the following day he was scheduled to preach at the Diamond Jubilee of East Waco Baptist Church. He was excited about returning to "the dear little Church that was my first pastorate, when I was a student at B. U. The memories of the dear people of the little Church, and of their never-ceasing kindnesses to us abidingly linger with us to gladden and bless us."[45]

The wonderful memories evoked by Truett's return to his first pastorate came during a time when another aspect of his ministry was producing bitter, painful feelings. Truett had been a member of the board of trustees of Baylor Hospital since 1905, when it was called the Texas Baptist Memorial Sanitarium. By January 21, 1921, the day on which the sanitarium's name was changed to Baylor Hospital, the hospital was surrounded by schools of medicine, dentistry, nursing, and pharmacy, all of which were under the authority of Baylor University's trustees.[46] Dallas's support for the schools began to wane, however, over the years, yet when a proposal was made in 1943 to move the schools of medicine and dentistry to Houston, Dallas officials objected and convinced Truett and several others to fight to keep the schools in Dallas.[47]

Truett fought tenaciously to keep the schools in Dallas, which did not surprise his friends or foes. As Leon McBeth observed, like "all mortals, he had feet of clay. He was known to prefer having his own way in both church and denominational affairs. Behind the scenes Truett could make opponents think twice before opposing his plans in public."[48] Truett could even make friends who opposed him think twice, as he did during meetings to discuss moving the schools of medicine and dentistry to Houston. His close friend J. M. Dawson supported the move and contended that "Truett...allowed local loyalties to cause him to resist outside pressures for the removal." Dawson noted that "[t]hrough a combination of circumstances it fell to me to combat the revered Truett and the whole Dallas contingent for an unforgettable, almost unendurable day." The Waco pastor noted that he and Truett "violently jostled" over the "unwelcome controversy," which was made more difficult because Dawson had to oppose "a man so superior, and one whom I loved profoundly." "In no sense," he continued, "did I forfeit Dr. Truett's regard."[49]

Despite Truett's vigorous opposition, on May 8, 1943, the hospital's trustees approved the move of the medicine and dentistry schools.[50] Regarding the vote, he noted in his diary: "The whole matter has given me more concern than my words can say. Now, I must leave the matter with God, whose promise in Romans 8:28 forever stands sure."[51]

### A Preacher to the End

Almost two months after the vote to move the schools of medicine and dentistry to Houston, the seventy-six-year-old Truett, despite a nagging pain in his left leg, traveled to Atlanta for another week-long revival at Druid Hills Baptist Church. His leg had started bothering him sometime in 1942. On September 15 of that year, Truett's physician noted that his patient had been experiencing "a moderate pain in the left leg...for several weeks."[52] Despite the pain, which aspirin relieved, Truett was in good health for a man of his age. Apparently, his 170/110 blood pressure did not cause any concern. The pain, however, continued to increase, and by the time Truett and Josephine arrived in Atlanta on July 1, 1943, he was a sick man. Newton picked them up at the train station.

Newton had first met Truett at the 1909 (Southern Baptist Convention) meeting in Louisville, Kentucky. In order for the seventeen-year-old Newton to attend the meeting, his mother had sold a heifer to pay for his train ticket. He left Sylvester, Georgia, with a free train ticket but with no way to pay for his room and board during his stay in Louisville. Newton quickly got a job as a page for Joshua Levering, the SBC president and former presidential candidate for the National Prohibition Party (1896). Levering introduced him to many important people during the week, the last being Truett. According to Newton, "Dr. Truett was...waiting to preach, and [Levering] introduced me to him. Dr. Truett took my hand and said, 'Young man, just keep following where He [God] leads you, and remember this: Jesus put it finally for all of us when he said, 'Father, not my will but Thine be done.'"[53]

Thirty-six years later, on an afternoon during the July 1943 revival, Truett and Newton sat outside of Newton's home, perhaps under the tree that J. H. Rushbrooke had dubbed "the Oak of Friendship."[54] The Dallas pastor, in failing health, returned again to the topic of God's will. "We were just sitting under that tree out there," Newton recalled during a 1973 interview for his oral memoirs, "and [Truett] said, 'Louie, when you come to have my funeral, if you can say in all consciousness that my thought has been to follow the will of God, Thy will be done, then I'll be happy.'"[55]

Despite being in constant pain while in Atlanta, Truett preached fourteen sermons. In an article written after the revival, Newton proclaimed that his friend's sermons represented "the greatest preaching I have ever heard. Nor am I alone in that opinion. Editors, educators, bankers, lawyers, doctors, merchants, farmers, scientists, engineers of the very first rank in our city and section have freely testified that his sermons this time were the ablest, the most powerful, the most appealing to which they have ever listened."[56] Newton did not mention anything about Truett's failing health; rather, he ended his article by noting that his friend had agreed to return to Druid Hills "next year for a season of ministry..., the Lord willing."[57]

After the 1943 revival, Truett and Josephine arrived back in Dallas on Tuesday, July 13. Two days later, he visited his doctor, who advised him to enter Baylor Hospital for "further diagnosis and treatment." Truett agreed and then canceled his preaching engagement in West Texas, "very much to my regret!"[58]

After preaching at FBC's Sunday evening service on July 18, Truett did not attend a church service for three and a half months. On Tuesday, July 20, 1943, he noted in his diary that his left leg had been bothering him "for more than a year, and has seemed to grow steadily worse. The

Drs. have sought to find the cause, and they have concluded that an operation on the leg is necessary. They insist that it need not be serious even though it may be painful. My prayer is that God will direct the whole matter, working His will in it all, for His glory!"[59] Around 8 p.m. on Wednesday, July 21, Truett entered Baylor Hospital for his operation, which was scheduled for the following day. In his last journal entry, he recorded that he and Josephine "trust that God's will [shall] guide in it all. We trust our all to Him, now and forevermore!"[60] During the operation the bone specialists who operated on Truett did not find anything wrong with his leg.[61] Following the surgery, however, his leg continued to bother him, and he spent six weeks recuperating in the hospital.

Truett finally returned home on September 1. The *Dallas Morning News* noted that his condition was "improving rapidly" and that he planned "to return to his pulpit Sept. 12 to preach his forty-sixth anniversary sermon."[62] His condition did not improve enough for him to preach on his anniversary or on any Sunday for several more weeks; however, on October 31, after a fourteen-week absence, he returned to his pulpit before an estimated crowd of 3,500. A. B. Tanco, an FBC member, recalled that memorable service:

> I was present on that Sunday morning when Dr. Truett returned to his pulpit.... That morning, he walked in slowly with the aid of a cane. There seemed to be a noticeable hush which went over the vast congregation. It seemed stunned and shocked. It seemed, for the first time, they realized they were seeing the beginning of the end of the career of the great Pastor. Everyone seemed to want to express his feelings and appreciation in some way. Finally, someone timidly started to applaud and the entire congregation followed until there was a mighty applause. Of course the great Pastor never approved of applause at a worship service, but there was a difference here and he felt it as he responded with a glorious smile which came over his weary face.[63]

In his sermon that morning Truett exhorted the congregation to be doers just like Jesus, whose attitude had been, "'What can I do for you?' His was not a patience of stoicism or sullenness. He went about doing good." Truett also reminded the congregation that God's will "is always best and safe. God's will is ever right and to go against it is ever wrong."[64]

After the sermon, the congregation sang "He Leadeth Me." Tanco recalled "that, after singing a verse or two, the Pastor said, 'Sing that last verse,' and then he went on and quoted the entire verse…. 'And when my task on earth is done, [When, by Thy grace, the victory's won, E'en death's cold wave I will not flee, Since God thro' Jordan leadeth me!]' He and everyone else realized that his task on earth was done."[65]

Returning to his pulpit lifted Truett's spirits. In a November 17 letter to Burton, Truett wrote, "For the past three Sundays I have been in my pulpit to my great joy, even as I hope to be there regularly from this time on. You will pray for me that I may find and follow God's will, faithfully, always, even as I would thus pray for you and yours and for your blessed work."[66]

Truett also attend the Baptist General Convention of Texas meeting, which was held at FBC in November. He offered the prayer on the evening that Dawson preached a sermon titled "The Christian View of Man." Outside the entrances to the church, J. Frank Norris and some members of his Fort Worth congregation distributed handbills and held up signs challenging the decision to allow the "heretic" Dawson to preach.[67]

Eventually, however, Truett became too weak to preach. After consulting with his family, he informed Robert H. Coleman that he wanted to take a leave of absence. At the deacons' meeting on Wednesday, January 5, 1944, Coleman reported that Truett's condition "was serious" but not "hopeless," and then he conveyed the pastor's request for a leave of absence. The deacons approved the request and voted to present it to the church, which also approved it later that evening during the church's monthly business meeting.[68]

In a report on his pastor's condition in April 1944, Coleman informed the public that doctors had suggested that Truett remain in bed. Although the seventy-six-year-old pastor had been suffering severely, he was now only experiencing "moderate" pain from "arthritis in his left limb." Coleman continued: "He is patient and brave and seeks to keep posted on all the work of his church and denomination and affairs, generally."[69]

Despite the respite from intense pain, Truett's health soon began to deteriorate. FBC members decided to do one last thing to express their love for their pastor. Since 1924, FBC had labored under an enormous building debt. By June 1943, the debt had been reduced to just under $100,000 ($1.2 million), and by March 1, 1944, it had been lowered to $50,000 ($589,040). In April, church members began to donate money to retire the debt by May 6, Truett's seventy-seventh birthday. The church raised $72,000 ($848,217) and presented Truett with the canceled note on his birthday.[70]

On Sunday, May 14, the church celebrated the retirement of its debt. Coleman preached, and Truett, as he had done the previous two Sundays, prayed from his bed at home via a special telephone hookup.[71] Tanco attended that service and "heard the last words which the Great Pastor delivered to his Church.... His final prayer closed with these words so familiar to those in the congregation: 'And now, may the blessings of God, bright like the light when the morning dawneth and gracious as the dew when the eventide cometh, abide with each of us today, tomorrow and forever.'"[72]

In late May, Newton, who had already made two visits to his dying friend, returned to Dallas. Truett constantly asked his long-time friend and colleague to pray with him "that I may be the Christian God would have me be." With tears in his eyes, Truett repeatedly told Newton that he was going to resign as FBC's pastor on June 4 because, he said, "it seems clearly the will of my Father, and that is all that concerns me now or ever has concerned me. His will, let us ever remember, is always safe, always right, always best."[73]

On Sunday, June 4, Coleman read Truett's resignation letter, which was addressed "To My Very Dear People." Truett informed his congregation that his illness had made it impossible for him to continue pastoring the church. He had not made such a drastic decision hastily, but had done so only "after weeks and even months of earnest prayer for Divine guidance, desiring only the highest welfare of our church. Her spiritual and missionary development has been, now for nearly forty-seven years, the dominant purpose of my life." He thanked FBC members for the "never-ceasing and overflowingly gracious consideration" they had shown to him and his family "through all the years." Truett ended his letter by quoting Philippians 1:8–11, a passage of scripture, he stressed, that "must forever be the expression of my heart to this church: 'God is my witness, how I long after you all in the tender mercies of Christ Jesus. And this I pray, that your love may abound yet more and more, in knowledge and all discernment; so that ye may approve the things that are excellent, that ye may be sincere and void of offense unto the day of Christ; being filled with the fruits of righteousness, which are through Jesus Christ, unto the glory and praise of God.'"[74]

After Coleman finished reading the letter, he and several other deacons spoke about Truett's long ministry at FBC. Then the church unanimously voted "lovingly and emphatically" to reject their pastor's resignation.[75]

As the days wore on, the pain in Truett's leg intensified, which caused him many sleepless nights. When a friend asked him if the nights seemed too long, Truett replied, "On the contrary, they are much too short. You see I begin every night by calling the roll of my friends. I walk with them again. I talk with them. I pray for them. And you see, I have so many friends that the dawn comes before I get around to all of them. The nights are far too short."[76]

Eventually, doctors had to medicate Truett heavily. They told his family that he might be difficult to control while unconscious and that he might even speak harshly, even to loved ones. Truett did not become unmanageable, nor did he speak any unkind words. He did, however, continue to preach even in his delirium, calling men and women to surrender their lives to Christ.[77] Thus, in a sense, Truett got his wish to be like his Grandfather Kimsey—preaching to the end.

At 11:50 p.m. on Friday, July 7, 1944, with his family by his side, Truett took "that last sleep" at his home in his beloved Dallas. No official cause of death was issued, but friends reported that he probably died from bone cancer in his left thigh.[78] Expressions of condolences and praise came from Baptists all over the world and from people of other denominations and faiths. J. H. Rushbrooke, president of the Baptist World Alliance, noted that "[a] prince and great man has fallen in our Israel.... He was a mighty evangelistic preacher, I think the greatest since Spurgeon.... He belonged...to the whole of the Christian world."[79] Several Dallas ministers also expressed their condolences when they heard of their colleague's death. Joseph P. Lynch, a Catholic bishop, wrote that Truett had "served [his] congregation in this city with loving efficiency. Dr. Truett's public life was spent in counseling the doubting, encouraging the sinner, warning the Godless, admonishing the frivolous and consoling the afflicted. As a citizen he was always ready to promote the American way of life and to encourage every enterprise helpful to the community. May his great soul find peace and refreshment in the Eternal Home." David Lefkowitz, rabbi of Temple Emanu-El, wrote that he had read of Truett's death "with an aching heart.... He was a great churchman, and above all, a great man, a great humanitarian. He above all others purified the soul of Dallas and lifted it to the heights. Whatever we in Dallas may do in the coming years along the lines of fineness of spirit, decency and human tolerance will be attributable to the leadership and spiritual uplift of Dr. Truett through the years." John M. Moore, a Methodist bishop who had known Truett for forty-two years, described his deceased friend as "a great Christian, citizen, evangelist, churchman. He was one of the...great men in the Baptist Church the last fifty years. He was a representative of the highest things in his own church and in Christianity. I held him in high admiration and in deep affection. He was the greatest asset that Dallas ever had." Harry T. Moore, the Episcopalian bishop who had argued against Truett's stand on prohibition before the Texas legislature's House Committee on Constitutional Amendments in February 1933, called Truett one of the greatest ministers Dallas ever had.[80]

Even Norris could not keep from joining the chorus of praises for Truett. The Fort Worth pastor described the voice of the man whom he had loved taunting as "one of the greatest, if not the greatest, carrying voices that was ever heard from the platform."[81] Moreover, Truett "was the last of the generation of giants among Texas Baptists" and had built "one of the world's greatest churches not only of this age but of all time."[82] Norris's words call to mind a sermon Truett preached on March 14, 1909, when he proclaimed, "Our trust in God, like that of Jesus, is to be open, known and read of all men. Even the tribute of our enemies should be that we are certainly on Christ's side."[83] Later in the sermon, Truett asked his congregation, "Are you living so that your enemies would say, 'One thing is certain, the man is for Christ'? O, what a blessed life if that is so!… [If you live like that,] you are living in the right way, you are living in the right way."[84]

On Monday, July 10, flags in Dallas flew at half-staff. The Commissioners Court ordered that all county work stop at 3:00 p.m. to allow county employees to attend the funeral. Many businesses closed, as did the courts. Perhaps as many as 20,000 people paid their respects as Truett's body lay in state in FBC's sanctuary from 11:30 a.m. until the funeral began at 4 p.m. Approximately 4,600 mourners filled FBC's sanctuary for the funeral, and another thousand listened to the service in Sunday-school rooms and outside the church building.[85] Many others listened to the service on the radio.

Deacons sat in the choir loft. The church's "silent friends" sat in a reserved section in one of the balconies and "heard" the service through an interpreter. A large contingent of African Americans attended the service and sat in their reserved section in a balcony. Next to the pulpit stood an arrangement with flowers spelling the words "Holy Bible" and "Thy Will Be Done." White roses covered the casket. Wreaths and sprays extended across the front of the sanctuary.

After the First Baptist Quartet sang "Rock of Ages," Eldred D. Head, president of Southwestern Baptist Theological Seminary in Fort Worth, Texas, read several passages of scripture. F. M. McConnell, editor emeritus of the *Baptist Standard,* then prayed and was followed by W. O. Lewis, general secretary of the Baptist World Alliance, who spoke briefly about

Truett's ministry among Baptists around the world. Coleman then gave an emotional eulogy for his beloved friend, whom he described as "the greatest soul I ever touched.... I loved him and honored him above any man on earth except my honored preacher-father and twice as much of my time has been spent with this dear pastor as I was ever permitted to spend with my own father."[86]

After Coleman spoke, Louie D. Newton, as he had promised, preached the funeral sermon. "Two texts emerge every time I think of Dr. George W. Truett," Newton told the mourners. "The first is found in that pattern prayer, which our blessed Savior and Lord gave us, in the Gospel of Matthew: 'Thy will be done.'... Every time one asks for the explanation of this marvelous and amazing man the answer is given fully and finally in these four, one-syllable words: 'Thy will be done.'" Newton remarked that he had heard Truett say "a thousand times" that "the will of God is always safe, and it is always right, and it is always best."[87] Another text that characterized Truett's life was Philippians 3:10: "that I may know Him." Newton remarked that Truett did not merely want to submit to God; he wanted to know God. "A man thus surrendered and a man thus committed can move the world nearer to God."[88]

Newton then described two aspects of the beloved pastor's life that represented his following God's will. Truett was a man of prayer, which was the key to his being a great preacher and an inspiration to the thousands who heard him. Furthermore, Truett made the Bible the "ruling guide of his faith and practice," for he believed that in that book anyone could find the will of God for every decision in life.[89]

Newton also felt compelled to mention Truett's great quest and care for souls. Truett "loved the souls of men with a passion beyond any man I have ever known in my life.... He sought them out anywhere, on the decks of ships, on speeding trains, in railway stations, anywhere, he was the great searcher for souls."[90]

As he drew his sermon to a close, Newton recounted a conversation he had had the day before at the Atlanta train station when an African-American porter asked Newton if he was "going to Dallas to bury our great preacher." Truett, the porter explained, "never rode on this train that I didn't feel like I was deeply honored if I could so much as shine his shoes, if I could so much as help him off of the train and onto the train. He was the greatest man I ever saw in all the world." After the train left the station, Newton sought out the porter and asked him why he thought Truett had been such a great man. The porter did not have to think long about his answer: "Mr. Newton, I tell you why he was such a great man. He had the love of God in his heart as no man I ever saw. He could speak to me, a black man, and he could speak to me about God with all the interest and care and power that one of my own race would have spoken to me. Now, you know that takes the love of God." Newton then challenged the congregation to "trace it if you will, trace the course of your great pastor and answer me this question: is not the secret of his influence in Dallas, and in Texas, and in the South, and in the nation, and out to the ends of the earth in the fact that he embodied the love of God as few men have embodied?" "God bless his memory," Newton said as he ended his sermon, "and bless you and keep us true to all he [Truett] taught us to do, until we too shall be called home with him and with the Lord."[91]

After the service many people drove to Grove Hill Cemetery, where Truett and Coleman had bought adjoining plots years before, for the burial. According to a *Dallas Morning News* reporter, "The funeral procession," which stretched three miles long, "was one of the largest, if not the largest, in the history of Dallas."[92] Six trucks carried flowers from the church and from the Truett home to the cemetery. At the gravesite, Coleman read a passage of scripture, and Newton closed the service with prayer. Then, before leaving the gravesite, Coleman quoted Mark Twain's eulogy to his daughter Susan:

> Warm summer sun, shine brightly here.
> Gentle southern breeze, blow softly here.
> Green sod above, lie light, lie light.
> Good night, great heart, good night.
> We'll see you in the morning.[93]

Eventually, all the mourners dispersed and returned to their homes, leaving Truett's remains at the cemetery. His fifty-four years as a Christian minister had finally come to an end. Death may have ended his ministry, but Truett had been adamant that his congregation never believe that death ended his life. In one sermon he stated his faith clearly and confidently: "You shall hear some day that the preacher before you is dead. Oh, no! His tongue will be quiet, his pulse will be still, his heart will have ceased its beating, but he will be alive—more alive than he is now, more alive than he has ever been in this world! He will have gone from this life; he will be where the conditions of life are perfect because God gives those who trust Him eternal life."[94]

# Chapter 8

# A Life of Abiding Interest

In his introduction to the autobiography of Mrs. William L. Williams, one of the founding members of First Baptist Church (FBC) in Dallas, George W. Truett wrote, "The record of any life, however humble or obscure, is invested with an abiding interest, while the record of a nobly good life teaches lessons and enforces obligations that are of more than ordinary moment to those who are privileged to know that life and study it in the light of its autobiographical history."[1] By any standard of measure, Truett's life was not only abidingly interesting but also nobly good.

Born in obscurity on a farm near rural Hayesville in southwestern North Carolina, Truett grew up in the home of loving parents where he learned lessons and developed habits that remained with him and guided him throughout the rest of his life. Working on the family farm, he learned the value and the necessity of hard work. His 1886 diary reveals him to have been a teenager who wanted to be constantly on the move. Downtime seemed to suffocate him. As a minister, Truett not only repeatedly preached the importance of hard work; he embodied it, almost to a fault. His numerous trips to cities across the United States, his extended preaching engagements across the world, and his ministry to his church and to the people of Dallas testify to Truett's philosophy that one's life should be dedicated to the glory of God and to the service of humanity.

As a young child and then as a young man, Truett worshiped at the Hayesville Baptist Church and at the nearby Methodist and Presbyterian churches, where he learned to love God, study the Bible, and respect the people and the work of other Protestant denominations. Although a committed Southern Baptist, Truett had an ecumenical spirit. He cooperated with anyone who would work with him toward the common good and for a common goal. Such a spirit endeared him to many people, including African Americans, Protestants, Catholics, and even non-believers. Not everyone loved Truett, including some fellow Baptists; some envied and despised him. But most of the people who knew him either loved him and/or respected him, even if they disagreed with him on certain points of theology.

While growing up and hearing the stories about his grandfather James Kimsey and listening to the sermons of his uncle Elijah (Uncle Lije) Kimsey and other ministers, Truett learned the power of words. As a teenager asking Baptists near his home in Hayesville to contribute money to buy Sunday-school literature, he learned how words—*his* words—could open people's wallets. When he became a minister, Truett used his gift of speech to persuade people to surrender their lives to Jesus and to raise millions of dollars for churches, the Texas Baptist Memorial Sanitarium, other benevolences, and Baptist colleges and universities.

Truett is perhaps best known for his advocacy of religious liberty. His 1920 address on the steps of the United States Capitol and his 1939 address at the Baptist World Alliance congress testify to his ability not only to state clearly and powerfully the concept of religious liberty but also to state Baptists' role in the genesis and spreading of such liberty. Yet his advocacy for religious liberty was not what set him apart from other Baptists, particularly pastors, for he did not say anything different than what many believed, although he was able to do so more passionately and forcefully. What set him apart from many other pastors was his understanding, and his embodiment of such an understanding, of stewardship.

Although Truett might not have been able to express completely early in life his attitude toward stewardship, his financial contributions to various Christian ministries and his time as a teacher passing on what his teachers had taught him eventually developed into the conviction, almost an obsession, that all of life was a matter of stewardship and service and that true living consists in giving rather than getting. "Oh, to live for others," Truett told his congregation in a 1909 sermon, "to lift up others, to make pale faces brighter, to make broken hearts lighter, to drive care and distress from human lives, to lay our money, our brains and our lives on the altar for others, as Jesus directs, and as He works with us, this is the highest privilege for us in this world."[2] While pastoring FBC, Truett received a good salary, yet he never accepted one of the several offers from churches that would have doubled or even tripled his salary. He had a reputation of helping anyone who needed his help, which often forced him to borrow money for his own and his family's personal needs. His life's savings consisted of a modest amount of life insurance and his books.[3] If the life of stewardship was a privileged one, then Truett lived a privileged life.

What Truett practiced in his personal life also affected his church's life. When he accepted the call of FBC in 1897, church polity stated that only 5 percent of total contributions could be given to outside causes. During Truett's first full year as FBC's pastor, the church gave 17 percent to such causes. When he arrived in Dallas, his church members thought monetarily in tens and twenties. He, however, thought in hundreds. Before too many years passed, both congregation and pastor thought in thousands. During Truett's forty-seven-year pastorate, FBC members contributed a little more than $6 million, of which 45 percent was given to outside causes. In twenty of those years, which included an eighteen-year stretch from 1904 to 1921, FBC members contributed more to outside causes than they did to their church's ministries. A church whose pastor cared nothing about acquiring personal wealth or security and whose members gave so sacrificially was a unique church. Truett led his congregation to be such a church, but his members had to be willing to be led.

Truett often acknowledged his indebtedness to his church members for their response to his leadership. For example, on September 10, 1922, his twenty-fifth anniversary as FBC's pastor, he told his congregation:

> My indebtedness to you, my fellow-workers for a quarter of a century, is
> deeper than can be told in words, and my indebtedness to these others, who
> have come along in these years, year after year and month after month, and
> Sunday after Sunday, and have linked their lives with us here, is immeasurable

and inexpressible. Whatever success or blessing may have attended the little ministry of the pastor over this church the past quarter of a century must be largely attributable to you, from the human viewpoint, and whatever the faults and imperfections of the ministry here—and they have been many—they have not been yours, nor due to you, but to him.[4]

Numerous individuals encouraged Truett throughout his life, and their friendship and support resulted in his effectiveness as a pastor and preacher. Although many could be named, four stand out. B. H. Carroll helped the North Carolina native get started in the ministry when, in 1890, he recognized in young Truett the tenacity that was required to retire Baylor University's debt. The hours Carroll spent mentoring, challenging, and encouraging his young protégé undoubtedly helped mold Truett into the preacher, leader, fundraiser, and statesman he would become.

C. C. Slaughter, whom Truett once described as having a "heart...larger than the vast prairies upon which his cattle graze,"[5] deserves to be numbered among Truett's influential fellow workers. Slaughter was Truett's friend, confidant, and benefactor. Whenever Truett embarked on a fundraising campaign at his church or for the Texas Baptist Memorial Sanitarium, he had the luxury of knowing that Slaughter, with his millions, was nearby and willing to give generously to the causes in which his pastor believed. Although thousands of other people heeded Truett's pleas to contribute sacrificially, having a multimillionaire in the congregation obviously aided the Dallas pastor's stellar reputation and effectiveness as a fundraiser.

Another of Truett's influential fellow workers was Robert H. Coleman. "I have never met a nobler, truer, better nor more useful man," Truett said of his assistant in 1936. "Others may have been more conspicuous than he, but none has been more truly useful and faithful. Prudent, courageous, sympathetic, zealous, optimistic, unselfish, faithful, his life is most nobly endowed, both by nature and by grace."[6] For nearly four decades Coleman assumed many of his pastor's duties during Truett's many absences from Dallas, and he vigorously promoted his pastor and his pastor's ministry. The two men were fiercely and affectionately loyal to each other. Truett undoubtedly could have achieved his success as a preacher without Coleman, but it could be argued that Truett could not have achieved it with a better friend than Coleman.

According to Truett, the most influential person in his adult life was his wife, Josephine. In 1927, at a banquet celebrating his thirtieth anniversary in Dallas, Truett called her "God's best gift to me in this world and my chief human inspiration through these years."[7] In her 1946 diary, Josephine, still grieving the loss of her spouse of fifty years, wrote a revealing, perhaps even sad, paragraph describing her complete devotion to her husband and his work: "As I stand & look down the hours & days & weeks & months of this New Year—it all seems empty to me. All my life I have never had a thought outside of my husband & his work. The last twenty[-]five years I have spent most of my time with him—thinking his thoughts, helping him work out his plans or trying to see his view point or let him see mine. We always 'got together' & then things were done. I miss him *so*, at home, at church, every where."[8] Josephine devoted her life to raising their three daughters and to supporting her husband's ministry. A college graduate, she obviously was intelligent and thoughtful. Her claim never to have had her own thoughts perhaps can be attributed to her grief. After all, she had been the foremost "human inspiration" behind the man who had inspired thousands.

The primary means by which Truett inspired people were his sermons, many of which were published after his death. From 1946 to 1952 William B. Eerdmans Publishing House published eight volumes of his sermons and addresses, all of which Powhatan W. James edited.[9] These easily accessible volumes gave readers a sense of Truett's preaching, but they eventually produced a cliché among Southern Baptists that "Truett was one of the most exciting preachers to hear and one of the most disappointing to read."[10] Clyde E. Fant, Jr., and William M. Pinson, Jr., attributed the genesis of the cliché to James's over-editing of the sermons and contended that if Truett's "sermons had been printed exactly as they were delivered, a different preacher might have emerged from the page."[11]

In addition to a legacy of inspirational preaching, Truett's stature among Baptists has continued through the years. Since his death, several Baptist organizations have memorialized the Truett name. FBC's seven-story educational building, the auditorium at Southwestern Baptist Theological Seminary, a college in Cleveland, Georgia, two church associations (one in North Carolina, the other in Tennessee), a Dallas elementary school, a children's home in Nazareth, Israel, and a seminary in Waco, Texas, all bear Truett's name.[12] The names of two churches also commemorate the famed Dallas minister: Truett Memorial Baptist Chapel in Dallas, Texas, and Truett Memorial Baptist Church in Hayesville, North Carolina. The Hayesville church was the one in which Truett made his profession of faith in 1886.[13]

One of the most fitting tributes to Truett's legacy occurred on November 30, 1950, when Dallas celebrated the opening of the George W. Truett Memorial Hospital. The 436-bed hospital cost $5.5 million ($47 million),[14] which had been donated by Dallas citizens and the Baptist General Convention of Texas. Public funds could have been used to defray some of the cost, but according to Wallace Bassett, a Dallas pastor and Baylor University trustee, Baptists "believe in the separation of church and state" and the hospital's "trustees would not take federal money to build this hospital."[15] A bronze bust of Truett was placed in the hospital's lobby. On the bust's stand were inscribed Truett's words describing his understanding of a faith-based hospital: "Never let it be said that Baylor Hospital has become just another boarding house for the sick. The science and knowledge of man must combine efforts with the Great Physician to render the ultimate in service to God and mankind."[16]

The first memorial to Truett came shortly after his death. FBC members wanted to mark their beloved pastor's grave with a monument befitting the man's stature, but the gravesite at Grove Hill Cemetery was too small for such a monument. Thus, on July 3, 1945, Truett's body was moved from Grove Hill to Hillcrest Memorial Cemetery (now Sparkman/Hillcrest Memorial Park) in Dallas, where a marble monument ten feet high and six feet wide now marks the graves of Truett and his wife.

Even death, apparently, could not keep Truett in one place very long. The engravings on the monument testify to the famous preacher's passions in life. The building of First Baptist Church is etched at the top of the monument and is followed by Truett's name and the years of his pastorate in Dallas. A quote from Truett follows: "My greatest desire is to help the people and to magnify the matchless name of Christ." The quote is followed by Josephine Jenkins Truett's name. Then, in four, one-syllable words, comes perhaps the most fitting testimony to the life of George W. Truett:

Thy Will Be Done[17]

# Notes

*Abbreviations*

AWRL: A Webb Roberts Library, Southwestern Baptist Theological Seminary, Fort
    Worth, Texas
DMN: *Dallas Morning News*
GWTML: George W. Truett Memorial Library, First Baptist Church, Dallas, Texas
MF: microfiche
SBHLA: Southern Baptist Historical Library and Archives, Nashville, Tennessee
TBHC: Texas Baptist Historical Commission, Dallas, Texas
TC: George W. Truett Collection, A. W. Roberts Library, Southwestern Baptist
    Theological Seminary, Fort Worth, Texas

---

*Chapter 1*

[1] Louie D. Newton, with A. Ronald Tonks, "Oral Memoirs of Louie D. Newton"
(Historical Commission, Southern Baptist Convention, SBHLA, Nashville, TN,
1973–1981) 22.

[2] J. Moran Kousser, "Reconstruction," in *The Oxford Companion to United States
History*, ed. Paul Boyer (Oxford: Oxford University Press, 2001) 653.

[3] Rudolph J. Vicoli, "Immigration," in *The Oxford Companion to United States
History*, 359.

[4] Powhatan W. James, *George W. Truett: A Biography* (Nashville: Broadman Press,
1939) 12; Margaret Walker Freel, *Our Heritage: The People of Cherokee County, North
Carolina, 1540–1955* (Asheville NC: Miller Printing Company, 1956; repr., Andrews
NC: Andrews Journal, 1973) 354–55; "Hayesville Baptist-Presbyterian Cemetery-Clay
Co.,              NC-Cemeteries,"              http://ftp.rootsweb.com/pub/
usgenweb/nc/clay/cemeteries/baptpres.txt?cj=1&o_xid=0002530104&o_lid=000253
0104&o_xt=1155785 (accessed October 3, 2007); George W. Truett to J. M.
Dawson, April 12, 1936, Joseph Martin Dawson Papers, SBHLA; "Death of J. Harvey
Truett," *DMN*, January 26, 1908; "Rev. Truett, 91, Dies at Home," *DMN*, July 22,
1946; George W. Truett to J. M. Dawson, March 8, 1941, Dawson Papers; "L. J.
Truett, 72, Brother of Cleric, Dies at McKinney," *DMN*, October 3, 1941.
Genealogical information on the Truett family can be found at the following websites:
"Schoaff Family Genealogy," http://www.schoaff.org (accessed July 10, 2007), and
"The      Truitt      Family,"      http://worldconnect.rootsweb.com/cgi-
bin/igm.cgi?op=GET&db=bgroves2&id=17477 (accessed March 3, 2007). Note that

the Truett name has several different spellings. For example, see the handwritten biographical information on the Truett family, TC 652/MF 628–657:4.

[5] James, *George W. Truett*, 6–7.

[6] Ibid., 7. Truett often referred to this event. See George W. Truett, "What Think Ye of Christ?" in *Some Vital Questions*, by George W. Truett, ed. Powhatan W. James (Grand Rapids MI: William B. Eerdmans Publishing House, 1946) 100; Joe W. Burton, "Preaching the Word," *Southern Baptist Home Missions* 12/11 (November 1941): 14, TC 438/MF 21–542:29; Joe W. Burton, *Prince of the Pulpit: A Pen Picture of George W. Truett at Work* (Grand Rapids MI: Zondervan Publishing House, 1946) 15; George W. Truett, "Trumpeting the Gospel," in *We Would See Jesus*, by George W. Truett, ed. J. B. Cranfill (New York: Fleming H. Revell Company, 1915) 74, available at http://www.archive.org/details/ wewouldseejesusa00trueuoft.

[7] See John Broadus, *A Treatise on the Preparation and Delivery of Sermons*, 2nd ed. (New York: Harper & Brothers, 1926) 493; John A. Broadus, "American Baptist Ministry of 100 Years Ago," *Baptist Quarterly* 9/1 (January 1875): 18–19.

[8] George W. Truett, "The Preacher as a Man" (address, Southwestern Baptist Theological Seminary, Fort Worth, Texas, February 18, 1914) 11, TC 1916/MF 1909–1970:2.

[9] James, *George W. Truett*, 8–9.

[10] Ibid., 9–10.

[11] Ethelene Dyer Jones, "Echoes of camp meetings and evangelist Rev. Elijah Kimsey," *Union Sentinel* (*Blairsville, GA*), May 4, 2006, http://www.unionsentinel. com/news/2006/0504/Front_Page/007.html (accessed July 2, 2007). See also Ferd McConnell's tribute to Kimsey in "Obituaries," *Christian Index*, July 16, 1896, 6.

[12] Robert H. Coleman, "George W. Truett…The Beloved," *Baptist Standard*, June 11, 1936, 35. George's brother Luther also held his parents in high esteem. In a 1915 letter to his father, Luther wrote, "Let me lay this tribute at your feet: There is no one living whose opinion I hold in such esteem as I do yours. Whatever of good there has been and is in my life, whatever of success I may have had, I owe to my parents. They have been the chief inspiration and the guiding star of my life. Upon you and mother I bestow all the love, honor and reverence of which I am capable." Luther Truett to Charles Truett, April 9, 1915, Notebook: Pastors: Truett: Pictures, Family, Ministry, GWTML.

[13] "Civil War Soldiers and Sailors System," http://www.itd.nps.gov/cwss/ soldiers.cfm (accessed October 3, 2007).

[14] "Charles L. Truett, 95, Called by Death," unidentified newspaper clipping, TC 653/MF 628–657:4.

[15] J. B. Cranfill, "A Glimpse at the Olden Time," *Baptist Standard*, May 30, 1901, 1, TC 654/MF 628–657:4.

[16] James, *George W. Truett*, 12; "Cherokee County, NC–Census–1860 Federal Census–Part 5," p. 204 (269A), see number 1346 Truett, http://ftp.rootsweb.com/pub/usgenweb/nc/cherokee/census/1860/1860cher5.txt (accessed October 3, 2007). The middle initials for Charles and his son William are incorrect on this website. Other Truetts, including Charles's widowed mother, also lived in Cherokee County in 1860. See "Cherokee County, NC–Census–1860 Federal Census–Part 4," p. 144 (239A)–p. 145 (239B), see number 958, http://ftp.rootsweb.com/pub/usgenweb/nc/cherokee/census/1860/1860cher4.txt (accessed October 3, 2007).

[17] For more on the formation of Clay County, see Carl S. Moore, *Clay County, NC: Then and Now: A Written and Pictorial History* (Franklin NC: Genealogy Publishing Service 2007) 37–39.

[18] E. C. Routh, "The Early Days of a Texas Pastor," *Baptist Standard*, September 3, 1914, 2; Coleman Craig, "Father of Dr. Truett Describes Early Days in North Carolina," *Baptist Standard*, April 26, 1923, 9, TC 655/MF 628–657:4; "Dr. Truett Underwent Many Hardships in His Youth," unidentified newspaper clipping, May 18, 1929, TC 172/MF 21–542:12.

[19] Pictures of the frame house can be found between pages 14 and 15 in James, *George W. Truett*. The Truett house still stands today, although it has had several refurbishments. In the small living area of the home, visitors can view photos of Truett, his wife, and his parents. Visitors can also ascend the small, narrow stairway to two bedrooms, one of which contains the bed in which George Truett was born.

[20] Charles E. Maddry, "A Visit to the Truett Home," unidentified newspaper clipping, September 11, 1929, TC 182/MF 21–542:13; James, *George W. Truett*, 15, 17.

[21] James, *George W. Truett*, 19, 21; J. B. Cranfill, "Life Sketch of George W. Truett," in Truett, *We Would See Jesus*, 9.

[22] George W. Truett, "How May We Know Jesus Better?" in *A Quest for Souls*, by George W. Truett, [ed. J. B. Cranfill] (New York: George H. Doran Company, 1917) 297, available at http://books.google.com/books?id=bMiGASqg YxUC&printsec=frontcover&dq=challenge+of+the+present.

[23] Ibid., 296–97.

[24] George W. Truett, untitled address to Grand Lodge of Texas, Waco, Texas, December 4, 1940, [5], TC 1964/MF 1909–1970:12. For Truett's membership in the Masons, see D. D. Tidwell, "Dr. George W. Truett," *Texas Grand Lodge Magazine*, March 1960, 113–14.

[25] "George W. Truett's Conversion and Call to the Ministry," *Baptist Messenger*, November 28, 1935, 3, TC 338/MF 21–542:22.

[26] George W. Truett, "The Mantle of Elijah," September 27, 1914, 4, TC 1822/MF 1809–1880:4.

[27] George W. Truett, "Elisha's Call to Service," in *On Eagle Wings*, by George W. Truett, ed. Powhatan W. James (Grand Rapids MI: William B. Eerdmans Publishing House, 1953) 54. At the conclusion of his description of Truett's preaching, Andrew Blackwood challenged young preachers with these words: "Young man, you have the same Bible and the same Gospel. Do you have the same simplicity and the same holy boldness? Do you enjoy the same indwelling presence and the same guidance of the Holy Spirit? That means the power of God in the life and work of a pastoral evangelist. Who will take up the mantle of George W. Truett?" Andrew Watterson Blackwood, *Preaching in Time of Reconstruction* (Great Neck NY: Pulpit Press, 1945) 54.

[28] James, *George W. Truett*, 18.

[29] Ibid., 22.

[30] Mark Leek, "History of Schools in Clay County, North Carolina," http://www.clayschools.org/ccshistory/ccshistory.htm (accessed July 10, 2007) [8]. Page numbers for this source refer to the screen page on which the information can be found. For more on Hicks, see Moore, *Clay County*, 97–98, and Guy Padgett, *A History of Clay County, North Carolina* ([Hayesville NC: Clay County Bicentennial Committee, 1976]) 85–86.

[31] Leek, "History of Schools in Clay County, North Carolina," 8–10.

[32] R. W. Prevost, "Students of John O. Hicks Recall Old Days in Clay," *Asheville-Citizen*, October 18, 1931, TC 223/MF 21–542:15; Padgett, *A History of Clay County*, 86–87; Moore, *Clay County*, 98.

[33] Charlsie Poe, "Classmate of George W. Truett," *Baptist Standard*, October 14, 1959, 8–9.

[34] James, *George W. Truett*, 15. B. H. Carroll also gives 1885 as the date when Truett finished his education at Hayesville Academy. B. H. Carroll, "Life Sketch of Rev. George W. Truett," *Baptist Standard*, July 14, 1892, 1, TC 649/MF 628–657:4.

[35] See George W. Truett, Diary, January 4, 1886, TC 662/MF 662–663:1, and many of the entries for winter and spring. Hereafter cited as Diary 1886. The diary entry for January 4 reads: "Started to school this morning to T. Neal Kitchens School [attendance] quite small to-day. Hope that our teacher will succeed in a permanent establishment of a thorough school." Truett did not identify the location of this school, but his diary entry for February 17 implies that the school was located in or near Hayesville: "Mr. Kitchens came to-day to board with us the remainder of the term. Expect to be greatly profited by his association." Truett did not mention Crooked Creek until his July 31 entry. Moreover, his August 1 entry implies that he was beginning a new phase in his life: "I must shortly start to 'Crooked Cr.' to begin school on to-morrow.... Trust that *success* may attend all my efforts, and that at the close of the term I may hear the welcome applaudit: 'Well done good and faithful servant.'"

[36] James, *George W. Truett*, 27.

[37] Poe, "Classmate of George W. Truett," 8.

[38] James, *George W. Truett*, 27–28.

[39] Rosalee Mills Appleby, "The Price of Power" (typed manuscript, n.d.) 3, Truett Baptist History File, SBHLA.

[40] Leon McBeth, *The First Baptist Church of Dallas: Centennial History, 1868–1968* (Grand Rapids MI: Zondervan Publishing House, 1968) 115; "Our Heritage," http://www.truettmemorialfbc.com/clientimages/33109/triuettpamphlet1.pdf (accessed April 12, 2007).

[41] James, *George W. Truett*, 23.

[42] George W. Truett, "What Does Salvation Involve?" in Truett, *Some Vital Questions*, 68.

[43] Joseph Martin Dawson, "President George W. Truett," *Christian Index*, June 15, 1939, 92; "Baptist Leader, Once a 'Clown Among Young People,' Product of North Carolina," *Dallas Times Herald*, September 12, 1926, TC 110/MF 21–542:8; Poe, "Classmate of George W. Truett," 8.

[44] Diary, April 3, 1886.

[45] Ibid., January 2, 1886.

[46] The amounts in parentheses represent the purchasing power in 2007. See Lawrence H. Officer and Samuel H. Williamson, "Purchasing Power of Money in the United States from 1774 to 2007," http://www.measuringworth.com.

[47] Diary, January 17, 1886.

[48] "George W. Truett's Conversion and Call to the Ministry," 3.

[49] Diary, April 18, 1886.

[50] Ibid., February 14, 1886.

[51] Ibid., March 28, April 11, April 16, and May 9, 1886.

[52] Ibid., March 14 and May 22, 1886.

[53] Ibid., May 31, 1886.

[54] Ibid., April 15, 16, and 19, 1886.

[55] Ibid., March 31, 1886.

[56] Ibid., January 30/31, 1886.

[57] Ibid., April 1, 1886.

[58] Ibid., April 15, 1886.

[59] Ibid., May 9, 1886.

[60] Ibid., May 29, 1886.

[61] Ibid., February 14, 1886. The date of this entry is probably incorrect. Truett says that Friday was February 14, but the fourteenth fell on a Sunday.

[62] Ibid., April 11, 1886. The date of this entry should probably be April 10.

[63] Ibid., [May 1], 1886.

[64] Ibid., May 27, 1886. This topic appears to have been a popular one, for Truett recorded that the same question had been debated on March 27.

[65] Ibid., May 14, 1886. Truett held similar views at least until 1906. See George W. Truett, untitled sermon on Dan. 3:16–18, August 12, 1906, 6, TC 1842/MF 1809–1880:9.

[66] Diary, March 7 and May 17, 1886.

[67] Ibid., April 24, 1886.

[68] Ibid., May 6, 1886.

[69] Ibid., June 10, 1886. This incident might be the one discussed in James, *George W. Truett*, 16, although Truett described killing a "large yellow rattlesnake" on September 16 while he and his father were again looking for cattle. See Diary, September 17, 1886.

[70] Diary, June 13, 1886.

[71] "Charles L. Truett, 95, Called by Death."

[72] Diary, June 10, 1886.

[73] Ibid., June 15, 1886.

[74] Ibid., [June] 22, 1886. Truett has May 22.

[75] Ibid., June 26, 1886.

[76] Ibid., June 28, 1886.

[77] Ibid., June 27, 1886.

[78] Ibid., July 3, 1886.

[79] Ibid., July 7, 1886.

[80] Ibid., July 20, 1886.

[81] Ibid., July 21, 1886.

[82] [A. C. Dixon], "Asheville, N.C. (George W. Truett)," Amzi Clarence Dixon Papers, SBHLA. See also [A. C. Dixon], "Asheville, N.C. (George W. Truett), From sermon 139-Fishing for Men," Dixon Papers; J. G. Pulliam to Mrs. A. C. Dixon, April 8, 1929, Dixon Papers.

[83] See Diary 1886 for the dates in this paragraph.

[84] See ibid., July 3, 8, 14, 16, 17, 19, and 20, 1886.

[85] Ibid., July 9, 14, and 16, 1886.

[86] Ibid., August 14, 1886. See also James, *George W. Truett*, 29.

[87] Diary, August 8, 1886.

[88] James, *George W. Truett*, 29–30.

[89] Diary, September 19, 1886.

[90] Ibid., September 26, 1886.

[91] Ibid., September 30, 1886.

[92] Ibid., October 3, 1886.

[93] "George W. Truett's Conversion and Call to the Ministry," 3; James, *George W. Truett*, 24.

[94] Diary, October 3, 1886.

[95] Truett, "What Does Salvation Involve?" 68.

[96] "George W. Truett's Conversion and Call to the Ministry," 3.

[97] Truett, "What Does Salvation Involve?" 68. See also George W. Truett, "Blessings," in Truett, *On Eagle Wings*, 109.

[98] "George W. Truett's Conversion and Call to the Ministry," 3.

[99] Ibid.

[100] Ibid.

[101] Diary, October 10, 1886.

[102] Ibid., October 17, 1886.

[103] Ibid.

[104] George W. Truett, "Stir up the Gift of God," in *Sermons from Paul*, by George W. Truett, ed. Powhatan W. James (Grand Rapids MI: William B. Eerdmans Publishing House, 1947) 161.

[105] Diary, 17 October 1886.

[106] Ibid., October 31, 1886.

[107] Ibid., November 28, 1886.

[108] Ibid., November 14, 1886.

[109] Ibid., November 28, 1886.

[110] Ibid.

[111] James, *George W. Truett*, 30–31.

[112] Ibid., 31–32. For a photograph of the building see between pages 30 and 31.

[113] Ibid., 31–34.

[114] George W. Truett, "Stir up the Gift of God," 168.

[115] Gainer Bryan, Jr., "The Moonshiner Who Heard Truett Pray," Notebook: Pastors; Truett Biographical Histories and Funeral, GWTML.

[116] James, *George W. Truett*, 32.

[117] Ibid., 33.

[118] "Dr. Truett Describes How Love Helped Him Win First Convert," *DMN*, March 10, 1941.

[119] Minutes, Hayesville (NC) Baptist Church, November 27, 1887, Truett Baptist History File.

[120] Ibid., n.d., 1887.

[121] Ibid., January 1, 1888.

[122] Ibid., May 26, 1888.

[123] William D. Upshaw, "From Mountain Home to Pulpit Throne," *Alabama Baptist*, August 1, 1935, 6, TC 335/MF 21–542:22.

[124] John E. White, "George W. Truett, the Man and Preacher," in Truett, *We Would See Jesus*, 17.

[125] Albert McClellan, *The Executive Committee of the Southern Baptist Convention, 1917–1984* (Nashville: Broadman Press, 1985) 86.

[126] "The Beginning of George Truett," *Golden Age*, May 6, 1909, 1, TC 23/MF 21–542:2.

[127] "Georgia Baptist Convention," *Christian Index*, May 2, 1889, 8. According to Ada Truett Gillespie, a niece of George Truett, the "impromptu" speech at the convention was prepared well in advance. She informed DeWitte Talmage Holland that her father, James L. Truett, helped George Truett on several occasions to prepare the speech. Ada Truett Gillespie to DeWitte Talmage Holland, n.d., in "A Rhetorical Analysis of the Preaching of George W. Truett," by DeWitte Talmage Holland (Ph.D. diss., Northwestern University, 1956) 130. Truett, however, maintained that McConnell's calling upon him to speak was unexpected. See George W. Truett, Diary, April 19, 1941, TC 668/MF 664–690:17.

[128] White, "George W. Truett, the Man and Preacher," 18; James, *George W. Truett*, 40.

[129] Newton, "Oral Memoirs," 27.

[130] Craig, "Father of Dr. Truett Describes Early Days in North Carolina," 9.

[131] "Mrs. Joan C. Truett," Notebook: Pastors: Truett: Pictures, Family, Ministry, GWTML.

[132] Ibid.; "J. H. Truett," *Baptist Standard*, February 1, 1900, 11; James, *George W. Truett*, 40–41.

[133] John S. Ramond, ed., *Among Southern Baptists*, vol.1 (Kansas City MO: Western Baptist Publishing Company, 1936) 506; "Mrs. James L. Truett Dies; Sister-in-Law of Dallas Minister," *DMN*, January 14, 1939.

[134] Autograph book with inscriptions from George W. Truett's students at Hiawassee, Georgia, May 1889, GWTML.

[135] James, *George W. Truett*, 41; "J. H. Truett," 1; Cranfill, "A Glimpse at the Olden Time," 1.

[136] Brian Hart, "Whitewright, Texas," in *Handbook of Texas Online*, http://www.tsha.utexas.edu/handbook/online/articles/WW/hjw10.html (accessed August 6, 2007).

[137] James, *George W. Truett*, 44.

[138] Ibid., 45.

[139] McBeth, *The First Baptist Church of Dallas*, 119; James, *George W. Truett*, 47–48.

[140] George W. Truett, "The Mission of Jesus," in *Who Is Jesus?* by George W. Truett, ed. Powhatan W. James (Grand Rapids MI: William B. Eerdmans Publishing House, 1952) 28.

[141] "George W. Truett's Conversion and Call to the Ministry," 3.

[142] George W. Gray, "Out of the Mountains Came This Great Preacher of the Plains," *American Magazine*, November 1925, 134, TC 106/MF 21–542:7.

[143] "George W. Truett's Conversion and Call to the Ministry," 3.

[144] Gray, "Out of the Mountains Came This Great Preacher of the Plains," 134.

[145] Ibid. Despite his public protests, Truett apparently had been struggling with his call to preach ever since his conversion. See Truett, "The Preacher as a Man," 2.

[146] "George W. Truett's Conversion and Call to the Ministry," 3.

[147] Coleman, "George W. Truett…The Beloved," *Baptist Standard*, 35.

[148] James, *George W. Truett*, 50.

[149] Cranfill, "Life Sketch of George W. Truett," 11.

[150] William D. Upshaw, "From Mountain Home to Pulpit Throne," 6.

[151] James, *George W. Truett*, 54–56.

## Chapter 2

[1] Robert G. Torbet, *A History of the Baptists*, 3rd ed. (Valley Forge PA: Judson Press, 1963) 425–26; Thomas A. Askew and Richard V. Pierard, *The American Church Experience: A Concise History* (Grand Rapids MI: Baker Academic, 2004) 129–32.

[2] Walter Rauschenbusch, *Christianity and the Social Crisis* (New York: MacMillan Co., 1907; repr., New York: Association Press, 1912) xiii.

[3] "Dr. Truett Missionary to Savages, Relatives of Dallasite Opine," *DMN*, December 20, 1933.

[4] J. B Cranfill to Powhatan James, July 27, 1937, TC 847/MF 736–1336:11.

[5] Harry Leon McBeth, *Texas Baptists: A Sesquicentennial History* (Dallas: Baptistway Press, 1998) 84.

[6] William D. Upshaw, "From Mountain Home to Pulpit Throne," *Alabama Baptist*, August 1, 1935, 6, TC 335/MF 21–542:22.

[7] Powhatan W. James, *George W. Truett: A Biography* (Nashville: Broadman Press, 1939) 56–58.

[8] B. H. Carroll and George W. Truett, "Account of a Great Battle," *Baptist Standard*, March 23, 1893, 1.

[9] Robert A. Baker, *Tell the Generations Following: A History of Southwestern Baptist Theological Seminary, 1903–1983* (Nashville: Broadman Press, 1983) 67–68.

[10] George W. Truett, "The Value of Life's Unrealized Purposes," in *On Eagle Wings*, by George W. Truett, ed. Powhatan W. James (Grand Rapids MI: William B. Eerdmans Publishing House, 1953) 179.

[11] [Illegible] Smith to George W. Truett, February 9, 1893, J. M. Carroll Collection, folder 689, AWRL. See also J. M. Carroll, *A History of Texas Baptists*, ed. J. B. Cranfill (Dallas: Baptist Standard Publishing Co., 1923) 896.

[12] George W. Truett, "Save the Cities," *Central Baptist*, April 25, 1907, 6, TC 556/MF 554–590:1.

[13] See J. W. Bruner, "Dr. B. H. Carroll's Money Creed" (Founder's Day address, Southwestern Baptist Theological Seminary, Fort Worth, Texas, January 27, 1942).

[14] Baker, *Tell the Generations Following*, 70.

[15] Thomas L. Watson, "Eschatology of B. H. Carroll" (Master's thesis, Southwestern Baptist Theological Seminary, 1960) 33–35.

[16] "An English Baptist's Appreciation of Pastor Truett," *Baptist Standard*, November 14, 1918, 5; "Writes Appreciation of Dr. G. W. Truett," *DMN*, November 3, 1918.

[17] See Alan J. Lefever, *Fighting the Good Fight: The Life and Work of Benajah Harvey Carroll* (Austin Texas: Eakin Press, 1994) 26–27, 44–51; L. R. Elliott, "Introduction: The Heart of Texas Baptist Life," in *Centennial Story of Texas Baptists*, ed. [L. R. Elliott] (Dallas: Executive Board of the Baptist General Convention of Texas, 1936) 11.

[18] J. N. Marshall, "George W. Truett," *Baptist Standard*, June 18, 1936, 1, TC 343/MF 21–542:22.

[19] Ibid. For Truett's intensity in the pulpit, see also J. B. Gambrell, "Geo. W. Truett, Preacher and Leader," *Baptist Standard*, January 16, 1913, 3, and Peter Clark Macfarlane, "The Apostle to the Texans," *Collier's*, January 16, 1913, 3, TC 24/MF 21–542:3. Macfarlane's article can also be found in the *DMN*, December 12, 1912.

[20] Macfarlane, "The Apostle to the Texans," 3.

[21] George T. Wood, "Studies of the American Pulpit: George W. Truett," *Homiletic Review* 93/2 (February 1927): 94, TC 114/MF 21–542:9. See also Gambrell, "Geo. W. Truett, Preacher and Leader," 3; George T. Wood, "Analytical Study of Six Representative Preachers," c. 1927, 4, TC 628/MF 628–657:1; and J. L. Rosser, "George Truett, Preacher," *Review and Expositor* 35/1 (January 1938): 15.

[22] The text for *Doing God's Will* was Joshua 17:5: "He left nothing undone of all the Lord had commanded Moses" (KJV). Truett preached on this verse on July 21, 1935 and on at least two occasions in the 1940s, the dates of which are listed in the text. The TC 1676/MF 1676:1 contains three lists of Truett's sermons and their dates. Because Truett did not title his sermons, these lists contain his sermon topics and usually quote the Bible verse or part of the verse about which he preached and occasionally identify the verse by citing the biblical book and chapter from which it was taken. The three sermon lists in the TC are: "Lists of Sermons and Addresses" (sermons and addresses from 1914 to 1918 and in 1920); "Sermon Topics of Dr. George W. Truett, Preached at the morning hour" (morning sermons from January 2, 1927 to July 18, 1943); and "Sermons by Dr. Geo. W. Truett, D. D." (some morning and evening sermons from 1914 to 1918).

[23] George W. Truett, *Doing God's Will* [audio recording] (Waco TX: Word, n.d.), AWRL and SBHLA.

[24] Ibid.

[25] James, *George W. Truett*, 53.

[26] Joseph Martin Dawson, "Pastor of the South's Largest Church," *Church Management*, October 1932, 16, TC 257/MF 21–542:17.

[27] George W. Truett to B. H. Carroll, May 20, 1891, in Lefever, *Fighting the Good Fight*, 55.

[28] Powhatan W. James, "George W. Truett," in *Ten Men from Baylor*, ed. J. M. Price, (Kansas City: Central Seminary Press, 1945) 162.

[29] No title, *Baptist Standard*, March 10, 1892, 4.

[30] Samuel P. Brooks, "Words of Appreciation about Dr. Geo. W. Truett at the Twenty Fifth Anniversary of His Pastorate of the First Baptist Church of Dallas," September 12, 1922, 2, TC 637/MF 628–657:2. See also "Dallas Honors Dr. Truett in Long Service," *DMN*, November 9, 1927.

[31] Brooks, "Words of Appreciation," 3.

[32] George W. Truett, "Baylor University," *Baptist Standard*, March 24, 1892, 5.

[33] George W. Truett, "Baylor University," *Baptist Standard*, April 14, 1892, 4.

[34] The amounts in parentheses represent the purchasing power in 2007. See Lawrence H. Officer and Samuel H. Williamson, "Purchasing Power of Money in the United States from 1774 to 2007," http://www.measuringworth.com.

[35] George W. Gray, "Out of the Mountains Came This Great Preacher of the Plains," *American Magazine*, November 1925, 136, 138, TC 106/MF 21–542:7.

[36] George W. Truett, "The Victory of Faith," in *Follow Thou Me*, by George W. Truett (Nashville: Broadman Press, n.d.) 24–25.

[37] Ibid., 25.

[38] "Vital quotes from Dr. Truett," October 18, 1892, TC 631/MF 628–657:1. These quotations are excerpts of letters from Truett to unidentified recipients.

[39] James, *George W. Truett*, 63–64.

[40] Diane Lindstrom, "Depressions, Economic," in *The Oxford Companion to United States History*, ed. Paul Boyer (Oxford: Oxford University Press, 2001) 184; Joseph R. Conlin, *The American Past: A Brief History* (San Diego: Harcourt Brace Jovanovich, Publishers, 1991) 415–16.

[41] J. B. Cranfill, *Dr. J. B. Cranfill's Chronicle* (New York: Fleming H. Revell, 1916) 435, available at http://books.google.com/books?id=6JwDAAAAYAA-J&pg=PP20&dq=j.+b.+cranfill#PPP19,M1.

[42] Carroll and Truett, "Account of a Great Battle," 1.

[43] Ibid.

[44] Ibid.

[45] Gray, "Out of the Mountains Came This Great Preacher of the Plains," 138.

[46] H. Leon McBeth, "Two Ways to Be Baptist," *Baptist History and Heritage* 32/2 (April 1997): 41.

[47] Brooks, "Words of Appreciation," 4.

[48] See DeWitte Talmage Holland, "A Rhetorical Analysis of the Preaching of George W. Truett" (Ph.D. diss., Northwestern University, 1956) 635. Holland titled the appendix in which he listed these classes, "Baylor Transcript of George W. Truett." Truett apparently dropped another class (Calculus) and was excused from another (Jr. Greek).

[49] Truett's notes for a Bible class can be found in the TC 1563/MF 1563–1575:1–3.

[50] W. C. Garrett, "What Dr. Truett Has Been to Me," TC 644/MF 628–657:3.

[51] Gray, "Out of the Mountains Came This Great Preacher of the Plains," 138.

[52] "Vital quotes from Dr. Truett," December 9, 1893.

[53] Ibid., February 24, 1894.

[54] Ibid.

[55] Holland, "A Rhetorical Analysis of the Preaching of George W. Truett," 154; *Manual of East Waco Baptist Church* (Waco: Knight Printing Co., 1896), 3, TC 651/MF 628–657:4; J. B. Cranfill, "Life Sketch of George W. Truett," in *We Would See Jesus*, by George W. Truett, ed. J. B. Cranfill (New York: Fleming H. Revell Company, 1915) 11–12, available at http://www.archive.org/details/ wewouldseejesusa00trueuoft.

[56] See her graduation announcement in the TC 1401/MF 1373–1403:3.

[57] George W. Truett, "The Inspiration of Ideals" (commencement address, Baylor University, Waco, Texas, June 1897) 1, TC 2/MF 2–20:1. See also George W. Truett, "The Inspiration of Ideals," in *The Inspiration of Ideals*, by George W. Truett, ed. Powhatan W. James (Grand Rapids MI: William B. Eerdmans Publishing House, 1950) 13–21.

[58] Ibid., 1. All references to "The Inspiration of Ideals" refer to the handwritten copy in the TC.

[59] Ibid.

[60] Ibid., 2–3.

[61] Ibid., 4.

[62] Ibid., 6.

[63] Ibid., 7–8.

[64] Ibid., 13.

[65] James, *George W. Truett*, 79.

[66] Deacons Minutes, First Baptist Church (FBC), Dallas, Texas, May 9, 1897.

[67] J. B. Gambrell, "The First Church, Dallas, Texas," *Watchman-Examiner*, May 8, 1919, 672, TC 34/MF 21–542:3.

[68] Joan Jenkins Perez, "Christopher Columbus Slaughter," in *Handbook of Texas Online*, http://www.tsha.utexas.edu/handbook/online/articles/SS/fsl1.html (accessed December 20, 2007).

[69] Cranfill, *Dr. J. B. Cranfill's Chronicle*, 487; Cranfill, "Life Sketch of George W. Truett," 12; Leon McBeth, *The First Baptist Church of Dallas: Centennial History (1868–1968)* Grand Rapids MI: Zondervan Publishing House, 1968) 112.

[70] "Local Notes," *DMN*, September 20, 1891.

[71] Minutes, First Baptist Church (FBC), Dallas, Texas, August 4, 1897.

[72] "A Pastor Called," *DMN*, August 8, 1897.

[73] "The Beginning of George Truett," *Golden Age*, May 6, 1909, 1, TC 23/MF 21–542:3.

[74] James, *George W. Truett*, 81.

[75] "First Baptist Church," *DMN*, August 29, 1897; "Accepted the Call," *DMN*, August 30, 1897; Minutes, FBC, Dallas, September 1, 1897.

[76] Minutes, FBC, Dallas, September 12, 1897.

[77] George W. Truett to Josephine Truett, September 20, 1897, TC 1337/MF 1337–1347:1.

[78] James, *George W. Truett*, 83. In his telling of the story, Joe W. Burton mentions different amounts of money. See Joe W. Burton, *Prince of the Pulpit: A Pen Picture of George W. Truett at Work* (Grand Rapids MI: Zondervan Publishing House, 1946) 73.

[79] G. Truett to J. Truett, September 20, 1897. The place in the letter at which Truett recorded the amount given at the morning service is ripped, but the amount appears to be $250.

[80] Lana Henderson, *Baylor University Medical Center: Yesterday, Today and Tomorrow* (Waco: Baylor University Press, 1978) 8.

[81] "Cleaner Dallas League," *DMN*, June 22, 1899.

[82] Henderson, *Baylor University Medical Center*, 9; Jackie McElhaney and Michael V. Hazel, "Dallas, Texas," in *Handbook of Texas Online*, http://www.tsha-online.org/handbook/online/articles/DD/hdd1.html (accessed December 20, 2007).

[83] Peter Wallace Agnew, "Religion and the Social Order in a Twentieth-Century City: Six Dallas Leaders" (Ph.D. diss., Southern Methodist University, 1999) 16, 27, 37–39.

[84] See page 4 of Truett's 1918 passport, TC 686/MF 664–690:42.

[85] George W. Truett, ["Response of Truett to the Baptist General Convention of Texas, Waco, Texas, 1898"], 5–6, TC 3/MF 2–21:1. "Ebenezer" means "stone of help" and was placed by Samuel between the cities of Mizpeh and Shen to commemorate an Israelite victory over the Philistines. See 1 Sam. 7:12.

[86] The details of the Arnold incident come from three sources: excerpts from George W. Baines's diary, which can be found in McBeth, *The First Baptist Church of Dallas*, 135–36; George W. Baines, "Chief Arnold's Taking Off," *DMN*, February 14,

1898; and ["Statement by W. M. Baines, son of George W. Baines, concerning the Arnold shooting"], April 24, 1959, TC 629/MF 628–657:1.

[87] ["Statement by W. M. Baines, son of George W. Baines, concerning the Arnold shooting"].

[88] Baines, "Chief Arnold's Taking Off."

[89] "Captain Arnold Wounded," *DMN*, February 5, 1898.

[90] J. M. Dawson, "Truett's Gethsemane now Revealed," [1958], 2, TC 629/MF 628–657:1.

[91] McBeth, *The First Baptist Church of Dallas*, 137. Truett might have referred to this time in his life in his sermon "The Ministry of Suffering," in *A Quest for Souls*, by George W. Truett, [ed. J. B. Cranfill] (New York: George H. Doran Company, 1917) 265, available at http://www.archive.org/details/questfor-souls009583mbp.

[92] "Church Notes," *DMN*, February 6, 1898.

[93] "Arnold Funeral," *DMN*, February 10, 1898.

[94] "Church Notes," *DMN*, February 20, 1898. See also "Texas News and Notes," *Baptist Standard*, February 24, 1898, 8.

[95] Gray, "Out of the Mountains Came This Great Preacher of the Plains," 138.

[96] McBeth, *The First Baptist Church of Dallas*, 137.

[97] James, *George W. Truett*, 88n2.

[98] George W. Truett to George W. Baines, February 25, 1898, in Dawson, "Truett's Gethsemane now Revealed," 3.

[99] Gray, "Out of the Mountains Came This Great Preacher of the Plains," 140. See also Dawson, "Truett's Gethsemane now Revealed," 3.

[100] Holland, "A Rhetorical Analysis of the Preaching of George W. Truett," 631. Holland (631–34) listed thirty-three examples of Truett's membership on committees and boards of institutions.

[101] Other honorary degrees included a D. D. from Southwestern Baptist University, Jackson, Tennessee (A. J. Crook to George W. Truett, June 7, 1902, TC 850/MF 736–1336:12); a Doctor of Laws from the University of Alabama (George H. Denny to George W. Truett, May 21, 1931, TC 874/MF 736–1336:14); a D. D. from McMaster University, Toronto, Canada ("D. D. Degree Given Truett," *DMN*, June 27, 1928); and a Doctor of Laws from Southern Methodist University, Dallas, Texas (Charles C. Selecman to George W. Truett, February 12, 1935, TC 1213/MF 736–1336:49). That people referred to Truett as "Dr. Truett," a practice he accepted, exasperated J. Frank Norris, who became an opponent of Truett. While editor and owner of the *Baptist Standard*, Norris complained, "Let us say Mr. Truett or Bro. Truett. Can you imagine 'Doctor' Spurgeon?" Whether Norris ever got over Truett's being called doctor is unknown; however, he did eventually overcome his animosity toward preachers being called doctor, for he subtitled his autobiography, *Life Story of Dr. J. Frank Norris*. See J. Frank Norris, *Inside History of First Baptist Church Fort*

*Worth and Temple Baptist Church Detroit: Life Story of Dr. J. Frank Norris* ([Fort Worth: n.p., n.d.]). For the Norris quote, see Presnall H. Wood and Floyd W. Thatcher, *Prophets with Pens* (Dallas: Baptist Standard Publishing, Co., 1969) 65. In 1923, F. S. Groner called attention to Norris's use of his honorary doctorates when he referred to "[t]he very Rev. Mr. Norris, D.D., D.D., D.D. (for he boasts that he has three pairs of D's." See F. S. Groner, "Editor Norris Greatly Embarrassed by Ecclesiastical Entanglements and High Financing Schemes," *Baptist Standard*, June 14, 1923, 9.

[102] "He Is Undecided," *DMN*, June 12, 1899.

[103] Ibid.

[104] "Editorial Brevities," *Baptist Standard*, June 22, 1899, 4.

[105] "Rev. George W. Truett," *Baptist Standard*, June 29, 1899, 4. This article of the *Standard* and the *Dallas Morning News* article "Rev. Truett Declined," June 28, 1899, contain Truett's rejection letter to B. H. Carroll, president of Baylor's board of trustees.

[106] "Is Asked to Decline," *DMN*, October 7, 1901. See also Minutes, FBC, October 6, 1901.

[107] "Declines the Call," *DMN*, October 14, 1901.

[108] Ibid.

[109] See TC 1361, 1362, 1363, 1365, and 1372/MF 1360–1372:1. See also "Dr. Truett Will Remain," *DMN*, April 6, 1903; "Dr. Truett Called to San Antonio *DMN*, February 19, 1904; and David Brian Whitlock, "Southern Baptists and Southern Culture: Three Visions of a Christian America, 1890–1945" (Ph.D. diss., Southern Baptist Theological Seminary, 1988) 234.

[110] John L. Peak et al., to George W. Truett, March 25, 1903, TC 1363/MF 1360–1372:1. Calvary eventually called Truett's cousin Ferd McConnell to be its pastor. See Louie Devotie Newton, "McConnell, Fernando Coello," in *Encyclopedia of Southern Baptists*, ed. Norman Wade Cox and Judson Boyce Allen, 2 vols. (Nashville: Broadman Press, 1958) 2:839.

[111] George W. Truett, "The Dedication of a Church," in Truett, *The Inspiration of Ideals*, 178.

[112] Katy Stokes, "Leander Randon Millican," in *Handbook of Texas Online*, http://www.tshaonline.org/handbook/online/articles/MM/fmi67.html (accessed January 21, 2008). These meetings still occur every July.

[113] For example, see the following articles, all of which appeared in the *DMN*: "Revival at Baptist Church," December 8, 1902; "Large Crowd at Revival," February 3, 1903; "Revival at Bryan Closes," May 1, 1904; "Revival Services at Cisco," July 24, 1905; "Revival at McKinney Begins," November 29, 1905; "Attendance at Revival," April 10, 1906; "Dr. Truett Returns," August 13, 1906; and "Many Hear Dr. Truett," April 15, 1907.

[114] "University of Texas," *DMN*, June 6, 1904.

[115] George W. Truett, "The Power of Convictions," in Truett, *The Inspiration of Ideals*, 50.

[116] Ibid., 51.

[117] Ibid., 62. Truett also preached the 1900 baccalaureate sermon to Texas A. & M.'s twenty-seven graduates and the 1907 commencement sermon at Furman University in South Carolina. See "A. and M. Commencement," *DMN*, June 2, 1900; "Commencement at A. and M.," *DMN*, June 11, 1900; and "Dr. Truett Is in Tennessee," *DMN*, June 3, 1907.

[118] George W. Truett, "The Leaf and the Life," in *God's Call to America*, by George W. Truett, ed. J. B. Cranfill (Philadelphia: Judson Press, 1923) 111–12. This address can also be found in the *Baptist Standard*, July 3, 1902, 6–8, and in Truett, *The Inspiration of Ideals*, 25–45. A handwritten copy of the address can be found in the TC 1894/MF 1881–1908:3–4.

[119] Ibid., 112–13. All references to "The Leaf and the Life" come from *God's Call to America*.

[120] Ibid., 113.

[121] Ibid., 114.

[122] Ibid., 115.

[123] Ibid., 121–22.

[124] Ibid., 125. Concerning this point, see George W. Truett, "Some Lessons from a Great Revival," *Baptist Standard*, March 29, 1900, 1, and Truett's "Welcome Address," in "And Still the Greatest," *Baptist Standard*, November 12, 1903, 1.

[125] Truett, "The Leaf and the Life," 126.

[126] Ibid., 128.

[127] Ibid., 130–31.

[128] Ibid., 139.

[129] "For Peace Congress," *DMN*, October 13, 1907; "State Peace Conference," *DMN*, October 28, 1907; "Texas Peace Conference," *DMN*, November 21, 1907.

[130] George W. Truett, "Why Save a Human Life?" in Truett, *God's Call to America*, 140. This address can also be found in the *Baptist Standard*, December 26, 1907, 1, and in the TC 558/MF 554–590:2.

[131] Ibid., 141. All references to "Why Save a Human Life?" come from *God's Call to America*.

[132] Ibid., 142.

[133] Ibid., 143.

[134] Ibid., 146.

[135] Ibid., 147.

[136] Ibid., 148.

[137] Ibid., 150.

[138] Ibid., 151. For Fritel's painting, see http://www.abchistory.cz/valky.htm (accessed August 7, 2007). The reference to nations beating their swords into ploughshares and their spears into pruning hooks comes from Isa. 2:4.

[139] George W. Truett to Josephine Truett, January 4, 1900, TC 1338/MF 1337–1347:1.

[140] George W. Truett to Josephine Truett, December 11, 1901, TC 1338/MF 1337–1347:1.

[141] Ibid.

[142] George W. Truett to Josephine Truett, June 28, [1902], TC 1338/MF 1337–1347:1.

[143] Henderson, *Baylor University Medical Center*, 8–10. See also Charles M. Rosser, *Doctors and Doctors, Wise and Otherwise: On the Firing Line Fifty Years* (Dallas: Mathis, Van Nort & Company, 1941) 141–46.

[144] Henderson, *Baylor University Medical Center*, 12–13.

[145] Rosser, *Doctors and Doctors*, 151–52.

[146] Minutes, FBC, December 15, 1897.

[147] Henderson, *Baylor University Medical Center*, 19.

[148] Ibid., 21–22.

[149] Adolf Lorenz to Charles M. Rosser, March 17, 1931, in Rosser, *Doctors and Doctors*, 182.

[150] "Speech by Guest," *DMN*, May 24, 1903.

[151] Ibid. Rosser quoted Truett as saying, "With our magnificently growing city, with our young though promising medical school, with our splendidly equipped medical profession, I raise the question: 'Is it not time to begin the erection of a great humanitarian hospital, one to which men of all creeds and those of none may come with equal confidence?'" Rosser, *Doctors and Doctors*, 183–84.

[152] Rosser, *Doctors and Doctors*, 183.

[153] Ibid., 184.

[154] "Dallas Gets Baylor," *DMN*, June 18, 1903; Charles T. Morrissey, "Baylor College of Medicine," in *Handbook of Texas Online*, http://www.tshaonline.org/handbook/online/articles/BB/kbb7.html (accessed January 25, 2008).

[155] "From Rev. Dr. Truett," *DMN*, June 19, 1903.

[156] George W. Truett, "Christianity's Companion, the Healing Art," *Baptist Standard*, December 3, 1904, 2. The text of this address can also be found under the title "The Texas Baptist Memorial Sanitarium" (N.p.: n.d.), TC 1913/MF 1909–1970:1.

[157] "Great Hospital Site," *DMN*, November 1, 1903.

[158] McBeth, *Texas Baptists*, 138.

[159] "Great Hospital Site."

[160] "Memorial Sanitarium," *DMN*, November 10, 1903; *Annual*, Baptist General Convention (BGCT), 1903, 65–66.

[161] Truett, "Christianity's Companion, the Healing Art," 2.

[162] See "Memorial Sanitarium Sure," *DMN*, November 13, 1904.

[163] Truett, "Christianity's Companion, the Healing Art," 2.

[164] Ibid.

[165] Ibid.

[166] Ibid.

[167] Ibid.

[168] Ibid.

[169] George W. Truett, "Let Us Keep It Going," *Baptist Standard*, March 2, 1905, 1, 5; Henderson, *Baylor University Medical Center*, 31.

[170] Gambrell, "Geo. W. Truett, Preacher and Leader," 3.

[171] George W. Truett to "My Dear Fellow Church Members," April 10, 1906, TC 1426/MF 1425–1431:1. For other letters concerning special offerings, see George W. Truett to "My Dear Christian Friend," October 17, 1901, TC 1431/MF 1425–1431:1, and George W. Truett to "My Dear Christian Friend," April 8, 1904, TC 1426/MF 1425–1431:1.

[172] For examples, see the following articles by Truett in the *Baptist Standard*: "Texas Baptist Affairs for 1901," December 20, 1900, 1, 5; "A Great Situation," August 14, 1902, 1, 5; "The Coming Waco Convention," October 2, 1902, 1; and "Responsibility of Texas Pastors," October 8, 1903, 1.

[173] Truett, "A Great Situation," 1. See also Truett, "Responsibility of Texas Pastors," 1.

[174] Truett, "The Coming Waco Convention," 1.

[175] Truett, "Christianity's Companion, the Healing Art," 3.

[176] Ibid.

[177] Ibid.

[178] [George W. Truett], "Notes for Sanitarium Campaign," 1904, TC 1574/MF 1563–1575: 3.

[179] [George W. Truett], "List of Names for the Texas Bapt. M. Sanitarium, 1904," TC 1574/ MF 1563–1575:12.

[180] Ibid., TC 1574/ MF 1563–1575:13.

[181] George W. Truett, J. B. Gambrell, and R. C. Buckner, "An Urgent Call to Action," *Baptist Standard*, June 22, 1905, 1.

[182] George W. Truett, "Concerning the Sanitarium," *Baptist Standard*, November 30, 1905, 1.

[183] *Annual*, BGCT, 1906, 69.

[184] *Annual*, BGCT, 1906, 70–71.

[185] George W. Truett, *The Larger Day for Texas Baptists* (N.p.: [1906]) 11, TC 1581/MF 1576–1595:2.

[186] Ibid.

[187] Ibid., 11–12.

[188] Ibid., 13.

[189] Ibid., 13–14.

[190] Thomas Robert Havins, "Benevolent Ministries," in *Centennial Story of Texas Baptists*, ed. [L. R. Elliott] (Dallas: Executive Board of the Baptist General Convention of Texas, 1936) 183.

[191] McBeth, *The First Baptist Church of Dallas*, 202; Holland, "A Rhetorical Analysis of the Preaching of George W. Truett," 49.

[192] John E. White, "George W. Truett, the Man and Preacher," in Truett, *We Would See Jesus*, 20.

[193] *Annual*, BGCT, 1896, 22.

[194] Ibid., 23.

[195] McBeth, *Texas Baptists*, 119.

[196] "Convention in Tears," *DMN*, November 9, 1897; McBeth, *Texas Baptists*, 120.

[197] George W. Truett, "A Word About the Lawsuit," *Baptist Standard*, December 11, 1902, 1. Truett made similar remarks in his welcome address at the 1903 BGCT meeting in Dallas. See George W. Truett, "Welcome Address," 4.

[198] McBeth, *Texas Baptists*, 120–21; "End of Famous Case," *DMN*, May 4, 1905. For an in-depth study of the entire controversy with Hayden, see Joe E. Early, *A Texas Baptist Power Struggle: The Hayden Controversy* (Denton TX: University of North Texas Press, 2005). This controversy is often called the Hayden-Cranfill controversy. Cranfill, however, preferred to call it "the Hell-raising of Hayden." See J. B Cranfill to Powhatan James, July 27, 1937, TC 847/MF 736–1336:11. Also in this letter Cranfill contended that the "Hayden lawyers…were all as mean as the devil."

[199] Samuel Tullock has questioned Norris's description of McKinney Avenue's growth during his pastorate. See Samuel K. Tullock, "The Transformation of American Fundamentalism: The Life and Career of John Franklyn Norris" (Ph.D. diss., University of Texas at Dallas, 1997), 52.

[200] John W. Storey, *Texas Baptist Leadership and Social Christianity, 1900–1980* (College Station: Texas A&M University Press, 1986) 46–47. See also Clovis Gwin Morris, "He Changed Things: The Life and Thought of J. Frank Norris" (Ph.D. diss., Texas Tech University, 1973) 45n18.

[201] "Address of J. Frank Norris," *DMN*, November 11, 1907.

[202] Norris, *Inside History of First Baptist Church Fort Worth and Temple Baptist Church Detroit*, 24–25.

[203] George W. Truett, "Response at SBC at Norfolk, 1898," 12, TC 1911/MF 1909–1970:1. See also Truett, ["Response of Truett to BGCT Convention, Waco, Texas, 1898"], 20. Truett also read the report of the committee on the work of the Sunday School Board at the 1898 SBC meeting. See *Annual*, Southern Baptist Convention (SBC), 1898, 23–24.

[204] *Annual*, SBC, 1898, 32.

[205] George W. Truett, "The Subject and the Object of the Gospel," in Truett, *We Would See Jesus*, 202.

[206] Ibid., 202. See also Truett, "The Leaf and the Life," 135–36.

[207] Truett, "The Subject and the Object of the Gospel," 203.

[208] Ibid., 212–13.

[209] Ibid., 214.

[210] *Annual*, SBC, 1903, 34.

[211] Eugene P. Alldredge, "Amazing Achievements of Dr. George W. Truett's Ministry, 1897–1941," *Quarterly Review* 1/4 (October–December 1941): 59.

[212] McBeth, *The First Baptist Church of Dallas*, 125.

[213] Ibid., 114.

[214] Ibid., 352.

[215] Ibid., 131.

[216] Ibid., 236.

[217] Ibid., 146.

*Chapter 3*

[1] Peter Wallace Agnew, "Religion and the Social Order in a Twentieth-Century City: Six Dallas Leaders" (Ph.D. diss., Southern Methodist University, 1999) 42.

[2] See "Gov. Woodrow Wilson Invited to Dallas," *DMN*, May 7, 1911; "Woodrow Wilson in Dallas Today," *DMN*, October 28, 1911; "Gov. Wilson Speaks at Baptist Church," *DMN*, October 29, 1911; George W. Truett, "'Excuse Making'," in *Follow Thou Me*, by George W. Truett (Nashville: Broadman Press, n.d.) 171.

[3] "War Is Right, Peace Wrong, Says German General," *New York Times*, April 21, 1912. See also Carlton Hayes, "The War of the Nations," *Political Science Quarterly* 29/4 (December 1914): 687–707.

[4] Friedrich von Bernhardi, *Germany and the Next War*, trans. Allen H. Powles (New York: Charles A. Eron, 1914) 18, available at http://books.google.com/books?id=eFhjHZ7DaocC&printsec=frontcover&dq=Allen+H.+Powles#PPA1920, M1.

[5] Ibid., 24.

[6] "War Is Right, Peace Wrong, Says German General."

[7] Robert T. Handy, *A Christian America: Protestant Hopes and Historical Realities*, 2nd ed. (New York: Oxford University Press, 1984) 111.

[8] William Warren Sweet, *The Story of Religion in America* (New York: Harper & Row, Publishers, 1930; repr., Grand Rapids MI: Baker Book House, 1983) 399–400.

[9] Darwin Payne, *Big D: Triumphs and Troubles of an American Supercity in the 20th Century* (Dallas: Three Forks Press, 1994) 31.

[10] Harry Leon McBeth, *Texas Baptists: A Sesquicentennial History* (Dallas: Baptistway Press, 1998) 122–24. The amounts in brackets here represent the purchasing power in 2007. Throughout the rest of the chapter, amounts in parentheses represent the purchasing power in 2007. See Lawrence H. Officer and Samuel H. Williamson, "Purchasing Power of Money in the United States from 1774 to 2007," http://www.measuringworth.com.

[11] "Needs Large Church Building," *DMN*, April 1, 1907.

[12] "Many Hear Dr. Truett," *DMN*, April 15, 1907. See also "Dr. Truett's Sermon," *DMN*, October 1, 1906, and "The Home in Heaven," *DMN*, February 3, 1908.

[13] "Addition to Cost Large Sum," *DMN*, May 2, 1907; "The First Baptist Church, Dallas, Texas," *Baptist Standard*, May 14, 1908, 16.

[14] Deacons Minutes, First Baptist Church (FBC), Dallas, Texas, March 2 and March 30, 1908.

[15] "Sin, Sorrow and Death Theme of Dr. Truett," *DMN*, December 14, 1908.

[16] Mrs. M. B. Slaughter, "Mrs. Geo. W. Truett's Bible Class," September 12, 1966, H. Leon McBeth Collection, box 11, "FBC Topic Reports" folder, TBHC.

[17] Leon McBeth, *The First Baptist Church of Dallas: Centennial History, 1868–1968* (Grand Rapids MI: Zondervan Publishing House, 1968) 142.

[18] Ibid., 145.

[19] Ibid., 146.

[20] DeWitte Talmage Holland, "A Rhetorical Analysis of the Preaching of George W. Truett" (Ph.D. diss., Northwestern University, 1956) 169.

[21] McBeth, *The First Baptist Church of Dallas*, 176.

[22] Ibid., 147. For other staff members during this period, see McBeth, *The First Baptist Church of Dallas*, 149.

[23] See, for example, George W. Truett to "My Dear Friend," October 16, 1913, TC 1450/MF 1450–1451:1.

[24] George W. Truett, "The True Neighbor," *Baptist Standard*, January 21, 1909, 2.

[25] George W. Truett, untitled sermon on Joshua 7:3 and 8:1, April 18, 1909, 4, TC 1818/MF 1809–1880:3.

[26] Ibid., 11.

[27] McBeth, *The First Baptist Church of Dallas*, 352; Eugene P. Alldredge, "Amazing Achievements of Dr. George W. Truett's Ministry, 1897–1941," *Quarterly Review* 1/4 (October–December 1941): 62.

[28] "Call to Dr. George W. Truett" *DMN*, February 15, 1910, 7; "Call to Dr. George W. Truett," *DMN*, February 2, 1915; "El Paso Wants Rev. Dr. Truett," *DMN*, October 11, 1910; Pulpit Committee of Greene Avenue Baptist Church, Brooklyn, New York, to George W. Truett, October 14, 1913, TC 1364/MF 1360–1372:1.

[29] George W. Truett, "Trumpeting the Gospel," in *We Would See Jesus*, by George W. Truett, ed. J. B. Cranfill (New York: Fleming H. Revell Company, 1915) 75, available at http://www.archive.org/details/wewouldseejesusa00trueuoft.

[30] Deacons Minutes, FBC, December 30, 1907; Minutes, First Baptist Church (FBC), Dallas, Texas, December 20, 1903; "Financial report for 1915," Notebook: Financial Reports 1910–1929, GWTML.

[31] J. B. Cranfill, "Life Sketch of George W. Truett," in Truett, *We Would See Jesus*, 14.

[32] McBeth, *The First Baptist Church of Dallas*, 192. See also George W. Gray, "Out of the Mountains Came This Great Preacher of the Plains," *American Magazine*, November 1925, 138, TC 106/MF 21–542:7.

[33] Josephine Nash to Keith E. Durso, February 26, 2008, in possession of the author.

[34] "Dr. George W. Truett's New Cadillac Eight," *DMN*, September 19, 1915; "The Cadillac Story," http://home.planet.nl/~nagte017/Cadillactext002.html (accessed February 5, 2008).

[35] "Reception Is Tendered Dr. George W. Truett," unidentified newspaper clipping, [September 17, 1915], TC 28/MF 21–542:3.

[36] "Death of J. Harvey Truett," *DMN*, January 26, 1908; "Death of Mrs. Rebecca Truett," *Baptist Standard*, August 10, 1911, 9; "Mother of Dr. Truett Dies," *DMN*, August 4, 1911.

[37] George W. Truett, "The Life and Work of B. H. Carroll," in *God's Call to America*, by George W. Truett, ed. J. B. Cranfill (Philadelphia: Judson Press, 1923) 68. This sermon is available at http://www.geocities.com/baptist_documents/ carroll.funeral.by.truitt.html. John Chrysostom (c. 350–407) preached in Antioch and was for a time bishop of Constantinople.

[38] Leon McBeth, "George W. Truett and Southwestern Seminary" (chapel address, Southwestern Baptist Theological Seminary, Fort Worth, Texas, March 16, 1971) 2, TC between 557 and 558/MF 554–590:1; Robert A. Baker, *Tell the Generations Following: A History of Southwestern Baptist Theological Seminary, 1903–1983* (Nashville: Broadman Press, 1983) 135–36.

[39] Baker, *Tell the Generations Following*, 145.

[40] McBeth, *Texas Baptists*, 148.

[41] B. H. Carroll to George W. Truett, March 30, 1909, TC 815/MF 736–1336:6.

[42] See Baker, *Tell the Generations Following*, 145–50.

[43] J. Frank Norris, *Inside History of First Baptist Church Fort Worth and Temple Baptist Church Detroit: Life Story of Dr. J. Frank Norris* ([Fort Worth: n.p., n.d.]) 32.

[44] Presnall H. Wood and Floyd W. Thatcher, *Prophets with Pens* (Dallas: Baptist Standard Publishing, Co., 1969) 61.

[45] McBeth, *Texas Baptists*, 135.

[46] Clovis Gwin Morris, "He Changed Things: The Life and Thought of J. Frank Norris" (Ph.D. diss., Texas Tech University, 1973) 70n60.

[47] Baker, *Tell the Generations Following*, 178–79.

[48] Morris, "He Changed Things," 89.

[49] For example, "Should a Prominent Fort Worth Banker Buy the High-Priced Silk Hose for Another Man's Wife?" See Mark G. Toulouse, "J. Frank Norris," in *Twentieth-Century Shapers of American Popular Religion*, ed. Charles H. Lippy (New York: Greenwood Press, 1989) 311.

[50] Morris, "He Changed Things," 116; C. Gwin Morris, "J. Frank Norris and the Baptist General Convention of Texas," *Texas Baptist History* 1 (1981): 2, 8.

[51] Morris, "He Changed Things," 33.

[52] Ibid., 117; Morris, "J. Frank Norris and the Baptist General Convention of Texas," 8.

[53] Baker, *Tell the Generations Following*, 179.

[54] See Morris, "He Changed Things," 95–110.

[55] "Rev. J. Frank Norris Is Found not Guilty," *DMN*, January 25, 1914.

[56] "Baylor University Home Coming," *Baptist Standard*, December 9, 1909, 2.

[57] George W. Truett, "The Baylor Home-Coming," in Truett, *God's Call to America*, 177. The address can also be found in the TC 4/MF 2–20:1. Truett would make similar remarks on June 16, 1920, in his address at Baylor's Diamond Jubilee. See George W. Truett, "Baylor's Diamond Jubilee," in Truett, *God's Call to America*, 191–208.

[58] Truett, "The Baylor Home-Coming," 181–87.

[59] Ibid., 188.

[60] Ibid., 189.

[61] Ibid., 190.

[62] George W. Truett et al., "Christian Union: A Deliverance by the Baptist General Convention of Texas," in *Christian Union Relative to Baptist Churches*, ed. J. M. Frost (Nashville: Sunday School Board of the Southern Baptist Convention, 1915) 35. The report can also be found in the TC 1888/MF 1881–1908:3, and in *A History of Texas Baptists*, by J. M. Carroll, ed. J. B. Cranfill (Dallas: Baptist Standard Publishing Co., 1923) 902–905. J. M. Dawson suggested that J. B. Gambrell wrote the report. See Joseph Martin Dawson, *A Century with Texas Baptists* (Nashville: Broadman Press, 1947) 73. However, in a letter to C. S. Wales, Truett stated, "My views on the subject of Christian Union are fully set out in the enclosed deliverance, which was adopted

some years ago by our Texas Convention." See George W. Truett to C. S. Wales, April 30, 1919, TC 1289/MF 736–1336:55.

[63] Truett et al., "Christian Union," 36.

[64] Ibid., 37–38.

[65] Ibid., 40.

[66] During the years from 1908 to 1916, Truett spoke to several non-Baptist organizations. When Lockett Adair, an evangelist, became ill during a January 1908 revival at Central Presbyterian Church in Dallas, the church asked Truett, not a Presbyterian minister, to fill the pulpit on at least two evenings ("When Refuge Fails," *DMN*, January 8, 1908; "Sermon by Dr. G. W. Truett," *DMN*, January 9, 1908). In fall 1908, Truett spoke to a group of Dallas newsboys ("Will Address Newsboys," *DMN*, November 20, 1908). In summer 1910, he travelled to Minnesota to speak at the Northwestern Bible Conference ("Rev. G. W. Truett Improving," *DMN*, August 14, 1910; "Dr. Truett Practically Well," *DMN*, August 12, 1910). In 1911, Truett spoke to Dallas's YMCA and YWCA, and he spent two weeks in Hamilton, New York, holding special meetings at Colgate University ("Rev. George W. Truett Preaches at Y. M. C. A.," *DMN*, January 2, 1911; "Dr. Truett to Young Women," *DMN*, June 12, 1911; E. B. Bryan to George W. Truett, March 22, 1911, TC 797/MF 736–1336:5). In 1915, Truett spoke to such diverse audiences as the Dallas Automobile Club, the University of Chicago, Northwestern University, Moody Bible Institute, and the Woman's Missionary Training School in Chicago ("Address Subject, 'Character,'" *DMN*, September 23, 1915; "Some Impressions of Two Trips," *Baptist Standard*, April 1, 1915, 4). First Presbyterian Church of Dallas invited Truett to preach when William M. Anderson, the church's pastor, was sick in September 1916 and then again after Anderson's death in November ("Ministry of Suffering Is Dr. Truett's Theme," *DMN*, September 18, 1916; George W. Truett, untitled sermon on Isaiah 15:10, September 17, 1916, TC 1835/MF 1809–1880:7; George W. Truett, untitled sermon on 2 Samuel 18:32, November 19, 1916, TC 1821/MF 1809–1880:3).

[67] For more on Truett's understanding of preaching and the role of preachers, see "Dr. Truett on the Preacher's Message," *Christian Index*, May 31, 1934, 9, TC 312/MF 21–542:20, and the following, all of which are by Truett: "Preaching," lecture notes, 1899, TC 1912/MF 1909–1970:1; "The Preacher and His Message," *Baptist Standard*, January 10, 1901, 7; "Bible Preaching and Preachers," *Baptist Standard*, February 7, 1901, 1; "A Chapter on Modern Preaching," *Baptist Standard*, June 4, 1901, 2; "The Trials and Joys of a Pastor's Life," *Baptist Standard*, October 24, 1901, 6–7; "A Message to Preachers," *Baptist Standard*, June 3, 1909, 1, 12–13, 16; "The Preacher as Shepherd," *Baptist Standard*, April 11, 1918, 7; "What We Preach," in *Sermons from Paul*, by George W. Truett, ed. Powhatan W. James (Grand Rapids MI: William B. Eerdmans Publishing House, 1947) 13–31; "Preachers and Preaching," in Truett, *Follow Thou Me*, 229–41; *On Preachers and Preaching* (N.p.: [1934]), TC

1940/MF 1909–1970:9; "Preachers and Preaching" (address, Southern Baptist Theological Seminary, Louisville, Kentucky, March 9, 1937), TC 1954/MF 1909–1970:10; and "The Preacher and His Message" (address, Southwestern Baptist Theological Seminary, Fort Worth, Texas, October 13, 1942) TC 589/MF 554–590:6, and TC 1966/MF 1909–1970:13.

[68] George W. Truett, "The Preacher as a Man" (address, Southwestern Baptist Theological Seminary, Fort Worth, Texas, February 18, 1914) 2, TC 1916/MF 1909–1970:2. See also his opening remarks in "The Preacher as a Soul Winner" (address, Southwestern Baptist Theological Seminary, Fort Worth, Texas, November 3, 1914) 2, TC 1915/MF 1909–1970:2.

[69] Truett, "The Preacher as a Man," 3–4.

[70] Ibid., 6.

[71] Ibid.

[72] Ibid., 7.

[73] Ibid., 8.

[74] George W. Truett, "The Preacher as a Student" (address, Southwestern Baptist Theological Seminary, Fort Worth, Texas, February 20, 1914) 3, TC 1917/MF 1909–1970:2.

[75] Ibid., 4.

[76] Ibid., 8.

[77] Ibid., 13.

[78] George W. Truett, "The Preacher in the Pulpit" (address, Southwestern Baptist Theological Seminary, Fort Worth, Texas, February 25, 1914) 1, TC 1917/MF 1909–1970:2.

[79] Ibid.

[80] Ibid., 5.

[81] Ibid., 6.

[82] Truett, "The Preacher as a Soul Winner," 4–5.

[83] Ibid., 4.

[84] Ibid., 6.

[85] Ibid., 7.

[86] Ibid., 10.

[87] Ibid., 12.

[88] Thomas Robert Havins, "Benevolent Ministries," in *Centennial Story of Texas Baptists*, ed. [L. R. Elliott] (Dallas: Executive Board of the Baptist General Convention of Texas, 1936) 185; McBeth, *Texas Baptists*, 138–39.

[89] George W. Truett, "Address by Rev. George W. Truett, D. D., at Banquet in Behalf of Baptist Sanitarium and Hospital, Houston, Texas, January 28, 1915," 3, TC 1919/MF 1909–1970:3.

[90] Ibid., 4.

[91] Ibid., 8. Note also the repetition of "Is it" (8), "History will not let us forget" (8–9), and "Selfishness is the" (10).

[92] Ibid., 10.

[93] Ibid., 11.

[94] Ibid., 18.

[95] Ibid. Truett had a handwritten copy of a slightly different version of this poem. See "What We Keep Is What We Give," TC 1620/MF 1613–1626:1.

[96] See "Chronology of Colleges and Universities," in *Teaching Them...: A Sesquicentennial Celebration of Texas Baptist Education*, ed. Jerry E. Dawson and John W. Storey ([Dallas]: Baptist General Convention of Texas, 1996) 7–10.

[97] John W. Storey, "Introduction," in Dawson and Storey, *Teaching Them*, 2.

[98] George. W. Truett, "Big Things for Baptists," *Baptist Standard*, May 29, 1913, 2.

[99] Ibid., 2–3. See also George W. Truett, "The Mantle of Elijah," 1 Kings 19:19, September 27, 1914, 12, TC 1822/MF 1809–1880:4.

[100] "First Church Gives Donation of $25,000," *DMN*, January 17, 1916; Robert A. Baker, *The Blossoming Desert: A Concise History of Texas Baptists* (Waco: Word Books, Publisher, 1970) 192. For one of Truett's addresses on behalf of the campaign, see George W. Truett, "Christian Education" (address, Brownwood, Texas, January 20, 1916) TC 1920/MF 1909–1970:3. See also his article "A Superb Opportunity," *Baptist Standard*, November 28, 1912, 4, written during a previous education fundraising campaign.

[101] Storey, "Introduction," 4; Baker, *The Blossoming Desert*, 192. See the following articles by Truett in the *Baptist Standard*: "Much at Stake Next Two Weeks," February 15, 1917, 6, 8; "The Third Big Drive," February 7, 1918; and "Once in a Life Time," February 21, 1918.

[102] George W. Truett to E. C. Dargan, February 18, 1909, Edwin C. Dargan Papers, SBHLA.

[103] George W. Truett to E. C. Dargan, April 20, 1909, Dargan Papers.

[104] John Jeter Hurt, "George Truett in Conway Arkansas," *Baptist Standard*, December 29, 1910, 3. See also "Praise for Dr. Truett," *DMN*, October 15, 1911, 22, for Truett's fundraising at South Side Baptist Church, Birmingham, Alabama.

[105] "Dr. Truett in New York," *DMN*, January 19, 1910.

[106] Edmund F. Merriam, "George W. Truett in Boston," *Watchman-Examiner*, September 3, 1914, 1171–72, TC 25/MF 21–542:3.

[107] George W. Truett to J. M. Frost, October 14, 1914, James Marion Frost Papers, SBHLA.

[108] "Some Impressions of Two Trips," *Baptist Standard*, April 1, 1915, 4.

[109] Richard H. Edmonds to Robert H. Coleman, September 3, 1912, TC 886/MF 736–1336:15.

[110] "Dallas Minister Stirs Baltimore," *DMN*, May 16, 1910.

[111] Ibid.

[112] Ibid.

[113] Ibid.

[114] Pamela R. Durso and Keith E. Durso, *The Story of Baptists in the United States* (Brentwood TN: Baptist History and Heritage Society, 2006) 149–50; John H. Y. Briggs, "From 1905 to the End of the First World War," in *Baptists Together in Christ, 1905–2005: A Hundred-Year History of the Baptist World Alliance*, ed. Richard V. Pierard (Falls Church VA: Baptist World Alliance, 2005) 20.

[115] George W. Truett to B. H. Carroll, April 14, 1911, B. H. Carroll Collection, folder 290, AWRL.

[116] Briggs, "From 1905 to the End of the First World War," 35.

[117] George W. Truett, "The Coming of the Kingdom in America," in *The Baptist World Alliance, Second Congress, The Baptist World Alliance, Second Congress, Philadelphia, June 19–25, 1911* (Philadelphia: Harper & Brother Company, 1911) 422, available at http://www.archive.org/details/recordofproceed00unknuoft. Truett's address can also be found under the same title in the *Baptist Standard*, October 23, 1911, 2–4, TC 1914/MF 1909–1970:1–2, and under the title "God's Call to America," in Truett, *God's Call to America*, 11–27. Truett also spoke on Tuesday afternoon, June 20, during the "Young People's Session." See George W. Truett, ["Remarks during the 'Young People's Session,' June 20, 1911, at the Baptist World Alliance Congress in Philadelphia"], in *The Baptist World Alliance, Second Congress, Philadelphia*, 95–99.

[118] George W. Truett, "The Coming of the Kingdom in America," 422.

[119] Ibid.

[120] Ibid., 423.

[121] Ibid.

[122] Ibid.

[123] Ibid., 424.

[124] Ibid.

[125] Ibid.

[126] Ibid., 425.

[127] Ibid.

[128] Ibid. 425–26.

[129] Ibid., 427.

[130] Ibid., 428.

[131] See George W. Truett to J. M. Frost, July 31, 1911, Frost Papers; George W. Truett to J. M. Frost, October 2, 1911, Frost Papers.

[132] Truett to Frost, October 2, 1911.

[133] Rufus B. Spain, *At Ease in Zion: A Social History of Southern Baptists 1865–1900* (Nashville: Vanderbilt University Press, 1967; repr., Tuscaloosa: University of Alabama Press, 2003) 211. See also Keith Harper, *The Quality of Mercy: Southern Baptists and Social Christianity, 1890–1920* (Tuscaloosa: The University of Alabama Press, 1996) 11–12.

[134] George W. Truett, "The Sin of Neutrality," *Baptist Standard*, July 23, 1914, 2.

[135] Ibid., 3.

[136] Harlan Julius Mathews, "Preaching and Preachers," in [Elliott], *Centennial Story of Texas Baptists*, 114.

[137] George W. Truett to E. C. Dargan, January 12, 1909, Dargan Papers.

[138] "Cowboys Make a Contribution," *DMN*, July 24, 1908.

[139] "Make Col. Slaughter Baptist Hospital Head," *DMN*, November 22, 1908.

[140] "Bro. Slaughter's Offer," *Baptist Standard*, February 11, 1909, 1; George W. Truett, "Now for the Top of the Hill," *Baptist Standard*, February 25, 1909, 1.

[141] Lana Henderson, *Baylor University Medical Center: Yesterday, Today and Tomorrow* (Waco: Baylor University Press, 1978) 36.

[142] Ibid., 40. See also Coleman Craig, "'On the Wing,'" *Baptist Review* (January-February 1974): 11.

[143] *Annual*, Baptist General Convention of Texas, 1910, 16–17.

[144] George W. Truett and J. B. Gambrell, "Sanitarium Charity Fund," *Baptist Standard*, January 5, 1911, 5.

[145] "Would Give $200,000 to Sanitarium Fund," *DMN*, November 23, 1913.

[146] Jackie McElhaney and Michael V. Hazel, "Dallas, Texas," in *Handbook of Texas Online*, http://www.tsha.utexas.edu/handbook/online/articles/DD/hdd1.html (accessed February 1, 2008).

[147] Morris, "He Changed Things," 65–66; C. Gwin Morris, "The Pulpit and Politics: J. Frank Norris as a Case Study" *Texas Baptist History* 7 (1987): 2; "Will Prepare Address Setting Forth Views," *DMN*, December 11, 1908.

[148] [George W. Truett], "General Pastors' Association Makes Appeal for Good Morals," *Baptist Standard*, January 7, 1909, 1.

[149] Ibid.

[150] Ibid.

[151] Morris, "He Changed Things," 65–66; Morris, "The Pulpit and Politics," 2.

[152] George W. Truett, "Healing the Demoniac," *Baptist Standard*, March 18, 1909, 2. See also "Many Legislators Hear Sermon by Dr. Truett," *DMN*, March 1, 1909.

[153] Truett, "Healing the Demoniac," 10.

[154] Ibid., 16.

[155] Morris, "He Changed Things," 68.

[156] [Truett], "General Pastors' Association Makes Appeal for Good Morals," 10.

[157] Ibid., 1.

[158] Kenneth K. Bailey, "Southern White Protestantism at the Turn of the Century," *American Historical Review* 68/3 (April 1963): 619.

[159] [Truett], "General Pastors' Association Makes Appeal for Good Morals," 10. Concerning this point, see "Dr. Truett's Sermon," *DMN*, December 18, 1905.

[160] "Dr. Truett Discusses Sunday Amusements," *DMN*, July 18, 1915; "City Laws Enforced as to Social Evil," *DMN*, October 28, 1915.

[161] "Dr. Truett Discusses Sunday Amusements."

[162] Payne, *Big D*, 31.

[163] "Dr. Truett to Enter Campaign," *DMN*, July 3, 1911.

[164] "Union Prohibition Services," *DMN*, July 7, 1911. See also "Dr. Truett at Denton," *DMN*, July 8, 1911.

[165] Rupert Norval Richardson, *Texas: The Lone Star State* (Englewood Cliffs NJ: Prentice-Hall, Inc., 1958) 287–88. The vote was 237,393 against the amendment, and 231,096 for it.

[166] George W. Truett to J. M. Frost, July 31, 1911, Frost Papers.

[167] John W. Storey, *Texas Baptist Leadership and Social Christianity, 1900–1980* (College Station: Texas A&M University Press, 1986) 96. If during the early twentieth century Texas Baptists had not yet arrived at the conclusion that African Americans were their equals, they did feel a responsibility to help them as best they could. Such an attitude has been characterized as being paternalistic, yet Texas Baptists, and Southern Baptists as well, could have done nothing; that was an option, but they did choose to help. Obviously, some African Americans thought such help was demeaning; others, however, appreciated it. For example, at the 1911 the Baptist World Alliance congress, G. P. Howard of the National Baptist Convention of the United States (Colored) said that his convention was "exceedingly grateful to God, [and] we are exceedingly grateful to the white people of the North and to the white people of the South and everybody else that has helped us in our struggle upward and onward." He also added that "whatever heights our white brethren go, we intend to go in the name of Christ, and we serve notice that you cannot crown Christ Lord of all without the Negro Baptists of this country helping you to do it." See his remarks in *The Baptist World Alliance, Second Congress*, 50.

[168] Truett, "The Coming of the Kingdom in America," 425.

[169] Henry Y. Warnock, "Prophets of Change: Some Southern Baptist Leaders and the Problem of Race, 1900–1921," *Baptist History and Heritage* 7/3 (July 1972): 173–74.

[170] David M. Reimers, *White Protestantism and the Negro* (New York: Oxford University Press, 1965) 53–54, 183.

[171] Bailey, "Southern White Protestantism at the Turn of the Century," 621.

[172] George W. Truett to W. H. Fuller, December 4, 1909, Baptist General Convention Archives, "Negro Work, 1896–1916" folder, AWRL.

[173] Truett, "Address by Rev. George W. Truett," 11.

[174] "Texas Colored Baptists," *DMN*, October 12, 1899.

[175] "To Help Their Own Race," *DMN*, July 5, 1903.

[176] Agnew, "Religion and the Social Order in a Twentieth-Century City," 130.

[177] "For Colored Orphanage," *DMN*, March 12, 1905.

[178] "Religious Campaign for Negroes Planned," *DMN*, December 6, 1911; "Negro Religious Campaign," *DMN*, January 1, 1912. See also "Negroes Will Hold Mass Meeting for Orphanage," *DMN*, June 6, 1922, and W. S. Willis to George W. Truett, June 10, 1929, TC 1320/MF 736–1336:59.

[179] George W. Truett, "Dealing with the Multitude," *Baptist Standard*, February 11, 1909, 1.

[180] Ibid. Some African Americans thought that relocating to Africa should be an option for them. On August 3, 1899, at the meeting of the American Methodist Episcopal Church held in Birmingham, Alabama, the committee on the state of the country recommended that another committee be established to petition the U.S. Congress to set aside $100,000 ($2,578,881) to secure ships to take any African American who wanted to emigrate to Africa at a reasonable cost to each person. See "Send Negroes to Africa," *DMN*, August 4, 1899.

[181] Charles Carroll, *The Negro a Beast* (St. Louis: American Book and Bible House, 1900) available at http://www.archive.org/details/thenegrobeastori00car-rich. If the title of Carroll's diatribe does not clarify the author's beliefs, the title of his final chapter does: "The Bible and Divine Revelation, as well as Reason, all Teach that the Negro is not Human." The BGCT condemned Carroll's book. See Storey, *Texas Baptist Leadership and Social Christianity*, 96, and Reimers, *White Protestantism and the Negro*, 28.

[182] Payne, *Big D*, 39.

[183] Peter W. Agnew, "Making Dallas Moral: Two Baptist Pastors," *Heritage News*, Summer 1987, 22.

[184] "Pastors Will Assist Fight on Reservation," *DMN*, September 16, 1913.

[185] Payne, *Big D*, 46; "Abate Social Evil Mass Meeting Topic," *DMN*, September 21, 1913.

[186] "Hold Mass Meeting against Social Evil," September 22, 1913.

[187] Ibid.

[188] Ibid.

[189] Ibid.

[190] Ibid.

[191] Payne, *Big D*, 47. See also 44–45.

[192] "All Walks of Life Pay Final Tribute to Dallas Surgeon," *DMN*, December 15, 1937. See also "Death Claims W. W. Samuell," http://www.dallaspioneer.org/stories/obituaries.php?ID=418 (accessed March 27, 2008). A Dallas high school and Dallas's largest public tennis center now bear Samuell's name. Truett wrote the following in his 1937 diary: "He [Samuell] was an outstanding personality, and his passing has called forth widespread tributes from the people." George W. Truett, Diary, December 14, 1937, TC 666/MF 664–690:10.

[193] Payne, *Big D*, 47.

[194] "Heir to Austro-Hungarian Throne Is Assassinated," *DMN*, June 29, 1914.

[195] George W. Truett, "Stirring the Nest," *Baptist Standard*, October 8, 1914, 5.

[196] Ibid.

[197] Ibid.

[198] "The Sinking of the *Lusitania*," *Baptist Standard*, May 13, 1915, 3–4.

[199] "$25,000 Donated for Building for Nurses," *DMN*, December 1, 1916.

[200] "500 Attend Banquet to George W. Truett," *DMN*, December 2, 1916.

[201] Ibid.

[202] Ibid.

[203] Ibid.

[204] Ibid.

[205] Ibid.

*Chapter 4*

[1] Joseph R. Conlin, *The American Past: A Brief History* (San Diego: Harcourt Brace Jovanovich, Publishers, 1991) 463.

[2] "Memoirs & Diaries: Account of the Assaults upon Fort Vaux, Verdun, June 1916," in *Encyclopedia of World War I*, http://www.firstworldwar.com/diaries/verdun_vaux.htm (accessed April 1, 2008).

[3] The amounts in parentheses represent the purchasing power in 2007. See Lawrence H. Officer and Samuel H. Williamson, "Purchasing Power of Money in the United States from 1774 to 2007," http://www.measuringworth.com.

[4] Conlin, *The American Past*, 463.

[5] *Annual*, Baptist General Convention of Texas (BGCT), 1917, 20.

[6] Woodrow Wilson, "Peace without Victory," in *The Annals of America, 1916–1928: World War and Prosperity*, vol. 14 (Chicago: Encyclopedia Britannica, Inc., 1976) 65.

[7] Ibid., 67.

[8] Martin Gilbert, *The First World War: A Complete History* (New York: Henry Holt and Company, 1994) 308.

[9] Ibid., 312; S. L. A. Marshall, *The American Heritage History of World War I* (New York: American Heritage Publishing Co., 1964) 204.

[10] [Woodrow Wilson], *The President's War Message: The Historic Address Delivered to the Congress of the United States by Woodrow Wilson, April 2nd, 1917* (San Francisco: Paul Elder and Company, 1917) 21.

[11] Ibid., 25–26.

[12] J. B. Cranfill, "George W. Truett, and His Work as Pastor, Builder and Leader," *Western Recorder*, January 26, 1928, 20, TC 149/MF 21-542:11.

[13] Robert D. Linder, "World War 1 (1914–1918)," in *Dictionary of Christianity in America*, ed. Daniel G. Reid, Robert D. Linder, Bruce L. Shelley, and Harry S. Stout (Downers Grove IL: InterVarsity Press, 1990) 1278–79.

[14] Robert T. Handy, *A Christian America: Protestant Hopes and Historical Realities*, 2nd ed. (New York: Oxford University Press, 1984) 130.

[15] Harry Emerson Fosdick, *The Challenge of the Present Crisis* (New York: Association Press, 1917), available at http://books.google.com/books?id=bMiGASqgYxUC&printsec=frontcover&dq=challenge+of+the+present. In his autobiography, Fosdick wrote that everything he had written in *The Challenge of the Present Crisis* was sincere, but that he repudiated everything he had written in defense of the war. See Harry Emerson Fosdick, *The Living of These Days: An Autobiography* (New York: Harper & Brothers, Publishers, 1956) 121.

[16] Handy, *A Christian America*, 132.

[17] Bill J. Leonard, *Baptist Ways: A History* (Valley Forge PA: Judson Press, 2003) 396–97.

[18] *Annual*, Southern Baptist Convention (SBC), 1918, 101.

[19] "Baptists to Begin Revival," *DMN*, April 1, 1917.

[20] See W. A. Criswell, *Fifty Years of Preaching at the Palace: Outstanding Sermons Preached by George W. Truett and W. A. Criswell* (Grand Rapids, MI: Zondervan Publishing House, 1969) 13–42.

[21] "Dr. Truett Conducting Revival in Fort Worth," *DMN*, June 12, 1917.

[22] George W. Truett, *A Quest for Souls*, [ed. J. B. Cranfill] (New York: George H. Doran Company, 1917), available at http://books.google.com/books?id=bMiGASqgYxUC&printsec=frontcover&dq=challenge+of+the+present.

[23] J. B. Cranfill, "Rev. Geo. W. Truett's Quest for Souls," *Baptist Standard*, June 20, 1918, 11.

[24] "Dr. Truett Will Address Soldiers in Guard Camps," *DMN*, June 26, 1917.

[25] "Pastor Truett Beginning His Twenty-first Year," *Baptist Standard*, September 13, 1917, 6.

[26] Ibid., 7.

[27] "Coliseum Filled at Closing Rally," *DMN*, September 17, 1917.

[28] George W. Truett, "The Passing of the Legalised Liquor Traffic," in *God's Call to America*, by George W. Truett, ed. J. B. Cranfill (Philadelphia: Judson Press, 1923) 152.

[29] Ibid., 155.

[30] Ibid., 155–57.

[31] Ibid., 157.

[32] Ibid., 158.

[33] Ibid., 159–60.

[34] Ibid., 164.

[35] Ibid., 168.

[36] Ibid., 168–69. Truett had at least one "saloon man" on his Christmas card list. See J. H. Sinchall to George W. Truett, January 1, 1916, TC 1229/MF 736–1336:50. Sinchall addressed the letter to his "Dear Friend Mr. Truett."

[37] "Complete Returns Give Local Option Majority of 1,851," *DMN*, September 15, 1917; "Dallas County Goes Dry by Majority of Nearly Two Thousand Votes," *DMN*, September 11, 1917.

[38] "Personal," *DMN*, October 9, 1917; Gaye L. McGlothlen, *A History of Immanuel Baptist Church, 1887–1986* (Nashville: Immanuel Baptist Church, 1987) 90.

[39] M. H. Wolfe, J. B. Gambrell, S. J. Porter, F. F. Brown, Jeff D. Ray, E. C. Routh, and George W. Truett, "An Address to Texas Baptists," *Baptist Standard*, September 27, 1917, 1. See also George W. Truett, "What Do Texas Baptists Say?" *Baptist Standard*, November 8, 1917, 1.

[40] "Dr. Truett Opens War Work Fund Campaign at S. M. I.," *DMN*, November 8, 1917.

[41] Donald Dawless, "Chaplains," in *The United States in the First World War: An Encyclopedia*, ed. Anne Cipriano Venzon (New York: Garland Publishing, Inc., 1995) 135; "Congress Passes the Chaplain Bill," *Christian Index*, April 18, 1918, 3.

[42] Nine Mjagkij, "Young Men's Christian Association/Young Women's Christian Association (YM/YWCA)," in *The United States in the First World War*, 810.

[43] George W. Truett, "Paper Read by Geo. W. Truett," in *Annual*, BGCT, 1917, 19.

[44] Ibid.

[45] "Texas Baptists Give Women Equal Rights," *DMN*, December 6, 1918.

[46] "Dr. Truett Declares that World Is Being Remade," *DMN*, January 9, 1918.

[47] "Men and Boys Take Notes on Lecture on War Bread," *DMN*, January 11, 1918.

[48] Ralph W. Steen, "World War I," in *Handbook of Texas Online*, http://www.tshaonline.org/handbook/online/articles/WW/qdw1.html (accessed April 12, 2008).

[49] "First Baptist Church Has Long Honor Roll," *DMN*, January 13, 1918.

[50] Leon McBeth, *The First Baptist Church of Dallas: Centennial History, 1868–1968* (Grand Rapids MI: Zondervan Publishing House, 1968) 158.

[51] "Dr. Truett Accepts Call to Go Abroad," *DMN*, June 3, 1918.

[52] "Dr. Truett Is Considering Invitation to Go to Europe," *DMN*, May 9, 1918.

[53] J. Michael Raley, "'On the Same Basis as the Men': The Campaign to Reinstate Women as Messengers to the Southern Baptist Convention, 1885-1918," *Journal of Southern Religion* 7 (2004), part 1, http://jsr.fsu.edu/Volume7/ Raley1.htm.

[54] Ibid., part 3. See also Leon McBeth, *Women in Baptist Life* (Nashville: Broadman Press, 1979) 111–12; *Annual*, SBC, 1917, 37–38, 62; and *Annual*, SBC, 1918, 15, 18.

[55] *Annual*, SBC, 1918, 73.

[56] Ibid., 75.

[57] George W. Truett, "The Leadership of God," *Baptist Standard*, August 8, 1918, 5.This sermon can also be found in the TC 1829/MF 1809-1880:6.

[58] Truett, "The Leadership of God," 5.

[59] Ibid.

[60] Ibid.

[61] Ibid. For brief descriptions of Germany's treatment of Belgium, see Bernard A. Cook, "Belgium, Occupation of, 1914–18," in *The European Powers in the First World War: An Encyclopedia*, ed. Spencer C. Tucker (New York: Garland Publishing Inc., 1996) 119–20, and Marshall, *The American Heritage History of World War I*, 96.

[62] Truett, "The Leadership of God," 5.

[63] Ibid.

[64] Ibid., 6.

[65] Ibid., 6–7, 25.

[66] Ibid., 25.

[67] "Dr. George W. Truett Accepts the Call Abroad," *Baptist Standard*, June 6, 1918, 8.

[68] Ibid.

[69] Ibid.

[70] Ibid. Truett's letter and the resolution granting him a leave of absence can also be found in "Dr. Truett Accepts Call to Go Abroad," *DMN*, June 3, 1918. For Truett's handwritten copy of the letter, see the TC 1582/MF 1576–1595:3.

[71] Joe W. Burton, *Prince of the Pulpit: A Pen Picture of George W. Truett at Work* (Grand Rapids MI: Zondervan Publishing House, 1946) 73.

[72] Ibid., 74; Thomas Robert Havins, "Benevolent Ministries," in *Centennial Story of Texas Baptists*, ed. [L. R. Elliott] (Dallas: Executive Board of the Baptist General Convention of Texas, 1936) 183–84.

[73] McBeth, *The First Baptist Church of Dallas*, 159.

[74] For example, see the following *DMN* articles: "Dr. Truett Praises Bravery of Soldiers," September 9, 1918; "Dr. Truett Writes His Impressions on Visit to Big War Hospital," September 19, 1918; "Dr. George W. Truett Writes of War Scenes,"

October 4, 1918; "Dr. Truett Meets Several Dallas Boys," October 15, 1918; and "Gen. Pershing Praised by Dr. Geo. W. Truett," December 29, 1918.

[75] George W. Truett to Josephine Truett, December 18, 1918. Truett's letters to Josephine during the war can be found in the TC 1337, 1339-1346/MF 1337-1346:1-8. (Note that the first MF card is incorrectly numbered as 1327-1347, and that the third card is incorrectly numbered 1237-1337.) Most of the letters are filed chronologically, but some, at least on the MF cards, are not. Card one contains TC 1337 (October 5, 1918, which is incorrectly dated 1915) and TC 1339 (August 18-19, 1918); card two, TC 1339 (August 21-31, 1918); card 3, TC 1340 (September 1-12, 1918) and TC 1341 (September 13-18, 1918); card four, TC 1341 (September 19-22, 1918), and TC 1342 (September 24-28, 1918, October 29, 1918, and September 30, 1918) and TC 1343 (October 2-3, 1918); card five, TC 1343 (October 4-13, 1918) and TC 1344 (October 16-24, 1918); card six, TC 1344 (October 26-27, 1918) and TC 1345 (one with no date, November 5, 7, 28, 1918, and December 2, 18-21, 1918); card seven, TC 1345 (December 22-24, 27-31, 1918) and TC 1346 (January 1, 5-7, 1919); and card eight, TC 1346 (January 8, 12-13, 16, 18-28, 1919).

[76] George W. Truett, Diary, July 9, 1918. Hereafter cited either as Diary 1918 or Diary 1919. Phil. 4:19 says, "But my God shall supply all your need according to his riches in glory by Christ Jesus" (KJV). Truett's diary for 1918-1919 can be found in the TC 665/MF 664-690:1-3. Card one contains January 1, 1919-February 9, 1919, and July 9, 1918-August 16, 1918; card 2, August 17, 1918-December 14, 1918; and card 3, December 15, 1918-December 31, 1918, and Memoranda.

[77] Diary, July 23, 1918.

[78] See Joseph L. Allen, *Love & Conflict: A Covenantal Model of Christian Ethics* (Nashville: Abingdon Press, 1984) 186–89. A third characteristic of the Crusade ethic, according to Allen, is that the forces of righteousness can act without moral restraint toward the forces of evil. Although Truett clearly accepted the first two characteristics of such an ethic, he probably would not condone acting without moral constraint. However, he certainly believed that Germany should be punished severely. See George W. Truett to Josephine Truett and their children, October 16, 1918, and George W. Truett, untitled sermon on 1 Peter 3:18, April 6, 1919, 9, TC 1880/MF 1809–1880:18–19.

[79] Diary, July 31, 1918.

[80] Ibid., July 19, 1918. The reference to the "Sword bathed in heaven" comes from Isa. 34:5, in which God declares, "my sword shall be bathed in heaven; behold it shall come down upon Idumea, and upon the people of my curse, to judgment" (KJV).

[81] Diary, July 30, 1918.

[82] Ibid., July 31, 1918.

[83] Ibid., August 2, 1918.

[84] Ibid., August 10, 1918.

[85] Ibid., August 11, 1918.

[86] Ibid., August 12 and 13, 1918; George W. Truett to Josephine Truett, August 18, 1918.

[87] George W. Truett to Josephine Truett, September 14, 1918; "Prominent Dallas Minister Arrives Safely in France," *DMN*, August 14, 1918. The *DMN* incorrectly reported Truett's destination.

[88] Diary, August 13, 1918.

[89] Ibid., August 18, 1918.

[90] G. Truett to J. Truett, August 18, 1918.

[91] George W. Truett to Josephine Truett, August 19, 1918. Truett incorrectly refers to Selecman as C. S.

[92] George W. Truett to Josephine Truett, August 23, 1918.

[93] Diary, August 24, 1918.

[94] Ibid., August 25, 1918.

[95] Ibid., August 26, 1918.

[96] George W. Truett to Josephine Truett, August 26, 1918.

[97] Diary, September 6, 1918.

[98] Ibid., September 22, 1918. See also his comments after a November 16 visit to a Catholic cathedral in Quimper, France. Diary, November 16, 1918.

[99] In Winchester the previous day, Truett preached three times at "the largest [camp] in the United Kingdom." See Diary, September 14, 1918.

[100] George W. Truett to Josephine Truett, September 14, 1918. Note that Truett recorded these events in his diary entry for September 15.

[101] G. Truett to J. Truett, September 14, 1918.

[102] "Dr. Truett Writes Mother about Son," *DMN*, October 16, 1918. See also Mrs. Albert Mann to George W. Truett, January 4, 1919, TC 1346/MF 1337–1347:7, and Cranfill, "George W. Truett, and His Work as Pastor, Builder and Leader," 20.

[103] See Coleman Craig, "Dr. George W. Truett as Pastor," TC 659/MF 658–1336:1, and Coleman Craig, "'On the Wing,'" *Baptist Review* (January–February 1974): 11.

[104] George W. Truett to Josephine Truett and their children, September 26, 1918. For more on Will and Agnes, see McBeth, *The First Baptist Church of Dallas*, 209–10, and Josephine Nash to Keith E. Durso, February 26, 2008, in possession of the author.

[105] George W. Truett to Josephine Truett and their children, September 27, 1918.

[106] George W. Truett to Josephine Truett and their children, October 13, 1918.

[107] George W. Truett, "The Last Call of Love," in *The Salt of the Earth*, by George W. Truett, ed. Powhatan W. James (Grand Rapids MI: William B. Eerdmans Publishing House, 1949) 118; "Pastor Truett at Home," *Baptist Standard*, February 13, 1919, 1.

[108] Marshall, *The American Heritage History of World War I*, 338; "Hold Leinster Attack Belies Peace Talk," *New York Times*, October 13, 1918; "'Town for Town' Cry Increases in London," *New York Times*, October 14, 1918.

[109] Diary, October 13, 1918.

[110] Ibid., October 14, 1918.

[111] Ibid., October 15, 1918.

[112] G. Truett to J. Truett and their children, October 16, 1918.

[113] Diary, October 16, 1918.

[114] Marshall, *The American Heritage History of World War I*, 214; "The Battle of Messines, 1917," in *Encyclopedia of World War I*, http://www.firstworldwar.com/battles/messines.htm (accessed April 1, 2008). This explosion followed twelve days (May 26–June 6) of bombardment, during which the 2,266 British guns lobbed 3.5 million shells on German positions. See Justin D. Murphy, "Ypres, Battle of," in *The United States in the First World War*, 813.

[115] Diary, October 17, 1918.

[116] George W. Truett to Josephine Truett and their children, October 17, 1918.

[117] George W. Truett to Josephine Truett and their children, October 18, 1918.

[118] Ibid. See also George W. Truett to Josephine Truett, October 27, 1918.

[119] Thomas J. Knock, "World War I," in *The Oxford Companion to United States History*, ed. Paul Boyer (Oxford: Oxford University Press, 2001) 845; Conlin, *The American Past*, 474. Most of the Texas servicemen who died during the war died in the United States, many from the 1918 flu epidemic. See Steen, "World War I."

[120] Diary, November 1, 1918.

[121] Ibid., November 3, 1918.

[122] George W. Truett to Josephine Truett and their children, November 5, 1918.

[123] Diary, November 7, 1918.

[124] Ibid., November 11, 1918.

[125] George W. Truett to Josephine Truett and their children, December 2, 1918. See also Powhatan W. James, *George W. Truett: A Biography* (Nashville: Broadman Press, 1939) 148–49.

[126] Diary, December 13, 1918.

[127] G. Truett to J. Truett, December 18, 1918.

[128] George W. Truett to Josephine Truett, December 22, 1918.

[129] Diary, December 24, 1918.

[130] James, *George W. Truett*, 147.

[131] Diary, December 25, 1918.

[132] George W. Truett to Josephine Truett and their children, January 6, 1919.

[133] Ibid.

[134] George W. Truett to Josephine Truett, January 7, 1919.

[135] George W. Truett to Josephine Truett, January 14, 1919.

[136] Diary, January 15, 1918.

[137] U.S. Constitution, amend. 18.

[138] "Celebrate Victory for Prohibition," *DMN*, January 18, 1919.

[139] Diary, January 17, 1918.

[140] Ibid., January 19, 1918.

[141] Ibid., January 28, 1918.

[142] Ibid., January 30, 1918. See "The Passing of Col. C. C. Slaughter," *Baptist Standard*, January 30, 1919, 7.

[143] Diary, January 31, 1918.

[144] Ibid., February 4, 1918.

[145] "Dr. Truett Is Given Reception at Church," *DMN*, February 5, 1919.

[146] For Truett's remarks at this gathering, see "Pastor Truett at Home," 1; "Dr. Truett Is Given Reception at Church," *DMN*, February 5, 1919; and George W. Truett, *The World War and Some of Its Lessons* (Dallas: Baptist Standard Publishing Co., 1919), TC 1585/MF 1576–1595:4.

[147] "Dr. Truett Guest at Citizens Banquet," *Baptist Standard*, February 13, 1919.

[148] Peter Wallace Agnew, "Religion and the Social Order in a Twentieth-Century City: Six Dallas Leaders" (Ph.D. diss., Southern Methodist University, 1999) 72.

[149] For excerpts from his Sunday morning sermon, see Coleman Craig, "Dr. Truett's First Sunday in Dallas," *Baptist Standard*, February 13, 1919, 18.

[150] George W. Truett, "Blessed Are the Peacemakers," *Baptist Standard*, July 10, 1919, 6.

[151] Ibid.

[152] Ibid.

[153] Ibid.

[154] Ibid., 6–7.

[155] Herbert Hoover, *America's First Crusade* (New York: Charles Scribner's Sons, 1942) 9–10.

[156] Ibid., 29.

[157] Marshall, *The American Heritage History of World War I*, 367–68; "Treaty of Versailles, 28 June 1919," in *Encyclopedia of World War I*, http://www.first-worldwar.com/source/versailles.htm (accessed April 1, 2008).

[158] U. S. Constitution, amend. 19; A. Elizabeth Taylor, "Women Suffrage," in *Handbook of Texas Online*, http://www.tshaonline.org/handbook/online/articles/WW/viw1.html (accessed April 14, 2008).

[159] Diary, February 9, 1919.

[160] *Annual*, SBC, 1919, 74.

[161] Glenn Thomas Carson, *Calling Out the Called: The Life and Work of Lee Rutland Scarborough* (Austin TX: Eakin Press, 1996) 56–57. For a list of the state goals and the proposed distribution of funds, see H. Leon McBeth, *The Baptist Heritage: Four*

*Centuries of Baptist Witness* (Nashville: Broadman Press, 1987) 619. For Truett's explanation of the benefits of and rationale for the campaign, see his article "Thinking in Millions," *Baptist Standard*, June 12, 1919, 1.

[162] "Says Baptist Drive Certain of Success," *DMN*, October 12, 1919.

[163] "Itinerary of Dr. Truett in Baptist Drive Given," *DMN*, October 22, 1919.

[164] George W. Truett to "My dear Brother Preacher," November 10, 1919, J. M. Carroll Collection, folder 689, AWRL.

[165] "Baptists Get Bulk of $16,000,000 Fund," *DMN*, December 1, 1919; Carson, *Calling Out the Called*, 67. Other sources place the figure at $507,850 ($6,086,626), which was given during the morning service. The discrepancy in amounts might be because these sources reported the money pledged at the morning worship service, whereas the *Dallas Morning News* reported the total given that day. Or one of the figures might be wrong. See James, *George W. Truett*, 166, and George W. Gray, "Out of the Mountains Came This Great Preacher of the Plains," *American Magazine*, November 1925, 138, TC 106/MF 21–542:7.

[166] Carson, *Calling Out the Called*, 67; Harry Leon McBeth, *Texas Baptists: A Sesquicentennial History* (Dallas: Baptistway Press, 1998) 164.

[167] Clovis Gwin Morris, "He Changed Things: The Life and Thought of J. Frank Norris" (Ph.D. diss., Texas Tech University, 1973) 133, 138n13.

[168] Carson, *Calling Out the Called*, 60.

[169] George W. Truett to Josephine Truett, August 22, 1918.

[170] George W. Truett, "The Importance of Co-operation," *Baptist Standard*, November 30, 1902, 2.

[171] Carson, *Calling Out the Called*, 66.

[172] McBeth, *The First Baptist Church of Dallas*, 352; Eugene P. Alldredge, "Amazing Achievements of Dr. George W. Truett's Ministry, 1897–1941," *Quarterly Review* 1/4 (October–December 1941): 62.

[173] Marshall, *The American Heritage History of World War I*, 344.

[174] Diary, the first page of the Memoranda section, 1918–1919.

*Chapter 5*

[1] Joseph R. Conlin, *The American Past: A Brief History* (San Diego: Harcourt Brace Jovanovich, Publishers, 1991) 483.

[2] The amounts in parentheses represent the purchasing power in 2007. See Lawrence H. Officer and Samuel H. Williamson, "Purchasing Power of Money in the United States from 1774 to 2007," http://www.measuringworth.com.

[3] Harry Leon McBeth, *Texas Baptists: A Sesquicentennial History* (Dallas: Baptistway Press, 1998) 154.

[4] George W. Truett, *Christian Education* (Birmingham AL: Education Board, Southern Baptist Convention, 1926) [9], TC 1929/MF 1909–1970:6–7.

[5] Ibid., [10].

[6] James J. Thompson, Jr., *Tried as by Fire: Southern Baptists and the Religious Controversies of the 1920s* (Macon GA: Mercer University Press, 1982) 143. Thompson noted that this letter could be found in Box 2 of the Norris Papers. A search of Box 2 by Taffey Hall, archivist at the SBHLA, did not yield this letter.

[7] [Curtis Lee Laws], "Convention Side Lights," *Watchman-Examiner,* July 1, 1920, 834.

[8] Pamela R. Durso and Keith E. Durso, *The Story of Baptists in the United States* (Brentwood TN: Baptist History and Heritage Society, 2006) 158–59.

[9] George M. Marsden, *Fundamentalism and American Culture: The Shaping of Twentieth-Century Evangelicalism: 1870–1925* (Oxford: Oxford University Press, 1980) 4.

[10] Thompson, Jr., *Tried as by Fire*, 140–41.

[11] Conlin, *The American Past*, 492–93. Many observers of the trial, particularly Darrow supporters, contended that the defense lawyer made Bryan look like a monkey during his testimony. In 1931, Darrow toured America, debating religious leaders. In Dallas, he found that C. C. Selecman, with whom Truett had become friends while a chaplain during World War, was a tougher opponent than Bryan. See Peter Wallace Agnew, "Religion and the Social Order in a Twentieth-Century City: Six Dallas Leaders" (Ph.D. diss., Southern Methodist University, 1999) 194–97; "Believer and Doubter Square Off for Action," *DMN*, March 18, 1931; and "Three Beliefs Turn Fires on Lone Agnostic," *DMN*, March 19, 1931.

[12] McBeth, *Texas Baptists*, 164.

[13] Leon McBeth, *The First Baptist Church of Dallas: Centennial History, 1868–1968* (Grand Rapids MI: Zondervan Publishing House, 1968) 145.

[14] *Annual,* Southern Baptist Convention (SBC), 1920, 51; Glenn Thomas Carson, *Calling Out the Called: The Life and Work of Lee Rutland Scarborough* (Austin TX: Eakin Press, 1996) 68.

[15] *Annual,* SBC, 1920, 57.

[16] Diane Lindstrom, "Depressions, Economic," in *The Oxford Companion to United States History*, ed. Paul Boyer (Oxford: Oxford University Press, 2001) 184.

[17] H. Leon McBeth, *The Baptist Heritage: Four Centuries of Baptist Witness* (Nashville: Broadman Press, 1987) 619.

[18] Robert A. Baker, *The Southern Baptist Convention and Its People, 1607–1972* (Nashville: Broadman Press 1974) 394.

[19] Clovis Gwin Morris, "He Changed Things: The Life and Thought of J. Frank Norris" (Ph.D. diss., Texas Tech University, 1973) 137.

[20] J. Frank Norris, *The Triple Major Operation in Detroit* ([Detroit: n.p.], 1935) 10.

[21] Ibid.

[22] Thompson, Jr., *Tried as by Fire*, 141.

[23] Morris, "He Changed Things," 203.

[24] Ibid., 204.

[25] George W. Truett, "World Call to Baptists," *Baptist Standard*, March 31, 1921, 1. For Truett's reference to the Macedonian call, see Acts 16:9.

[26] *Annual*, SBC, 1921, 35.

[27] *Annual*, SBC, 1922, 26.

[28] Ibid., 23.

[29] L. R. Scarborough, "The Fruits of Norrisism," in Carson, *Calling Out the Called*, 130.

[30] F. S. Groner, "Concerning 'Agreements,' 'Treaties,' and 'Scraps of Paper,'" *Baptist Standard*, October 12, 1923, 1.

[31] Morris, "He Changed Things," 139–41. Morris (141) lists other allegations made by Norris. See also Gwin Morris, "J. Frank Norris: Rascal or Reformer?" *Baptist History and Heritage* 3/3 (Autumn 1998): 31–32.

[32] Robert A. Baker, *The Blossoming Desert: A Concise History of Texas Baptists* (Waco: Word Books, Publisher, 1970) 197; Rosalie Beck, "1920–1929: Recession, Norris Fail to Derail Texans," *Baptist Standard*, November 17, 1999, http://www.baptiststandard.com/1999/11_17/pages/cent_1920.html (accessed May 12, 2008).

[33] George W. Truett, "Some Frank Words with Texas Baptists," *Baptist Standard*, October 19, 1922, 33. Truett's article was reprinted in *Texas Baptist History* 1 (1981): 65–68.

[34] Truett, "Some Frank Words with Texas Baptists," 33.

[35] Ibid., 34.

[36] *Annual*, SBC, 1923, 28.

[37] George W. Truett, "An Adequate Gospel for a Lost World," in *Third Baptist World Congress: Stockholm, July 21–27, 1923*, ed. W. T. Whitley (London: Kingsgate, 1923) 114–23. The sermon can also be found under the title "An Adequate Gospel," *Baptist Standard*, August 30, 1923, 7–10. Truett also gave a brief response to the greetings from a Swedish pastor, A. Hagström. See George W. Truett, ["Response to Greetings at the Baptist World Alliance, Stockholm, Sweden, July 21, 1923"], in *Third Baptist World Congress*, 6.

[38] "Pastor Describes European Journey," *DMN*, October 4, 1923. While in Jerusalem, Truett wrote a letter to his church. See George W. Truett to "My Very Dear Friends," August 16, 1923, in Notebook: Pastors: Christmas Letters and Correspondence, GWTML. This trip to Europe was Truett's third. In 1920, Truett, J. B. Gambrell, M. H. Wolfe, chair of the FBC deacons, and others travelled to Europe to attend conferences of the SBC's Foreign Mission Board. See "M. H. Wolfe to Attend European Convention," *DMN*, June 4, 1920; "Truett Tells of Visit in Europe,"

*DMN*, August 19, 1920; and "European Churches Need Assistance of Americans," *DMN*, September 21, 1920.

[39] J. Matthew Harder to George W. Truett, November 2, 1923, TC 954/MF 736–1336:21.

[40] Ibid.

[41] *Annual*, SBC 1924, 28.

[42] George W. Truett, "Texas Baptists Not Deceived," *Baptist Standard*, October 30, 1924, 3.

[43] Ibid.

[44] Morris, "He Changed Things,"192–93; Robert A. Baker, *Tell the Generations Following: A History of Southwestern Baptist Theological Seminary, 1903–1983* (Nashville: Broadman Press, 1983) 225. After Norris promised to change some of his church's policies, he asked the association to seat messengers from First Baptist, Fort Worth, at the 1924 associational meeting. Not wanting to appear to be unforgiving, the association relented and even invited Norris to preach at the meeting. He used part of the Ten Commandments as his text, and in an attempt to flatter Jeff D. Ray, a professor of preaching at Southwestern Baptist Theological Seminary who was sitting in the front row, Norris quipped that if Ray were preaching the sermon, he would undoubtedly captivate the congregation by his eloquence. When Norris paused to take a breath, Ray rose from his seat, pointed his finger at Norris, and said, "If I were up there preaching to you on a commandment, I would take the text, 'Thou shalt not *lie*!'" After the audience stopped laughing, Norris merely blinked and continued preaching as if nothing had happened. The association expelled Norris's church again in 1925. See Baker, *Tell the Generations Following*, 227–28.

[45] *Annual*, Baptist General Convention of Texas (BGCT), 1924, 25.

[46] Ibid.

[47] H. Leon McBeth, "Two Ways to Be Baptist," *Baptist History and Heritage* 32/2 (April 1997): 43.

[48] *Annual*, SBC, 1925, 25.

[49] Ibid., 23.

[50] Ibid., 23–24.

[51] McBeth, *The Baptist Heritage*, 621.

[52] Beck, "1920–1929: Recession, Norris Fail to Derail Texans"; *Annual*, SBC, 1925, 23.

[53] McBeth, *The First Baptist Church of Dallas*, 145.

[54] "Some Impressions of the Convention," *Baptist Standard*, May 27, 1920, 8.

[55] J. B. Gambrell, [foreword] to "Baptists and Religious Liberty," by George W. Truett in *God's Call to America*, by George W. Truett, ed. J. B. Cranfill (Philadelphia: Judson Press, 1923) 28.

[56] Ibid., 29; J. B. Cranfill, "A Historic Address," *Baptist Standard*, June 3, 1920, 5.

[57] *Annual*, SBC, 1920, 115.

[58] George W. Truett, "Baptists and Religious Liberty," in Truett, *God's Call to America*, 30. This address can also be found in *The Inspiration of Ideals*, by George W. Truett, ed. Powhatan W. James (Grand Rapids MI: William B. Eerdmans Publishing House, 1950) 85–112, and most of the address can be found at http://www.bjcpa.org/resources/pubs/pub_truett_address.htm. All references refer to the address in *God's Call to America*. To help him prepare his address, Truett used Charles F. James's *Documentary History of the Struggle for Religious Liberty in Virginia*, a copy of which Truett's son-in-law Powhatan W. James loaned him. See Powhatan W. James to J. M. Dawson, July 16, 1954, Joseph Martin Dawson Papers, SBHLA.

[59] Truett, "Baptists and Religious Liberty," 31.

[60] Ibid., 32.

[61] Ibid.

[62] Ibid., 33.

[63] Ibid.

[64] Ibid., 34.

[65] Ibid., 34–35. The Bible verse is Rom. 14:9, KJV.

[66] Ibid., 36–37. For Truett's reference to the "High Priest," see the ninth chapter of Hebrews; for the "veil," see Ex. 26:31–33; Matt. 27:51; Mark 15:38; Heb. 9:3; and Eph. 2:11–12.

[67] Ibid., 38.

[68] Ibid.

[69] Ibid., 39.

[70] Ibid.

[71] Ibid., 39–40.

[72] Ibid., 40.

[73] Ibid., 43–44. The Bible verse quoted by Truett can be found in Matt. 22:21 and Luke 20:25, KJV.

[74] Ibid., 44.

[75] Ibid.

[76] Ibid., 48.

[77] Ibid.

[78] Ibid., 50.

[79] Ibid., 51.

[80] Ibid., 52.

[81] Ibid.

[82] Ibid., 54–56. Cain's question can be found in Gen. 4:9.

[83] Ibid., 59.

[84] Ibid., 59–60. For the complete poem, see Alfred Noyes, *Collected Poems*, vol. 3 (New York: Frederick A. Stokes Company, 1920) 220–22, available at

http://books.google.com/books?id=MzERAAAAYAAJ&printsec=frontcover&dq=alfr ed+noyes.

[85] Truett, "Baptists and Religious Liberty," 62.

[86] Ibid., 63.

[87] Ibid., 64.

[88] Ibid., 65.

[89] Ibid., 65–66.

[90] Ibid., 66.

[91] Ibid., 66–67. Whittier's poem "The Moral Warfare" can be found in his *The Poetical Works of John Greenleaf Whittier* (Boston: Houghton, Mifflin and Company, 1880) 74, available at http://books.google.com/books?id=ns4-MAAAAYAAJ&printsec=frontcover&dq=whittier.

[92] Gambrell, [foreword] to "Baptists and Religious Liberty," 28.

[93] "Some Impressions of the Convention," *Baptist Standard*, May 27, 1920, 8.

[94] John D. Erwin, "Baptists Favor League of Nations," *Tennessean*, May 21, 1920, TC 37/MF 21–542:3.

[95] E. J. Forrester, "Truett on the Capitol Steps," typed manuscript, [1920], [1], TC 545/MF 543–553:1.

[96] Ibid., [2].

[97] "Syllabus of Errors," http://www.traditionalcatholic.net/Tradition/Pope/Pius_IX/The_Syllabus_of_Errors,_1864.html (accessed June 3, 2008). The propositions noted in the text read:

15. Every man is free to embrace and profess that religion which, guided by the light of reason, he shall consider true.

17. Good hope at least is to be entertained of the eternal salvation of all those who are not at all in the true [Catholic] Church of Christ.

18. Protestantism is nothing more than another form of the same true Christian religion, in which form it is given to please God equally as in the Catholic Church.

24. The Church has not the power of using force, nor has she any temporal power, direct or indirect.

47. The best theory of civil society requires that popular schools open to children of every class of the people, and, generally, all public institutes intended for instruction in letters and philosophical sciences and for carrying on the education of youth, should be freed from all ecclesiastical authority, control and interference, and should be fully subjected to the civil and political power at the pleasure of the rulers, and according to the standard of the prevalent opinions of the age.

48. Catholics may approve of the system of educating youth unconnected with Catholic faith and the power of the Church, and which regards the knowledge of merely natural things, and only, or at least primarily, the ends of earthly social life.

55. The Church ought to be separated from the State, and the State from the Church.

77. In the present day it is no longer expedient that the Catholic religion should be held as the only religion of the State, to the exclusion of all other forms of worship.

78. Hence it has been wisely decided by law, in some Catholic countries, that persons coming to reside therein shall enjoy the public exercise of their own peculiar worship.

79. Moreover, it is false that the civil liberty of every form of worship, and the full power, given to all, of overtly and publicly manifesting any opinions whatsoever and thoughts, conduce more easily to corrupt the morals and minds of the people, and to propagate the pest of indifferentism.

[98] On this point, see Henry Vedder, *Baptist "Bigotry and Intolerance": A Reply to Cardinal Gibbons* (Chester PA: published by the author, 1909).

[99] "Dr. Truett Makes Statement," *DMN*, November 21, 1905. See also "Statement by Father Hayes," *DMN*, November 17, 1905.

[100] See Durso and Durso, *The Story of Baptists in the United States*, 105–19.

[101] Joseph Martin Dawson, *A Thousand Months to Remember: An Autobiography* (Waco TX: Baylor University Press, 1964) 132.

[102] Everett Gill, *A. T. Robertson: A Biography* (New York: Macmillan Co., 1943) 181.

[103] John W. Storey, *Texas Baptist Leadership and Social Christianity, 1900–1980* (College Station: Texas A&M University Press, 1986) 46–48.

[104] H. Leon McBeth, "John Frank Norris: Texas Tornado," *Baptist History and Heritage* 32/2 (April 1997): 31.

[105] Ibid.

[106] Morris, "He Changed Things," 151–53; Storey, *Texas Baptist Leadership and Social Christianity*, 53–54.

[107] Morris, "He Changed Things," 155.

[108] Ibid., 157–58.

[109] "Heresy Committee Ready to Report," *DMN*, July 21, 1922.

[110] *Annual*, BGCT, 1922, 152.

[111] Ibid., 157–58.

[112] Storey, *Texas Baptist Leadership and Social Christianity*, 56.

[113] Morris, "He Changed Things," 220–37.

[114] *Annual*, SBC, 1925, 76.

[115] Jesse C. Fletcher, *The Southern Baptist Convention: A Sesquicentennial History* (Nashville: Broadman & Holman Publishers, 1994) 143.

[116] George W. Truett, "The Power of Convictions," in Truett, *The Inspiration of Ideals*, 52.

[117] John T. Boland to George W. Truett, April 27, 1926, TC 782/MF 736–1336:4.

[118] George W. Truett to John T. Boland, May 7, 1926, TC 782/MF 736–1336:4.

[119] George W. Truett to C. P. Stealey, March 3, 1926, TC 1252/MF 736–1336:52. See also George W. Truett to W. L. Dearing, April 4, 1930, TC 872/MF 736–1336:14.

[120] Alva N. Turner to George W. Truett, August 29, 1927, TC 1280/MF 736–1336:55. See also L. E. Jarrell to George W. Truett, September 14, 1927, TC 999/MF 736–1336:25.

[121] George W. Truett to A. N. Hall, April 18, 1921, TC 951. See also "Dr. Shailer Mathews Lectures at Sherman," *DMN*, March 25, 1921; "Open Forum Will Hear Dr. Mathews," *DMN*, March 27, 1921; and "Forum Holds Last Session of Season," *DMN*, March 28, 1921. In a 1935 sermon, Norris also referred to Mathews's appearance in the pulpit of FBC. See Norris, *The Triple Major Operation in Detroit*, 9, and J. Frank Norris, *Inside History of First Baptist Church Fort Worth and Temple Baptist Church Detroit: Life Story of Dr. J. Frank Norris* ([Fort Worth: n.p., n.d.]) 159.

[122] Dawson, *A Thousand Months to Remember*, 121.

[123] Ibid., 97. See also 159.

[124] Morris, "He Changed Things," 45n18.

[125] George W. Truett to J. M. Dawson, April 22, 1929, Dawson Papers.

[126] David Brian Whitlock, "Southern Baptists and Southern Culture: Three Visions of a Christian America, 1890–1945" (Ph.D. diss., Southern Baptist Theological Seminary, 1988) 288.

[127] Fletcher, *The Southern Baptist Convention*, 144.

[128] Baker, *The Southern Baptist Convention and Its People*, 394. The BGCT also incurred an enormous debt. See McBeth, *Texas Baptists* (Dallas: Baptistway Press, 1998) 155–56.

[129] "Appraisement of the Convention," *Biblical Recorder*, May 18, 1927, 6, TC 117/MF 21–542:9; "Bouquets for the Deserving," *Baptist and Reflector*, May 19, 1927, 2, TC 116/MF 21–542:9.

[130] J. E. Dillard, "Moments with Readers," *Alabama Baptist*, May 19, 1927, 7.

[131] Claude W. Duke to George W. Truett, May 25, 1927, TC 881/MF 736–1336:14. In his comment about "the creed making convention policy," Duke was probably referring to the adoption of the Baptist Faith and Message at the 1925 meeting.

[132] Fletcher, *The Southern Baptist Convention*, 148.

[133] For the text of this message, see *Fourth Baptist World Congress, Toronto, Canada, 23–29 June 1928*, ed. W. T. Whitley (Toronto Canada: Stewart Printing Service, [1928]) 55–63. Truett also read Z. T. Cody's paper, "The Vital Principles of the Baptist Faith." See *Fourth Baptist World Congress*, 106–111.

[134] Joe W. Burton, "The Preacher and Missions," *Southern Baptist Home Missions* 13/4 (April 1942): 13, TC 446/MF 21–542:30; Joe W. Burton, *Prince of the Pulpit: A Pen Picture of George W. Truett at Work* (Grand Rapids MI: Zondervan Publishing House, 1946) 78.

[135] Burton, "The Preacher and Missions," 13; Burton, *Prince of the Pulpit*, 78.

[136] Louie D. Newton, with A. Ronald Tonks, "Oral Memoirs of Louie D. Newton" (Historical Commission, Southern Baptist Convention, SBHLA, Nashville, TN, 1973–1981) 208.

[137] Burton, "The Preacher and Missions," 13; Burton, *Prince of the Pulpit*, 78; W. W. Barnes, "Carnes's Defalcation," in *Encyclopedia of Southern Baptists*, ed. Norman Wade Cox and Judson Boyce Allen (Nashville: Broadman Press, 1958) 1:232. For more on the Carnes defalcation, see *Annual*, 1929, 67–71, and "Minutes, Reports, Correspondence, Etc.–1928," 38–40, 52–54, 58–59, Executive Committee Records, box 72 A, folder 9, SBHLA.

[138] George W. Truett and Arch C. Cree, "Facing Baptist Honor Day with Sacrificial Purpose," *Baptist Standard*, November 8, 1928, 1.

[139] Burton, "The Preacher and Missions," 13; Burton, *Prince of the Pulpit*, 79; Barnes, "Carnes's Defalcation," 1:232. Carnes was arrested in Winnipeg, Canada, a couple of months after his crime was discovered. At that time he owned $3,357,193.71 ($40.6 million) worth of real estate. See "Bad Angel," *Time*, October 8, 1928, http://www.time.com/time/magazine/article/0,9171,928165,00.html?iid=chix-sphere (accessed June 16, 2008).

[140] "Truett for President," in "Letters from Readers," *DMN*, February 23, 1928.

[141] "Cullen Thomas Raps Baptists about Politics," *DMN*, August 19, 1928. See also "Truett Speaks on Prohibition," *DMN*, December 2, 1927, TC 563/MF 554–590:2; George W. Truett, "The Sin of Omission," in *On Eagle Wings*, by George W. Truett, ed. Powhatan W. James (Grand Rapids MI: William B. Eerdmans Publishing House, 1953) 118; "Dr. Truett Gives Stand in Campaign," *DMN*, September 30, 1928, TC 165/MF 21–542:12; George W. Truett, "Christian Citizenship and Baptists," *Baptist Standard*, October 4, 1928, 3; "Dr. Truett Denies Giving Indorsement," *DMN*, July 23, 1924; and the TC 787/MF 736–1336:4 for the following letters: W. A. Bowen to George W. Truett, April 20, 1920, and George W. Truett to W. A. Bowen, April 24, 1920.

[142] "Dr. Truett Gives Stand in Campaign."

[143] "Another Example of Tammanycrat Misrepresentation," *Fundamentalist*, October 5, 1928, 1.

[144] Ibid., 2, 7.

[145] Morris, "He Changed Things," 339. Norris was not the only preacher who urged people to vote against Smith. For example, in October 1928, the president of Southern Methodist University, C. C. Selecman, told a crowd of 300 in Denton,

Texas, that he did not preach about politics from the pulpit because people were intelligent enough to know how to vote; nevertheless, "I do not propose to surrender my right of free speech and I have a right to express my opinions outside the pulpit without submitting to the brass collar and lash of the political boss. I claim to be one of the best Democrats in Texas. But when party loyalty conflicts with my patriotism, then my patriotism is first and my party loyalty second." Selecman encouraged everyone, even Democrats, to vote for Hoover. "Dr. Selecman Asks Support for Hoover," *DMN*, October 28, 1928. See also "Clergy Oppose Smith Election," *DMN*, October 29, 1928.

[146] Appendix: "Presidential Elections, 1789–1989," in Conlin, *The American Past*, n.p.

[147] Conlin, *The American Past*, 497. For an example of one author who praised the messianic qualities of business, see Edward E. Purinton, "Business as the Savior of the Community," http://historymatters.gmu.edu/d/5049/ (accessed June 20, 2008).

[148] *Annual*, SBC, 1929, 91.

[149] Ibid., 38.

[150] J. W. Porter to George W. Truett, April 27, 1929, TC 1159/MF 736–1336:39.

[151] "Bible Is Quoted to Prevent Woman Talking to Baptists; She Wins and Pastor Leaves," *DMN*, May 12, 1929. See also "Women Brethren," *Time*, May 20, 1929, http://www.time.com/time/magazine/article/0,9171,723668,00.html    (accessed March 20, 2007).

[152] George W. Truett to E. H. Owen, April 6, 1929, TC 1139/MF 736–1336:36. See also E. H. Owen to George W. Truett, April 3, 1929, TC 1139/MF 736–1336:36.

[153] Wedding announcement, TC 1675/MF 1657–1675:3; "Social Affairs," *DMN*, August 31, 1924; "Miss Truett Soon to Wed R. L. Milliken," *DMN*, February 27, 1927; "Miss Truett Becomes Bride," *DMN*, April 23, 1927; and D. A. Teal, "Early History of the First Baptist Church and Its Friends," typed manuscript, n.d., [5–6], GWTML.

[154] See the newspaper clippings in the TC 67–79/MF 21–542:5–6.

[155] McBeth, *The First Baptist Church of Dallas*, 352; Eugene P. Alldredge, "Amazing Achievements of Dr. George W. Truett's Ministry, 1897–1941," *Quarterly Review* 1/4 (October–December 1941): 62.

[156] McBeth, *The First Baptist Church of Dallas*, 352.

[157] A. B. Macdonald, "A Great Pastor and Organization Give Dallas a Monster Church," *Kansas City Star*, March 31, 1929, TC 171/MF 21–542:12.

[158] For Truett's salary during the 1920s, see the financial reports in Notebook: Financial Reports 1910–1929, GWTML, and Minutes, First Baptist Church (FBC), Dallas, Texas.

[159] Mrs. [Oscar] Marchman, interview by H. Leon McBeth, [1966], H. Leon McBetth Collection, box 11, "Interview" folder, TBHC. Mrs. Marchman was one of

Josephine Truett's sisters. According to one FBC deacon, "It does not make any difference how much salary we pay Bro. Truett. It all comes back to the Church. If we would pay him $100,000 a year, he would give it all back to the objects represented by the Church." See B. F. Riley, *History of the Baptists of Texas* (Dallas: published for the author, 1907) 327.

[160] Macdonald, "A Great Pastor and Organization Give Dallas a Monster Church." See also Newton, "Oral Memoirs," 238–39.

[161] See "Father Hears Sermon on Radio," *DMN*, December 18, 1921; "Sermons Sent Out on Wings of Air," *DMN*, December 24, 1921; McBeth, *The First Baptist Church of Dallas*, 153–154, 179–80.

[162] See McBeth, *The First Baptist Church of Dallas*, 162–67; Macdonald, "A Great Pastor and Organization Give Dallas a Monster Church."

[163] Coleman Craig, "Father of Dr. Truett Describes Early Days in North Carolina," *Baptist Standard*, April 26, 1923, 10.

[164] Adelia Brown, "Truett and Leavell in Georgia," *Baptist Standard*, July 8, 1920, 12. Mary Davidson had a similar experience. She recalled passing Truett in a hallway at FBC when she was eleven or twelve years old: "When his eyes met mine, I felt that I was looking into the face of God and he knew everything I had ever done wrong." Mary Davidson to Keith E. Durso, n.d., 2008, in possession of the author.

[165] "First Baptist Church, Dallas, Texas. Thursday Night, September 14, 1922. Mayor Sawnie Aldredge, Chairman," 7, Notebook: Pastors: Truett: 25th Anniversary, GWTML. Truett received hundreds of telegrams and letters congratulating him for his twenty-five years of service at FBC. See "Pastor Observes Silver Anniversary," *DMN*, September 12, 1922. Many of these telegrams and letters can be found in the TC 701–712/MF 701–717:1–6.

[166] "First Baptist Church, Dallas, Texas. Thursday Night, September 14, 1922. Mayor Sawnie Aldredge, Chairman,"16.

[167] David Lefkowitz to George W. Truett, January 30, 1929, TC 1037/MF 736–1336:28. See also the remarks by Alex Sanger, a Jewish businessman, during the 1922 banquet. "First Baptist Church, Dallas, Texas. Thursday Night, September 14, 1922. Mayor Sawnie Aldredge, Chairman,"17–18.

[168] Macdonald, "A Great Pastor and Organization Give Dallas a Monster Church." See also Viola Else to George W. and Josephine Truett, November 10, 1935, TC 9143/MF 736–1336:17.

[169] Joe W. Burton, "The Preacher and His Appointments," *Southern Baptist Home Missions* 13/1 (January 1942): 13, TC 442/MF 21–542:29; Burton, *Prince of the Pulpit*, 40.

[170] "Charles L. Truett, 95, Called by Death," unidentified newspaper clipping, TC 653/MF 628–657:4. Truett preached Gambrell's funeral sermon. See George W.

Truett, "Dr. J. B. Gambrell, the Great Southern Baptist Commoner," in Truett, *God's Call to America*, 92–109.

[171] Josephine Nash to Keith E. Durso, March 22, 2008, in possession of the author.

[172] W. C. Biting to George W. Truett, February 28, 1928, TC 776/MF 736–1336:3. For two other letters criticizing Truett and his responses, see Mrs. A. D. Gentry to George W. Truett, March 28, 1929; George W. Truett to Mrs. A. D. Gentry, April 6, 1929, TC93/MF 736–1336:19; DeWitt McMurray to George W. Truett, November 9, 1935; and George W. Truett to DeWitt McMurray, November 13, 1935, TC 1088/MF 736–1336:32.

[173] J. Frank Norris to Victor I. Masters, April 22, 1929, L. R. Scarborough Collection, AWRL, folder 264/MF 207–296:8.

[174] Ibid.

[175] Ibid. See also J. Frank Norris to Victor I. Masters, n.d., J. Frank Norris Papers, SBHLA, box 27, folder 1228.

[176] Morris, "He Changed Things," 318; McBeth, "John Frank Norris: Texas Tornado," 35. McBeth said that Norris fired two shots while Chipps was on the floor. The following day, Norris preached a sermon on Romans 8:28: "And we know that all things work together for good to them that love God, to them who are the called according to His purpose" (KJV). This sermon can be found in the *Searchlight*, July 23, 1926, 1, 5. In his autobiography, Norris expressed his sorrow for killing Chipps and regretted the "unfortunate dark tragedy that fell across" his life. Nevertheless, he never experienced "one tinge of remorse." See J. Frank Norris, *Inside History of First Baptist Church Fort Worth and Temple Baptist Church Detroit: Life Story of Dr. J. Frank Norris* ([Fort Worth: n.p., n.d.]) 94–95.

[177] Morris, "He Changed Things," 328–31. See also "Not Guilty, Jury Finds Dr. Norris in Quick Verdict," *DMN*, January 26, 1927.

[178] Scarborough wrote, "I do not believe that the New Testament will recognize an evangelism by killing…. I do not believe that any 2,000 people in Fort Worth or surrounding country have joined his church since his smoking pistol carried to his grave an unarmed man, Mr. Chipps." L. R. Scarborough, ["Remarks concerning J. Frank Norris, 1931"], 14, L. R. Scarborough Collection, folder 198/MF 155–206:10, AWRL. See also Morris, "He Changed Things," 327–28, 332–33.

[179] Norris to Victor I. Masters, April 22, 1929.

[180] J. B. Cranfill, "George W. Truett, and His Work as Pastor, Builder and Leader," *Western Recorder*, January 26, 1928, 20, TC 149/MF 21–542:11. See also George W. Truett to W. F. Matheny, March 27, 1930, TC 1069/MF 736–1336:31.

[181] "Deluge of Selling Crashes Stock in Last Hour of Trading," *DMN*, October 24, 1929. See also "Prices of Stocks Collapse during Wild Selling Orgy; Bankers

Minimize Danger," *DMN*, October 29, 1929; and "Frantic Stock Selling Stampede Is Checked by Bankers' Buying," *DMN*, October 30, 1929.

[182] Norris to Masters, April 22, 1929.

Chapter 6: Owing Himself to the World, 1930–1939

*Chapter 6*

[1] David Thompson, *World History from 1914 to 1961*, 2nd ed. (London: Oxford University Press, 1963) 129.

[2] Ibid., 130.

[3] Harry Leon McBeth, *Texas Baptists: A Sesquicentennial History* (Dallas: Baptistway Press, 1998) 194.

[4] The amounts in parentheses represent the purchasing power in 2007. See Lawrence H. Officer and Samuel H. Williamson, "Purchasing Power of Money in the United States from 1774 to 2007," http://www.measuringworth.com.

[5] Robert A. Baker, *The Blossoming Desert: A Concise History of Texas Baptists* (Waco: Word Books, Publisher, 1970) 212.

[6] Robert A. Baker, *The Southern Baptist Convention and Its People, 1607–1972* (Nashville: Broadman Press 1974) 396.

[7] Leon McBeth, *The First Baptist Church of Dallas: Centennial History, 1868–1968* (Grand Rapids MI: Zondervan Publishing House, 1968) 352; Eugene P. Alldredge, "Amazing Achievements of Dr. George W. Truett's Ministry, 1897–1941," *Quarterly Review* 1/4 (October–December 1941): 62.

[8] See Clerk's Book, First Baptist Church, Dallas, Texas, 1931–1935, and 1936–1940, GWTML.

[9] Joseph R. Conlin, *The American Past: A Brief History* (San Diego: Harcourt Brace Jovanovich, Publishers, 1991) 506.

[10] Jackie McElhaney and Michael V. Hazel, "Dallas, Texas," in *Handbook of Texas Online*, http://www.tshaonline.org/handbook/online/articles/DD/hdd1.html (accessed December 20, 2007); Darwin Payne, *Big D: Triumphs and Troubles of an American Supercity in the 20th Century* (Dallas: Three Forks Press, 1994) 144.

[11] "Truett Calls on All Dallas to Help Needy," *DMN*, December 15, 1931.

[12] McBeth, *Texas Baptists*, 195.

[13] "Pastor Truett Beginning His Twenty-first Year," *Baptist Standard*, September 13, 1917, 6.

[14] A. T. Robertson, "Dr. George W. Truett in Louisville," *Watchman-Examiner*, April 3, 1930, 442. Much of this article also appeared in the *Baptist Standard*, April 10, 1930, 3. See also John R. Sampey, *Memoirs of John R. Sampey* (Nashville: Broadman Press, 1947) 212.

[15] Robertson, "Dr. George W. Truett in Louisville," 442.

[16] "Dr. Truett in Florida," *Baptist Standard*, March 20, 1930, 2.

[17] John R. Sampey to George W. Truett, March 24, 1930, TC 1205/MF 736–1336. See also Benjamin F. Procter to W. J. McGlothlin, February 13, 1930, TC 1083/MF 736–1336.

[18] H. Leon McBeth, "George W. Truett: Baptist Statesman," *Baptist History and Heritage* 32/2 (April 1997): 20.

[19] Powhatan W. James, *George W. Truett: A Biography* (Nashville: Broadman Press, 1939) 197.

[20] Ibid., 198–99.

[21] "Dr. Truett's Mission," *Baptist Standard*, July 24, 1930, 4.

[22] William A. Brown, "Triumphs of Redeeming Grace," *Baptist Standard*, September 11, 1930, 1.

[23] Ibid.

[24] Gaye L. McGlothlen, *A History of Immanuel Baptist Church, 1887–1986* (Nashville: Immanuel Baptist Church, 1987) 95; George W. Truett, *Follow Thou Me* (Nashville: Broadman Press, n.d.).

[25] George W. Truett, "A Convenient Season," in *The Salt of the Earth*, by George W. Truett, ed. Powhatan W. James (Grand Rapids MI: William B. Eerdmans Publishing House, 1949) 146.

[26] Peter Wallace Agnew, "Religion and the Social Order in a Twentieth-Century City: Six Dallas Leaders" (Ph.D. diss., Southern Methodist University, 1999) 78.

[27] "Liquor Argued Pro and Con by Dallas Pastors," *DMN*, February 8, 1933.

[28] Ibid.

[29] Ibid.

[30] Jack S. Blocker, Jr., "Temperance and Prohibition," in *The Oxford Companion to United States History*, ed. Paul Boyer (Oxford: Oxford University Press, 2001) 773; Richard F. Hamm, "Eighteenth Amendment," in *The Oxford Companion to United States History*, 217.

[31] D. W. Bebbington, "C. H. Spurgeon," in *Eerdmans' Handbook to the History of Christianity*, ed. Tim Dowley (Grand Rapids MI: Wm. B. Eerdmans Publishing Co., 1977) 529.

[32] "Truett Compared to Spurgeon by London Minister," *DMN*, May 6, 1934.

[33] George W. Truett, "C. H. Spurgeon Centenary," in *The Inspiration of Ideals*, by George W. Truett, ed. Powhatan W. James (Grand Rapids MI: William B. Eerdmans Publishing House, 1950) 149. Parts of this address can also be found at http://members.aol.com/pilgrimpub/centnary.htm (accessed July 7, 2008).

[34] Truett, "C. H. Spurgeon Centenary," 149.

[35] Ibid., 154, 156.

[36] Ibid., 159–60.

[37] Ibid., 165.

[38] Martin Gilbert, *History of the Twentieth Century* (New York: William Morrow, 2001) 219

[39] Erich Geldbach, "The Years of Anxiety and World War II," in *Baptists Together in Christ, 1905–2005: A Hundred-Year History of the Baptist World Alliance*, ed. Richard V. Pierard (Falls Church VA: Baptist World Alliance, 2005) 76–79.

[40] Ibid., 80. See the picture in the *Baptist Standard*, September 1, 1934, 6, and June 11, 1936, 34.

[41] George W. Truett, "Closing Words," in *Fifth Baptist World Congress, Berlin, August 4–10, 1934*, ed. J. H. Rushbrooke (London: Baptist World Alliance, 1934) 217.

[42] Ibid.

[43] "Baptists Meeting in Berlin Treated with Great Courtesy, Coleman Tells Congregation," *DMN*, September 3, 1934. See also "The Declaration of the Reichsbischof," in *Fifth Baptist World Congress*, 228–29.

[44] Geldbach, "The Years of Anxiety and World War II," 83.

[45] See the dedicatory page in *Centennial Story of Texas Baptists*, ed. [L. R. Elliott] (Dallas: Executive Board of the Baptist General Convention of Texas, 1936).

[46] J. Frank Norris, *The Triple Major Operation in Detroit* ([Detroit: n.p.], 1935) 8; J. Frank Norris, *Inside History of First Baptist Church Fort Worth and Temple Baptist Church Detroit: Life Story of Dr. J. Frank Norris* ([Fort Worth: n.p., n.d.]) 158.

[47] Norris, *The Triple Major Operation in Detroit*, 8–9; Norris, *Inside History of First Baptist Church Fort Worth and Temple Baptist Church Detroit*, 158–59.

[48] J. Frank Norris to Victor I. Masters, April 22, 1929, L. R. Scarborough Collection, AWRL, folder 264/MF 207–296:8.

[49] John Graham to J. Frank Norris, February 18, 1931, J. Frank Norris Papers, box 2, folder 1849, SBHLA.

[50] David M. Gardner, "Dr. Truett Preaches to All America in St. Petersburg, Florida," *Baptist Standard*, February 12, 1931, 5–6, TC 206/MF 21–542:14. See also George W. Truett to W. F. Matheny, March 27, 1930, TC 1069/MF 736–1336:31, and George W. Truett to W. L. Dearing, April 4, 1930, TC 872/MF 736–1336:14.

[51] J. Frank Norris to John Graham, February 23, 1931, Norris Papers, box 2, folder 1849. See also J. Frank Norris to Clarence Martin, February 23, 1931, Norris Papers, box 2, folder 1849, and "A sympathizer" to J. Frank Norris, n.d., Norris Papers, box 2, folder 1849. The "sympathizer" was probably an FBC member, for his letter is filed in the Norris Papers with an April 23, 1931, form letter from Truett in which the last name of the recipients has been deleted.

[52] J. N. Marshall, "George W. Truett," *Baptist Standard*, June 18, 1936, 5, TC 343/MF 21–542:22. Other names Norris called Truett included: "the infallible Baptist pope" (J. Frank Norris to E. P. Alldredge, April 28, 1930, Norris Papers, box 1, folder 35); "poor fool" (J. Frank Norris to Louis Entzminger, June 5, 1931,

Scarborough Collection, folder 264/MF 207–296:8); "tyrant" (J. Frank Norris to C. P. Stealey, April 4, 1931, Scarborough Collection, folder 266/MF 207–296:8); and "pathetic figure" (J. Frank Norris to Victor I. Masters, January 8, 1933, Scarborough Collection, folder 267/MF 207–296:9)

[53] Marshall, "George W. Truett," 5.

[54] DeWitte Talmage Holland, "A Rhetorical Analysis of the Preaching of George W. Truett" (Ph.D. diss., Northwestern University, 1956) 180. Holland cited Truett's daily journal for February 12, 1938. Holland noted that Powhatan W. James had allowed him to use Truett's pocket diaries for 1937 and 1941 and his daily journals for 1938 and 1942 (Holland, "A Rhetorical Analysis of the Preaching of George W. Truett," 34). Unfortunately, the 1938 diary is not in the TC.

[55] Ibid., 177.

[56] Robert H. Coleman's grandson Robert O. Coleman donated this letter to Southwestern Baptist Theological Seminary on October 6, 1981.

[57] J. Frank Norris to George W. Truett, March 9, 1940, TC 1133/MF 736–1336:35.

[58] Ibid.

[59] Ibid.

[60] Ibid.

[61] McBeth, *The First Baptist Church of Dallas*, 190.

[62] Holland, "A Rhetorical Analysis of the Preaching of George W. Truett," 180–81; McBeth, *The First Baptist Church of Dallas*, 190. Other Baptists also chose not to mention Norris's name. In a 1924 letter to Truett, for example, Robert H. (R. H.) Pitt, editor of the *Religious Herald*, referred to Norris as "the unspeakable editor" who used the methods of an "assassin." "I do not like to use abusive language of anybody," Pitt confided to his friend, "but surely none of us can mistake the presence in our neighborhood of a plain ordinary skunk." R. H. Pitt to George W. Truett, April 22, 1924, TC 1154/MF 736–1336:37.

[63] Gwin Morris, "J. Frank Norris: Rascal or Reformer?" *Baptist History and Heritage* 3/3 (Autumn 1998): 33.

[64] J. T. Harrington to George W. Truett, October 31, 1935, TC 959/MF 736–1336:22.

[65] George W. Truett, "What Think Ye of Christ?" in *Some Vital Questions*, by George W. Truett, ed. Powhatan W. James (Grand Rapids MI: William B. Eerdmans Publishing House, 1946) 103.

[66] "President George Truett," *Baptist Standard*, August 3, 1939, 3.

[67] Mildred Lively, interview by Marvin Jarvis Mosley, n.d., in "Pastoral Ministry of Dr. George W. Truett," by Marvin Jarvis Mosley (Master's thesis, Southwestern Baptist Theological Seminary, 1971) 48.

[68] George W. Truett, "Impressions of a World Tour," *Baptist Messenger*, May 28, 1936, 28, TC 568/MF 554–590:2.

[69] Truett, "What Think Ye of Christ?" 106.

[70] Truett, "Impressions of a World Tour," *Baptist Messenger*, 28.

[71] Josephine Truett, "Words from the Far East," *Baptist Standard*, April 9, 1936, 6.

[72] Truett, "Impressions of a World Tour," 6.

[73] James, *George W. Truett*, 222.

[74] "Sermons on Ship Mark Voyage for Dr. George Truett," *DMN*, March 28, 1936.

[75] "Chinese Trek Miles for Sermon," *DMN*, May 22, 1936.

[76] "Letter from Dr. Truett to Robert H. Coleman," *Baptist Standard*, April 9, 1936, 1, TC 567/MF 554–590:2.

[77] Bill J. Leonard, *Baptist Ways: A History* (Valley Forge PA: Judson Press, 2003) 356.

[78] "Letter from Dr. Truett to Robert H. Coleman," 1.

[79] Truett, "Impressions of a World Tour," 6.

[80] "Church Filled for Return of World Pastor," *DMN*, May 25, 1936.

[81] George W. Truett to J. M. Dawson, April 12, 1936, Joseph Martin Dawson Papers, SBHLA.

[82] George W. Truett to T. L. Holcomb, June 15, 1936, Thomas Luther Holcombe Papers, SBHLA.

[83] "The National Preaching Mission," *Christian Index*, September 24, 1936, 10, TC 349/MF 21–542:22; "Reformation Ideas Urged to Aid World," *DMN*, December 2, 1935.

[84] "Preaching Team," *Time*, September 28, 1936, http://www.time.com/time/magazine/article/0,9171,756733,00.html (accessed September 4, 2007).

[85] Deacons Minutes, First Baptist Church, Dallas, Texas, June 1, 1936.

[86] Mary E. Ponce de Leon to George W. Truett, August 20, 1936, TC 1038/MF 736–1336:28.

[87] Ibid.

[88] George W. Truett to Jerry E. Lambdin, July 26, 1933, Jerry Elmer Lambdin Papers, SBHLA.

[89] Jessie Truett James, interview by DeWitte Talmage Holland, August 1955, in Holland, "A Rhetorical Analysis of the Preaching of George W. Truett," 184.

[90] J. B. Cranfill, "George W. Truett, Minister," *Holland's*, November 1937, 9, TC 393/MF 21–542:26.

[91] W. O. Vaught, Jr., "Memorable Events from the Life of George W. Truett," *Proclaim* (April–June 1978): 12. See also James, *George W. Truett*, 232–33, and George W. Truett, "Baptists and World Conditions," *Baptist Messenger*, November 25, 1937, 11, TC 574/MF 554–590:3. For Jones's understanding of Christian unity, see Stephen

A. Graham, *Ordinary Man, Extraordinary Mission: The Life and Work of E. Stanley Jones* (Nashville: Abingdon Press, 2005) 243–45.

[92] See the following articles in the *Dallas Morning News*: "Praises Preaching Mission," November 3, 1936; "Preaching Mission First Day's Crowds Estimated at 10,850," November 16, 1936; "National Preaching Missioners Heard by 70,000 Here," November 18, 1936; and "Mission Aims to Save U. S. from Dry Rot," December 1, 1936.

[93] George W. Truett, Diary, January 15, 1937, TC 666/MF 664–690:3. Hereafter cited as Diary 1937.

[94] Ibid., January 24, 1937, TC 666/MF 664–690:3.

[95] Ibid., May 6, 1937, TC 666/MF 664–690:5.

[96] "$15,000 Love Token Presented Baptist Pastor," *DMN*, May 19, 1937.

[97] Diary, May 18, 1937, TC 666/MF 664–690:5

[98] Ibid., May 28, 1937, TC 666/MF 664–690:5.

[99] George W. Truett to J. M. Dawson, June 10, 1937, Dawson Papers.

[100] J. H. Rushbrooke, "Dr. Truett in Britain," *Baptist Standard*, August 5, 1937, 9.

[101] George W. Truett, "Baptists and World Conditions," *Baptist Messenger*, November 25, 1937, 11, TC 567/MF 554–590:3; George W. Truett, "Tour of Dr. and Mrs. George W. Truett to British Isles and Europe," *Western Recorder*, September 30, 1937, 4.

[102] Diary, June 31, 1937, TC 666/MF 664–690:6.

[103] Truett, "Baptists and World Conditions," 11.

[104] Ibid.

[105] George W. Truett, "World's Largest Challenge to Religious Liberty Is Europe," *Western Recorder*, October 7, 1937, 3, TC 383/MF 21–542:25.

[106] Gilbert, *History of the Twentieth Century*, 224.

[107] Diary, July 26, 1937, TC 666/MF 664–690:6.

[108] Truett, "World's Largest Challenge to Religious Liberty Is Europe," 3. Emphasis in the original.

[109] Diary, August 2, 1937, TC 666/MF 664–690:6.

[110] Truett, "World's Largest Challenge to Religious Liberty Is Europe," 3; Truett, "Baptists and World Conditions," 15.

[111] Ibid., September 1, 1937, TC 666/MF 664–690:7.

[112] Ibid., September 9, 1937, TC 666/MF 664–690:7.

[113] Truett, "World's Largest Challenge to Religious Liberty Is Europe," 4.

[114] Ibid.

[115] See *Baptist Standard*, September 9, 1937, 11.

[116] [F. M. McConnell], "The Pastor's Wife," *Baptist Standard*, September 9, 1937, 9.

[117] "Dr. Truett Ill in Hospital," *DMN*, May 2, 1938; "Baptist World Leader Touched by Sympathy," *DMN*, May 22, 1938. Truett was hospitalized again in December after contracting a severe cold while preaching in Denver, Colorado. See "Crowded Church Greets Dr. Truett on Return," *DMN*, January 2, 1939.

[118] Josephine Truett to Powhatan W. James, July [n. d.], 1938, TC 632/MF628–657:1.

[119] Holland, "A Rhetorical Analysis of the Preaching of George W. Truett," 616.

[120] See ibid., 614–18.

[121] Don Norman, "Building for the New Year," *Baptist Student*, February 1937, 3.

[122] Frank H. Leavell to George W. Truett, November 23, 1937, TC 1036/MF 736–1336:28. See also A. T. Hardy to George W. Truett, September 20, 1938, TC 954/MF 736–1336:21, and Louie D. Newton to George W. Truett, January 12, 1938, TC 1094 MF 736–1336:32.

[123] Frank H. Leavell to George W. Truett, November 23, 1937, TC 1036/MF 736–1336:28.

[124] "Mission Snagged," *Time*, October 19, 1936, http://www.time.com/time/magazine/article/0,9171,756785,00.html (September 4, 2007).

[125] George W. Truett to Wilfrid L. McKay, March 5, 1937, TC 1085/ MF 736–1336:32. See also Louie D. Newton to George W. Truett, January 12, 1938, TC 1094/MF 736–1336:32.

[126] M. McElroy Flynn to George W. Truett, September 12, 1938, TC 9143/MF 736–1336:17. See also Daniel L. Reed to George W. Truett, September 27, 1938, TC 1174/MF 736–1336:39.

[127] Ernest A. Payne, *Baptists Speak to the World: A Description and Interpretation of the Sixth Baptist World Congress, Atlanta, 1939* (London: Carey Press, [1939]) 15.

[128] Geldbach, "The Years of Anxiety and World War II," 90; "The Congress and Its Setting: Incidents, Impressions and Evaluations," in *Sixth Baptist World Congress, Atlanta, Georgia, U.S.A., July 22–28, 1939*, ed. J. H. Rushbrooke (Atlanta: Baptist World Alliance, 1939) 292–93; "Messengers in Atlanta," *Time*, July 31, 1939, http://www.time.com/time/magazine/article/0,9171,761791,00. html (accessed March 20, 2007).

[129] George W. Truett, Diary, July 23, 1939, TC 667/MF 664–690:12. Hereafter cited as Diary 1939.

[130] Payne, *Baptists Speak to the World*, 28.

[131] Geldbach, "The Years of Anxiety and World War II," 90. On the last day of the congress, Lacy Kirk Williams, an African-American minister and president of the National Baptist Convention, U.S.A., Inc., expressed his convention's "gratitude to Atlanta citizens as a whole, the local entertainment committee," under the leadership of Louie D. Newton, and "a generous press, all of which have spared no pains to make this the peer of any of the former Congresses of this Alliance." Despite a few

unfortunate incidents, everyone had "enabled Baptists of the world to try to be one in spirit and to help form in Christ that real brotherhood that will banish from the earth all of its ills which today yet sorely and passionately grieve our common Lord Jesus Christ." See "Minutes," in *Sixth Baptist World Congress*, 17–18.

[132] Louie D. Newton, "Dr. Truett on Old Atlanta," *Atlanta Constitution*, June 10, 1940.

[133] "Messengers in Atlanta."

[134] "Sixty Nations Send Baptists to Convention," *DMN*, July 19, 1939.

[135] Diary, July 22, 1939, TC 667/MF 664–690:12.

[136] "Messengers in Atlanta"; Betty Mathis, "125 Roar Atlanta's Welcome as Baptist Congress Opens with Parade," *Atlanta Constitution*, July 23, 1939; Payne, *Baptists Speak to the World*, 14; Joseph Martin Dawson, *A Century with Texas Baptists* (Nashville: Broadman Press, 1947) 97. A photo of the swastika can be found in Payne, *Baptists Speak to the World*, between 22 and 23.

[137] Louie D. Newton, with A. Ronald Tonks, "Oral Memoirs of Louie D. Newton" (Historical Commission, Southern Baptist Convention, SBHLA, Nashville, TN, 1973–1981) 162.

[138] Payne, *Baptists Speak to the World*, 14.

[139] George W. Truett, *President's Address: 6th Baptist World Congress* [audio recording] (N.p.: Baptist World Alliance, 1939), AWRL. The text of the address, which differs in many places from the actual address, can be found in *Sixth Baptist World Congress*, 22–36; TC18/MF 2–20:6; and TC 1962/MF 1909–1970:11–12. Excerpts of the address can be found in Quinn Pugh, "George W. Truett: Prophet of Freedom, Herald of Faith, 1867–1944," http://www.bwa-baptist-heritage.org/r_truett.htm (accessed February 4, 2008).

[140] Conlin, *The American Past*, 527–28; Gilbert, *History of the Twentieth Century*, 201, 250–55.

[141] The poet's name is unknown.

[142] Truett, *President's Address*.

[143] Ibid.

[144] Ibid.

[145] Ibid.

[146] Ibid.

[147] Ibid.

[148] See John Bunyan, *A Confession of My Faith, and a Reason of My Practice, Etc.*, in *The Works of John Bunyan*, ed. George Offor, vol. 2 (London: Blackie and Sone, 1862) 594.

[149] Truett, *President's Address*.

[150] Ibid.

[151] Ibid.

[152] Ibid.

[153] Ibid.

[154] Ibid.

[155] John Howard (1726–1790), Baptist philanthropist and prison reformer.

[156] John Clifford (1836–1923), British Baptist pastor and first president of the Baptist World Alliance.

[157] Alexander MacLaren (1826–1910), British Baptist pastor.

[158] William Carey (1761–1834), British Baptist missionary to India (1793–1834).

[159] Adoniram Judson (1788–1850), Baptist missionary to Burma (1813–1850).

[160] Luther Rice (1783–1836), Baptist promoter of foreign missions and education.

[161] John E. Clough (1836–1910), Baptist missionary to India (1864–1905).

[162] Robert H. Pitt (1853–1937), editor of the *Religious Herald*.

[163] Augustus Strong (1836–1921), Baptist theologian.

[164] John Hope (1868–1936), first African-American president of Morehouse College, in Atlanta, Georgia.

[165] Truett, *President's Address*.

[166] Ibid.

[167] Ps. 30:5.

[168] Truett, *President's Address*. The hymn is "All Hail the Power of Jesus' Name."

[169] Edwin Gaustad, e-mail to Keith E. Durso, August 15, 2007, in possession of the author.

[170] Diary, July 23, 1939, TC 667/MF 664–690:12.

[171] C. C. Whitmire to George W. Truett, July 24, 1939, TC 1313/MF 736–1336:58.

[172] Anonymous to George W. Truett, n.d., [1939], TC 1313/MF 736–1336:58. "Johnnie Smyth" is John Smyth, one of the founders of the Baptist denomination. The phrase *STULTORUM INFINITUS EST NUMERSUS* comes from the Latin Vulgate, Eccl. 1:15.

[173] Diary, September 20, 1938, in Holland, "A Rhetorical Analysis of the Preaching of George W. Truett," 87.

[174] George W. Truett to Joseph M. Dawson, April 18, 1939, Dawson Papers.

[175] J. Truett to James, July [n. d.], 1938.

[176] [George W. Truett], *These Gracious Years: Being the Year-end Messages and Addresses of Dr. George W. Truett* (Nashville: Sunday School Board of the Southern Baptist Convention, 1929) 8.

[177] George W. Truett, "Preachers and Preaching," in Truett, *Follow Thou Me*, 230. See Charles Wesley's hymn "Jesus, the Name High over All," http://www.puritansermons.com/poetry/wesley12.htm (accessed July 29, 2008).

*Chapter 7*

[1] Joseph Martin Dawson, *A Thousand Months to Remember: An Autobiography* (Waco TX: Baylor University Press, 1964) 121.

[2] "Hidden History of Dallas," http://www.dallasnews.com/s/dws/spe/2002/hiddenhistory/timeline.htm#1940s (accessed August 14, 2008).

[3] George W. Truett, "Trumpeting the Gospel," in *We Would See Jesus*, by George W. Truett, ed. J. B. Cranfill (New York: Fleming H. Revell Company, 1915) 74, available at http://www.archive.org/details/wewouldseejesusa00trueuoft.

[4] George W. Truett, "The Passing of the Legalised Liquor Traffic," in *God's Call to America*, by George W. Truett, ed. J. B. Cranfill (Philadelphia: Judson Press, 1923) 152. See also his remarks in "First Baptist Church, Dallas, Texas. Thursday Night, September 14, 1922. Mayor Sawnie Aldredge, Chairman," 2, Notebook: Pastors: Truett: 25th Anniversary, GWTML.

[5] Peter Clark Macfarlane, "The Apostle to the Texans," *Collier's*, January 16, 1913, 21, TC 24/MF 21–542:3.

[6] J. B. Gambrell, "Geo. W. Truett, Preacher and Leader," *Baptist Standard*, January 16, 1913, 3.

[7] Eugene P. Alldredge, "Amazing Achievements of Dr. George W. Truett's Ministry, 1897–1941," *Quarterly Review* 1/4 (October–December 1941): 63.

[8] DeWitte Talmage Holland, "A Rhetorical Analysis of the Preaching of George W. Truett" (Ph.D. diss., Northwestern University, 1956) 28, 35–36, 377.

[9] Joe W. Burton, "The Preacher and His Appointments," *Southern Baptist Home Missions* 13/1 (January 1942): 13, TC 442/MF 21–542:29; Joe W. Burton, *Prince of the Pulpit: A Pen Picture of George W. Truett at Work* (Grand Rapids MI: Zondervan Publishing House, 1946) 35.

[10] A. B. Tanco to W. A. Criswell, December 27, 1954, H. Leon McBeth Collection, box 11, "Speeches on FBC, Texas Baptists" folder, TBHC; Frank B. Spangler, interview by H. Leon McBeth, [1966], McBeth Collection, box 11, "Interview" folder.

[11] The amounts in parentheses represent the purchasing power in 2007. See Lawrence H. Officer and Samuel H. Williamson, "Purchasing Power of Money in the United States from 1774 to 2007," http://www.measuringworth.com.

[12] Leon McBeth, *The First Baptist Church of Dallas: Centennial History, 1868–1968* (Grand Rapids MI: Zondervan Publishing House, 1968) 352.

[13] Powhatan W. James, *George W. Truett: A Biography* (Nashville: Broadman Press, 1939) 236.

[14] Joe W. Burton, "The Preacher in His Study," *Southern Baptist Home Missions* 12/12 (December 1941): 12, TC 440/MF 21–542:29; Burton, *Prince of the Pulpit*, 24.

---

[15] George W. Truett, Diary, January 18, 1941, TC 668/MF 664–690:16. Hereafter cited as Diary 1941. See also Diary, September 27, 1941, TC 668/MF 664–690:20.

[16] Burton, "The Preacher in His Study," 12; Burton, *Prince of the Pulpit*, 23–24.

[17] "Truett Books Bequeathed to Seminary," *DMN*, August 8, 1944; Holland, "A Rhetorical Analysis of the Preaching of George W. Truett," 11; McBeth, *The First Baptist Church of Dallas*, 193–94; Joe W. Burton, "The Preacher and His Appointments," *Southern Baptist Home Missions* 13/1 (January 1942): 13, TC 442/MF 21–542:29; Burton, *Prince of the Pulpit*, 37–38.

[18] Burton, "The Preacher in His Study," 13; Burton, *Prince of the Pulpit*, 27.

[19] A. B. Macdonald, "A Great Pastor and Organization Give Dallas a Monster Church," *Kansas City Star*, March 31, 1929, TC 171/MF 21-542:12. Compare the deacon's comment about FBC's services with Nels Anderson's description of the services at J. Frank Norris's church in Fort Worth. In a 1926 article for the *New Republic*, Anderson described Norris as "a stunt performer, a display artist, and a clown in his own circus." See Clovis Gwin Morris, "He Changed Things: The Life and Thought of J. Frank Norris" (Ph.D. diss., Texas Tech University, 1973) 322n53.

[20] Josephine Nash to Keith E. Durso, February 26, 2008, in possession of the author. Nash's mother, Mrs. Oscar Marchman, was one of Josephine Truett's sisters. See also Grace E. Wilson, interview by Keith E. Durso, January 27, 2008, in possession of the author.

[21] Nash to Durso, February 26, 2008.

[22] L. H. Tapscott, interview by DeWitte Talmage Holland, August 1955, in Holland, "A Rhetorical Analysis of the Preaching of George W. Truett," 99.

[23] Diary, March 29, 1941, TC 668/MF 664–690.17.

[24] Wilson, interview.

[25] Jessie Truett James, interview by DeWitte Talmage Holland, August 1955, in Holland, "A Rhetorical Analysis of the Preaching of George W. Truett," 370–71. See also James, *George W. Truett*, 254; Burton, "The Preacher in His Study," 13; and Burton, *Prince of the Pulpit*, 26.

[26] George W. Truett, Diary, September 27, 1937, TC 666/ MF 664–690:17.

[27] See Diary, May 7, 1941, TC 668/MF 664–690:17, and George W. Truett, Diary, April 8, 1942, TC 669/MF 664–690:23. Hereafter cited as Diary 1942.

[28] Joe W. Burton, "Aflame for Souls," *Southern Baptist Home Missions* 13/3 (March 1942): 11; Burton, *Prince of the Pulpit*, 63.

[29] Marvin Jarvis Mosley, "Pastoral Ministry of Dr. George W. Truett" (Master's thesis, Southwestern Baptist Theological Seminary, 1971) 16-17.

[30] Diary, December 28 and 29, 1942, TC 669/MF 664–690:27.

[31] Diary, February 14, 1941, TC 668/MF 664–690:16.

[32] Ibid., July 17, 1941, TC 668/MF 664–690:19.

[33] Ibid., October 2, 1941, TC 668/MF 664–690:20.

[34] Manon Seawell, "Dr. Truett Receives Just Tribute," *Baptist Standard*, February 22, 1940, 2. See also "State, National Figures Honor Dr. Truett at Belton Banquet," *DMN*, February 17, 1940.

[35] Seawell, "Dr. Truett Receives Just Tribute," 2.

[36] Ibid.

[37] Ibid.

[38] Diary, December 7, 1941, TC 668/MF 664–690:21.

[39] McBeth, *The First Baptist Church of Dallas*, 184.

[40] George W. Truett, "Why Be Discouraged?" in *Some Vital Questions*, by George W. Truett, ed. Powhatan W. James (Grand Rapids MI: William B. Eerdmans Publishing House, 1946) 92–93.

[41] Ibid., 96.

[42] Diary, April 19, 1941, TC 668/MF 664–690:17.

[43] Diary, January 15, 1942, TC 669/MF 664–690:22.

[44] Louie D. Newton, "For Sixty Years His Fruit Faileth Not," *Atlanta Constitution*, April 19, 1941; Ralph McGill, "Pastor of Same Church 60 Years Honored by Vast Throng Here," *Atlanta Constitution*, April 20, 1941; Powhatan W. James, *George W. Truett: A Biography*, rev. ed. (Nashville: Broadman Press, 1945) 296–97.

[45] George W. Truett, Diary, May 2, 1943, TC 670/MF 664–690:30. Hereafter cited as Diary 1943.

[46] "Sanitarium to Be Known as Baylor," *DMN*, June 17, 1920, 4; Lana Henderson, *Baylor University Medical Center: Yesterday, Today and Tomorrow* (Waco: Baylor University Press, 1978) 59–61.

[47] Dawson, *A Thousand Months to Remember*, 173.

[48] McBeth, *The First Baptist Church of Dallas*, 190–91. In a 1949 letter to J. Frank Norris, for example, Victor I. Masters wrote that he had admired Truett's "single but great gift—in the pulpit," but Masters, still bitter about the Dallas pastor's determined support of the "stupid 75-million Campaign" of 1919–1924, went on to describe Truett as "an intolerant bull-whip." Victor I. Masters to J. Frank Norris, May 8, 1949, J. Frank Norris Papers, box 27, folder 1230, SBHLA.

[49] Dawson, *A Thousand Months to Remember*, 173.

[50] For more on the removal of the schools to Houston, see Henderson, *Baylor University Medical Center*, 96–106; "Foundation School to Open on June 21; Baylor Trustees Vote to Move to Houston," *DMN*, May 9, 1943; "Pat Neff Tells about Baylor College Move," *DMN*, May 30, 1943; and Diary April 17, 26, and 27, 1943, TC 670/MF 664–690:29.

[51] Diary, May 8, 1943, TC 670/MF 664–690:30. Rom. 8:28: "And we know that all things work together for good to them that love God, to them who are the called according to his purpose" (KJV).

[52] "Report of Examination of Dr. George W. Truett, September 15, 1942," TC 664/MF 664–690:1.

[53] Louie D. Newton, with A. Ronald Tonks, "Oral Memoirs of Louie D. Newton" (Historical Commission, Southern Baptist Convention, SBHLA, Nashville, TN, 1973–1981) 22. See also Louie Devotie Newton, *Why I Am a Baptist* (New York: Thomas Nelson & Sons, 1957) 61–64.

[54] Ernest A. Payne, *James Henry Rushbrooke, 1870–1947: A Baptist Greatheart* (London: Carey Kingsgate Press Limited, 1954) 54.

[55] Newton, "Oral Memoirs," 22.

[56] Louie D. Newton, "Dr. Geo. W. Truett at Druid Hills," *Baptist Standard*, July 22, 1943, 2.

[57] Ibid., 15.

[58] Diary, July 15, 1943, TC 670/MF 664–690:31.

[59] Ibid., July 20, 1943, TC 670/MF 664–690:31.

[60] Ibid., July 21, 1943, TC 670/MF 664–690:31.

[61] "George Truett Still Confined to Sickbed," *DMN*, April 13, 1944.

[62] "Dr. Truett Returns after Leg Operation," *DMN*, September 2, 1943.

[63] Tanco to Criswell, December 27, 1954.

[64] "Dr. Truett Gets Ovation on Return," *DMN*, November 1, 1943.

[65] Tanco to Criswell, December 27, 1954.

[66] George W. Truett to Joe W. Burton, November 17, 1943, George W. Truett Papers, SBHLA.

[67] Dawson, *A Thousand Months to Remember*, 133.

[68] Deacons Minutes, First Baptist Church (FBC), Dallas, Texas, January 5, 1944; "Dr. Truett Given Leave by His Church," *DMN*, January 6, 1944.

[69] "George Truett Still Confined to Sickbed."

[70] Deacons Minutes, FBC, June 25, 1943; James, *George W. Truett*, rev. ed., 302.

[71] James, *George W. Truett*, rev. ed., 302–303.

[72] Tanco to Criswell, December 27, 1954.

[73] Louie D. Newton, "Thy Will, O Lord, Be Done," *Baptist Standard*, June 15, 1944, 1.

[74] George W. Truett to the First Baptist Church, Dallas, Texas, n.d., 1944, McBeth Collection, box 11, "Speeches on FBC, Texas Baptists" folder. Truett's letter can also be found in "Dr. Truett's Resignation Is Rejected," *DMN*, June 5, 1944, TC 463/MF 21–542:31.

[75] "Dr. Truett's Resignation Is Rejected."

[76] Harold Dye, "The Nights Are Too Short," *Baptist New Mexican*, June 29, 1944, 1, TC 466/MF 21–542:31.

[77] Unidentified clipping, George W. Truett Baptist History File, SBHLA.

[78] McBeth, *The First Baptist Church of Dallas*, 210.

[79] "Head of Baptist World Alliance Sends Sympathy From London," *DMN*, July 10, 1944, TC 485/MF 21–542:32.

[80] "All Creeds Join In Many Tributes Paid Dr. Truett," *DMN*, July 9, 1944, TC 496/MF 21–542:34.

[81] [J. Frank Norris], "Dr. George W. Truett Dead," *Fundamentalist*, July 21, 1944, 1.

[82] Ibid., 5.

[83] George W. Truett, untitled sermon on Matthew 27:43, March 14, 1909, [4], TC 1852/MF 1809-1880:12.

[84] Ibid., 5.

[85] Lois Sager, "Christendom Bows Its Head As Dr. Truett Laid to Rest," *DMN*, July 11, 1944, TC 502/MF 21–542:35.

[86] *Funeral of Dr. George W. Truett* [audio recording] (N.p.: Radio and Television Commission, Southern Baptist Convention, 1944), AWRL. For excerpts of much of what was said at the funeral, see Sager, "Christendom Bows Its Head As Dr. Truett Laid to Rest."

[87] *Funeral of Dr. George W. Truett.*

[88] Ibid.

[89] Ibid.

[90] Ibid.

[91] Ibid.

[92] Sager, "Christendom Bows Its Head As Dr. Truett Laid to Rest."

[93] Ibid. Twain's eulogy can be found at http://www.design.caltech.edu/erik/Misc/Twain_eulogy.html (accessed April 14, 2007). This eulogy appears to have been an adaptation of Robert Richardson's poem, "Annette." See Robert Richardson, *Willow and Wattle* (Edinburgh: John Grant, 1893) 35, http://books.google.com/books?id=DvMOAAAAIAAJ&printsec=frontcover&dq= willow+and+wattle.

[94] George W. Truett, "Count Your Blessings," in *On Eagle Wings*, by George W. Truett, ed. Powhatan W. James (Grand Rapids MI: William B. Eerdmans Publishing House, 1953) 106–107.

### Chapter 8

[1] George W. Truett, foreword to *Golden Years: An Autobiography* by Mrs. William L. Williams (Dallas: Baptist Standard Publishing Company, 1921) 7.

[2] George W. Truett, "Dealing with the Multitude," *Baptist Standard*, February 11, 1909, 5.

[3] Powhatan W. James, *George W. Truett: A Biography* (Nashville: Broadman Press, 1939) 181.

[4] George W. Truett, untitled sermon on Romans 9:33, September 10, 1922, 1–2, Notebook: Pastors: Truett: 25th Anniversary, GWTML. See also "First Baptist Church, Dallas, Texas. Thursday Night, September 14, 1922. Mayor Sawnie Aldredge, Chairman," 25–26, Notebook: Pastors: Truett: 25th Anniversary, GWTML.

[5] "500 Attend Banquet to George W. Truett," *DMN*, December 2, 1916.

[6] Manon Seawell, "Robert H. Coleman…Abounds in Effective Service," *Baptist Standard*, June 11, 1936, 36.

[7] "Dallas Honors Dr. Truett in Long Service," *DMN*, November 9, 1927.

[8] Josephine Truett, Diary, January 1, 1946, TC 673/MF 664–690:31.

[9] See *Some Vital Questions* (1946); *Sermons from Paul* (1947); *The Prophet's* Mantle (1948); *The Salt of the Earth* (1949); *The Inspiration of Ideals* (1950); *Who Is Jesus?* (1952); *On Eagle Wings* 1953); and *After His Likeness* (1954). In 1980, Broadman Press published these eight volumes in a four-volume set titled *George W. Truett Library*. Also published posthumously were Truett's Christmas messages from 1929 to 1943. See George W. Truett, *Christmas Messages* (Chicago: Moody Bible Institute, 1945).

[10] Clyde E. Fant, Jr., and William M. Pinson, Jr., "George Washington Truett," in *20 Centuries of Great Preaching: An Encyclopedia of Preaching*, ed. Clyde E. Fant, Jr., and William M. Pinson, Jr. (Waco TX: Word Books, Publisher, 1971) 137.

[11] Ibid., 137–38. See the examples they provide on 138–39. Compare also the edited version of Truett's sermon on Mark 8:36 in *Who Is Jesus?*, 81–92, with the stenographically recorded version, found in TC 1928/MF1909–1970:6.

[12] For much of the information contained in this paragraph, see the following: Truett Auditorium (Robert A. Baker, *Tell the Generations Following: A History of Southwestern Baptist Theological Seminary, 1903–1983* [Nashville: Broadman Press, 1983], 293–94); "About TMC," http://www.truett.edu/templates/ custruett/ details.asp?id=26811&PID=140506 (accessed September 1, 2008); the Truett Baptist Associations (http://www.truettba.com/templates/System/details.asp?id=20878&PID =213732 and http://www.jstba.com/ [both accessed August 21, 2008]); George W. Truett Home for Children (David Smith, "Baptists in the Holy Land," *Jerusalem Post* [online edition], March 8, 2007, http://www.jpost.com/servlet/Satellite?cid= 1173173963207&pagename=JPost%2FJPArticle%2FShowFull [accessed March 11, 2007]); and George W. Truett Theological Seminary (http://www.baylor.edu/ truett/ index.php?id=596 [accessed August 21, 2008]).

[13] Carl S. Moore, *Clay County, NC: Then and Now: A Written and Pictorial History* (Franklin NC: Genealogy Publishing Service 2007) 113. Two other churches once bore Truett's name. The name of Truett Baptist Church, founded in 1953 in Edgewater, Colorado, was changed in 1989 to Rose Acres Baptist Church. The name

of Truett Memorial Baptist Church, founded in 1945 in Long Beach, California, was changed in 2007 to The Neighborhood Church. The church's worship center is called "The George W. Truett Worship Center." See "Rose Acres Baptist Church," http://www.co.jefferson.co.us/placenames/search3.cfm?ps_oid=    113199&search= (accessed August 21, 2008), and Robert Francisco, e-mail message to Keith E. Durso, August 20, 2008, in possession of the author.

[14] The amount in parentheses represents the purchasing power in 2007. See Lawrence H. Officer and Samuel H. Williamson, "Purchasing Power of Money in the United States from 1774 to 2007," http://www.measuringworth.com.

[15] Bullock, "Truett Hospital Has Opening, Dedication," *DMN*, 127.

[16] Henderson, *Baylor University Medical Center*, 129.

[17] See "George W. Truett," http://www.findagrave.com/cgi-bin/fg.cgi?page=gr&GSsr=41&GSmpid=557&GRid=19945& (accessed August 14, 2008).

# Bibliography

Many citations in the bibliography contain "TC" and "MF" references. For example, in the TC 1929/MF 1909–1970:6–7 citation, "TC" refers to the Truett Collection; "1929" refers to the folder number; "MF" refers to the microfiche card of the TC; "1909–1970" refers to the group of files to which the folder belongs; and "6–7" refers to the specific microfiche cards that contain the document cited.

*Abbreviations*

AWRL: AWebb Roberts Library, Southwestern Baptist Theological Seminary, Fort Worth, Texas
DMN: *Dallas Morning News*
GWTML: George W. Truett Memorial Library, First Baptist Church, Dallas, Texas
MF: microfiche
SBHLA: Southern Baptist Historical Library and Archives, Nashville, Tennessee
TBHC: Texas Baptist Historical Commission, Dallas, Texas
TC: George W. Truett Collection, A. W. Roberts Library, Southwestern Baptist Theological Seminary, Fort Worth, Texas

*Primary Sources*

Books, Addresses, Pamphlets, and Internet Sources
Truett, George W. "An Adequate Gospel for a Lost World." In *Third Baptist World Congress: Stockholm, July 21–27, 1923*, edited by W. T. Whitley, 114–23. London: Kingsgate, 1923.
———. *After His Likeness*, edited by Powhatan W. James. Grand Rapids MI: William B. Eerdmans Publishing House, 1954.
———. *The Baptist Message and Mission for the World Today*. Nashville: Sunday School Board, [1939].
———. "Baptists and Religious Liberty." http://www.bjcpa.org/resources/pubs/pub_truett_address.htm.
———. *Be Still and Know that I Am God*. Atlanta: Radio Committee, Southern Baptist Convention, 1943. Baptist Hour Sermons. Box 5.6. SBHLA.
———. "Charles Haddon Spurgeon Centenary." http://members.aol.com/pilgrimpub/centnary.htm.

———. *Christian Education*. Birmingham AL: Education Board, Southern Baptist Convention, 1926. TC 1929/MF 1909–1970:6–7.

———. *Christmas Messages*. Chicago: Moody Bible Institute, 1945.

———. *Christ's Answer to World Need*. Atlanta: Radio Committee, Southern Baptist Convention, 1943. Baptist Hour Sermons. Box 1.3b. SBHLA.

———. "Closing Words." In *Fifth Baptist World Congress, Berlin, August 4–10, 1934*, edited by J. H. Rushbrooke, 215–17. London: Baptist World Alliance, 1934.

———. "The Coming of the Kingdom in America." In *The Baptist World Alliance, Second Congress, Philadelphia, June 19–25, 1911*, 421–29. Philadelphia: Harper & Brother Company, 1911. Available at http://www.archive.org/details/recordofproceed00unknuoft.

———. *The Conquest of Fear*. Atlanta: Radio Committee, Southern Baptist Convention, 1942. Baptist Hour Sermons. Box 1.1a. SBHLA.

———. *Follow Thou Me*. Nashville: Broadman Press, n.d.

———. Foreword to *Golden Years: An Autobiography*, by Mrs. W. L. Williams, 7–9. Dallas: Baptist Standard Publishing Company, 1921.

———. *George W. Truett Library*, edited by Powhatan W. James. 4 volumes. Nashville TN: Broadman Press, 1980.

———. *God's Call to America*, edited by J. B. Cranfill. Philadelphia: Judson Press, 1923.

———. *The Inspiration of Ideals*, edited by Powhatan W. James. Grand Rapids MI: William B. Eerdmans Publishing House, 1950.

———. Introduction to *The Doctrines of Our Faith*, by E. C. Dargan, 9–16. Nashville: Sunday School Board, Southern Baptist Convention, 1905.

———. Introduction to *Young People's Pilgrim's Progress*, by John Bunyan, edited by S. J. Reid, 7–8. New York: Fleming H. Revell Company, [c. 1914].

———. *The Larger Day for Texas Baptists*. N.p.: [1906]. TC 1581/MF 1576–1595:2.

———. "Loyal to the Name." In *No Other Name: Proceedings of the First Southwide B.Y.P.U. Conference, Memphis, Tennessee, December 31, 1929–January 2, 1930*, 79–85. Nashville: Sunday School Board, Southern Baptist Convention, 1930.

———. *On Eagle Wings*, edited by Powhatan W. James. Grand Rapids MI: William B. Eerdmans Publishing House, 1953.

———. *On Preachers and Preaching*. N.p.: [1934]. TC 1940/MF 1909–1970:9.

———. *Our Adequate and Abiding Gospel*. Atlanta: Radio Committee, Southern Baptist Convention, 1942. Baptist Hour Sermons. Box 1.1a. SBHLA.

———. "Paper Read by George W. Truett." In *Annual*, Baptist General Convention of Texas, 1917, 19.

———. *The Prophet's Mantle*, edited by Powhatan W. James. Grand Rapids MI: William B. Eerdmans Publishing House, 1948.

———. *A Quest for Souls*, [edited by J. B. Cranfill]. New York: George H. Doran Company, 1917. Available at http://www.archive.org/details/questforsouls009583mbp.

———. ["Remarks during the 'Young People's Session,' June 20, 1911, at the Baptist World Alliance Congress in Philadelphia"]. In *The Baptist World Alliance, Second Congress, Philadelphia, June 19–25, 1911*, 95–99. Philadelphia: Harper & Brother Company, 1911. Available at http://www.archive.org/details/recordofproceed00unknuoft.

———. ["Response to Greetings, July 21, 1923, at the Baptist World Alliance Congress in Stockholm"]. In *Third Baptist World Congress: Stockholm, July 21–27, 1923*, edited by W. T. Whitley, 6. London: Kingsgate, 1923.

———. *The Salt of the Earth*, edited by Powhatan W. James. Grand Rapids MI: William B. Eerdmans Publishing House, 1949.

———. *Sermons from Paul*, edited by Powhatan W. James. Grand Rapids MI: William B. Eerdmans Publishing House, 1947.

———. *Some Vital Questions*, edited by Powhatan W. James. Grand Rapids MI: William B. Eerdmans Publishing House, 1946.

———. *The Supper of Our Lord*. Dallas: B. J. Robert Book Company, n.d. TC 1873/MF 1809–1880:17.

———. "The Texas Baptist Memorial Sanitarium." N.p.: n.d. TC 1913/MF 1909–1970:1.

———. *These Gracious Years: Being the Year-end Messages and Addresses of Dr. George W. Truett*. Nashville: Sunday School Board of the Southern Baptist Convention, 1929.

———. *Tribute of the Church to Scouting*. Atlanta: Radio Committee, Southern Baptist Convention, 1943. Baptist Hour Sermons. Box 5.6. SBHLA.

———. *We Would See Jesus*, edited by J. B. Cranfill. New York: Fleming H. Revell Company, 1915. Available at http://www.archive.org/details/wewouldseejesusa00trueuoft.

———. *Who Is Jesus?* edited by Powhatan W. James. Grand Rapids MI: William B. Eerdmans Publishing House, 1952.

Truett, George W., et al. "Christian Union: A Deliverance by the Baptist General Convention of Texas." In *Christian Union Relative to Baptist Churches*, edited by J. M. Frost, 35–42. Nashville: Sunday School Board of the Southern Baptist Convention, 1915.

Truett, George W., J. H. Rushbrooke, and Clifton D. Gray. "A Postscript to the Congress." In *Fifth Baptist World Congress, Berlin, August 4–10, 1934*, edited by J. H. Rushbrooke, 251. London: Baptist World Alliance, 1934.

Articles
Truett, George W. "Christian Education." *Homiletic Review* 93 (February 1927): 148–51.

———. "My Deep Conviction." *Sunday School Builder* (November 1934): 5.

———. "New Year 1928." *Southwestern Evangel* (January 1928): 111.

———. "Preparing Worthily for New Orleans Convention." *Southwestern Evangel* (May 1930): 249–50.

———. "A Quarter of a Century of World History." *Review and Expositor* 22/1 (January 1925): 49–67.

———. "Some Frank Words with Texas Baptists." *Texas Baptist History* 1 (1981): 65–68.

———. "Vitalization of Home Mission Work." *Home Field* (January 1912): 8–9.

———. "Who Is Jesus?" *Quarterly Review* 16/3 (July–September 1956): 64–69.

———. "Why Christ Died." *Christ for the World Messenger* 12/8 (September 1954): 2–7. TC 1872/MF 1809–1880:16.

Audio Recordings
Truett, George W. *Abraham and Lot.* Waco TX: Word, n.d. SBHLA and AWRL.

———. *Art Not Thou One of His Disciples?* Waco TX: Word, n.d. SBHLA.

———. *As It Was with Moses, So It Will Be with Thee.* Waco TX: Word, n.d. SBHLA and AWRL.

———. *Be Still and Know That I Am God.* Waco TX: Word, n.d. SBHLA and AWRL.

———. *The Business of Christians.* Waco TX: Word, n.d. SBHLA and AWRL.

———. *Christ's Answer to World Need.* Parts 1 and 2. Waco TX: Word, n.d. SBHLA and AWRL.

———. *Christ's Death and Resurrection.* Waco TX: Word, n.d. SBHLA and AWRL.

———. *Christ's Method in the World.* Waco TX: Word, n.d. SBHLA.

———. *Christ's Standard of Greatness.* N.p.: Radio and Television Commission, Southern Baptist Convention, n.d. AWRL.

———. *Conquest of Fear.* Waco TX: Word, n.d. SBHLA and AWRL.

———. *The Day of Trouble.* Waco TX: Word, n.d. SBHLA and AWRL.

———. *Dedication of Life to Christ.* Dallas: First Baptist Church, 1937. AWRL.

———. *Doing God's Will.* Waco TX: Word, n.d. SBHLA and AWRL.

———. *Duty*. Waco TX: Word, n.d. SBHLA and AWRL.

———. *Easter Sermon*. Waco TX: Word, n.d. SBHLA.

———. *Elisha—In Tune with God*. Waco TX: Word, n.d. SBHLA and AWRL.

———. *Except You Go with God*. Waco TX: Word, n.d. SBHLA and AWRL.

———. *The Fear of Elijah*. Waco TX: Word, n.d. SBHLA and AWRL.

———. *God Provides Leaders*. Waco TX: Word, n.d. SBHLA and AWRL.

———. *God's Presence with His People Is the Supreme Matter*. Waco TX: Word, n.d.
SBHLA.

———. *God's Providence in Life*. Waco TX: Word, n.d. SBHLA and AWRL.

———. *Graduation no. 1*. N.p.: Radio and Television Commission, Southern Baptist
Convention, n.d. AWRL.

———. *Graduation no. 2*. N.p.: Radio and Television Commission, Southern Baptist
Convention, n.d. AWRL.

———. *Hazard Your Life for Christ*. Waco TX: Word, n.d. SBHLA and AWRL.

———. *How Shall We Escape If We Neglect Salvation?* Waco TX: Word, n.d. SBHLA
and AWRL.

———. *If Christ Had Not Come*. Waco TX: Word, n.d. SBHLA and AWRL.

———. *In Tune with God*. N.p.: Radio and Television Commission, Southern
Baptist Convention, n.d. AWRL.

———. *Is Prayer Profitable?* Waco TX: Word, n.d. SBHLA and AWRL.

———. *It Pays to Do Right*. Waco TX: Word, n.d. SBHLA and AWRL.

———. *Joshua's Resolution*. Waco TX: Word, n.d. SBHLA and AWRL.

———. *The Kind of Men Needed Today*. Waco TX: Word, n.d. SBHLA and AWRL.

———. *Lessons from Esther*. Waco TX: Word, n.d. SBHLA and AWRL.

———. *Life's Middle Time*. Waco TX: Word, n.d. SBHLA.

———. *Life's Most Important Prayer*. Waco TX: Word, n.d. SBHLA.

———. *Marvelous Possibilities of Property*. N.p.: Radio and Television Commission,
Southern Baptist Convention, n.d. AWRL.

———. *The Most Important Book in the World*. Waco TX: Word, n.d. SBHLA and
AWRL.

———. *Mother's Day*. Waco TX: Word, n.d. SBHLA and AWRL.

———. *Need for Encouragement*. Waco TX: Word, n.d. SBHLA and AWRL.

———. *Our Burden Threefold*. Waco TX: Word, n.d. SBHLA and AWRL.

———. *The Power of Choice*. Waco TX: Word, n.d. SBHLA.

———. *President's Address: 6th Baptist World Congress*. N.p.: Baptist World Alliance,
1939. AWRL.

———. *The Principle of Stewardship*. Waco TX: Word, n.d. SBHLA and AWRL.

———. *The Regulating Principle of Life*. Dallas: First Baptist Church, 1938. AWRL.

———. *The Right Attitude toward Church.* Dallas: First Baptist Church, 1938. AWRL.

———. *The Spiritual Recovery of the Home.* Waco TX: Word, n.d. SBHLA and AWRL.

———. *Standing on the Other Side.* Waco TX: Word, n.d. SBHLA and AWRL.

———. *Stewardship.* Waco TX: Word, n.d. SBHLA and AWRL.

———. *Tell the World about Jesus.* Waco TX: Word, n.d. SBHLA and AWRL.

———. *The Temptation of Abraham.* Waco TX: Word, n.d. SBHLA and AWRL.

———. *This One Thing I Do.* Waco TX: Word, n.d. SBHLA and AWRL.

———. *The Transforming Influence of Public Worship.* Waco TX: Word, n.d. SBHLA and AWRL.

———. *True Meaning and Mission of Life.* Waco TX: Word, n.d. SBHLA and AWRL.

———. *Two Supreme Reasons for Following Christ.* Dallas: First Baptist Church, 1939. AWRL.

———. *The Virtues of Patience.* Waco TX: Word, n.d. SBHLA and AWRL.

———. *The Unjust Steward.* Waco TX: Word, n.d. SBHLA and AWRL.

———. *Victories and Defeats.* Waco TX: Word, n.d. SBHLA.

———. *A Well-Ordered Life.* Waco TX: Word, n.d. SBHLA and AWRL.

———. *What Think Ye of Christ?* Waco TX: Word, n.d. SBHLA and AWRL.

———. *Who Do You Say That I Am?* Waco TX: Word, n.d. SBHLA and AWRL.

———. *A Worthy Offering for Christ.* Waco TX: Word, n.d. SBHLA and AWRL.

———. *Would You Have Your Life Count?* Waco TX: Word, n.d. SBHLA and AWRL.

———. *Ye Are Not Your Own.* Waco TX: Word, n.d. SBHLA and AWRL.

———. *You Know Not What Ye Ask.* Waco TX: Word, n.d. SBHLA and AWRL.

Collections and Files

Notebook: Dr. George W. Truett. Druid Hills Baptist Church, Atlanta, Georgia.

Notebook: Pastors: Christmas Letters and Correspondence. GWTML.

Notebook: Pastors: Truett: Pictures, Family, Ministry. GWTML.

Notebook: Pastors: Truett: 25th Anniversary. GWTML.

Truett, George W., Baptist History File. SBHLA.

Truett, George W., Biographical File. TBHC.

Truett, George W., Collection. AWRL. (MF is located at SBHLA; TBHC; Baylor University, Waco, Texas; and Southern Baptist Theological Seminary, Louisville, Kentucky.)

Truett, George W., Papers. SBHLA.

Unpublished Works

Truett, George W. "Address by Rev. George W. Truett, D. D., at Banquet in Behalf of Baptist Sanitarium and Hospital, Houston, Texas, January 28, 1915." TC 1919/MF 1909–1970:3.

———. Autograph book with inscriptions from George W. Truett's students at Hiawassee, Georgia, May 1889. GWTML.

———. "Christian Education." Address, Brownwood, Texas, January 20, 1916. TC 1920/MF 1909–1970:3.

———. Diary 1886. TC 662/MF 662–663:1.

———. Diary 1918–1919. TC 665/MF 664–690:1–3.

———. Diary 1937. TC 666/MF 664–690:3–10.

———. Diary 1939. TC 667/MF 664–690:9–15.

———. Diary 1941. TC 668/MF 664–690:15–21.

———. Diary 1942. TC 669/MF 664–690:21–27.

———. Diary 1943. TC 670/MF 664–690:28–31.

———. "The Inspiration of Ideals." Commencement address, Baylor University, Waco, Texas, June 1897. TC 2/MF 2–20:1.

———. "List of Names for the Texas Bapt. M. Sanitarium, 1904." TC 1574/MF 1563–1575:12–13.

———. "The Making of the Right Kind of Life." Baccalaureate sermon, Rice Institute, Houston Texas, June 10, 1917. George W. Truett Biographical File. TBHC.

———. "The Mantle of Elijah." September 27, 1914. TC 1822/MF 1809–1880:4.

———. "Notes for Sanitarium Campaign." 1904. TC 1574/MF 1563–1575:3.

———. "The Preacher as a Man." Address, Southwestern Baptist Theological Seminary, Fort Worth, Texas, February 18, 1914. TC 1916/MF 1909–1970:2.

———. "The Preacher as a Soul Winner." Address, Southwestern Baptist Theological Seminary, Fort Worth, Texas, November 3, 1914. TC 1915/MF 1909–1970:2.

———. "The Preacher as a Student." Address, Southwestern Baptist Theological Seminary, Fort Worth, Texas, February 20, 1914. TC 1917/MF 1909–1970:2.

———. "The Preacher in the Pulpit." Address, Southwestern Baptist Theological Seminary, Fort Worth, Texas, February 25, 1914. TC 1917/MF 1909–1970:2–3.

———. "Preachers and Preaching." Address, Southern Baptist Theological Seminary, Louisville, Kentucky, March 9, 1937. TC 1954/MF 1909–1970:10.

———. "Preaching." Lecture notes, 1899. TC 1912/MF 1909–1970:1.

———. "Response at SBC at Norfolk, 1898." TC 1911/MF 1909–1970:1.

———. ["Response of Truett to the Baptist General Convention of Texas, Waco, Texas, 1898"]. TC 3/MF 2–21:1.

———. Truett's 1918 passport. TC 686/MF 664–690:42.

———. Untitled address to Grand Lodge of Texas, Waco, Texas, December 4, 1940. TC 1964/MF 1909–1970:12.

———. Untitled sermon on Daniel 3:16–18, August 12, 1906. TC 1842/MF 1809–1880:8–9.

———. Untitled sermon on 1 Peter 3:18, April 6, 1919. TC 1880/MF 1809–1880:18–19.

———. Untitled sermon on Matthew 27:43, March 14, 1909. TC 1852/MF 1809–1880:12.

———. Untitled sermon on Romans 9:33, September 10, 1922. Notebook: Pastors: Truett: 25th Anniversary. GWTML.

*Secondary Sources*

Books, Addresses, Pamphlets, and Internet Sources

"About TMC." http://www.truett.edu/templates/custruett/details.asp?id=26811&PID=140506.

Ahlstrom, Sidney E. *A Religious History of the American People.* Volume 2. New York: Image Books, 1975.

Allen, Joseph L. *Love & Conflict: A Covenantal Model of Christian Ethics.* Nashville: Abingdon Press, 1984.

Askew, Thomas A., and Richard V. Pierard. *The American Church Experience: A Concise History.* Grand Rapids MI: Baker Academic, 2004.

Baker, Robert A. *The Blossoming Desert: A Concise History of Texas Baptists.* Waco: Word Books, Publisher, 1970.

———. *The Southern Baptist Convention and Its People, 1607–1972.* Nashville: Broadman Press, 1974.

———. *Tell the Generations Following: A History of Southwestern Baptist Theological Seminary, 1903–1983.* Nashville: Broadman Press, 1983.

*The Baptist World Alliance, Second Congress, Philadelphia, June 19–25, 1911.* Philadelphia: Harper & Brother Company, 1911. Available at http://www.archive.org/details/recordofproceed00unknuoft.

Barnes, William Wright. *The Southern Baptist Convention, 1845–1953.* Nashville: Broadman Press, 1954.

Bebbington, D. W. "C. H. Spurgeon." In *Eerdmans' Handbook to the History of Christianity*, edited by Tim Dowley, 529. Grand Rapids MI: Wm. B. Eerdmans Publishing Co., 1977.

Bernhardi, Friedrich von. *Germany and the Next War*, translated by Allen H. Powles. New York: Charles A. Eron, 1914. Available at http://books.google.com/books?id=eFhjHZ7DaocC&printsec=frontcover&dq=Allen+H.+Powles#PPA1920,M1.

Blackwood, Andrew Watterson. *Preaching in Time of Reconstruction*. Great Neck NY: Pulpit Press, 1945.

Broadus, John. *A Treatise on the Preparation and Delivery of Sermons*. 2nd edition. New York: Harper & Brothers, 1926.

Burton, Joe W. *Prince of the Pulpit: A Pen Picture of George W. Truett at Work*. Grand Rapids MI: Zondervan Publishing House, 1946.

Carroll, Charles. *The Negro a Beast*. St. Louis: American Book and Bible House, 1900. Available at http://www.archive.org/details/thenegrobeastori00carrrich.

Carroll, J. M. *A History of Texas Baptists*, edited by J. B. Cranfill. Dallas: Baptist Standard Publishing Co., 1923.

Carson, Glenn Thomas. *Calling Out the Called: The Life and Work of Lee Rutland Scarborough*. Austin TX: Eakin Press, 1996.

"Cherokee County, NC–Census–1860 Federal Census–Part 4," p.144 (239A)–p.145 (239B). http://ftp.rootsweb.com/pub/usgenweb/nc/cherokee/census/1860/1860cher4.txt.

"Cherokee County, NC–Census–1860 Federal Census–Part 5." http://ftp.rootsweb.com/pub/usgenweb/nc/cherokee/census/1860/1860cher5.txt.

"Civil War Soldiers and Sailors System." http://www.itd.nps.gov/cwss/soldiers.cfm.

Conlin, Joseph R. *The American Past: A Brief History*. San Diego: Harcourt Brace Jovanovich, Publishers, 1991.

Cranfill, J. B. *Dr. J. B. Cranfill's Chronicle*. New York: Fleming H. Revell, 1916. Available at http://books.google.com/books?id=6JwDAAAAYAAJ&pg=PP20&dq=j.+b.+cranfill#PPP19,M1.

———. "Life Sketch of George W. Truett." In *We Would See Jesus*, by George W. Truett, edited by J. B. Cranfill, 9–15. New York: Fleming H. Revell Company, 1915. Available at http://www.archive.org/details/wewouldseejesusa00trueuoft.

Criswell, W. A. *Fifty Years of Preaching at the Palace: Outstanding Sermons Preached by George W. Truett and W. A. Criswell.* Grand Rapids MI: Zondervan Publishing House, 1969.

Dawson, Jerry E., and John W. Storey, editors. *Teaching Them…: A Sesquicentennial Celebration of Texas Baptist Education.* [Dallas]: Baptist General Convention of Texas, 1996.

Dawson, Joseph Martin. *A Century with Texas Baptists.* Nashville: Broadman Press, 1947.

———. *A Thousand Months to Remember: An Autobiography.* Waco TX: Baylor University Press, 1964.

Durso, Pamela R., and Keith E. Durso. *The Story of Baptists in the United States.* Brentwood TN: Baptist History and Heritage Society, 2006.

Early, Joe E. *A Texas Baptist Power Struggle: The Hayden Controversy.* Denton TX: University of North Texas Press, 2005.

[Elliott, L. R.], editor. *Centennial Story of Texas Baptists.* Dallas: Executive Board of the Baptist General Convention of Texas, 1936.

Entzminger, Louis. *The J. Frank Norris I Have Known for 34 Years.* N.p.: n.d.

Fant, Jr., Clyde E., and William M. Pinson, Jr. "George Washington Truett." In *20 Centuries of Great Preaching: An Encyclopedia of Preaching,* edited by Clyde E. Fant, Jr., and William M. Pinson, Jr., 8:129–43. Waco TX: Word Books, Publisher, 1971.

Fletcher, Jesse C. *The Southern Baptist Convention: A Sesquicentennial History.* Nashville: Broadman & Holman Publishers, 1994.

Fosdick, Harry Emerson. *The Challenge of the Present Crisis.* New York: Association Press, 1917. Available at http://books.google.com/books?id=bMiGASqgYxUC&printsec=frontcover&dq=challenge+of+the+present.

———. *The Living of These Days: An Autobiography.* New York: Harper & Brothers, Publishers, 1956.

*Fourth Baptist World Congress, Toronto, Canada, 23–29 June 1928,* edited by W. T. Whitley. Toronto Canada: Stewart Printing Service, [1928].

Freel, Margaret Walker. *Our Heritage: The People of Cherokee County, North Carolina, 1540–1955.* Asheville NC: Miller Printing Company, 1956; reprint, Andrews NC: Andrews Journal, 1973.

Gaustad, Edwin Scott. *The Baptist Tradition of Religious Liberty in America.* Waco TX: J. M. Dawson Institute of Church-State Studies, n.d.

Gilbert, Martin. *The First World War: A Complete History.* New York: Henry Holt and Company, 1994.

————. *History of the Twentieth Century.* New York: William Morrow, 2001.

Handy, Robert T. *A Christian America: Protestant Hopes and Historical Realities.* 2nd edition. New York: Oxford University Press, 1984.

Hankins, Barry. *God's Rascal: J. Frank Norris & the Beginnings of Southern Fundamentalism.* Lexington: The University Press of Kentucky, 1996.

Harper, Keith. *The Quality of Mercy: Southern Baptists and Social Christianity, 1890–1920.* Tuscaloosa: The University of Alabama Press, 1996.

Harvey, Paul. *Redeeming the South: Religious Cultures and Racial Identities among Southern Baptists, 1865–1925.* Chapel Hill: University of North Carolina Press, 1997.

"Hayesville Baptist-Presbyterian Cemetery-Clay Co., NC-Cemeteries." http://ftp.rootsweb.com/pub/usgenweb/nc/clay/cemeteries/baptpres.txt?cj=1&o_xid=0002530104&o_lid=0002530104&o_xt=1155785.

Henderson, Lana. *Baylor University Medical Center: Yesterday, Today and Tomorrow.* Waco TX: Baylor University Press, 1978.

"Hidden History of Dallas." http://www.dallasnews.com/s/dws/spe/2002/hiddenhistory/timeline.htm#1940s.

Hoover, Herbert. *America's First Crusade.* New York: Charles Scribner's Sons, 1942.

Huggins, Maloy A. *A History of North Carolina Baptists, 1727–1932.* Raleigh: The General Board, Baptist State Convention of North Carolina, 1967.

James, Powhatan W. *Fifty Years of Baylor University Hospital.* Dallas: Baylor University Hospital, 1953.

————. "George W. Truett." In *Ten Men from Baylor,* edited by J. M. Price, 161–76. Kansas City: Central Seminary Press, 1945.

————. *George W. Truett: A Biography.* Nashville: Broadman Press, 1939.

————. *George W. Truett: A Biography.* Revised edition. New York: Macmillan Company, 1945.

Larsen, David L. *The Company of the Preachers: A History of Biblical Preaching from the Old Testament to the Modern Era.* Volume 2. Grand Rapids MI: Kregel Publications, 1998.

Lefever, Alan J. *Fighting the Good Fight: The Life and Work of Benajah Harvey Carroll.* Austin TX: Eakin Press, 1994.

Leonard, Bill J. *Baptist Ways: A History.* Valley Forge PA: Judson Press, 2003.

Lippy, Charles H., editor. *Twentieth-Century Shapers of American Popular Religion.* New York: Greenwood Press, 1989.

*Manual of East Waco Baptist Church.* Waco: Knight Printing Co., 1896. TC 651/MF 628-657:4.

Marsden, George M. *Fundamentalism and American Culture: The Shaping of Twentieth-Century Evangelicalism: 1870–1925*. Oxford: Oxford University Press, 1980.

Marshall, S. L. A. *The American Heritage History of World War I*. New York: American Heritage Publishing Co., 1964.

McBeth, H. Leon. *The Baptist Heritage: Four Centuries of Baptist Witness*. Nashville: Broadman Press, 1987.

———. *The First Baptist Church of Dallas: Centennial History (1868–1968)*. Grand Rapids MI: Zondervan Publishing House, 1968.

———. *Texas Baptists: A Sesquicentennial History*. Dallas: Baptistway Press, 1998.

———. *Women in Baptist Life*. Nashville: Broadman Press, 1979.

McClellan, Albert. *The Executive Committee of the Southern Baptist Convention, 1917–1984*. Nashville: Broadman Press, 1985.

McGlothlen, Gaye L. *A History of Immanuel Baptist Church, 1887–1986*. Nashville: Immanuel Baptist Church, 1987.

*Men of All Creeds May Come*. N.p: 1950. Notebook: Pastors: Truett: Pictures, Family, Ministry. GWTML.

Miller, Glenn T. "Baptists World Outreach and U.S. Foreign Affairs." In *Baptists and the American Experience*, edited by James E. Wood, Jr., 153–84. Valley Forge PA: Judson Press, 1976.

Moore, Carl S. *Clay County, NC: Then and Now: A Written and Pictorial History*. Franklin NC: Genealogy Publishing Service, 2007.

Murrah, David J. *C. C. Slaughter: Rancher, Banker, Baptist*. Austin: University of Texas Press, 1981.

Newton, Joseph Fort. *Some Living Masters of the Pulpit*. New York: George H. Doran Company, 1923.

Newton, Louie Devotie. *Why I Am a Baptist*. New York: Thomas Nelson & Sons, 1957.

Niebuhr, H. Richard. *The Kingdom of God in America*. New York: Harper & Row, Publishers, 1937; reprint New York: Harper Torchbook, 1959.

Norris, J. Frank. *Inside History of First Baptist Church Fort Worth and Temple Baptist Church Detroit: Life Story of Dr. J. Frank Norris*. [Fort Worth: n.p., n.d.].

———. *The Triple Major Operation in Detroit*. [Detroit: n.p.], 1935.

Officer, Lawrence H., and Samuel H. Williamson. "Purchasing Power of Money in the United States from 1774 to 2007." http://www.measuringworth.com.

"Our Heritage."
http://www.truettmemorialfbc.com/clientimages/33109/triuettpamphlet1.pdf.

Padgett, Guy. *A History of Clay County, North Carolina*. [Hayesville NC: Clay County Bicentennial Committee, 1976].

Payne, Darwin. *Big D: Triumphs and Troubles of an American Supercity in the 20th Century*. Dallas: Three Forks Press, 1994.

Payne, Ernest A. *Baptists Speak to the World: A Description and Interpretation of the Sixth Baptist World Congress, Atlanta, 1939*. London: Carey Press, [1939].

———. *James Henry Rushbrooke, 1870–1947: A Baptist Greatheart*. London: Carey Kingsgate Press Limited, 1954.

Pierard, Richard V., editor. *Baptists Together in Christ, 1905–2005: A Hundred-Year History of the Baptist World Alliance*. Falls Church VA: Baptist World Alliance, 2005.

Piper, John F., Jr. *The American Churches in World War I*. Athens: Ohio University Press, 1985.

Powell, Paul W. "A Tribute to George W. Truett: Texas Baptists' Gift to the World." In *Looking at Life through the Rear View Mirror*, by Paul W. Powell, 113–24. Tyler TX: published by the author, 2006.

Pugh, Quinn. "George W. Truett: Prophet of Freedom, Herald of Faith, 1867–1944." http://www.bwa-baptist-heritage.org/r_truett.htm.

Ramond, John S., editor. *Among Southern Baptists*. Volume 1. Kansas City MO: Western Baptist Publishing Company, 1936.

Rauschenbusch, Walter. *Christianity and the Social Crisis*. New York: MacMillan Co., 1907; reprint, New York: Association Press, 1912.

Reimers, David M. *White Protestantism and the Negro*. New York: Oxford University Press, 1965.

Richardson, Rupert Norval. *Texas: The Lone Star State*. Englewood Cliffs NJ: Prentice-Hall, Inc., 1958.

Riley, B. F. *History of the Baptists of Texas*. Dallas: published for the author, 1907.

Rosser, Charles M. *Doctors and Doctors, Wise and Otherwise: On the Firing Line Fifty Years*. Dallas: Mathis, Van Nort & Company, 1941.

Routh, Porter. *Meet the Presidents*. Nashville: Broadman Press, 1953.

Rushbrooke, J. H., editor. *Sixth Baptist World Congress, Atlanta, Georgia, U.S.A., July 22–28, 1939*. Atlanta: Baptist World Alliance, 1939.

Sampey, John R. *Memoirs of John R. Sampey*. Nashville: Broadman Press, 1947.

Scarborough, L. R. "The Fruits of Norrisism." In *Calling Out the Called: The Life and Work of Lee Rutland Scarborough*, by Glenn Thomas Carson, 120–32. Austin TX: Eakin Press, 1996.

"Schoaff Family Genealogy." http://www.schoaff.org.

Spain, Rufus B. *At Ease in Zion: A Social History of Southern Baptists 1865–1900*. Nashville: Vanderbilt University Press, 1967; reprint Tuscaloosa: University of Alabama Press, 2003.

Storey, John W. *Texas Baptist Leadership and Social Christianity, 1900–1980.* College Station: Texas A&M University Press, 1986.

Stroope, Mike W. "George W. Truett: The World His Parish." In *The Truett Pulpit: Sermons Preached During Worship in the Paul Powell Chapel at George W. Truett Theological Seminary, 2006–2007,* edited by Elizabeth Grasham-Reeves, 83–92. [Waco TX: The Kyle Lake Center for Effective Preaching at Truett Seminary], 2007.

Sweet, William Warren. *The Story of Religion in America.* New York: Harper & Row, Publishers, 1930; reprint Grand Rapids MI: Baker Book House, 1983.

"Syllabus of Errors." http://www.traditionalcatholic.net/Tradition/Pope/Pius_IX/The_Syllabus_of_Errors,_1864.html.

Thompson, James J., Jr. *Tried As by Fire: Southern Baptists and the Religious Controversies of the 1920s.* Macon GA: Mercer University Press, 1982.

Torbet, Robert G. *A History of the Baptists.* 3rd ed. Valley Forge PA: Judson Press, 1963.

"The Truett Family." http://worldconnect.rootsweb.com/cgi-bin/igm.cgi?op=GET&db=bgroves2&id=I7477.

Vedder, Henry. *Baptist "Bigotry and Intolerance": A Reply to Cardinal Gibbons.* Chester PA: published by the author, 1909.

Weaver, C. Douglas. *Second to None: A History of Second-Ponce de Leon Baptist Church.* Brentwood TN: Baptist History and Heritage Society; Nashville: Fields Publishing, 2004.

Wilson, Woodrow. "Peace without Victory." In *The Annals of America, 1916–1928: World War and Prosperity.* Volume 14. Chicago: Encyclopedia Britannica, Inc., 1976.

————. *The President's War Message: The Historic Address Delivered to the Congress of the United States by Woodrow Wilson, April 2nd, 1917.* San Francisco: Paul Elder and Company, 1917.

Wood, Presnall H., and Floyd W. Thatcher. *Prophets with Pens.* Dallas: Baptist Standard Publishing, Co., 1969.


Articles

Agnew, Peter W. "Making Dallas Moral: Two Baptist Pastors." *Heritage News* (Summer 1987): 19–25.

Alexander, Charles T. "Dr. George W. Truett." *Southern Baptist Home Missions* 13/3 (March 1942): 10.

Alldredge, Eugene P. "Amazing Achievements of Dr. George W. Truett's Ministry, 1897–1941." *Quarterly Review* 1/4 (October–December 1941): 59–64.

"Bad Angel." *Time*, October 8, 1928. Available at http://www.time.com/time/magazine/article/0,9171,928165,00.html?iid=chix-sphere.

Bailey, Kenneth K. "Southern White Protestantism at the Turn of the Century." *American Historical Review* 68/3 (April 1963): 618–35.

"Baptists in St. Louis." *Time*, June 1, 1936. Available at http://www.time.com/time/magazine/article/0,9171,756173,00.html.

Broadus, John A. "American Baptist Ministry of 100 Years Ago." *Baptist Quarterly* 9/1 (January 1875): 1-20.

Burton, Joe W. "Aflame for Souls." *Southern Baptist Home Missions* 13/3 (March 1942): 10–11, 16.

————. "The Preacher and His Appointments." *Southern Baptist Home Missions* 13/1 (January 1942): 12–13. TC 442/MF 21–542:29.

————. "The Preacher and Missions." *Southern Baptist Home Missions* 13/4 (April 1942): 12–13. TC 446/MF 21–542:30.

————. "The Preacher and the Troubled." *Southern Baptist Home Missions* 13/2 (February 1942): 10–11. TC 444/MF 21–542:29.

————. "The Preacher in His Study." *Southern Baptist Home Missions* 12/12 (December 1941): 12–13. TC 440/MF 21–542:29.

————. "Preaching the Word." *Southern Baptist Home Missions* 12/11 (November 1941): 14–16. TC 438/MF 21–542:29.

Chatfield, Charles. "World War I and the Liberal Pacifist in the United States." *American Historical Review* 75/7 (December 1970): 1920–37.

Craig, Coleman. "The Funeral Service of Dr. George W. Truett." *Baptist Review* (May-June 1973): 14.

Cranfill, J. B. "George W. Truett, Minister." *Holland's* (November 1937): 9. TC 393/MF 21–542:26.

Crowell, Grace Noll. "To George W. Truett." *Southern Baptist Home Missions* 12/11 (November 1941): 1.

Daniel, Wallace L. "Leadership and Recent Controversies over Religious Liberty." *Journal of Church and State* 49/4 (Autumn 2007): 649–62.

Dawson, Joseph Martin. "Pastor of the South's Largest Church." *Church Management* (October 1932): 15–16, 18. TC 257/MF 21–542:17.

"Federal Council's Biennial." *Time*, December 12, 1936. Available at http://www.time.com/time/magazine/article/0,9171,757215,00.html.

Fine, Robert L. "The History of Institutional Ethics at Baylor University Medical Center." *Proceedings* (Baylor University Medical Center) 17/1 (January 2004): 73–82. http://www.pubmedcentral.nih.gov/articlerender.fcgi?artid=1200643.

"George W. Truett." http://www.findagrave.com/cgi-bin/fg.cgi?page=gr&GSsr=41&GSmpid=557&GRid=19945&.

Gray, George W. "Out of the Mountains Came This Great Preacher of the Plains." *American Magazine* (November 1925): 16, 134, 136, 138, 140, 143–44, 147. TC 106/MF 21–542:8.

Hayes, Carlton. "The War of the Nations." *Political Science Quarterly* 29/4 (December 1914): 687–707.

Holcomb, J. David. "'A Millstone Hanged about His Neck': George W. Truett, Anti-Catholicism, and Baptist Conceptions of Religious Liberty." *Baptist History and Heritage* 43/2 (Summer/Fall 2008): 68–81.

James, Powhatan W. "George W. Truett." *Quarterly Review* 16/3 (July–September 1956): 61–64.

Jones, Ronald Coy. "History of the Department of Surgery at Baylor University Medical Center." *Proceedings* (Baylor University Medical Center) 17/2 (April 2004): 130–67. http://www.pubmedcentral.nih.gov/articlerender.fcgi?artid=1200650.

Leavell, Frank H. "Dr. George Washington Truett, D.D., LL.D." *Baptist Student* (September-October 1928): 3–4, 14–15.

Macfarlane, Peter Clark. "The Apostle to the Texans." *Collier's* (January 16, 1913): 2–3. TC 24/MF 21–542:3

McBeth, H. Leon. "George W. Truett: Baptist Statesman." *Baptist History and Heritage* 32/2 (April 1997): 9–22.

———. "John Frank Norris: Texas Tornado." *Baptist History and Heritage* 32/2 (April 1997): 23–38.

———. "Two Ways to Be a Baptist." *Baptist History and Heritage* 32/2 (April 1997): 39–53.

———. "Two Ways to Be a Baptist: An Introduction." *Baptist History and Heritage* 32/2 (April 1997): 7–8.

"Messengers in Atlanta." *Time*, July 31, 1939. Available at http://www.time.com/time/magazine/article/0,9171,761791,00.html.

"Mission Snagged." *Time*, October 19, 1936. Available at http://www.time.com/time/magazine/article/0,9171,756785,00.html.

"Mission's End." *Time*, December 14, 1936. Available at http://www.time.com/time/magazine/article/0,9171,757146,00.html.

"Moratorium." *Time*, August 17, 1936. Available at
    http://www.time.com/time/magazine/article/0,9171,756481,00.html.

Morris, C. Gwin. "J. Frank Norris and the Baptist General Convention of Texas."
    *Texas Baptist History* 1 (1981): 1–34.

———. "J. Frank Norris: Rascal or Reformer?" *Baptist History and Heritage* 3/3
    (Autumn 1998): 21–40.

———. "The Pulpit and Politics: J. Frank Norris As a Case Study." *Texas Baptist
    History* 7 (1987): 1–19.

Norman, Don. "Building for the New Year." *Baptist Student* (February 1937): 2–3.

Piper, John F., Jr. "The American Churches in World War I." *Journal of the American
    Academy of Religion* 38/2 (June 1970): 147–55.

Pitts, William L. "Truett, George Washington." *Texas Baptist History* 1 (1981): 62–
    63.

"Preaching Team." *Time*, September 28, 1936. Available at
    http://www.time.com/time/magazine/article/0,9171,756733,00.html.

Raley, J. Michael. "'On the Same Basis As the Men': The Campaign to Reinstate
    Women As Messengers to the Southern Baptist Convention, 1885–1918." Parts
    1–3. *Journal of Southern Religion* 7 (2004). http://jsr.fsu.edu/Volume7/Raley-
    1.htm.

Rosser, J. L. "George Truett, Preacher." *Review and Expositor* 35/1 (January 1938): 3–
    23.

Shurden, Walter B. "Reaction to Paper of Henry Warnock." *Baptist History and
    Heritage* 7/3 (July 1972): 184–85.

"Southern Baptists." *Time*, May 28, 1934. Available at
    http.//www.time.com/time/magazine/article/0,9171,754156,00.html.

Tidwell, D. D. "Dr. George W. Truett." *Texas Grand Lodge Magazine* (March 1960):
    113–14. George W. Truett Baptist History File. SBHLA.

Vaught, W. O., Jr. "Memorable Events from the Life of George Truett." *Proclaim*
    (April–June 1978): 11–12.

Warnock, Henry Y. "Prophets of Change: Some Southern Baptist Leaders and the
    Problem of Race, 1900–1921." *Baptist History and Heritage* 7/3 (July 1972): 172–
    83.

"Women Brethren." *Time*, May 20, 1929. Available at
    http://www.time.com/time/magazine/article/0,9171,723668,00.html.

Wood, George T. "Studies of the American Pulpit: George W. Truett." *Homiletic
    Review* 93/2 (February 1927): 89, 90–94. TC 114//MF 21–542:9.

Young, Doyle L. "Leadership That Motivates: A Study in the Life of George W.
    Truett." *Baptist History and Heritage* 20/1 (January 1985): 45–51.

Encyclopedias and Dictionaries

*American National Biography Online.* Oxford University Press, 2005.
    http://www.anb.org.ezproxy.baylor.edu/articles/home.html.
*Dictionary of Baptists in America,* edited by Bill J. Leonard. Downers Grove IL:
    InterVarsity Press, 1994.
*Dictionary of Christianity in America,* edited by Daniel G. Reid, Robert D. Linder,
    Bruce L. Shelley, and Harry S. Stout. Downers Grove IL: InterVarsity Press, 1990.
*Dictionary of North Carolina Biography.* Volume 6, T-Z, edited by William Stevens
    Powell. Chapel Hill: University of North Carolina Press, 1996.
*Encyclopedia of Southern Baptists,* edited by Norman Wade Cox and Judson Boyce
    Allen. Volumes 1 and 2. Nashville: Broadman Press, 1958.
*Encyclopedia of Southern Baptists,* edited by Davis Collier Woolley. Volume 3,
    supplement. Nashville: Broadman Press, 1971.
*Encyclopedia of Southern Baptists,* edited by Lynn Edward May, Jr., Charles Stephen
    Bond, Jr., and Charles William Deweese. Volume 4, Supplement. Nashville:
    Broadman Press, 1982.
*Encyclopedia of World War I.* http://www.firstworldwar.com/atoz/index.htm.
*The European Powers in the First World War: An Encyclopedia,* edited by Spencer C.
    Tucker. New York: Garland Publishing Inc., 1996.
*Handbook of Texas Online.* http://www.tshaonline.org.
*The United States in the First World War: An Encyclopedia,* edited by Anne Cipriano
    Venzon. New York: Garland Publishing, Inc., 1995.
*The Oxford Companion to United States History,* edited by Paul Boyer. Oxford: Oxford
    University Press, 2001.

Newspapers
*Alabama Baptist,* 1927, 1935, 1944
*Asheville-Citizen,* 1931
*Atlanta Constitution,* 1939–1940, 1942
*Baptist, The,* 1928
*Baptist and Reflector,* 1927
*Baptist Messenger,* 1935, 1937, 1944
*Baptist New Mexican,* 1944
*Baptist Standard,* 1892–1893, 1898–1944, 1956, 1959, 1999
*Biblical Recorder,* 1927
*Birmingham Post,* 1933
*Central Baptist,* 1907

*Christian Index*, 1889, 1896, 1918, 1923, 1934, 1936, 1937, 1939
*Dallas Morning News*, 1891, 1896–1944, 1946, 1950, 2007
*Dallas Times Herald*, 1926
*Florida Baptist Witness*, 1944
*Fundamentalist*, 1928, 1932, 1944
*Golden Age*, 1909
*Illinois Baptist*, 1944
*Kansas City Star*, 1929
*New York Times*, 1912, 1918
*Religious Herald*, 1918, 1929
*Searchlight*, 1919–1920, 1926
*Southwestern News*, 1944
*Tennessean*, 1920
*Union Sentinel* (*Blairsville, GA*), 2006
*Watchman-Examiner*, 1914, 1919, 1930
*Western Recorder*, 1927–1928, 1930, 1937


Audio Recordings
*Funeral of Dr. George W. Truett.* N.p.: Radio and Television Commission, Southern
    Baptist Convention, 1944. AWRL.


Annuals
*Annual.* Baptist General Convention of Texas, 1893, 1896, 1903, 1906–1907
*Annual.* Southern Baptist Convention, 1898, 1901, 1902, 1903, 1905, 1906, 1907,
    1909, 1917, 1918, 1919, 1945


Minutes
Clerk's Book. First Baptist Church, Dallas, Texas, 1926–1930, 1931–1935, 1936–
    1940. GWTML.
Deacons Minutes. First Baptist Church, Dallas, Texas, 1897–1944. GWTML.
Minutes. First Baptist Church, Dallas, Texas, 1897–1944. GWTML.
Minutes. Hayesville (NC) Baptist Church, 1887–1888. George W. Truett Baptist
    History File. SBHLA.
"Minutes, Reports, Correspondence, Etc.–1928." Executive Committee Records. Box
    72A, folder 9. SBHLA.


Collections and Files
Alldredge, Eugene Perry. Papers. SBHLA.

Allen, Clifton Judson. Papers. SBHLA.

Baptist Hour Sermons. SBHLA.

Carroll, B. H., Collection. AWRL.

Carroll, J. M., Collection. AWRL.

Dargan, Edwin C., Papers. SBHLA.

Dawson, Joseph Martin. Papers. SBHLA.

Dixon, Amzi Clarence. Papers. SBHLA.

Frost, James Marion. Papers. SBHLA.

Holcombe, Thomas Luther. Papers. SBHLA.

Lambdin, Jerry Elmer. Papers. SBHLA.

Leavell, Landrum Pinson. Papers. SBHLA.

McBeth, H. Leon. Collection. TBHC.

Mullins, Edgar Young. Papers. SBHLA.

Norris, J. Frank. Papers. SBHLA. (MF is located at TBHC; Baylor University, Waco, Texas; and Southern Baptist Theological Seminary, Louisville, Kentucky.)

Notebook: Financial Reports 1910–1929. GWTML.

Notebook: Pastors: Truett: Biographical Histories and Funeral. GWTML.

Paschall, Henry Franklin. Papers. SBHLA.

Scarborough, L. R., Collection. AWRL. (MF is located at TBHC.)

Van Ness, I. J., Papers. SBHLA.

Warren, Caspar Carl. Papers. SBHLA.


Unpublished Works

Agnew, Peter Wallace. "Religion and the Social Order in a Twentieth-Century City: Six Dallas Leaders." Ph.D. dissertation, Southern Methodist University, 1999.

Appleby, Rosalee Mills. "The Price of Power." Typed manuscript, n.d. George W. Truett Baptist History File. SBHLA.

Brannon, Richard S. "George W. Truett, Evangelist." Master's thesis, Southwestern Baptist Theological Seminary, 1954.

Brannon, Richard S. "George Washington Truett and His Preaching." Ph.D. dissertation, Southwestern Baptist Theological Seminary, 1956.

Brooks, Samuel P. "Words of Appreciation about Dr. Geo. W. Truett at the Twenty Fifth Anniversary of His Pastorate of the First Baptist Church of Dallas." September 12, 1922. TC 637/MF 628–657:2.

Bruner, J. W. "Dr. B. H. Carroll's Money Creed." Founder's Day address, Southwestern Baptist Theological Seminary, Fort Worth, Texas, January 27, 1942. AWRL.

Bryant, Thurmon F.. "The Ethics of George Washington Truett," Ph.D. dissertation, Southwestern Baptist Theological Seminary, 1959.

Canipe, Christopher L. "A Captive Church in the Land of the Free: E. Y. Mullins, Walter Rauschenbusch, George Truett, and the Rise of Baptist Democracy, 1900–1925." Ph.D. dissertation, Baylor University, 2004.

Choi, Jung Ki. "The Use of the Functional Elements of Preaching in Selected Sermons of George Washington Truett and Harry Emerson Fosdick: Centering around Illustration." Master's thesis, Southwestern Baptist Theological Seminary, 2003.

Dawson, J. M. "Truett's Gethsemane Now Revealed." [1958]. TC 629/MF 628–657:1.

"First Baptist Church, Dallas, Texas. Thursday Night, September 14, 1922. Mayor Sawnie Aldredge, Chairman." Notebook: Pastors: Truett: 25th Anniversary, GWTML.

Forrester, E. J. "Truett on the Capitol Steps." Typed manuscript, [1920]. TC 545/MF 543–553:1.

Garrett, W. C. "What Dr. Truett Has Been to Me." TC 644/MF 628–657:3.

"George W. Truett, D.D.: LL.D." Henry Franklin Paschall Papers. SBHLA.

Harvey, Paul William. "Southern Baptists and Southern Culture, 1865–1920." Ph.D. dissertation, University of California at Berkeley, 1992.

Holland, DeWitte Talmage. "A Rhetorical Analysis of the Preaching of George W. Truett." Ph.D. dissertation, Northwestern University, 1956.

Ivey, Harvey Duane. "The Concept of Stewardship Reflected in the Preaching of George W. Truett." Master's thesis, New Orleans Baptist Theological Seminary, 1965.

James, Powhatan W. "Address of Powhatan W. James Delivered on 'Truett Day' at the Southwestern Baptist Theological Seminary, February 19, 1954." AWRL.

Leek, Mark. "History of Schools in Clay County, North Carolina." http://www.clayschools.org/ccshistory/ccshistory.htm.

Loftis, Joe Dowell. "Pastoral Themes in the Life and Ministry of George Washington Truett: An Evaluation in Light of the Pastoral Theology of Thomas C. Oden." Ph.D. dissertation, Southwestern Baptist Theological Seminary, 1994.

McBeth, Leon. "George W. Truett and Southwestern Seminary." Chapel address, Southwestern Baptist Theological Seminary, Fort Worth, Texas, March 16, 1971. TC between 557 and 558/MF 554–590:1.

Morris, Clovis Gwin. "He Changed Things: The Life and Thought of J. Frank Norris." Ph.D. dissertation, Texas Tech University, 1973.

Mosley, Marvin Jarvis. "Pastoral Ministry of Dr. George W. Truett." Master's thesis, Southwestern Baptist Theological Seminary, 1971.

Newton, Louie D., with A. Ronald Tonks. "Oral Memoirs of Louie D. Newton." Historical Commission, Southern Baptist Convention, SBHLA, Nashville, TN, 1973–1981.

Pigott, Kelly David. "A Comparison of the Leadership of George W. Truett and J. Frank Norris in Church, Denominational, Interdenominational, and Political Affairs." Ph.D. dissertation, Southwestern Baptist Theological Seminary, 1993.

"Report of Examination of Dr. George W. Truett," September 15, 1942. TC 664/MF 664–690:1.

"Resolutions by the Trustees of Baylor University in Commemoration of Dr. George W. Truett." TC 659/MF 658–661:1.

Slaughter, Mrs. M. B. "Mrs. Geo. W. Truett's Bible Class," September 12, 1966. H. Leon McBeth Collection, "FBC Topic Reports" folder, TBHC.

["Statement by W. M. Baines, son of George W. Baines, concerning the Arnold shooting"], April 24, 1959. TC 629/MF 628–657:1.

Teal, D. A. "Early History of the First Baptist Church and Its Friends." Typed manuscript, n.d., GWTML.

Truett, Josephine. Diary 1946. TC 673/MF 664–690:31.

Tullock, Samuel K. "The Transformation of American Fundamentalism: The Life and Career of John Franklyn Norris." Ph.D. dissertation, University of Texas at Dallas, 1997.

Watson, Thomas L. "Eschatology of B. H. Carroll." Master's thesis, Southwestern Baptist Theological Seminary, 1960.

Wheeler, David Edward. "An Evaluation of the Evangelism of George W. Truett As Related to His Ministry at the First Baptist Church, Dallas, Texas." Ph.D. dissertation, Southwestern Baptist Theological Seminary, 1994.

Whitlock, David Brian. "Southern Baptists and Southern Culture: Three Visions of a Christian America, 1890–1945." Ph.D. dissertation, Southern Baptist Theological Seminary, 1988.

# Index

Young Men's Christian Association
    (YMCA), 131, 134, 136, 150, 151,
    296n66. *See also* National War
    Work Council
Young Women's Christian Association
    (YWCA), 296n66
Ypres, France, 148
Zimmermann, Arthur, 129
Zimmermann telegram, 129
Zondervan Publishing House, 242